Praise for *Ol*

"Dan Black, respected [former] editor of *Legion Magazine*,
and John Boileau, a retired army colonel and the author of ten
books, tell the compelling story of Canada's war effort through
these underage witnesses... Perhaps the greatest strength of *Old
Enough to Fight* is that these stories may resonate deeply with
today's youth and help them connect with the war of one hundred years ago."
— Tim Cook, winner of the Governor General's History Award
      for Popular Media, writing in *Canada's History Magazine*

"*Old Enough to Fight* grips the imagination by its vivid portrayal
of the youngsters through whose eyes one sees unimaginable
conditions on the Western Front."
— *Halifax Chronicle-Herald*

"The boys' backgrounds are fully developed, and their testimony is skilfully woven into the bloody battles and routine
horrors of trench warfare. The human element extends the
book's appeal to readers beyond those whose interest is primar-
ily military... destined to be an immediate success."
— *Atlantic Books Today*

"The authors include excerpts from the boys' letters home,
which include vivid descriptions of trench warfare, battles, and
the constant discomfort in which the soldiers lived. They were
cold, wet, hungry, ill, and often lonley for home, and the letters
make that plain."
— *Maritime Forces Atlantic Trident*

OLD ENOUGH TO FIGHT

CANADA'S BOY SOLDIERS IN THE FIRST WORLD WAR

DAN BLACK AND JOHN BOILEAU

FOREWORD BY ROMÉO DALLAIRE

JAMES LORIMER & COMPANY LTD., PUBLISHERS
TORONTO

Copyright © 2015, 2013 by Dan Black and John Boileau.
First published in the United States in 2014.
Maps drawn by Jason Duprau.
For image credits, see page 434.

James Lorimer & Company Ltd., Publishers acknowledges the support of the Ontario Arts Council. We acknowledge the support of the Canada Council for the Arts, which last year invested $24.3 million in writing and publishing throughout Canada. We acknowledge the Government of Ontario through the Ontario Media Development Corporation's Ontario Book Initiative.

Cover design: Tyler Cleroux

Library and Archives Canada Cataloguing in Publication

Black, Dan, 1957-, author
    Old enough to fight : Canada's boy soldiers in the First World War / Dan Black and John Boileau ; foreword by Roméo Dallaire.

Includes bibliographical references and index.
Issued in print and electronic formats.
ISBN 978-1-4594-0541-7 (bound).--ISBN 1-4594-0542-4 (epub).--
ISBN 978-1-4594-0955-2 (paperback)

    1. World War, 1914-1918--Personal narratives, Canadian. 2. World War, 1914-1918--Participation, Juvenile. 3. Child soldiers--Canada--Biography. 4. World War, 1914-1918--Sources. I. Boileau, John, author II. Title.

D639.C4B63 2013   940.3083'510971   C2013-904170-2
                                                   C2013-904171-0

James Lorimer & Company Ltd., Publishers
317 Adelaide Street West, Suite 1002
Toronto, ON, Canada
M5V 1P9
www.lorimer.ca

Printed and bound in Canada.

In memory of the boy soldiers who fought and died for Canada.

"No young man believes he shall ever die."

— *William Hazlitt (English literary critic*
and essayist, 1778-1830)

CONTENTS

LIST OF MAPS
See map section
following page 144

Map I: The Colonial Wars, 1604–1902

Map II: Ypres Salient, 1914–18

Map III: Second Battle of Ypres Gas Attack, 24 April 1915

Map IV: Festubert, 15–31 May 1915

Map V: The Battle of Mount Sorrel, 2–13 June 1916

Map VI: The Somme Battles: Courcelette,
15 September 1916

Map VII: The Somme Battles: Thiepval Ridge,
26 September 1916

Map VIII: The Somme Battles: Ancre Heights,
1 October 1916

Map IX: Vimy Ridge, 9–12 April 1917

Map X: Hill 70 and Lens, 15–25 August 1917

Map XI: Passchendaele, 26 October–10 November 1917

Map XII: Spring Offensives, March–July 1918

Map XIII: Amiens, 8–18 August 1918

Map XIV: Arras, 26 August–5 September 1918

Map XV: Canal du Nord and Cambrai,
27 September–11 October 1918

Map XVI: The Final Advance: Cambrai to Mons,
12 October–11 November 1918

CANADIAN CORPS INFANTRY DIVISIONS, BRIGADES, AND BATTALIONS

1st Canadian Division

    1st Brigade

        1st (Western Ontario) Battalion

        2nd (Eastern Ontario) Battalion

        3rd (Toronto Regiment) Battalion

        4th (Central Ontario) Battalion

    2nd Brigade

        5th (Western Cavalry) Battalion

        7th (1st British Columbia) Battalion

        8th (90th Winnipeg Rifles) Battalion

        10th (Calgary-Winnipeg) Battalion

    3rd Brigade

        13th (Royal Highlanders of Canada) Battalion

        14th (Royal Montreal Regiment) Battalion

        15th (48th Highlanders of Canada) Battalion

        16th (Canadian Scottish) Battalion

2nd Canadian Division

    4th Brigade

        18th (Western Ontario) Battalion

        19th (Central Ontario) Battalion

        20th (Central Ontario) Battalion

        21st (Eastern Ontario) Battalion

    5th Brigade

        22nd (French Canadian) Battalion

        24th (Victoria Rifles of Canada) Battalion

        25th (Nova Scotia Rifles) Battalion

26th (New Brunswick) Battalion

6th Brigade

27th (City of Winnipeg) Battalion

28th (Northwest) Battalion

29th (Vancouver) Battalion

31st (Alberta) Battalion

3rd Canadian Division

7th Brigade

Royal Canadian Regiment

Princess Patricia's Canadian Light Infantry

42nd (Royal Highlanders of Canada) Battalion

49th (Edmonton Regiment) Battalion

8th Brigade

1st (Saskatchewan) Battalion Canadian Mounted Rifles

2nd (British Columbia) Battalion Canadian Mounted Rifles

4th (Central Ontario) Battalion Canadian Mounted Rifles

5th (Quebec) Battalion Canadian Mounted Rifles

9th Brigade

43rd (Cameron Highlanders of Canada) Battalion

52nd (New Ontario) Battalion

58th (Central Ontario) Battalion

60th (Victoria Rifles of Canada) Battalion (replaced by 116th (Ontario County) Battalion April 1917)

4th Canadian Division

10th Brigade

44th (Manitoba) Battalion (redesignated "New

Brunswick" August 1918)

46th (South Saskatchewan) Battalion

47th (British Columbia) Battalion (redesignated "Western Ontario" February 1918)

50th (Calgary) Battalion

11th Brigade

54th (Kootenay) Battalion (redesignated "Central Ontario" August 1917)

75th (Mississauga) Battalion

87th (Canadian Grenadier Guards) Battalion

102nd (North British Columbians) Battalion (redesignated "Central Ontario" August 1917)

12th Brigade

38th (Ottawa) Battalion

72nd (Seaforth Highlanders of Canada) Battalion

73rd (Royal Highlanders of Canada) Battalion (replaced by 85th (Nova Scotia Highlanders) Battalion April 1917)

78th (Winnipeg Grenadiers) Battalion

THE BOY SOLDIERS

Several boy soldiers in this book appear in more than one chapter. This list serves as a quick reference for recalling basic details about their service.

Brown, Archie — 78th (Winnipeg Grenadiers) Battalion; normal school student from Macdonald, Manitoba; enrolled age sixteen.

Brown, Gordon — 46th (South Saskatchewan) Battalion; farmhand from Redvers, Saskatchewan; enrolled age seventeen.

Cadenhead, John — 102nd (North British Columbians) Battalion; student from Vancouver; enrolled age sixteen.

Claydon, Fred — 43rd (Cameron Highlanders of Canada) Battalion; farm labourer from Elkhorn, Manitoba; enrolled age sixteen.

Henley, Roy — 42nd (Royal Highlanders of Canada) Battalion; farmhand from Alliston, Ontario; enrolled twice — ages thirteen and fifteen.

King, Walter — 5th (Western Cavalry) Battalion; schoolteacher from Wainwright, Alberta; enrolled age seventeen.

Lawson, Gordon — Princess Patricia's Canadian Light Infantry; farmer from Winnipeg; enrolled age seventeen.

Low, David — 43rd (Cameron Highlanders of Canada) Battalion; clerk from Winnipeg; enrolled age sixteen.

MacArthur, J. H. — 7th (1st British Columbia) Battalion; occupation unknown, from Vancouver; enrolled age sixteen.

Moir, David — 7th Brigade Machine Gun Company; clerk from Winnipeg; enrolled age seventeen.

Moore, Percival — 38th (Ottawa) Battalion; schoolboy from

Carleton Place, Ontario; enrolled age fifteen; missing in action at Vimy Ridge April 9, 1917, presumed dead (age sixteen).

Ogilvie, Will — 21st Howitzer Battery; student from Lakefield, Ontario; enrolled age seventeen.

Parsons, M. E. — 2nd (British Columbia) Battalion Canadian Mounted Rifles; farm boy from Winnipeg; enrolled age seventeen.

Ricketts, Tommy, VC —Royal Newfoundland Regiment; schoolboy from Middle Arm, Newfoundland; enrolled age fifteen.

Salisbury, Howard — 21st (Eastern Ontario) Battalion; wood turner from Kingston, Ontario; enrolled age fifteen.

Searle, Morris — 18th (Western Ontario) Battalion; mail carrier (Eaton's department store) from Toronto; enrolled age seventeen.

Smith, Cyril — 54th (Kootenay) Battalion; ranch hand from Port Hammond, British Columbia; enrolled age sixteen.

Syrett, Vic — 46th (South Saskatchewan) Battalion; bricklayer from Regina; enrolled age sixteen.

Thompson, Robert — Canadian Mounted Rifles; schoolboy from Hillier, Ontario; enrolled three times — twice at age fourteen and once at fifteen.

Waldron, David — 58th (Central Ontario) Battalion; clerk from Toronto; enrolled age sixteen.

FOREWORD

It is quite the opportunity to write the foreword to this unique
historical account of the roles Canada's boy soldiers played during
the First World War. The invitation from authors John Boileau
and Dan Black emerged due to the personal connections I have
held with both. John Boileau and I served a number of years
together in the Canadian military, and Dan Black and I first met
several years ago and again in 2011 when he interviewed me for an
article in *Legion Magazine*. I was duly impressed with his profes-
sionalism and passion.

The authors provide us with a tangible human face and first-
order documentation for the global discussion of the issue of
child soldiers. So very often we think of child soldiers as African
boys armed with AK-47s, and we fail to recognize the deep connections we have to far off lands over many years. In addition,
we fail to see that the child soldier can be depicted through
the faces of our very own children. This book sheds light on a
Canadian connection to the issues faced by children in armed

combat and the moral dilemmas that result. These stories resonate with many who have served in the Canadian Forces but need
to be recounted, not only for the historical record, but for the
Canadian public to digest.

I grew up in a military family; my father was a strict disciplin-
arian. I was used to order, uniforms, and shining boots. When I
went to high school, I was obliged to join the army cadet corps,
and take part in weekly drill parades. At the end of the school year
I volunteered and was chosen for army cadet summer camps. It
seemed like a chance for adventure, a chance to fulfil my fantasies
of being a gallant, noble, and fearless warrior. However, we were
children in a very adult business. Amazingly, the fact that we were
learning warlike skills with weapons that were taller than us never
really registered.

In the vastness of the tented camp, among thousands of other
boys, in the all-encompassing way of life, in a real expression
of belonging, of supporting others and being counted on and
supported by others, too, I found my soul. Unabashedly and
generously offered such richness by the army — the institution,
its ethos, and its people — I responded with zeal. I found my
vocation there: that world of the army cadet linked seamlessly —
astonishingly — with the imaginary world of my childhood.

Many of the stories in this book reveal stories of enthusiastic
boys who volunteered to join the war effort. There are stories
such as those of John G. Wright, who went to great lengths to
plead his case at the age of sixteen to Prime Minister Sir Robert
Borden. Others found creative ways to conceal their age. Those
involved in war are often left with indelible scars and memories,
and no matter who you are or how professionally prepared you
may be, war will change your very being. The children involved
in Canada's war effort may have entered as innocent boys looking
for adventure, honour, and purpose, but they underwent a mat-
uration that many would not have originally anticipated.

The reasons that made it possible for boys to join the Canadian military were the sheer lack of eligible males, the large number of unemployed youth that sought financial means and purpose, and the overall lack of preparation and recruiting rigour for a Canadian war effort. Additionally, the ethos of indoctrination of boys and young men into the military life was viewed as a positive effort to enhance the professionalization of the military. Military service was also seen to be of great personal benefit to the boys themselves: "Boys will be boys."

Most interesting is the evolution in Canadian thinking on the involvement of children in armed conflict. As Chapter 2 tells us, "more Canadians were concerned about the issue of whether or not soldiers should be able to buy a beer in a wet canteen than they were about boy soldiers killing and possibly being killed in the frontline trenches." It took many years before the world would pay attention and start earnestly putting effort into ending the use of children as soldiers. In 1989 the world adopted the *United Nations Convention of the Rights of the Child*, which clearly stipulates a child is any person under the age of eighteen years. Canada was at the forefront of international legislation such as the *Optional Protocol on the Involvement of Children in Armed Conflict* (2000) and the *Paris Principles and Guidelines on Children Associated with Armed Forces or Groups* (2007). The *Optional Protocol* aims to ensure that states take all feasible measures to ensure armed groups do not allow members that are below eighteen years of age to take a direct part in hostilities. Voluntary recruitment into national armed forces under the age of eighteen must ensure the following minimum safeguards: a) such recruitment is genuinely voluntary; b) such recruitment is carried out with the informed consent of the person's parents or legal guardians; c) such persons are fully informed of the duties involved in such military service; and d) such persons provide reliable proof of age prior to acceptance into national military service. Many countries also add the restriction that no personnel under eighteen years of age are deployed in combat operations.

During my tenure as Force Commander of the United Nations Assistance Mission for Rwanda in 1994, I was faced with the reality of the modern use of child soldiers by armed groups. This seemed so very distant from my boyhood experiences with the cadets and the home I had found within the Canadian Forces. Looking into the eyes of these children, some of them the same age as my son, gave me insight into the similarities of all children yet haunted me with the need to ensure no child ever has to undertake the acts these children were forced to commit. This experience would eventually lead me in my quest to eradicate the use of children as weapons of war through the founding of the Roméo Dallaire Child Soldiers Initiative, now housed at Dalhousie University in Halifax.

It is most striking to read the accounts of parents whose boys had been part of the war effort. Some had consented, others had not, but all worried about the well-being of their beloved children. For no matter where you stand on this issue, the human factor must be understood. This book makes it abundantly clear that children must have room to protect their young lives, and the eternal lives of their souls.

— Senator Roméo Dallaire, OC, CMM, GOQ, MSC, CD, LOM (US), Lieutenant-General (Ret'd)

PREFACE

We knew the story of Canada's boy soldiers would resonate with Canadians by the enthusiastic response we got from everyone with whom we discussed our ideas, from ordinary citizens to professional historians. It is easy to understand why. These courageous young men, who joined the military as young as ten,[1] personify in many ways our natural idealization of childhood and our nostalgia for it. In the face of repeated rebuffs, several of them persevered — one way or the other — to evade their parents, fool the recruiters, and join up. Others went overseas with the full knowledge and blessing of their parents. No matter how they got there, they fought — and many died — for Canada. Yet their story is not simply military history; it is as much social history, and even family history.

Our research into the First World War experience shows the majority of these young boys headed overseas with the same strong resolve felt by a lot of soldiers. They went off, promising to "do their bit" and return home — probably within a year — with the "great adventure" behind them. For most, that romantic notion was wiped out the second they arrived on the Western Front. Disease and death did not discriminate. Boys died just as quickly and as horribly as older men, while count-less others suffered ghastly physical and psychological wounds. Many of these boys "cracked up" under pressure or got into trouble on account of their youthful pride, but overall Canada's boy soldiers hung in and displayed great courage under fire. We have found fine examples of boys who — in the heat of battle — made a seamless transition from follower to leader to hero. Their bravery earned them medals, but more importantly it earned the respect of fellow soldiers, many of whom were old enough to be their fathers.

Although boy soldiers are well known in the context of the history of the British army and have been the subject of a num-ber of books, to date no one has attempted to tell the entire story of boy soldiers in the framework of the Canadian military. We sincerely hope this book — and its companion volume to follow with stories of post–First World War boy soldiers (and sailors and airmen) — will fill a void that has existed for far too long.

DRB   JBB
Merrickville, Ontario   "Lindisfarne"
                             Glen Margaret, Nova Scotia

April 22, 2013 — the ninety-eighth anniversary
of Canada's baptism of fire in the First World War
at the Second Battle of Ypres.

THE BOY SOLDIER TRADITION

Drummer Thomas Flynn ran toward the enemy position, swept up in the excitement of the moment. The sounds of rifle and cannon fire rent the air, thick with black smoke and swirling, choking dust. Acrid cordite filled Flynn's mouth and nostrils as he and 170 of his compatriots in the 64th Regiment charged shouting and yelling toward some of the twenty thousand sepoy mutineers who were besieging Cawnpore (now Kanpur) in northern India. The British garrison, on the banks of the Ganges River about 450 kilometres southwest of Delhi, had already been surrounded once before during the Indian Mutiny, until it was relieved by a force under Sir Colin Campbell in July 1857. When Campbell subsequently moved on with most of his soldiers to relieve nearby Lucknow, the rebels promptly besieged the town again, finding it now garrisoned by a small force that included the 64th. One rebel gun battery, roughly nine hundred metres away up a steep ravine, was particularly troublesome.[1]

On November 28 the 64th Regiment was ordered to capture that battery and destroy its guns. During the attack, Flynn was wounded but carried on. Suddenly, the Irish lad found himself facing two rebel artillerymen manning their gun. Without hesitation, Flynn sprang upon them before they had time to react. After a short and deadly hand-to-hand combat, the mutineers lay still on the ground and the cannon was Flynn's. The surviving mutineers fled to safety in some nearby houses and gardens. For his gallantry, the young drummer boy was one of the first recipients of the Victoria Cross, the British Empire's highest award for bravery in the face of the enemy. Flynn was fifteen years and three months old. He and hospital apprentice Andrew Fitzgibbon, who was the same age when he performed his brave act on August 21, 1860, were the youngest recipients ever of the Victoria Cross.[2]

Thomas Flynn was only thirteen when he joined the 64th Regiment. This in and of itself was neither remarkable nor unique, as the employment of children in wars and military campaigns is as old as warfare itself. Records from antiquity indicate youths were taken on campaign along with soldiers' families, not only to provide essential support to the fighting men in the days before military logistics were fully developed, but also as armed combatants. Throughout medieval England, squires began training for their roles as military assistants to knights as early as twelve. Even before England created the New Model Army in 1645, drummer and bugle boys accompanied soldiers into battle. Soon, other boys began to be employed as assistants to certain army tradesmen, such as farriers and tailors. In 1683, King Charles II started the system by which about two-thirds of initial officer commissions and subsequent promotions in the army (except for promotion to staff and general ranks) were by purchase and that became the path by which many boys entered the army to become officers.[3] In Canada, although the French had

The Victoria Cross, the highest award for gallantry in the British Empire/Commonwealth, was instituted in 1856. By mid-2013, it had only been awarded 1,361 times.

been the first to employ boy soldiers here, the tradition of using boy soldiers was inherited from the British, who along with most other nations employed minors in various military roles even before armies, navies, and air forces were formally organized.

The two most famous generals in Canadian colonial history — James Wolfe and Louis-Joseph de Montcalm — began their careers as boy soldiers. In 1741, Wolfe received his first military appointment at fourteen as a second lieutenant in the 1st Regiment of Marines, although he never served with the unit. The next year he exchanged that appointment to join the 12th Foot as an ensign. At sixteen Wolfe underwent his baptism of fire at the Battle of Dettingen in Bavaria and was subsequently promoted lieutenant before becoming a captain in the 4th Foot when he was only seventeen. After the British success at Louisbourg in 1758 during the Seven Years' War, Wolfe was appointed major-general and land commander of the expedition against Quebec in 1759 (see Map I).[4]

The French military commander at Quebec, Montcalm, started his military career in 1721 at the age of nine as an ensign in the Regiment d'Hainaut and obtained his captaincy at seventeen. He saw his first action in 1733 during the War of the Polish Succession and was appointed major-general in 1756 to command French troops in North America, replacing a predecessor who had been captured.[5] Despite his military experience, Montcalm gave up the advantage that Quebec's stout walls provided and went out to challenge the British head-on. When the British and French met on the Plains of Abraham on September 13, 1759, the fate of Canada was decided in fifteen minutes. The British were victorious, Wolfe was dead, and Montcalm was mortally wounded. In 1763 Canada passed into British hands by the Treaty of Paris that ended the Seven Years' War.

This portrait of James Wolfe, the future conqueror of Canada, was painted when he was about fifteen, a year after he joined the army.

In February 1793, the lieutenant-governors of Nova Scotia, New Brunswick, and Newfoundland received dispatches from the British army's adjutant-general authorizing them to "take necessary steps for raising and forming from among inhabitants ... a corps not exceeding 600 men ... with the usual establishment of commissioned and non-commissioned officers." Recruiting started immediately in the three colonies to create these units for provincial service. In July, Lieutenant-Governor Thomas Carleton of New Brunswick reported to London that two hundred men had enlisted. One of the first to join was seventeen-year-old Jabish Squiers, who was living on his own after his family of Connecticut Loyalists had decided to return to New England. After enrolling in March 1793, Squiers rose through the ranks from private to colour-sergeant to sergeant-major. As a sergeant he earned three shillings and sixpence a day.[6] In 1810, the New Brunswick Regiment received a rare

A mounted Major-General Louis-Joseph de Montcalm leads his troops into battle to face the British on the Plains of Abraham, September 13, 1759.

distinction when it was approved as a British line regiment and renamed the 104th Foot.

Although the 104th existed for only seven years before being disbanded in 1817, its muster rolls record a total of 168 names as drummers, buglers, or boy soldiers. Additionally, an unknown number of privates would have enlisted as young as fifteen. British regiments were permitted under certain circumstances to enrol boys, and the authorities took care not to miss any opportunity to increase their regiment's numerical strength. A letter on the subject from the War Office in October 1805 noted, "His Royal Highness is pleased to accede to you enlisting Boys from ten to fourteen for unlimited Service; for each of whom two thirds Bounty will be allowed, but none are to be taken who are not very promising in their appearance as to growth." Elsewhere in the letter permission was given to recruit five boys for each company, but a later dispatch of May 1810 states that the commander-in-chief approved increasing this number to ten.[7]

Between December 1805 and October 1806, recruiting parties enrolled twenty-two boys. The total number of boys attached to the regiment in August 1808 was forty-six, while the greatest number noted in the records at any one time was sixty-three, in the quarterly return for September 1810. Zebedee Squiers, the eldest son of Sergeant Jabish Squiers, joined the regiment on February 20, 1809, having reached the age of ten. Judged "fit to carry arms" at fifteen years, but still unofficially referred to as "lads," these boys were transferred to the list of private men at a private's pay. A private's pay in 1812 was sixpence a day for his first seven years' service.[8] Nearly forty of the 104th's boy soldiers eventually achieved senior non-commissioned rank.[9]

During the War of 1812, most of the 104th marched from Saint John and Fredericton to Quebec City and on to Kingston in the dead of winter in 1813, an amazing feat of endurance. Zebedee Squiers, who was thirteen or fourteen years old at the time, was — unlike his father — spared the pain of frozen feet. He remained at Fredericton until spring, when the rest of the regiment travelled by boat to Upper Canada. From Kingston, water transport took the unit to the Niagara Peninsula where it engaged in several battles. Among the boys from the 104th killed in action were James Hayward and Nelson Pearson. Hayward, who enlisted on June 15, 1809, died on May 29, 1813, during fighting at Sacket's Harbour, New York. Pearson, who had more than four years of service, fell on August 15, 1814, at Fort Erie. Boy soldier Joseph St. Germain was somewhat luckier. Taken prisoner on the same day Pearson was killed, he was released by the Americans eight months later, and was discharged from the army in May 1817.[10]

Several of Britain's senior officers in command of British forces, Canadian militia, and native allies during the War of 1812 had begun their careers as boy soldiers. The most famous is Major-General Sir Isaac Brock, who helped to turn back the

British regulars, Canadian militia, and native warriors push on at the Battle of Queenston Heights as a dying Major-General Isaac Brock urges them forward.

American invasion at Queenston Heights but died in the fighting. At fifteen, Brock purchased an ensigncy in the 8th Foot, a vacancy caused by the promotion of his eldest brother. He came from a moderately wealthy Channel Islands family and excelled at swimming and boxing at school, although he was also noted for his extreme gentleness. In 1791, Brock joined the 49th Foot, a unit linked to much of his subsequent career. His first experience with battle was not until 1799, when he was thirty years old. He came to Canada in 1802, as commanding officer of the 49th and remained here (except for a lengthy period of leave in England) for the rest of his career — and his life. In 1811, Brock was promoted major-general and appointed administrator of Upper Canada, making him the senior military and civilian authority in the colony. A big man at six feet and two inches, his

Lieutenant-Colonel Charles de Salaberry rallies his Canadian militia and native allies to turn back the American invaders at the Battle of Châteauguay, October 26, 1813.

physical stature and position leading a small group of soldiers in a counterattack — along with the bright red coatee he was wearing — probably proved an irresistible target to the American sharpshooter who shot him full in the heart.[11]

A French Canadian who joined the British army as a boy was Charles-Michel d'Irumberry de Salaberry, carrying on a long family tradition of military service first for France and then — after the Conquest — for Britain. At fourteen, Charles followed his father's footsteps into the 44th Foot as a volunteer. At sixteen, thanks to the good graces of family friend Prince Edward, he received an ensign's commission in the 60th Foot, then stationed in the West Indies. In 1810, de Salaberry was posted to Canada, where he successfully raised the Voltigeurs Canadiens on the eve of the War of 1812. At the Battle of Châteauguay on October 26, 1813, de Salaberry commanded a mixed force of sixteen hundred

The 1870 Red River Expedition involved forty-seven back-breaking portages between Thunder Bay and Fort Garry, such as this one at Kakabeka Falls.

Canadian militiamen and native warriors that met and quickly turned back a four-thousand-man American invasion force headed for Montreal.[12]

Although the War of 1812 marked the last time Canada and the United States went to war against each other, some American citizens supported the rebellions of 1837, and especially the raids of 1866 and 1870 conducted by the Fenian Brotherhood, an organization of Irish-Americans who were dedicated to taking the British out of British North America. The Fenian Raids drew one of the most remarkable Canadians of the Victorian Age into the militia when he joined the 35th (Simcoe) Battalion of Infantry as a seventeen-year-old boy. Sam Steele went on to an illustrious military and mounted police career in a story that could have come out of the pages of *Boy's Own Annual*.

Steele served in the 1st Ontario Battalion of Rifles during the Red River Expedition of 1870 and joined the newly-formed Permanent Force artillery at Kingston on his return from Manitoba, becoming an instructor. When the North West

Mounted Police (NWMP) was formed in 1873, he immediately applied to join it and made his way west with the first contingent, in October, as a staff constable. He rose steadily through the Mounties' ranks and along the way became responsible for policing the line of the Canadian Pacific Railway as it was built across the Prairies and into British Columbia. During the Louis Riel–led North-West Rebellion of 1885, Steele was in charge of the mounted troops and scouts of the Alberta Field Force.[13]

Major-General Frederick Middleton, a British officer who began his own career as a boy soldier and was the general officer commanding the Canadian Militia at the time of the rebellion, was directed by Prime Minister Sir John A. Macdonald to take charge of the entire operation.[14] To put down the rebellion, Middleton formed the North-West Field Force, made up of regulars, mobilized militiamen, Mounties, locally raised units, and others, and divided it into three columns. Middleton personally commanded the nine-hundred-man Batoche column, which included Winnipeg's 90th Rifles. Serving in the Rifles was Bugler Billy Buchanan, aged fifteen, the youngest soldier in the column. Like many other boys, Buchanan, a farm lad, had lied about his age in order to be taken along.

As Middleton's column made its way down both sides of the South Saskatchewan River, Gabriel Dumont, Louis Riel's chief lieutenant, set up an ambush with around 150 men at Fish Creek, a coulee on the east side of the river roughly twenty kilometres south of the rebels' capital and main stronghold at Batoche. When Middleton's scouts approached the coulee early on April 24, the rebels opened fire. In the skirmishing that followed the soldiers tried repeatedly — and unsuccessfully — to drive Dumont's men from the coulee. At one serious juncture in the fighting, Middleton's men were nearly overrun by the rebels, who had set fire to the prairie. Using smoke as a cover, the rebels attacked, but the soldiers advanced and beat out the flames. "If anything

The capture of Batoche on May 12, 1885, marked the last major battle of the North-West Rebellion and broke the back of the uprising.

had been required," Middleton said later, "to keep the men steady at this rather critical moment, it would have been found in the extraordinarily composed and cool behavior of William Buchanan, a little bugler of the Ninetieth, who while calmly distributing ammunition along the line, kept calling out in his childish shrill voice, 'Now, boys, who's for more cartridges?'" As night fell at Fish Creek, both commanders pulled back. The army had ten killed and forty-five wounded in the fighting compared to four dead and one wounded for the Métis. More importantly, the ambush caused Middleton to pause for two weeks before he resumed his advance on Batoche. For his courage under fire, Buchanan was mentioned in dispatches.[15]

After some relatively quiet peacetime policing once the North-West Rebellion was put down by early July, Sam Steele was ordered north in January 1898 to assist in establishing law and order among the thousands of prospectors who flocked to the Yukon in search of gold. Then, when the Second Boer War broke out in October 1899, Steele immediately volunteered and was offered command of a new mounted unit being raised privately by Lord Strathcona. Steele recruited the men for Strathcona's Horse from western Canada and managed to include a solid leavening of NWMP officers and NCOs. After a successful year the Strathcona's returned to Canada in 1901 for disbandment. A few months later, Steele was back in South Africa as divisional commander in the South African Constabulary, a paramilitary police force charged with overseeing a safe return to peace. He returned to Canada and succeeded in having the Strathcona's reactivated as a permanent force cavalry regiment, to be known as Lord Strathcona's Horse (Royal Canadians).

When the First World War broke out, Steele, then sixty-three, hoped to be given command of the Canadian Division, but was rejected by the minister of militia and defence, Sam Hughes, on the grounds of age. He was, however, promoted major-general, and put in charge of training in western Canada. When a second Canadian division was formed, Hughes offered Steele command of it, only to be vetoed by Lord Kitchener, again because of Steele's age. The obstreperous Hughes, even though he was not too keen on Steele, then insisted on making the appointment. A compromise saw Steele command 2nd Canadian Division until it was sent to France under Major-General Richard Turner, a Victoria Cross recipient from the Boer War. Steele was then given command of England's Southeastern District, which included the principal Canadian training camp at Shorncliffe. He retained this appointment until March 1917, retired, and was knighted in early 1918. He died shortly afterwards, a victim of the influenza epidemic. His military and Mountie careers spanned fifty-three years.[16]

The Boer War marked the first time Canada deployed soldiers overseas, after the tiny Boer republics of Transvaal and the Orange Free State made good on their threats and attacked the British territories of Cape Colony and Natal at the southern tip of Africa in October 1899. Although reluctant to provide men to fight in one of Britain's imperial wars, mainly due to pressure from his fellow French Canadians, Prime Minister Sir Wilfrid Laurier finally agreed to a volunteer contingent of a thousand men. Recruited, examined, organized, clothed, equipped, concentrated, and dispatched in an amazing sixteen days, the 2nd (Special Service) Battalion, Royal Canadian Regiment, arrived in South Africa in December.[17] It contained several boy soldiers in its ranks, one of whom features prominently in one of Canada's most iconic works of war art.

Douglas Williams was a bugler in Toronto's Queen Own Rifles, the second-oldest infantry regiment in Canada. When war broke out in South Africa, the five-foot-three fourteen-year-old promptly joined the first contingent and eagerly sailed off to battle. Early on Sunday morning, February 18, the Canadians reached Paardeberg Drift (ford) on the Modder River, part of a thirty-seven-thousand-man force under Field Marshal Lord Roberts. Nearly five thousand Boers under General Piet Cronje were dug into defensive positions along the river bank. At the time, Lord Kitchener was temporarily in command because Roberts was ill, and he was chafing at the bit to assault the Boers. But, because the terrain was so open, the Boers' firing pits so well-concealed and protected, and the Boers so expert in long-range marksmanship, none of the British units succeeded in breaking through.

Frustrated with the lack of progress, Kitchener ordered a British unit, the Duke of Cornwall's Light Infantry, to assist the Canadians, who had advanced too far toward the Boer lines and were pinned down for hours by accurate rifle fire and forced to endure heat, hunger, thirst, insects, wounded and decaying bodies, and even an icy rainstorm.[18] Williams described what happened late that afternoon:

The Cornwalls had moved up to within about 100

yards of our rear, and we heard them getting orders to fix bayonets and be ready to rush. Bayonets were fixed, straps were tightened and we were ready. Soon I heard the Cornwalls getting ready to charge, and looking back saw them coming on the run. The orders came from the centre for the Canadians to charge. It was plain that by the time the order had got the length of our line (about half a mile) that the Cornwalls would be past us, and not wanting any regiment to beat us at the finish, when we had led all day, I jumped up and blew the Canadian regimental call, and then the charge. I sounded four times, namely, to the right, left, rear and the front.[19]

On another occasion, Williams stated that the last time he blew, "we were moving forward so rapidly that I was stumbling as I pumped out the notes."[20] Unfortunately, the bravery of the Cornwalls and the Canadians resulted in the dismounted equivalent of the Charge of the Light Brigade (during the Crimean War) and the wild rush ended in failure. "Bloody Sunday" was the costliest battle for Canada since the War of 1812 — twenty-one killed and sixty wounded.[21] Canada's revenge came a few days later when the Royal Canadian Regiment relieved a British unit in the front lines only 550 metres from the dug-in Boers. The raw Canadians undertook one of the most difficult operations in warfare — a night attack, but the assault failed when the Boers detected the advancing soldiers and opened fire around 2:45 a.m. on February 27. When verbal orders rang out commanding the soldiers to "Retire and bring back your wounded!" most of the soldiers were only too happy to oblige, but the two companies from the Maritimes either did not hear the order or purposely chose to ignore it.

At dawn the Maritimers discovered they now overlooked the enemy and could fire into the main Boer position as well as

The Dawn of Majuba Day *saw the Royal Canadian Regiment avenge a Boer victory over the British during the First Boer War nineteen years earlier.*

into Boer dugouts in the river bank. After trading a few shots, the Boers in the forward trenches shouted that they wanted to surrender. This was followed by a lone Boer's coming out with a white flag. The leading Canadian and British troops advanced cautiously, bayonets fixed, past the Boer trenches, and into the main position. The Canadian victory was depicted by British artist R. Caton Woodville in his popular painting, *The Dawn of Majuba Day.* Standing at attention near the centre of the picture is the diminutive Douglas Williams, blowing his bugle. After the battle, Lord Roberts praised the soldiers of the Royal Canadian Regiment, noting that "Canadian now stands for bravery, dash, and courage."[22]

Edward "Mickey" McCormick was another young boy who wanted to join the army and fight the Boers. In February 1900, the fourteen-year-old made his way to Ottawa from Toronto, hoping to join Strathcona's Horse, the new regiment he heard was being formed. McCormick had even written to the unit's commanding officer (CO), the legendary Sam Steele, claiming to be sixteen, a qualified trumpeter, and an experienced rider. He was none of these. In Ottawa, the Strathcona's regimental sergeant-major paraded McCormick before the CO, who sternly demanded a militia trumpeter's certificate and a letter from his mother. It was obvious Steele knew the boy had none of these — and was underage as well. As the sergeant-major started to march the teenager out, Steele called to him, "Just a minute, McCormick. Your mother wrote to me and I know she really doesn't want you to come, but you'd leave home anyway. So I'll have to be a father to you as well as your colonel and keep you out of trouble." To keep an eye on McCormick, Steele appointed him as his trumpeter and orderly. Undoubtedly, Steele recalled the day thirty-six years earlier, when he himself had claimed he was older than he was, so he could join the army.[23]

In South Africa, in the third week of August 1900, British forces moved together in a pincer movement against General Louis Botha's army in the eastern Transvaal. General Redvers Buller tried to force his way through the Boer lines with a massive artillery bombardment by forty guns. McCormick witnessed the firepower of the guns, which made "it look like the eruption of Mount Vesuvius, as smoke, dirt, rocks and sulphurous gasses shot up from the position."[24] Later, in the third week of October, the Strathcona's were eighty kilometres west of Johannesburg on remounts, moving to assist in the relief of a British brigade besieged at Frederikstad. As the relief column arrived, the blockaded British counterattacked the now under-strength

A trooper of Strathcona's Horse holds his comrades' mounts as the regiment performs flank guard duties for a large column of British soldiers (detail).

Boers, supported by a heavy artillery bombardment. The Boers broke and fled across an open field, where many were killed.

After the battle, McCormick walked among the Boer dead that littered the field, when he noticed "a boy younger than himself, a fine looking boy, perhaps not over thirteen years old. His wide open blue eyes looking at the sun." Through an open shirt, "a swarm of flies covered his bloody intestines oozing out of a hole in his navel." Tears welled up in McCormick's eyes as he stood by the boy, brushing the flies away, happy that he "carried no rifle and had no part in the battle. A few metres away lay another dead Boer, his Mauser rifle beside him [and] his left arm stretched towards the boy." McCormick was convinced the boy was the man's son. The memory of tragedy of the small scene that had played out on the battlefield stayed with him for the rest of his life.[25]

Although McCormick returned safely to Canada with the Strathcona's, the excitement he had experienced during the Boer War led him to enlist again, this time in the 2nd Regiment, Canadian Mounted Rifles. He was seventeen by now and served again as a bugler with fellow trumpeter Douglas Williams. Along with these two, about a quarter of the men in 2 CMR had previous service in South Africa. McCormick and Williams fought in Canada's last battle of the war, at Harts River, in March 1902, when a joint Anglo-Canadian force was ambushed, surrounded, and subjected to several attacks before the Boers unexpectedly withdrew. For the Canadians, it was second only to Paardeberg in casualties: eleven killed, forty-three wounded, and seven missing.[26] On the night following the battle, McCormick played the last post as several of his companions were laid to rest in the South African soil. His was the last Canadian unit to see combat. Other units arrived afterwards, but by then the war was over.

The Boer War heralded a considerable change in the Canadian government's outlook on defence issues. Not only had troops been deployed overseas for the first time, in support of a British war, but now Canada finally agreed to Britain's long-standing demands that she defend her own borders. The challenge was to create a force capable of doing this, given the financial constraints of a still-developing nation that had other priorities. The solution was a citizen's army of volunteers that could rapidly mobilize when needed. With an eye to the recently ended Boer War, such a force could also supply a contingent of volunteers for any imperial conflict. On October 8, 1903, Minister of Militia and Defence Frederick Borden explained his plan to the House of Commons. One hundred thousand men would be ready for military service, but only 40 per cent of them would undergo annual military training. The remaining 60 per cent, although committed to serve in wartime, would not drill but would become trained riflemen. These figures required an expansion in both the Permanent Force and the Non-Permanent Active Militia (NPAM), that portion of the reserve force that drilled and trained on a regular basis.

Hand-in-hand with militia growth was an unprecedented expansion of paramilitary organizations. While rifle associations, cadet corps, and militia officer organizations had existed for several years, they were largely unknown by the majority of Canadians and survived without government support. After the Boer War, these paramilitary bodies suddenly resonated with their countrymen and received financial assistance from the Department of Militia and Defence, which viewed such groups as sources for an expanded national army. In a wider sense, they also reflected a common belief among Canadians generally that military training would produce healthy, law-abiding, and better citizens.[27]

While many young boys and men joined the new rifle clubs that sprang up around the country, the organization that had the greatest effect on youth was the cadet movement. Several cadet corps had been formed in Canada beginning in the 1860s, based on the English model and spurred by the threat of an American invasion during and immediately after the Civil War. At first, schoolboys donned uniforms and organized into what were essentially drill companies. Although the *Militia Act* of 1868 promised cadets and their instructors arms and military manuals, it was not until 1879 that regulations were promulgated setting up a system for organizing and supplying corps attached to schools. But with a miniscule budget, there was still little the Department of Militia and Defence could do in concrete terms to help the cadet movement.

It was the impetus of the Boer War that finally triggered the much-needed support. In the same House of Commons policy

Toronto public school cadets and their instructors during an 1899 trip to Tampa, Florida.

announcement that marked an increase to the militia, Borden explained his views on the importance of cadets in providing future members and leaders for the expanded reserve force. He noted that boys were able to learn military skills much faster than adults and promised to advance the development of youth training. He was as good as his word.

That same year, Borden allowed cadet instructors to hold militia rank for the first time and added cadet corps to the annual Militia List (the official government document detailing all military units and their locations across the country), which gave them formal recognition. All corps were to be connected to a school or organized as independent units. The next year, the *Militia Act* of 1904 confirmed these arrangements and over the next several years the government encouraged the formation of new corps by a generous provision of rifles, ammunition, and arcade rifle-practice machines. New units proliferated, and by 1908 there were 145 corps with nine thousand boys, a 40 per cent increase in the number of units in four years. By now, Borden had begun to initiate a much broader scheme for training youth, which appealed to Canadians because it not only provided young boys with physical exercise, discipline, and a sense of patriotism, but with military training as well.

Borden's plan, based on a successful example from Australia, was to provide a better system of military training for youth through the schools. Because education was a provincial responsibility, Borden had to work with the provinces. Progress was slow, but by the spring of 1907 he had met with every provincial premier or minister of education and had general agreement that some form of physical training for all boys and girls, as well as military drill for older boys, was desirable. Only Nova Scotia concluded an agreement that year, and physical and military training were introduced into the curriculum that fall, with the resulting formation of cadet corps.

Borden sought and received the financial assistance of Lord Strathcona to further his training scheme during a visit to England in 1908. Strathcona, the Canadian High Commissioner in London at the time, was an ardent imperialist with strong military leanings. The idea immediately appealed to him, and with a large personal fortune made through such iconic Canadian institutions as the Hudson's Bay Company, the Canadian Pacific Railway, and the Bank of Montreal, he provided a $250,000 trust fund (later doubled to $500,000) to support this training. His letter supporting the scheme noted he attached "the greatest importance to the advantages of physical training and elementary drill for all children of both sexes" and was particularly anxious that "the special value of military drill, including rifle shooting for boys capable of using rifles should be constantly borne in mind." Strathcona not only wanted "to help to improve the physical and intellectual capabilities of children by inculcating habits of alertness, orderliness and prompt obedience, but also to bring up the boys to patriotism and to a realization that the first duty of a free citizen is to be prepared to defend his country."[28]

Combining Strathcona's private funding with money from his department, Borden launched his new campaign in March 1909. As he explained in the House of Commons, all male and female teachers graduating from provincial normal schools (as teacher's colleges were then known), would be required to hold a certificate in physical training, while in addition all male graduates would "be encouraged" to hold a certificate in military training. Boys and girls would receive compulsory physical training in their early years in elementary schools, followed by voluntary military training for boys as they reached the upper levels of grade school and entered high school. Male teachers who provided the military training would hold militia commissions and receive an annual stipend. Permanent Force personnel would provide instruction at normal schools and would eventually conduct the annual inspections of cadet corps.

At first, the provinces were slow to accept Borden's offer, perhaps over concerns that such a drastic departure from the previous curriculum would be criticized, but by 1911 they had all signed on. The bombastic Sam Hughes replaced Borden in 1911 and added incentives to the program. He lowered the age for free issues of ammunition to fourteen from fifteen and allowed any cadet able to load a rifle to obtain shooting-gallery ammunition. Annual bonuses were given each corps to assist in the purchase and upkeep of uniforms, signalling equipment was issued to all corps, and bayonets were distributed to some cadets. But Hughes's most important achievement was amending the *Militia Act* to allow cadets to be sent to summer camps separate from militia ones. Such encouragement and positive measures saw the number of cadets rise from fifteen thousand in 1910 to nearly forty-five thousand in early 1913, supervised by more than twelve thousand teachers and cadet instructors.[29]

Cadets and officers of the Church Lads' Brigade, St. John's, Newfoundland, about 1910.

In Newfoundland, a separate and distinct cadet movement arose based on the English model of the Church Lads' Brigade, which had been established in 1891. The island's cadets were a function of the way the educational system had developed there, under which all schools were maintained on a strictly sectarian basis. This system was a logical extension of the schools' efforts to see to the physical and moral welfare of the youth in their charge, whereby boys and young men would receive "guidance and training that would help mould their character and develop them into good citizens."[30] Four separate organizations were formed: the Church Lads' Brigade in 1892 by the Anglican Church, the Catholic Cadet Corps in 1896, the Methodist Guards Brigade in 1900, and the Newfoundland Highlanders in 1907 by the Presbyterian Church.

Initially formed in St. John's, some of the corps later expanded to other parts of the island. The aim of these organizations was to oversee the physical, mental, and moral welfare of their members. Their founders believed this could best be accomplished through an organization patterned along semi-military lines, where the habits of discipline, self-reliance, cooperation, and obedience to authority would be developed. Programs included physical and gymnastics exercises, as well as sports and other recreational activities. Military training usually consisted of signalling, basic medical instruction such as first aid and stretcher-bearing, drill, marching, and rifle shooting. Several corps held summer camps, to which the cadets normally marched, and many of them formed military bands. A spirit of competition was encouraged by annual contests between the various corps. Apart from a small Royal Naval Reserve, the church brigades were almost the only source of recruits with some form of military training for any future war effort involving Newfoundland.[31]

The pre-war efforts of Canada and Newfoundland in offering some form of military training to schoolboys provided a large recruiting pool to draw on when the First World War broke out in August 1914. More than forty-four thousand cadets or ex-cadets served in the Canadian Expeditionary Force (CEF), of whom twenty-five were awarded the Victoria Cross.[32] A comparable situation existed in Newfoundland, where of the more than seven hundred men who had volunteered by the end of August, considerably more than half had been members of the various church brigades. Additionally, the Royal Newfoundland Regiment's only Victoria Cross recipient had been a member of the Church Lads' Brigade.[33] But the unheard-of carnage, bloodshed, and destruction about to occur during the First World War were a far cry from the peacetime drilling, marching, and camping these young boys had experienced as cadets.

CHAPTER 1

"TAKE A WALK AROUND THE BLOCK."
Recruiting Boy Soldiers, 1914–1918

Although there had been some warning signs, the outbreak of war in the summer of 1914 was largely unexpected, particularly within the British Empire.[1] At the beginning of the year, British Chancellor of the Exchequer David Lloyd George had declared that the time was the most opportune in twenty years for a reconsideration of the whole question of armaments. He described relations with Germany as "infinitely more friendly than they have been for years."[2] In June, during a debate in the Canadian House of Commons about a proposed increase to the size of the militia, a Member of Parliament said, "There is no danger in sight; why then raise the Militia of this country to the enormous figure of between 75,000 and 80,000 men? There is no reason for it; there is no emergency in sight, and there will be none in our day and generation."[3] How wrong he was.

The spark that ignited the war was the assassination of Archduke Franz Ferdinand, nephew and heir of Franz Josef, the

Sir Wilfrid Laurier was Canada's seventh prime minister and was in office from 1896 to 1911. This full-length portrait was painted in 1913.

eighty-eight-year-old Habsburg Emperor of Austria and King of Hungary, during a state visit to the Bosnian capital of Sarajevo on June 28, 1914. The attack was carried out by nineteen-year-old Gavrilo Princip, a member of the Bosnian Serb nationalist group "Black Hand," which was dedicated to freeing Bosnia from Austria-Hungary so it could become a part of Serbia. In reaction to the assassination, and after many lengthy and secret discussions, Austria sent Serbia an ultimatum with fifteen demands on July 23, which required an answer within forty-eight hours. Events over the next two weeks moved swiftly and — many believe —

inexorably, as most of Europe mobilized. According to respected American historian Barbara Tuchman, the general staffs of the major European powers "were pounding the table for the signal to move lest their opponents gain an hour's head start,"[4] driven by the self-imposed relentlessness of railway timetables designed to move vast numbers of troops to the front lines.

It was not enough that Serbia humiliated itself and unexpectedly agreed to most of Austria's demands; Austria declared war on Serbia on July 29. On August 2, military patrols from Austria's ally, Germany, crossed the French border and several skirmishes ensued. Germany demanded free passage through Belgium, which the little country refused. The next day, Germany declared war on France. On August 4, Britain delivered an ultimatum to Germany demanding it honour the treaty protecting Belgium's neutrality. Seven hours before the demand expired, the Kaiser's troops entered Belgium. German Chancellor Theobald von Bethmann-Hollweg's reply to the British ultimatum, dismissing the treaty as "a scrap of paper,"[5] resounded around the world. Britain declared war on Germany at eleven o'clock that night and by midnight five great empires — Austro-Hungarian, German, Russian, British, and French — were at war.

With the European war begun in earnest and since Canada was a British colony, then, as Prime Minister Sir Wilfrid Laurier had put it in 1910, "When Britain is at war, Canada is at war. There is no distinction."[6] Canada, however, was ill-prepared to fight any war, anywhere. To begin with, it did not have nearly enough regular enlisted men. The Canadian Army Permanent Force (the full-time regular component) consisted of some 3,110 officers and men. On the plus side, various reforms and increases in the military budget had resulted in a larger, better-equipped militia than ever before.

As the unusually hot summer of 1914 unfolded, the government felt it was necessary — due to the rapidly worsening international situation after mid-July — to order creation of militia detachments as local protection forces on both coasts and elsewhere. At the same time, it also made preparations to field a Canadian contingent for overseas service. On July 30, Colonel Sam Hughes, the minister of militia and defence, held an emergency meeting of the Militia Council, which included the deputy minister and senior military officers. They concluded that if war came, a first contingent of at least twenty thousand men would be sent abroad. The governor general and the prime minister approved.

On August 1, as German troops marched toward the French border, the governor general, His Royal Highness Field Marshal the Duke of Connaught, cabled Lewis Harcourt, the secretary of state for the colonies, noting that while a peaceful solution to the difficult international situation was earnestly hoped for, he was conveying the firm assurance that if war broke out, "the Canadian people will be united in a common resolve to put forth every effort and to make every sacrifice necessary to ensure the integrity and maintain the honour of our empire."[7]

On August 4, the government issued an order in council that put the Royal Canadian Navy (RCN) on active service and placed the navy's sailors and its two warships, His Majesty's Canadian Ships *Niobe* and *Rainbow* at the disposal of the Royal Navy (RN). At 8:45 that evening, the news that war had broken out with Germany arrived in a cable addressed to the governor general. The next day, the Duke of Connaught (who, ironically, also held the German titles of Duke of Saxony and Prince of Saxe-Coburg and Gotha), issued a formal proclamation in the *Canada Gazette*.

Canada was officially at war. The next four years would absorb a generation of young men — thousands of them under the age of eighteen.

Militia training at Camp Sewell (later Camp Hughes), Manitoba, in late July 1914, two weeks before the declaration of war.

On August 6, 1914, a cable from Secretary of State for the Colonies Lewis Harcourt to Governor General the Duke of Connaught noted that the British government "gratefully accepts offer of your Ministers to send Expeditionary Force to this country and would be glad if it could be despatched as soon as possible."[8] The suggested force was a division of about 22,500 men.[9] With this number in mind, military staff in Ottawa prepared to implement the country's mobilization plan, drawn up in 1911 by Colonel Willoughby Gwatkin, a British officer permanently seconded to Canada that year.[10] His plan detailed the mobilization of an infantry division and a mounted brigade for "active service in a civilized country in a temperate climate"[11] — almost exactly what the British had requested. But neither the governor general, the prime minister, the chief of the general staff, militia council, nor anyone else had reckoned with Sam Hughes, who had his own ideas.

As aggressive as he was unpredictable, Sam Hughes was minister of militia and defence for the first twenty-seven months of the First World War.

Colonel Samuel Hughes was a sixty-one-year-old Ontario editor, soldier, and politician. Argumentative, egotistical, stubborn — as well as supremely confident of his own military prowess, Hughes had been elected to Parliament in 1892 as the Conservative member for Victoria North, a rural Ontario riding east of Lake Simcoe. A long-serving militia officer, he was convinced his fellow citizen-soldiers were far superior to insular regulars. In 1899, he had bullied his way to a staff job in the Boer War in South Africa, and by October 1911 he was minister of militia and defence in Robert Borden's government. Because of Hughes, the mobilization for overseas service at the outbreak of war turned out to be a chaotic, confused affair that became highly politicized as the minister hired and fired, promoted and demoted on the spot. He completely disregarded the existing pre-war mobilization plans drawn up by the professionals, deciding instead to personally oversee the mobilization according to his own ideas.

As a result, dozens of traditional and storied named regiments were bypassed and soulless numbered battalions created instead, with many of their soldiers, at least initially, drawn from existing militia units. Eventually, 260 separate infantry battalions and thirteen regiments of mounted rifles were formed, along with hundreds of units in the support and service arms. At its peak establishment of four divisions in the field, the Canadian Corps — the fighting arm of the CEF — required only forty-eight battalions, less than 20 percent of the total available.[12] This left the vast majority of CEF infantry and mounted rifles battalions to the soul-destroying fate of being broken up in England to provide reinforcement drafts for the Corps on the Western Front in France and Flanders. Not only was this a crushing blow to the units involved, it was an extremely inefficient use of men and money. Indeed, it took several weeks to sort out the mass confusion caused by Hughes's meddling; all of it occurring as thousands of men poured into Valcartier, the massive mobilization camp located on the rough and sandy plain northwest of Quebec City.

Meanwhile, across the country, men and boys were volunteering in large numbers and, in many instances, militia units volunteered to a man. To be selected, infantrymen, artillery drivers, Army Service Corps and Army Medical Corps recruits had to stand a minimum of five-feet-three-inches tall with a chest measuring at least thirty-three and a half inches, except for artillery drivers, whose minimum chest measurement had to be thirty-four and a half inches. Others had to be bigger to handle the heavy work expected of them. Engineer sappers and drivers had to have a minimum height of five feet four inches and a chest measurement of thirty-four and a half inches, while artillery gunners and pioneers had to stand at least five feet seven inches with a thirty-four-and-a-half-inch chest circumference.

Age limits were eighteen (later raised to nineteen) to forty-five years and a high standard was expected in musketry and general proficiency. Under-eighteens could be accepted if they had a signed letter of consent from a parent, although this did not guarantee acceptance if the individual were undersize or otherwise unsuitable for service. Interestingly, applicants had to enter their birth date on the attestation form and to declare that such answers were true, but no birth certificates had to be produced unless specifically requested. Instead, examining doctors entered the prospective enrolees' apparent age in years and months, which was "to be determined according to the instructions given in the Regulations for Army Medical Services." Such a system left the door wide open to overstating the age of those under eighteen. Applicants were to be selected from, in order, single men, then married men without families, and then married men with families. No married man could join without the written consent of his wife. The term of service was for the duration of the war and soldiers were to have the same status as British regulars.[13]

The standard of medical examinations varied across the country, often depending on the abilities or interest of unit medical officers or civilian practitioners, who were paid fifty cents a head.[14] A huge number of potential recruits were turned down — perhaps as high as 40 percent of all those who tried to join, which would amount to several hundred thousand men. There were many reasons for medical rejection, among them weak eyesight, poor hearing, bad teeth, or flat feet. Despite these standards, some individuals still managed to enrol who clearly did not meet the criteria, including in several instances boys whose physical development clearly marked them as too young to enlist.

Perhaps the most blatant example was Russell Mick, of Pembroke, Ontario. On March 17, 1916, Mick wandered into the local

BUSHMEN AND SAWMILL HANDS
WANTED
JOIN THE
224TH CANADIAN FORESTRY BATTALION
ALEXANDER McDOUGALL   HEADQUARTERS
LT. COL.   43 BANK ST. OTTAWA

Forestry battalions, like the 224th, drew on the lumbering skills — real or imagined — of Canadian men.

recruiting centre claiming a birth date of April 4, 1898, making him two weeks short of his eighteenth birthday. Although he was only sixteen, and despite his apparent age being recorded as seventeen, he was duly enrolled in the 224th Forestry Battalion. As well as being too young, Mick weighed only eighty pounds and was suffering from infantile paralysis, which rendered him largely incapable of movement. Despite the boy's obvious physical shortcomings, a medical officer certified on Mick's attestation form that he had examined him and that he "does not present any of the causes of rejection specified in the Regulations for Army Medical Services" and that "he can see at the required distance with either eye; his heart and lungs are healthy; he has the free use of his joints and limbs…"[15]

A month later, Mick was sent to England, where he went into hospital and was eventually returned to Canada as an "undesirable." His case was used in the House of Commons as an example of poor screening. Mick himself was undeterred and — almost unbelievably — on February 20, 1917, re-enrolled into the CEF, again at Pembroke. This time he joined a Field Ambulance Depot, claiming a birth date of June 6, 1898 (this time his apparent age was recorded as eighteen). He even noted his previous service with the 224th Battalion, which should have raised some obvious questions among the recruiting staff.[16]

Ottawa, meanwhile, got a bargain when it came to recruiting. Without the government's having to spend a cent, militia units essentially did all the recruiting for the army and paid for it from their regimental funds. According to the *Toronto Daily Star*, it cost an average of $13,384 to raise a thousand-man infantry battalion, which included advertising and the cost of instruments for the band.[17] A number of groups such as women's associations, recruiting organizations, and various instant patriotic societies, helped by raising money and hosting highly jingoistic meetings — and by keeping an eye out for potential recruits.

The initial patriotic fervour that sparked enlistment during the opening months of the war began to wane fairly quickly. As early as January 1915, a reduction in the number of recruits from certain parts of the country, such as the Maritimes — and, most noticeably, Quebec — was observed. In response, the Department of Militia and Defence made various changes to its recruiting standards and policies. In July it lowered its minimum standards for height for all corps except artillery to a minimum of five feet two inches (artillery was lowered to five feet four inches) and for chest circumference by half an inch, to a range between thirty-three and thirty-four inches.

The right of parents to take their underage sons out of the army was discontinued in the summer of 1915, after a court ruled

This recruiting poster, based on the importance of friends, would have exerted a particularly powerful influence on young boys — whether intended or not.

that a pact existed between the army and an enrolled soldier, regardless of his age.[18] Nevertheless, parental persistence could still — as in the case of Robert Thompson of Hillier, Ontario — get a son out of the service. In August the requirement for a married man to have his wife's permission to join was dropped and the right of a soldier to buy his way out after enlisting (fifteen dollars during the first three months of service; if after three months, then two dollars per month for the unexpired period of one year's service), which had been approved only in March, was rescinded. By that fall, many militia units had run out of money for recruiting and the first accusations against the government were made by various recruiting organizations for not helping them. Additionally, demands for some kind of national registration or conscription began to be heard at patriotic rallies, to

Canada's eighth prime minister, Sir Robert Borden, served from 1911 to 1920 and successfully led the country through the First World War.

ensure that men who tried to shirk their duty could be identified and urged to enlist.[19]

Astonishingly, even boys younger than ten tried to enlist. In 1916, nine-year-old Milton Brown arrived at a Regina recruiting office in an attempt to join the 195th Battalion. He told recruiters he wanted to be overseas with his father, and figured if he enrolled he could get transferred to his father's company. Instead of rejecting him outright, the recruiters sent him home to get his mother's permission. Remarkably, the lad returned the next day with the required letter, signed by his mother. Although he was turned down by the 195th, young Milton applied to the 217th Battalion — where he was rejected again.[20]

Despite a general minimum age restriction of eighteen, Tim Cook, First World War historian at the Canadian War Museum, estimates that out of the 424,589 who served overseas in the Canadian Expeditionary Force (CEF), as many as twenty thousand underage soldiers made it to Europe[21], and another several thousand never left Canada. Additionally, when the true age of an unknown number of boys was discovered during or after the enrolment process, they were either turned away or released.

Later, as the war ground on and more recruits were needed to replace previously unheard of casualties on the Western Front, recruiters were not as fussy. When many boys stated their true age to recruiting sergeants, they were frequently told "to take a walk around the block."[22] In other words, they were deliberately invited to pause, to think about it, and then to falsify their ages so they could be enlisted. Even before the outbreak of war it was common for boys who had been told to come back in a year or two to ignore the advice; they simply approached a different recruiting sergeant.

For other lads the route overseas was more challenging. Many were stopped in their tracks, some even after they had enrolled. Frank Bell spent only a short time in the army, and never did get his wish. Born in the eastern Ontario town of Lancaster in 1901, Bell enlisted at age fifteen in the spring of 1916. He looked older than his years, but just as he was about to go overseas his brother forced him to confess his true age to military officials and he was released. The young man's adventures did not end there. Searching for a job, Bell moved to Montreal, where he found work as an electrician in a powerhouse. By the time conscription went into effect in 1917, he had experienced a serious run-in with authorities because he was *not* in the army. "I was picked up one night and put in jail overnight because I didn't have my discharge papers with me. By this time I was about seventeen. I was dying to get into the army, but they wouldn't take me. So I was picked up by these civilian police. They weren't the regular police force, they were a special corps that went around at night picking up young men and putting them in the army — press gang is really what they were."

After a cold night in jail, Bell — at the point of a bayonet — forcefully declined the opportunity to help mop the cell's grimy floor, explaining to a soldier-warder that "I joined the army voluntarily... I was no God-damned conscript." Bell's protest

Three young men from the Ottawa area who enrolled in the 77th Battalion pose formally in 1914. L-R: Duff Crerar, Elmo Sully, and Ross Campbell.

worked; he was allowed to call his workplace, which sent someone to his boarding house to retrieve his discharge papers so he could finally get out of jail. Interestingly, Bell had been carrying his birth certificate all along, "but they wouldn't believe it."[23]

Other lads anxious to get overseas took different approaches. John G. Wright was one of them. Not willing to take "no" for an answer, Wright, whose father had already served overseas and whose brother was still there, wrote to Prime Minister Sir Robert Borden, noting he was "the only one left to do something for my country." His handwritten plea came on April 18, 1918 — after huge battlefield loses and insufficient replacements had forced the government to introduce conscription eight months earlier. "I am only a boy of sixteen years and want to give my life for my country. I have tried many times and failed... And, Sir, if you only knew how I am going crazy to do something to gain honour. I am strong and healthy. I have never had any sickness in my life. I was just reading in the paper this morning and saw that you said 'Canadians must hold the line.' They cannot do it without men. Please will you give me a position in that line? I don't call myself a man but I might help to hold that line. So please give me a chance, the line is more valuable than my life."[24]

Even with such a heartfelt pitch, Wright failed to get in, presumably on account of being so honest about his age. Yet, at a time when birth certificates were less common than they are today — and in most cases were not required at recruiting centres — big, brawny boys who had, like Robert Thompson, spent their childhood working in factories, forests, or on farms could easily be mistaken for being old enough to join, and so their chances of getting overseas were much greater.

Born in England in 1899 and orphaned at an early age, Burton Woods was eleven when he was sent to Canada by Fegan's Homes, an English Christian charity dedicated to the welfare of orphans and abandoned street urchins. He had been working on a farm for five years when war erupted. Then, as he explained it, "I run away and joined the army, and I gave my age as eighteen. I was between fourteen and fifteen. I didn't wash or anything or shine my shoes or clean anything. I looked just tough, you know, like a regular farm boy." Getting into the army delighted Woods. On the farm he had been earning just five dollars a year plus his keep; in the army he got a dollar and ten cents a day, as well as uniforms, quarters, and rations. He served as a sniper overseas and survived the war.[25]

The reasons these and thousands of other boy soldiers joined the CEF were numerous. Some enrolled almost out of desperation, so they could escape poverty, menial, mind-numbing jobs, or the hell-hole of an orphanage or foster home. Others were searching for adventure, weaned on stories from such popular contemporary publications as *Boy's Own Annual*. Some — like their older comrades — enlisted out of a strong sense of patriotism, wanting to be part of the "just crusade" of the great British Empire, of which Canada was an integral part. This was especially true of adolescent boys who had rudimentary military training in drill and shooting by having served either in the militia or as members of the forty-five-thousand-strong cadet movement. Undoubtedly, peer pressure also played a role, a standard element in the coming of age of males. And, in common with young men everywhere, Canadian boys believed they were invincible; war was a game, not a deadly contest. Later, as the war continued and the casualties rose, some boys joined to avenge the loss of a father, older brother, or other relative. Whatever their motives — patriotism, adventure, escape, revenge, optimism — they came about as a result of their youthful thinking and the global conflagration that had its beginning half a world away from Canada.

CHAPTER 2

" . . . ABOUT A THIRD OF THE BOYS HAD BEEN TO FRANCE AND THEY WERE GLAD TO BE BACK."
Overseas, but Underage, 1914 – 1918

On September 26, 1914, sixteen-year-old Private George McCahon stood on the docks at Quebec City amid scenes of mass confusion. Being younger and shorter than the men around him, it is most likely he had to crane his neck to get a better view of the thousands of soldiers who, like him, were waiting to board an odd assortment of thirty-one transports and luxury passenger liners, newly painted in their wartime grey. It must have seemed to McCahon, and indeed to many others, that none of the higher-ups knew much about loading ships, as evidenced by the huge traffic jams along the docks, and the on-again-off-again transfer of soldiers and cargo. Ultimately, it would take a week to load everything, including the men, nearly 7,700 horses, 127 guns, hundreds of wagons, and even a wartime gift to Great Britain of more than 135,000 sacks of flour.[1] Many times the cheering, which had greeted the soldiers as they marched along the cobblestone streets of the old city to the waterfront, drowned out the brass bands and choirs trying to entertain the boys of the first Canadian contingent: Canada's initial contribution to the war overseas.

As each ship was finally loaded and moved out into the St. Lawrence River, a great flotilla formed — destined to sail down-river to Gaspé Harbour where it would be joined by four light cruisers of the Royal Navy. At 3 p.m. on October 3, the ships and their escorts began their 4,025-kilometre journey across the North Atlantic into fading daylight toward England, making history as the largest convoy ever to sail from Canada. The weather was warm and the sea calm as the armada sailed through the night and past the Dominion of Newfoundland, where at 11 a.m. it was joined by the passenger liner SS *Florizel* carrying The First Five Hundred, the name given to the initial group of Newfoundland volunteers.[2] Assigned to third-class steerage and mixed among the lower ranks in all of the ships were an unknown number of boy soldiers, including McCahon; the first of several thousand teenage boys — and, in a few cases, boys still in their pre-teens — who left or ran away from home during the First World War.[3]

On arrival in England, soldiers were surprised to discover that the age limits for going to the front were different from those for recruitment. Recruits could be eighteen to forty-five, but only those between nineteen and forty-two were sent to the trenches, according to the standards established by the British.[4] As a result, thousands of eighteen-year-old Canadian boys who had legally enrolled were suddenly too young to go to France. But, more often than not, units simply ignored this stricture, especially if the eighteen-year-old in question "was considered a good soldier."[5] Perhaps not unexpectedly, boy soldiers were frequently considered "good soldiers," as they were usually mentally and physically fit, robust, adaptive, resilient, easily trained, well-disciplined, and appreciative. It is also true that many of these teenagers worked hard at portraying themselves as being much older than their actual years, lest they be discovered and sent home. On the Western Front, many took on the mannerisms of older men, eager to swear, drink, smoke, and tough it out without complaint.

Surprisingly, the question of boy soldiers at the front never became an important issue to the vast majority of Canadians. It was not raised in the House of Commons until April 1916, when the prime minister responded to a question about boy soldiers in the CEF by stating he had "always understood that the policy is not to enlist boys under 18" but agreed to look into it.[6] Borden's response seems to have satisfied MPs, and very few similar questions arose for the rest of the war. Paradoxically — and perhaps perversely — more Canadians were concerned about whether or not soldiers should be able to buy a beer in a wet canteen than they were about boy soldiers killing and possibly being killed in front-line trenches.[7]

Certainly, the parents of some of these boys wrote letters to the authorities in an attempt to have them returned home. The stated reason was usually that the boy was needed to help on the family farm — regarded as essential war work — especially if other male family members were also serving or otherwise unavailable. Most requests were ignored or stalling tactics employed, such as requiring evidence of age. Some boys were killed in action waiting for this proof of age to arrive. Despite insistence by military headquarters staff that boy soldiers were to be withdrawn from the front, units still continued to wilfully ignore the order, concerned about losing well-trained soldiers.

One lad was — if nothing else — persistent in his determination to enlist. Robert Clarence Thompson of Hillier, Ontario, had just turned fourteen less than three months earlier and was a student at Prince Edward Collegiate Institute in nearby Picton when he enrolled, caught up in the patriotic fervour of the time. He explained his reasons on four pages of pencilled, handwritten notes, titled "Why I Should Enlist," which not only reflect his motivation

Robert Thompson, from Hillier, Ontario, was, if nothing else, a determined individual. He managed to enroll twice at age fourteen and once at fifteen.

for joining, but also show an understanding of the issues beyond his years. "There are many reasons why I should enlist for overseas service," he began. "The fate of the empire is at stake and Great Britain needs all of her men to go and fight for liberty's course. If the Allies win, which should and must be the case you will come home crowned with glory and proud to say that you have fought for your king and country. A man has got to die once and why not die a hero rather than a coward?"[8]

At school Thompson wore short pants, but he was wearing a pair of borrowed trousers when he walked into the Brockville, Ontario, recruiting centre of the 59th Battalion on February 25, 1916. The trousers helped create the impression he was a working man, rather than a schoolboy. On his attestation papers he claimed he was born on December 12, 1897 — he had actually been born in December 1901 — and listed his occupation as "factory hand." He also stated he had spent a year in cadets. At five-feet-six-inches tall, with a chest of thirty-six inches, Thompson's physique easily exceeded minimum enrolment standards. His ploy — coupled with his confidence and appearance — worked; recruiting personnel quickly noted his "apparent age" as eighteen.[9]

One of eight sons of Robert Wesley and Grace Thompson, pro-
prietors of the Cloverdale Cheese Factory in nearby Wellington,
Thompson was well on his way when his father discovered what
his namesake had done, and managed to convince authorities
to release the boy after a few day's service. But the venturesome
Thompson quickly discovered a systemic shortcoming that
allowed many youngsters to enrol: recruiting centre personnel
did not cross-reference rejected individuals with other recruiters. And so, less than three weeks after his original enlistment,
Thompson re-enrolled in the CEF on March 16, 1916 — this
time in the 155th Battalion, headquartered in Belleville. Although
he listed his occupation as "student," and claimed the same date
of birth as the first time (December 12, 1897), his apparent age
was noted as nineteen on his new attestation form.[10] After initial
training, Thompson sailed with his battalion from Halifax on
October 18 in the former German immigrant ship *Northland* and
arrived at Liverpool ten days later. After six months training in
Britain, he was sent to France.

Fred Claydon felt the urge to join the army at an early age and
had no trouble being accepted. Before enlisting at age sixteen in
1915, Claydon was better off than orphaned farm boy Burton
Woods, earning a hundred dollars a year — plus clothes and
board — thrashing wheat and herding sheep on his grandfather's
ranch northwest of Elkhorn, Manitoba.[11] Still, what Claydon
earned in 1910 was well below the average annual wage paid to
farm workers.[12] "There was no money in them days," he recalled,
adding it was common for ranchers to loan out their hired help
to neighbouring farms in exchange for other work or as a way of
paying off a debt. Claydon, who never attended school, worked
mostly outdoors, and when he was not herding or thrashing he
was "nutting" rams or tramping wool, occasionally stopping to
scratch at the tick bites on his arms and legs. Joining the infantry
took him away from that — in the direction of adventure. But

he would never forget the long and dangerous work or the brutal winter weather that toughened him for his years on the Western Front. Howling winds — strong enough to knock a grown man off his feet — and sub-zero temperatures were never enough to keep a boy from his work which, even on the coldest of days, included riding an ox into town to pick up the mail.

Roy Edward Henley also got overseas — more than once, and lived to tell about it. In an interview many years after the war, Henley claimed he was born on September 21, 1902, and was ten when he was shipped off to relatives in Canada. He had spent the first decade of his life at Dymchurch, Kent, not far from the Romney Marshes made infamous by bootleggers. "It was the family business," Henley recalled, "...smuggling French wine and tobacco" into England. In central Ontario, relatives tried to interest the boy in farming, but "farming and I don't mix," he remembered. So Henley struck out for Toronto, where he joined the Royal Canadian Dragoons as a trumpeter in 1915. He was thirteen, but passed for sixteen. "They were looking for bodies," he remembered. "They looked in one ear and if they couldn't see through, well, you were in."[13]

In 1916, Henley made it through training and to England, where he contracted pneumonia. Then, "when they caught up with my age I was sent back to Canada,"[14] where he re-enrolled at Montreal on March 24, 1917, claiming a birth date of September 29, 1898. He stated his trade as teamster,[15] which may be the reason he was taken on strength of the Canadian Army Service Corps, the branch of the service responsible for the delivery of supplies, most of which were hauled by horses and wagons. Henley made it to England again, and eventually got to France where he was wounded while serving with the 42nd (Royal Highlanders of Canada) Battalion.

Once a boy was withdrawn from the trenches, the problem then became where to hold him. While many were employed in

The cookhouse at Witley Camp, Surrey, was typical of the cooking facilities provided to Canadians stationed at army camps in England.

rear areas — some still within the range of enemy fire — most were sent to England for additional training until they turned nineteen and could legally rejoin their units. By the end of 1916, more than five thousand such adolescents were spread throughout reserve or training units in England.[16] When the COs of these units began asking what to do with these boys, the headquarters of the Overseas Military Forces of Canada (OMFC) in London issued new orders in January 1917. Boys under sixteen and a half would be returned to Canada, unless they were buglers or drummers, while those older would be sent to the 5th Division, which remained in England. About fifteen hundred boy soldiers were working in the Forestry Corps, either in England or on the continent. Hundreds of boys were sent home in response to this directive, but the vast majority remained in uniform.

Meanwhile, as early as September 1916, discussions had taken place about forming a special unit to hold adolescents. At the end of December that year, the 34th Battalion at Brighton held about eight hundred boy soldiers in it, making it an unofficial "boys' battalion." On July 28, 1917, this informal status was formalized with the creation of a special boys' battalion at Bramshott, Surrey (known to soldiers and locals alike as "Mudsplosh Camp"[17]), designated the Young Soldiers Battalion (YSB), and commanded by Lieutenant-Colonel Daniel MacKay.[18]

MacKay, a thirty-nine-year-old surgeon from Manitoba, had originally joined the 27th (City of Winnipeg) Battalion on October 25, 1914, shortly after the war broke out. When he joined the CEF he was a member of Winnipeg's 79th Cameron Highlanders, and had previously served with 17th Field Battery and 16th Field Ambulance. MacKay was appointed the 27th Battalion's second-in-command, followed by service at the 6th Brigade headquarters until he was transferred to the medical corps in February 1916.[19] The 27th, which had been raised in response to the mobilization of a second Canadian contingent, preceded overseas in May 1915, arrived in France in mid-September as part of 2nd Canadian Division's 6th Brigade, and entered the line for the first time on October 1, in the Ypres Salient.[20] MacKay returned to Canada in the spring of 1916 and was promoted to lieutenant colonel on June 1 to become the CO of the 196th Battalion. Based in Winnipeg, the 196th recruited in universities throughout western Canada during the winter of 1915–16. After sailing to England in the fall of 1916, the unit was absorbed into the 19th Reserve Battalion. MacKay became CO of the YSB in October 1917.

Headquarters ordered all units, including those at the front, to transfer boy soldiers to the YSB, which quickly reached its maximum allowable strength of one thousand adolescents. Those over the quota were attached to various other units, such as medical, railway, or forestry, providing they were kept out of harm's way; although that was easier said than done, especially for those assigned duties in France. At the YSB, the daily schedule included military training, physical fitness, and discipline. MacKay was solicitous of his young charges and especially concerned about creating an environment where proper morals could be instilled. He established "cheerful, well furnished reading and games rooms" and allowed access to dry canteens, but placed wet canteens out of bounds.[21] He even persuaded authorities that developing boys had different dietary requirements than adults and obtained extra rations.

The training at the YSB was thorough, intense, and relevant to what the young soldiers could expect in the trenches. For those who had already survived the daily grind of front-line life it was hardly new, but for fresh arrivals from Canada it was a revelation. More formal education also played a part in the boys' training, and they were encouraged to enrol in the Khaki University, which allowed several to complete high school courses. Roy Henley, the Ontario boy who enrolled at age thirteen, was never sent to the YSB, although he remembered how good it was. "It was the smartest battalion in the Canadian forces because all they did was drill, and they gave them one third more rations ... because they were growing boys. Some of the smartest RSMs (regimental sergeant majors) came out of that boys battalion..."[22]

At Bramshott, there were several opportunities outside the camp for the boys' entertainment. One of the best remembered was "Tin Town," the nickname for a nearby straggle of corrugated-iron huts that had been hurriedly erected along the narrow London to Portsmouth road to serve the camp and its soldiers. While many of these establishments, such as the Salvation Army and the YMCA, were concerned with the soldiers' welfare; or, like a Royal Post office and the Midland Bank, with seeing to their needs; others — cafés and shops — were designed to separate soldiers from their money.

Charlie Edwards (left) and Aubrey Rumbold pose as soldiers while wearing Canadian headdress at Bramshott Camp, 1916. Charlie's mother ran the "Tin Town Café."

As local Charles Edwards recalled, "There were no sidewalks, just mud! — the shops had to put down duckboards by their entrances." When Edwards was five years old, his mother, Mabel, ran the "Tin Town Café," as she did from 1915. Edwards had the run of the place and was given a pass that read "Chief Butterfly Catcher to Canadian Army." The appetites of soldiers, looking for a change from the monotony of army rations, were prodigious. His mother had a truck-load of two-kilogram loaves of bread delivered daily and about four horse-drawn carts of mineral water a week. Tea or coffee was a penny a cup, while a sandwich or a piece of cake was two pence. All the men called Mrs. Edwards "Mother" and voted her place the most popular in the camp. After the end of the war, when demobilization delays led to some looting and arson in early 1919, soldiers turned out to protect her shop.[23]

By June 1918 there remained only 1,269 "officially identified"

The A3, the main London-Portsmouth Road, ran through "Tintown," a straggle of corrugated iron huts hurriedly erected to serve Canadian soldiers at Bramshott Camp.

soldiers under eighteen in the CEF: 755 in the YSB, 136 in the Forestry Corps, 131 in the Army Medical Corps, 99 in reserve battalions, and 148 in other units.[24] How many "unidentified" adolescents there still were is unknown, but it was in the thousands. As MacKay's young charges moved toward their nineteenth birthdays, the inevitable transfer to fighting units at the front loomed over them. Six months before that date, boys were moved into the battalion's D Company, while their final three months were spent in a reserve battalion undergoing intense training. By the end of the YSB's existence in 1918, 568 of its adolescents had been sent to the continent.[25] The rest stayed in England and continued training until the war ended.

One of those who never made it to the front from the YSB was John Babcock, who, when he died on February 18, 2010, at age 109, was Canada's last surviving soldier of the First World War — and one of only two or three worldwide. "Jack" Babcock was born north of Kingston, Ontario, in rural Frontenac County on July 23, 1900. When he was fifteen, he was impressed by a lieutenant and a sergeant on a recruiting drive in the nearby village of Perth

Road in January 1916. "They spoke about the British Cavalry and the charge of the Light Brigade," he recalled. "How they charged the Russian guns and sabred the gunners. I was impressed. I joined up."[26] Babcock also admitted to a more practical consideration: "I would get a dollar and ten cents a day — good money. On the farm I was only getting fifty cents a day."

Although he admitted his correct birth date, his attestation form noted his apparent age as eighteen and he was enrolled in the 146th Battalion in early February.[27] In June, the battalion moved to Valcartier, where Babcock underwent a second medical examination. Although he was declared physically fit, his age made him unsuitable for overseas service. About forty other soldiers in the unit were also declared unfit to go overseas. When their names were posted, for some reason Babcock's was not among them. Not waiting for further explanation, he grabbed his kit bag and fell in with the troops as they boarded a train for Halifax.

Unfortunately for Babcock, as the 146th Battalion boarded its ship, his company commander was standing by the gangway, recognized him, and waved him off. He was sent to the city's Wellington Barracks, where he soon grew bored of general duties, such as loading stores onto vehicles. Two weeks later, when the Royal Canadian Regiment (RCR) called for fifty volunteers for a reinforcement draft, Babcock stepped forward, claimed he was eighteen, and was finally on his way to England in October 1916.

Overseas, Babcock was taken on strength of the RCR and Princess Patricia's Canadian Light Infantry (PPCLI) Depot for additional training, the normal procedure for soldiers newly-arrived from Canada. Mixed in with the raw recruits were several veterans of the RCR and PPCLI awaiting return to the front. Babcock used every opportunity to learn from these experienced soldiers through their stories and actions. In January 1917 he was transferred briefly to the 7th Reserve Battalion before being sent

A fifteen-year-old John Babcock — rifle at the ready — poses front and centre with his mates from D Company, 146th Battalion, at Camp Valcartier, 1916.

to the 26th Reserve Battalion.

Once again his real age was discovered and Babcock was sent to the YSB in August 1917, which eventually held about thirteen hundred — some three hundred more than its maximum allowable strength. "I remember that about a third of the boys had been to France and they were glad to be back," Babcock explained. "Who the hell would want to be shot at all the time?" Yet, "Nobody was scared to go to France. We knew we'd be shot at, but we didn't know any better." He was promoted Acting Lance Corporal in September, lost his single stripe in March 1918 for "Neglect of Duty" but won it back in October.

On MacKay's recommendation, the decision was taken to disband the YSB and, in early November 1918, 981 of its members were transferred to Kinmel Park Camp in North Wales to begin demobilization. It was a dreadful place: foul weather, bad food, substandard accommodation, mindless activities, and delays

Beginning in 1915 the government asked Canadians to buy Victory Bonds to help finance its massive and unprecedented war effort.

in shipping only added to the tense atmosphere that already permeated the camp. But it was here that Babcock finally did see some action — of sorts. He and his buddies had been invited to a dance but were barred from entry by a bunch of British officer cadets. The Canadians, some of them veterans of combat, were not about to be denied the chance to meet some young women. Armed with an assortment of bricks and fence posts, and fuelled by alcohol, they charged the dance hall.

According to Babcock, "We got into a beef with some British soldiers and they armed themselves with rifles and bayonets. One fellow got a little obstreperous and they stuck a bayonet through his thigh."[28] After a bit of property damage and a few non-lethal personal injuries, the Canadian officers convinced their youthful soldiers to return to their barracks. While Babcock was at Kinmel, with eight months to go before his nineteenth birthday, the war ended. He never made it to the front. It was always a source of extreme disappointment to him and he often referred to himself as a "tin soldier" because of it. "I never got to fight. I don't consider myself to be a veteran, because I never got to fight."

But thousands of other boy soldiers did get to fight and experience the harsh reality of trench life in France and Flanders. From the opening gas attacks against 1st Canadian Division at Ypres in 1915, through the slugfest of the Somme in 1916, to the victories at Vimy Ridge and Passchendaele in 1917, to the glories of Canada's Hundred Days in the closing months of the war in 1918 — along with several other lesser-known but just as fierce battles — boy soldiers were there and played their full part as Canadian soldiers in "the war to end all wars."

CHAPTER 3

"GOODBYE MOTHER, FORGIVE ME."
Second Ypres, April 1915

The last twenty-four hours offered Private Donald Gordon a lot to write home about. To begin with, the Manitoba teenager, who had lied about his age when he enrolled at Valcartier in September 1914, did not expect to be riding a double-decker bus from the battalion's billets at Abeele to the outskirts of Ypres. Another surprise for the former gardener was the 8th (90th Winnipeg Rifles) Battalion's dangerous nighttime march on April 14, 1915, through the battered Belgian city toward the front, where guides had met the exhausted soldiers around midnight to lead them into shallow trenches. As the five-foot-six, blue-eyed Gordon marched past shell holes and piles of debris, a few large enemy shells — known as "coal boxes" for the black smoke they produced — smashed into the populated city. While Gordon had enrolled against his parents' wishes, the guilt he felt from that was perhaps less than what he would have felt if he had not signed up. Besides, thousands of other lads — even younger than him — had got past the recruiting sergeants by fudging their birth dates.[1]

Within two months of the German army's invasion of neutral Belgium on August 3, 1914, 30,617 males — many still in their teens and others well beyond the oldest permitted age for enrolment — had joined the CEF and were on their way overseas. It took eleven days for the thirty-one ships of the Canadian armada to cross the Atlantic and drop anchor off Plymouth and Devonport harbours in mid-October 1914. Waiting on the quay — sporting a thick, but well-managed moustache — was the Canadian contingent's new commander, fifty-five-year-old Lieutenant-General Sir Edwin Alderson, who had commanded Canadians during the South African War.[2] From the crowded railings on board ship, the men could see that the wharf was abuzz with the same kind of chaos as during their embarkation at Quebec. It would take nine days to unload the vessels, and patience had run dry amid rumours that the war would be over before the first soldier set foot in Britain, let alone France.[3] Men griped, tempers flared, and fights broke out — mostly over deteriorating food and accommodations. On shore, the good citizens of Plymouth — dressed in their Sunday finery — maintained a patriotic welcoming vigil, providing the men with moral support as well as some pleasant views for sore eyes. Some of the brave citizens even rowed fresh fruit and vegetables out to the ship-bound men, the vast majority of whom were British-born, making good on a promised homecoming.

Finally unloaded, the first contingent travelled seven hours by train to the edges of the British Army training area at Salisbury, 145 kilometres southwest of London. A week's leave followed, during which many found good company in local pubs where the taps ran free and where drunken brawls and frisky encounters with local girls took some shine off the Canadian reputation.

Bruised egos and sore heads, however, would be far less painful than what the men would endure during their first winter on Salisbury Plain. The rain began falling on the training ground in October and continued into February. Throughout winter, the rolling countryside was a sea of mud, made worse by the movement of thousands of soldiers and their rotting Canadian-made boots. The mud and oily dampness saturated clothes and skin, and without sufficient heating fuel most men elected to sleep in their clammy clothes rather than face the uncomfortable task of climbing back into them — minus body heat — in the morning. Worst of all were the penetrating winds that whipped across the open countryside, chilling men to the core as they fought to keep their non-waterproof bell tents from ripping or blowing over.[4] Metal and wooden huts set on cement risers were erected toward the end of the year, but with forty men to a hut it was easy for disease to spread. "As the weather became increasingly wet and cold, and with the transfer of the men to the huts a virulent type (of meningitis) disease appeared," wrote Colonel Kenneth Cameron of the Canadian Army Medical Corps. "During the second fortnight of December, 15 cases were reported…"[5]

Throughout the war, diseases, especially meningitis and pneumonia, proved fatal for several young Canadian lads undergoing training in England and Canada. Doctors and nurses worked around the clock but could do little to alleviate the severe suffering.[6] Outside the crowded hospital wards, thousands of others fought colds and the flu while sticking to a demanding training regime that for the infantry included long route marches, musketry, bayonet drill, and field exercises.

Among those weighed down but undaunted by the muck and rigours of drill was sixteen-year-old Private J. H. MacArthur of Vancouver, who had been fourteen when he enrolled in 1912 with the Duke of Connaught's Rifle Regiment. Initially, MacArthur made the mistake of telling the unit's recruiting sergeant he was sixteen, at which point he was asked to leave and come back in two years. Anxious to join the unit in time for an upcoming visit by the well-travelled Governor General, the Duke of Connaught, MacArthur returned in two weeks, reporting an age of eighteen to a different sergeant major. "So they take me in. I go through a medical, and in a week's time I'm thrown a uniform..." Unlike many under-aged soldiers, MacArthur did not have to worry about a parent's pulling him out. "I didn't have any family. That was one reason I went in. I figured that if anything happened to me, nobody would be the loser outside of my sister." An orphan since the age of two, MacArthur lived with one set of relatives while his sister lived with the other.

At Valcartier, MacArthur was assigned to the 7th (1st British Columbia) Battalion. He was handed equipment and lined up for inoculation and weeks of hard drill. "The inoculation was an odd thing... The fellow next to me was a big ox of a man, and he fainted while the man in front of him got the needle in his arm. I thought, 'What kind of soldier is he?'" By early October, MacArthur was aboard the SS *Virginia,* part of the first contingent sailing to England. He recalled the trip as a "wonder affair" with more than thirty ships, three destroyers and a couple of smaller escorts. It also marked the first time he encountered lice, and to a city boy that was a huge shock. "I found out later it was nothing at all to what I had to put up with [in the trenches]."

On Salisbury Plain, while enduring one of the bitterest winters ever to hit England, MacArthur figured he was tough and smart enough to escape further suspicion about how old he was, until he came under the sharp gaze of Queen Mary during a "royal" regimental review. Looking the young soldier up and down, the Queen paused long enough to ask him his age. "Nineteen, your Majesty," said MacArthur. The Queen responded by shaking her head and telling him he was "a naughty boy." From then on, MacArthur would remember it as a "royal reprimand."[7]

The 18,500-man-strong Canadian Division, led by the pipes of the 13th (Royal Highlanders of Canada) Battalion, comes ashore at Saint-Nazaire, France, on February 15, 1915.

On February 4, 1915, MacArthur and the thousands of other soldiers did not mind the rain as they lined up again, this time to be inspected by the king. Considered ready for battle, the saluting Canadians marched past George V, oblivious to the icy rain pelting their faces, but mindful of their commitment to fight. Three days later, the 1st, 2nd, and 3rd Brigades boarded ships at Avonmouth and headed to France, enduring a fierce winter gale before landing at Saint-Nazaire. Green, but grateful for surviving the wild voyage, the 18,500 officers and men inhaled the fresh salty air as they assembled on the docks and then marched two kilometres to a railway station where they boarded unheated boxcars with signs that read, in French: "Men 40, horses 8." Forty-three hours later, after numerous stops and the ear-popping screech of steel on steel, the men were deposited in northern France at Hazebrouck, destined for billets and then a six-thousand-metre sector at Fleurbaix, roughly five kilometres south of Armentières.[8] For the first time, the Canadian Division would slip into

This recruiting poster combines the dash of horse artillery with references to heroes, men, and uniforms.

the mud and water of Flanders — occupying dangerously shallow trenches built up about a metre and a half above the ground with sods and sandbags.

Like many of his buddies, young Donald Gordon had not had much time to ponder the larger scope of the war.[9] The teenager's focus was on survival and living up to manly expectations of being in the infantry. Still, many men were aware of the month-long First Battle of Ypres that had been fought by the British Army the previous fall, during the "race to the sea," as the two sides scrambled to outflank each other. The result, in addition to a horrendous loss of life, was a 750-kilometre-long line of trenches, stretching from the North Sea to the Swiss border. In the Canadian sector — near the medieval town of Ypres — the fighting had created a large bulge or semi-circular salient into German-held territory north, east, and south of the town. To the east and south, where the ground rose slightly over a series of small ridges, this marginally higher ground afforded the enemy a good view of any activity between the Allied line and the town (see Map II).

By mid-April there were six divisions deployed along the front lines of the salient: two French ones on the northern flank, the Canadians on the northeast, a British one in the apex of the bulge, and two more British ones on the southeast flank. The French 45th Algerian Division was immediately north of the Canadians and the British 28th Division to the south. Brigadier-General Arthur Currie's 2nd Brigade, which consisted of the 5th (Western Cavalry), 7th, 8th, and 10th (Calgary-Winnipeg) Battalions, manned the right half of the forty-five-hundred-metre Canadian section with the 5th and 8th Battalions holding the front lines. To their left was Brigadier-General Richard Turner's 3rd Brigade, made up of the 13th (Royal Highlanders of Canada), 14th (Royal Montreal Regiment), 15th (48th Highlanders of Canada), and 16th (Canadian Scottish) Battalions, with the 13th and 15th in the front lines. Brigadier-General Malcolm Mercer's 1st Brigade, containing the 1st (Western Ontario), 2nd (Eastern Ontario), 3rd (Toronto Regiment), and 4th (Central Ontario) Battalions, was in reserve.

Like the other battalions of 2nd Brigade, Donald Gordon's 8th Battalion was separated from the enemy by a slender strip of no man's land. The weather by then was warm, and the humid air reeked of the bloated and decaying corpses that littered the battlefield. Other human remains lay half buried or slowly became exposed beneath men's feet in the sodden trenches or from within crumbling trench walls. Mixed into this assault on the senses was the unmistakable, eye-watering stench of urine and feces left behind by French soldiers who had not bothered to build latrines.[10]

The trench walls, which under normal circumstances consisted of a parapet and rear parados, were dangerously low because of the high water table. The haphazard and hasty placement of rotting sandbags increased the height of the walls, but did not eliminate the danger of shrapnel or sniper bullets, which claimed a small, but steady toll. Snipers zeroed in on the gaps between the sandbags, targeting soldiers too foolish or too green to keep their heads down. The dangerous and difficult work of repairing the trenches was a top priority for the Canadians, who worked quietly under cover of darkness, using what materials they could scrounge. During the day the men would sit back on their heels, mesmerized by the air show above the battlefield.

Although younger than many of his mates, Gordon pulled his weight, even if still hounded by the guilt of going against his parents' wishes. During his slow journey to the front, his conscience caused him to pick up a pencil, open a page in the Bible he kept under his tunic, and scrawl four short words: "Goodbye Mother, Forgive Me." His choice of words was prophetic, because the sniper's bullet that found him on April 15, 1915, killed him instantly.[11] It happened in the few seconds his blue eyes were drawn away from his position in the crowded trench to the flying machines above.[12]

Seventeen-year-old Private William Campbell of Carleton Place, Ontario, had barely enough time to fire a letter off to his mother after arriving on the Western Front with the 2nd Battalion. Part of 1st Brigade, his unit was heading into reserve near Ypres on April 21, 1915, when he wrote that he was "just beginning to realize what this war means to the Belgian people." The sympathetic teenager described scores of displaced citizens, including old women with heavy sacks on their backs, and farmers with horses and wagons loaded high with personal effects — all of them making their way past the troops and ruined houses in a desperate bid to get away from the indiscriminate shelling that had destroyed much of Ypres, including its magnificent centrepiece — the five-hundred-year-old Cloth Hall. "I don't suppose any of them know where they are going to get a house of any kind to sleep in again," wrote Campbell, who preferred to use his middle name, Lockhard. "It makes a person vow vengeance on those who are causing their suffering."[13]

But Campbell's sadness was trumped by the rising anger he felt as he watched wounded soldiers being hauled out of the line. These grisly scenes frightened him, but strengthened his resolve to get the enemy: "there won't be any fun in it . . . for the Germans seem to be determined to break through now or never." He closed his letter by promising to write again soon, but his time was running out.[14]

The blue-eyed, five-foot-six-inch youth had enrolled at Valcartier on September 23, 1914, and was with the contingent when it sailed out of Quebec.[15] He was a quick study, and his superiors and fellow soldiers were impressed by his accurate shooting. To them, he was someone they could count on. In the salient, Campbell was tapped to be part of a risky assignment; a sniper team that would creep out into no man's land and establish shooting positions in the ruins of a bombed-out house. The team's job was to "shoot off all stray Germans who were inclined to creep up and study our position," explained Private James McGill, in a letter written after the battle.[16]

The snipers held their positions for three days, knowing at any moment they could be blown to bits by enemy shelling. Instead, on April 22 the house drew the attention of German infantry, which advanced toward it on the right and the left. The men took aim and fired, but were soon cut off. With some of his men wounded, the captain decided it was time to withdraw. "We were obliged to get back to our trenches as quickly and quietly as possible so the Captain sent six of us out at first and watched the results," McGill wrote.

Seventeen-year-old William Lockhard Campbell, from Carleton Place, Ontario, was killed by a sniper's bullet during the Second Battle of Ypres.

Fatal shots ripped through the retreating men, dropping some of them in their tracks. The wounded lay helplessly exposed until they died or were taken prisoner. "Poor Lockhard met his death by a bullet in the head," recalled McGill. "It was instant . . . causing no pain, which was a blessing when we think of what some of the boys suffered . . ." McGill wrote his letter while recovering from wounds in a hospital bed in England. Young Campbell, though, died a soldier. His body was never recovered from the battlefield.[17]

Worse days lay ahead. Late on the afternoon of April 22, the German guns turned their attention to the French, and at 5 p.m. a greenish-yellow cloud drifted over from the German lines, released from 5,730 cylinders. It was the first use of poison gas on the Western Front. The French line broke as terrified soldiers — clutching their burning throats — died choking and gasping in their trenches. Others fled to the rear, creating a gap of more than six kilometres to the left of the Canadians. Three German divisions poured through the breach.

The gas dissipated, but not before flowing over the Canadian lines, where it caused a few casualties. The situation quickly became confused as the proverbial "fog of war" descended on the Canadians, compounded by cut telephone lines and conflicting reports. Few realized that the Germans, after advancing roughly three kilometres into the French sector, had halted for the night. In an attempt to stabilize the situation, Alderson ordered a counterattack against Kitchener's Wood, west of the village of Saint-Julien.

The 10th and 16th Battalions moved off at midnight in eight ranks; about sixteen hundred untested troops in one of the most difficult operations of war — a night attack. A sudden charge — illuminated by German flares — was met with withering machine-gun fire. The next morning, less than five hundred men answered roll call as they huddled in a trench south of Kitchener's Wood. Over eleven hundred had been killed, wounded, or captured. The attack failed, not for lack of courage, but because it was poorly planned, uncoordinated, and undertaken by troops with no experience in night attacks. Two attacks in broad daylight later on April 23, by the 1st and 4th Battalions, against entrenched German positions on Mauser Ridge, west of Kitchener's Wood, lost 858 men without capturing the ridge. They did, though, close the open flank. Elsewhere, the Canadians managed to hold on, while British units were sent in piecemeal to plug the gaps.

Amid the chaos, sixteen-year-old Sergeant John Wilfred McKay of No. 2 Field Ambulance, Canadian Army Medical Corps (CAMC), was an example of courage under fire.[18] Employed as a canvas cutter before the war, McKay experienced rapid promotion in the CAMC. He had enrolled at Valcartier on September

23, 1914, and sailed from Quebec on the SS *Cassandra*. Before leaving, he stipulated that twenty dollars from his monthly pay go to his mother Annie, who remained busy on the home front with his three younger siblings. McKay's father, who was also named John and who was also serving as a sergeant in the same unit, was in his early forties.

Lieutenant-Colonel D. W. McPherson, CO of the 2nd Canadian Field Ambulance, would have high praise for those who worked beyond the point of exhaustion to care for the wounded. With blood-smeared hands, tunics, and faces, these officers and men faced horrible situations while trying to save lives. The blood was also mixed into the mud clinging to the boots worn by the exhausted stretcher-bearers who continually sought out the wounded while bravely risking their own death. The five-foot-eight McKay worked non-stop at a dressing station that was constantly under fire. He helped treat and evacuate dozens of wounded men, some with arms and legs missing and others with their insides blown out. The lucky ones were treated and sent further behind the line to hospitals in Poperinghe and Vlamertinghe. Finally, enemy fire also caught McKay; wounded in both arms, he died two days after being hit. Rightly, he would be remembered not so much for his youth, but for receiving a Mentioned in Despatches for his "gallant and distinguished service in the field."[19]

Sixteen-year-old Private George McCahon, who had embarked with the first Canadian contingent from Quebec City in the fall of 1914, was also in the Ypres Salient — fighting for his life. He was with the 13th (Royal Highlanders of Canada) Battalion. To the right of the 13th, three other Canadian battalions — the 5th (Western Cavalry), 8th (90th Winnipeg Rifles), and 15th (48th Highlanders of Canada) — were also holding the line, opposite German forces to the east.

At exactly 4 a.m. on Saturday, April 24, the Germans resumed

Canadian soldiers man their trenches near Ypres as the French retreat in front of the advancing Germans, who drop aircraft flares to direct their artillery.

their vicious pounding of the shallow Canadian trenches, and minutes later unleashed the second poison gas attack of the war, directly at the 8th and 15th Battalions. Advancing behind the lethal cloud, German infantry crossed no man's land and penetrated the Canadian lines. Some men in the 8th Battalion managed to escape the deadly vapour by holding urine-soaked handkerchiefs or rags over their mouths and noses. Those not ripped apart by shells or slowly and painfully suffocated by Germany's new weapon fought on from their poisoned trenches and shallow pits, many blinded by the searing gas and frustrated by Ross rifles that jammed. The first wave of German infantry that crashed into the corner held by the 13th Battalion was repelled, but the second thrust was heavier and bloodier. Canadians fell, and McCahon was hit (see Map III).

Wounded in the right elbow and buttocks, the teenager seemed destined for surgery and recovery in a hospital bed behind the lines. But before he could be pulled off the battlefield his fate was decided: he was hit again — this time seriously, in the leg. On April 29, the five-foot-four, 127-pound soldier was evacuated over bumpy roads through a succession of over-crowded medical aid posts to No. 11 Stationary Hospital nearly a hundred kilometres away behind the lines at Boulogne, France.

There is no record of what McCahon thought about as his young life slipped away, but in his head was a fading timeline of choices he had made: His decision to "do the right thing" and enlist in September 1914 and have twenty-five dollars drawn off his monthly pay to assist his widowed mother; his commitment to board the massive troopship at Quebec that fall; and his more recent resolve to hang on as best he could during those moments of terror, alongside chums who never made it off the torn and contaminated battlefield. They were men who treated him like a soldier — despite his age.[20]

Private Bill Barrett of the 7th Battalion was also in the salient — and unceremoniously introduced to another untested gas-avoidance technique. The fifteen-year-old, who would survive the war to become a district fire chief in Vancouver, was up on the fire step — taking aim at the enemy — when an older soldier reached over and shoved his face into the mud. The young lad from Fort Langley, British Columbia, remembered he almost drowned as the poisonous cloud blew past and seeped into the trench behind him. For soldiers a mere arm's length away, crouching down in the bottom of the trenches to reload the rifles for the shooters, there was no escape.[21] With stinging eyes and burning throats they fell while the fighting survivors were pushed back. The situation got more confused as weakened and isolated battalions, companies and platoons, fighting on against nearly overwhelming odds, lost contact with what was happening around them. Soldiers cried in frustration as their Ross rifles jammed within metres of the advancing enemy. Whenever possible, the Canadians threw them away and salvaged Lee-Enfields from dead British soldiers.

Fifteen-year-old William Barrett, from Fort Langley, British Columbia, survived the Second Battle of Ypres — and the rest of the war — to return home safely.

"Some men, who in the ordinary routine of life were considered strong, were confused and could give no help; others, as junior as lance-corporals and privates, unknown previously, proved themselves leaders, rallying their comrades, taking them into and out of trying situations with coolness and skill."[22] Barrett, who had run away from home before enrolling in September 1914, was a tough, no-nonsense kid who could both impress and disappoint. He was promoted to lance corporal after Second Ypres, but was later charged for having beaten a soldier "with his bare hands" because "the man refused to go up onto the firing platform." While answering to that charge, Barrett was asked if 1899 was the year of his birth. The question came as a surprise because he had told military authorities — when he enrolled in Vancouver —

Richard Jack's monumental painting of the Second Battle of Ypres was the first work commissioned by the Canadian War Memorials Fund, established by Lord Beaverbrook.

that he was born on July 9, 1896. With the truth now catching up to him, he admitted he was sixteen. But instead of getting a one-way ticket home, he was reverted to private and returned to the front — a judgment that suited him fine.

That same year Barrett earned the nickname "Bluey" after polishing off a bottle of wine, which left him drunkenly singing "I am blue" to his trench mates. On the plus side, Bluey demonstrated his survival skills one night on a patrol in no man's land. The sun was just beginning to rise when the shelling started. He and a buddy had no place to go, except into a shell hole filled with smelly water. All through the day they remained nearly motionless on their backs with just their faces above the murky waterline. They had no way of knowing what lay beneath them in that foul place, but when it was dark enough they pulled themselves out and crawled back to their lines, where they surprised even the strongest cynics.[23]

In addition to those who could rise to the occasion and find ways to cope, there were some who had had enough or who just could not deal with the horror and exhaustion. "One young lad, not more than seventeen or eighteen years of age, threw himself headlong into one of the forts on the top of the garrison, his whole body trembling and heaving like an animal chased to the death. All he could gasp was 'It's Hell up there — I'm done, I'm done for!' He was quietened down, and it was learned from him that his battalion had marched the whole of the previous night towards the battlefield, reached there a little before daylight and gone straight into the attack."[24]

With shells and bullets flying at them or just over their heads, and with the heavier-than-air gas seeping around their feet and legs in the poorly-constructed trenches, soldiers either broke down or relied on their final reserves of adrenalin to get through, knowing the next instant could prove fatal. J. H. MacArthur, the young soldier who had been royally reprimanded by Queen Mary, continued to hold the line as the Germans advanced and the Ross rifles jammed. "The Ross was a very good sporting rifle but it had an open breech ... and dust and dirt would get in the mechanism of the bolt," MacArthur recalled. He also remembered an incident when, on the run and dodging bullets, he and another man became separated. A bullet slammed into his buddy, briefly knocking him over, but his position as he went down told MacArthur exactly where the enemy was hiding. Within seconds, the two Canadians had their bayonets in the German rifleman. "He was just putting the bolt [of his rifle] home to take another shot at one or the other of us," remembered MacArthur.[25]

By April 27, British units had relieved the exhausted Canadians, who remained in the salient but were not involved again in the heavy fighting. In their introduction to battle, the men of the Canadian Division, supported by nearby British battalions, had stubbornly fought through two gas attacks, jammed rifles, water shortages, and a serious lack of communications as the enemy pushed toward Ypres. The Canadians were surrounded and dealt

This scene of destroyed houses in the war-ravaged city of Ypres was painted by future Group of Seven artist A. Y. Jackson.

one devastating blow after another, but a kilometre or so south of the Saint-Julien-Ypres Road, the resistance paid off and the line held.[26] Ypres was heavily damaged, but it did not fall, and the costly defensive operation had also saved the British divisions in the salient from being cut off and destroyed.[27]

After the battle, the British War Office noted that the Canadians' "gallantry and determination undoubtedly saved the situation," but it was at an incredibly high price. While the Canadians had established a reputation as first-class troops, the division, which had a front-line strength of roughly ten thousand, suffered 6,037 casualties, including nearly two thousand killed and hundreds taken prisoner. At the end of April, the battered Canadians withdrew westward through the town's ruins for a well-deserved respite.

CHAPTER 4

"THE HARD WORK AGREED WITH HIM. AND SINCE HE HAS BEEN IN FRANCE HE HAS GROWN THREE INCHES."

Neuve Chapelle, Festubert, Givenchy and Ploegsteert, May – December 1915

After a two-week break from front-line duty in the spring of 1915, the Canadian Division was fighting again, this time as part of a French and British offensive aimed at breaking through the German lines, which had become even more fortified. When the British phase of the offensive ended in failure after twelve hours and more than eleven thousand casualties, the British First Army commander, General Sir Douglas Haig, decided to narrow his attack frontage to five kilometres between Neuve Chapelle and Festubert. After a sixty-hour preliminary artillery bombardment, the British attacked at midnight on May 15. This forced the enemy to withdraw along a three-kilometre front to a second line of defence. Haig misinterpreted this tactical withdrawal as a weakening of German resolve and ordered the attacks intensified.

To support this, the Canadian Division moved forward to relieve the British 7th Division, and over the next several days Canadian

A 1915 recruiting poster uses the names of battles from Second Ypres, as well as Festubert and Givenchy, to encourage men to join the colours.

units launched attacks in conditions that were impossible for victory: flat, muddy, and unrecognizable terrain — crossed by drainage ditches and dominated by German positions on higher ground — forward trenches that were nothing more than indentations in the mud, and grossly inaccurate maps that had been printed with south at the top and east to the left. Despite these and other frustrations, the first Canadian attack was launched by the 14th (Royal Montreal Regiment) and 16th (Canadian Scottish) Battalions of Turner's 3rd Brigade at 5:25 p.m. on May 18, just thirty minutes after a failed British attack to the north. With the Germans fully alerted, both battalions ran into concentrated rifle and machine-gun fire that stopped them after four hundred metres. One salvo of enemy artillery killed or wounded nearly fifty highlanders (see Map IV).

The wounded lay where they fell, exposed throughout the night to shellfire and the pouring rain. On the 14th Battalion's front, fifteen-year-old bugler Anthony Ginley ran the risk of sudden death while guiding stretcher-bearers into no man's land. The teenager's actions under intense shelling and machine-gun fire impressed the older soldiers, especially those who had watched comrades fall. "He had enlisted at fourteen in the ranks," remembered Sergeant Fred Bagnall of Hazel Grove, Prince Edward Island. "When just turned fifteen he had dragged a wounded man into the trench and guided stretcher-bearers to other wounded at Festubert under heavy fire. Later it was decided that he was too young to fight..."[1]

Private Ginley's actions drew the attention of officers, and he was pulled out of the line as an underaged soldier. While biding his time in England before being shipped home for discharge, word of his time on the Western Front fed the public's patriotic appetite and its imagination. One London newspaper published his photograph, which Bagnall spotted while on leave. The sergeant also ran into the lad in one of the city's popular clubs. "He was more like a mascot. Everyone made a fuss over him, but were very kind to him."[2]

Ginley's front-line service was also of interest to Canadian news reporters. A cable by Canadian Associated Press published in the October 4, 1915, edition of the *Toronto World* newspaper featured the headline: "Boy Bugler Gets Off On Furlough: Anthony Ginley, Who Won Distinction At Front, Visits Cliveden Hospital." The cable, written from London on October 2, stated the "boy bugler of the Royal Montreal Regiment, whose persistence won for him a place with the regiment at the front, and who ... has been recommended for the Distinguished Conduct Medal, caused a mild sensation on arriving unexpectedly at the Cliveden Canadian Hospital, giving evidence of recent association with the trenches, and bearing a rifle and uniform."[3]

The story noted that Ginley had not come to Cliveden for

Canadian soldiers on leave wait at a YMCA canteen in a London railway station for a train that will take them back to their camps.

treatment, but to meet the quartermaster of the hospital whose wife back in Canada had cared to write to him at the front. The newspaper account described Ginley as being an orphan of Scottish parentage, noting his father had died when he was eighteen months old, and he had travelled from Scotland to Canada with his mother, who had also died a few years later. Alone and without means, Ginley persevered and found work on a farm near Ottawa, where he was employed by a retired major who volunteered for service soon after the outbreak of war. The newspaper noted "the boy was also eager to go," but "was so young that the major declined to give consent." The major did, however, suggest Anthony could join the 14th Montreal Regiment "as a bugler." Ginley embraced the idea and was soon welcomed into the army and on his way overseas, arriving in England and then crossing to France in February 1915. "He was allowed to shoulder a rifle," the article noted. "The hard work agreed with him. And since he has been in France he has grown three inches."[4]

One teen who never made it off the battlefield that May was seventeen-year-old Private Kenneth Cameron of Victoria, British Columbia. First reported as missing in action on May 18, he was — by May 22 — listed as killed in action. Cameron had enrolled with the 16th Battalion on September 22, 1914, and arrived in France three months before he was killed. Descriptions of the fighting faced by Cameron's 16th and the other Canadian battalions during their time at Festubert offer some of the grimmest accounts of the war, and show how easy it was to go missing, even if only for a few hours or days. "Smashed rifles, torn, blood-stained equipment and clothing were strewn over the battlefield. The dead, mainly British, lay thick around… One man stood in the trench, in an eerily life-like attitude, the hand up to the head where the fatal bomb fragment had pierced, as if listening to the movement of the oncoming enemy; some were locked together in an embrace of death with the bayonet through one or other of the bodies." Above the grotesque, the grim stench of death permeated the air, but men got used to living among the dead.[5] "We had to walk over dead bodies and sleep beside them," noted a diarist with the 14th Battalion.[6]

A second attack on the evening of May 20 involved Currie's 2nd Brigade, ordered to seize a strongpoint designated K.5, which jutted into no man's land. Third Brigade, meanwhile, was to capture eight hundred metres of the new German line, including a small orchard. The Canadians advanced into a storm of machine-gun fire. In 2nd Brigade's sector, two companies of the 10th (Calgary-Winnipeg) Battalion advanced only a hundred metres into no man's land before their leading elements were cut to pieces and the attack halted. To their left the 15th (48th

Highlanders) made some progress before being forced to dig in, while the 16th captured the orchard — renamed Canadian Orchard in their honour.

On the evening of May 21, the same two 10th Battalion companies attacked K.5. One company was cut down, but the other seized nearly four hundred metres of enemy line. Reinforcements from the 5th (Western Cavalry) arrived, and together — during the night — they beat back several counterattacks. By noon, heavy German shelling forced the Canadians to abandon all but one hundred metres of the captured trench.

Although his attestation paper lists him as being twenty, Private Frederick Heffernan was sixteen when he went missing and was later presumed killed in action on May 22, 1915.[7] Born in England, Heffernan had moved with his parents to Canada, settling out west where he worked as a carpenter before enrolling with the 32nd Battalion at Winnipeg on December 16, 1914. The tall and fit teen was his mother's only son, and after getting to France in late April was taken on strength by the 10th Battalion. For him, there had not been much time to write home, but he certainly held his mother close to his heart, stipulating that fifteen dollars from his monthly pay be sent to her.

Meanwhile, Haig personally rebuked Alderson and his senior staff officer for the failure of the May 21 attacks, and ordered another. It began at 2:30 a.m. on May 24, when two 5th Battalion companies assaulted K.5 and forced the Germans from the strongpoint at a cost of 268 men. The 7th (1st British Columbia) Battalion sent reinforcements, and that night a company from 1st Brigade's 3rd (Toronto Regiment) Battalion attacked from the Canadian Orchard to capture 275 metres of trench. Unfortunately, four enemy machine guns caught the company in the open and cut it down.

On May 31, the Canadians left Festubert for the Givenchy sector, three kilometres to the south. The fruitless and frustrating

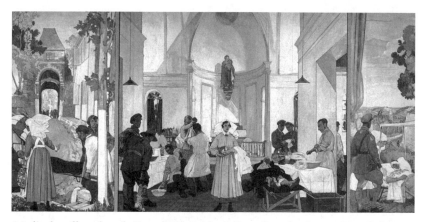

Medical staff tend to their patients at No. 3 Canadian Stationary Hospital, set up in a fifteenth-century citadel outside Doullens, north of Amiens.

attacks at Festubert had cost them 2,605 casualties — a huge price to pay for some twelve hundred square metres of mud, now filled with hundreds of decomposing Canadian corpses, many of which would be lost forever.

Seventeen-year-old Private Frank Burnley of Halifax was serving with the 13th Battalion when he collapsed after being shot through the head. The bullet did not kill him right away, and he managed to hang on while being evacuated over rough roads to the Canadian hospital in Boulogne, France, where he took his last breath on June 1. Getting into the army had been easy for Burnley, staying alive at the front had not. The tough, five-foot-five Nova Scotia coal miner, who had previous militia experience, easily passed the medical while being poked and prodded at Valcartier in August. He listed his age as 19 years, 142 days, but the record shows he was two years younger than that when he died.[8] After crossing the Atlantic with the first contingent and settling at Larkhill, Burnley was transferred in late January from the 17th to the 13th Battalion. A month after landing in France he was pulled out of the line and treated at No. 4 Stationary Hospital in Saint-Omer for an ingrown toenail on his left foot, most likely a condition painfully aggravated by soggy boots. Less than four weeks later, on March 27, he was hospitalized again, this time at No. 14 General Hospital with a slight case of the measles. Burnley came to the attention of medical authorities again on May 2 when he was treated for myalgia (sore muscles) before rejoining his unit at the front just days before he was shot on May 26.[9]

The Canadians' move to Givenchy brought a welcome change; in contrast to the waterlogged lines at Festubert, the trenches were dry. The Canadians had roughly nine hundred metres of front to hold, and their next mission — which was in support of a larger British assault — would be to capture two German strongpoints designated H.2 and H.3. At 5:45 p.m. on June 15, two 18-pounder guns opposite H.2 fired over open sights directly at the German parapet, followed thirteen minutes later by an exploding mine. The massive explosion killed several 1st (Western Ontario) Battalion soldiers in bombing parties — small groups of soldiers that moved forward to throw "bombs" (as grenades were then called) into enemy positions — who were waiting nearby to lead their comrades forward. Unfortunately, H.2 remained undamaged. The Germans reacted and bombarded the Canadian front lines, causing additional casualties in 1st Battalion and knocking out both 18-pounders.

The Germans recovered and mounted a series of counterattacks to regain lost trenches. As daylight began to fade, the German attempts grew in intensity. The 2nd (Eastern Ontario) and 3rd Battalions tried to get reinforcements forward, but they could barely make it into no man's land. Without the much-needed reinforcements and almost out of ammunition, 1st Battalion had to withdraw. Late the next afternoon 3rd Battalion attempted another attack but was stopped cold. Givenchy had cost four hundred Canadian casualties.

The brave but fruitless fighting through May and June afforded the overworked surgeons and nurses some of their first experiences with the effects of trench warfare. In four days, nearly four hundred soldiers were admitted to No. 1 Canadian General Hospital (CGH). Most of them had arrived directly from the field without passing through the casualty clearing stations. "They had had first aid and anti-tetanic serum given, but the filth had not been removed from their persons nor the foreign bodies from their tissue," notes the hospital's official history, which also describes the challenges doctors faced to find the "most rational line of treatment" for wounds that often defied description. Of the 663 wounded brought into the hospital during June, nineteen died and 525 were evacuated to England. Among the first Canadians to die at No. 1 CGH was Private Robert Marsh of the 15th Battalion, who had enrolled at age seventeen and been pulled off the battlefield with a shattered arm that later had to be amputated. Doctors monitoring the British-born soldier's progress describe how he suddenly collapsed and died on June 17.[10] Marsh, who had enrolled at Valcartier in September 1914, was the ninth death in hospital up to that point.

When the French ended their offensive on June 19, the British halted any further attacks. The next week the Canadians marched northwards to the Ploegsteert sector, dubbed "Plugstreet" by the British. For the next nine months, they remained in this relatively quiet area of Belgium where a "live-and-let-live" attitude existed on both sides. Activity was largely limited to night patrols and to improving the ever-expanding trench system.

The CEF, meanwhile, was expanding in more ways than one. Lieutenant-Colonel Raymond Brutinel's 1st Motor Machine Gun Brigade — a Canadian innovation — arrived in late June, combining mobility with firepower. A second Canadian contingent was in France by mid-September, signalling the establishment of the Canadian Corps under Alderson. The Canadian Army's expansion to corps size introduced new responsibilities over a much wider front. By late September 1915, that front had been

Soldiers raise their caps on rifles to cheer King George V on Salisbury Plain during a visit to Canadian units.

extended five kilometres north of Ploegsteert to the village of Kemmel. Almost four months of rain began in late October while the corps consolidated its enlarged frontage in trenches that soon either flooded or collapsed. When temperatures fell to near freezing, trench life became miserable again, brightened only by a daily tot of rum and a visit to the divisional baths every ten days. Later, shorter periods of leave were granted for visits to towns in the rear.

Other key developments saw Currie elevated to the newly named 1st Canadian Division and Turner put in charge of the 2nd Canadian Division. Like 1st Division, 2nd Division consisted of three brigades — the 4th, 5th, and 6th — and a divisional cavalry squadron. Each brigade had four infantry battalions. The 4th, under British Brigadier-General Lord Brooke, consisted of the 18th (Western Ontario), 19th (Central Ontario), 20th (Central Ontario), and 21st (Eastern Ontario) Battalions. Brigadier-General David Watson commanded 5th Brigade comprising the 22nd (French Canadian), 24th (Victoria Rifles of Canada), 25th (Nova Scotia Rifles), and 26th (New Brunswick) Battalions. Under the command of Brigadier-General Huntley Ketchen, the units of 6th Brigade were the 27th (City of Winnipeg), 28th (Northwest), 29th (Vancouver), and 31st (Alberta) Battalions.

Hunkered down in the freezing mud with 13th Platoon, D Company, 21st Battalion, Private Howard Salisbury of Kingston, Ontario, stole moments between front-line duties to write home.[11] Only fifteen when he arrived in England in May 1915, Salisbury was less than a month past his sixteenth birthday when he set foot on the Western Front in mid-September. While writing home to his sister Phyllis, he stared down at the stationery supplied by the Canadian National Council of Young Men's Christian Associations. He either missed or ignored much of the warning contained in the letterhead, instructing those at the front to not mention "rank, battalion, brigade or the names of places, expected operations, movements or numbers of troops . . . or make specific reference to the moral or physical condition of troops."

A quarter of an inch shy of five-foot-seven, Salisbury began by jotting down his regimental number, rank, and battalion name. Fortunately, he had picked a rare sunny day to write to Phyllis, who had recently written to him. "We are in the trenches again and it is pretty miserable owing to too much rain, but we have been supplied with rain cloaks," he reported on November 11, 1915. "Yesterday, we had some rain, and then a hailstorm, and then there was a magnificent rainbow." He also reported he had written in early October to just about everyone in the family, but had not heard from anyone recently except her. He informed Phyllis that he loved receiving her letters because she filled them with hometown news others did not think to include.[12]

"We hardly ever know when it is Sunday here," Salisbury wrote, "and if we think of it we usually observe it by working a little harder." He told her that leave passes were expected to start December 15, "but if they work it in alphabetical order my turn won't come until April or May." Before closing he told his sister he was sending her a handmade kerchief for her birthday, and would like her to say hello to his schoolteacher, Miss Booth. "I hope she and all the class are well. Our artillery is sending the Germans some hot stuff now."[13]

Salisbury wrote home again on December 4, advising Phyllis he had just received her last letter. "The raining season looked like it was clearing up at one time, but it is raining again today. For about a week the ground was frozen hard but it has thawed out again and is muddier than ever." To illustrate his point, he compared the trenches at the front to those used for training exercises back home in Ontario. "You might get some idea of what we have to go through by seeing those trenches at Barriefield," he wrote, "but I bet they didn't show miniature rivers running through them or big families of rats . . ."[14]

With so much rain, the heavy work to repair the trench works and establish new dugouts continued. Through muddy slush men hauled heavy lumber and other supplies to front-line positions while exposed to enemy fire. "The other night we had to carry twenty-foot beams up to the frontline from the reserve line which is about a three-quarter of a mile walk ... it certainly was some job," wrote Salisbury. "We couldn't go by the communication trench as the beams wouldn't take the corners so we went by overland route. First the hail started and it would cut your face, then you would fall in about every shell hole you could find — fall and about break your shoulder when you popped down every time a flare light went up. When you came to a tunnel or an old trench you would put your plank down, walk across it and then pick it up again, and all the time the bullets were whistling unpleasantly close to our ears. We certainly were some sorry sights when we got back to our dugouts."[15]

No Man's Land *by Maurice Cullen depicts the grim scene all too familiar to soldiers serving on the Western Front.*

Salisbury may have been just putting on a brave face when he told his sister he "likes this life... In fact, I'm thriving on it," proudly adding that the heavy artillery is putting "some coal boxes in the German's front line." The last part of his letter, however, may have undone his good intentions, in particular his note that the shelling is making "it difficult to focus on this letter... You can tell how many times a shell landed in the ... front line by t he many mistakes ... in this letter. Give my love to the family. Your loving brother, Howard."[16]

CHAPTER 5

"I DUCKED AND TRIED TO GET MY HEAD IN A HOLE A PEANUT WOULD NOT FIT IN."

Saint-Eloi and Mount Sorrel, December 1915–June 1916

Private David O'Brien was well into his Great War experience by the time he arrived on the Western Front in January 1916. In his memoir he recalls enrolling in Ottawa at age fourteen after quitting work as a baker. On his attestation paper, signed on June 3, 1915, he swore he was much older, born on December 25, 1897. "I wrote a letter giving consent to my enlistment and signed my mother's name to it [because] they would not enlist me without her consent."[1]

O'Brien's wartime service began with the 5th Princess Louise Dragoon Guards and ended three kilometres east of Ypres, Belgium, at Mount Sorrel with the 8th Canadian Infantry Brigade's 4th (Central Ontario) Battalion Canadian Mounted Rifles (4th CMR).[2]

His first serious taste of infantry training occurred at Bramshott Camp in southern England, where it was tough for any adventuresome lad to resist the temptations of London only seventy

This Victory Bonds poster was produced in both French and English versions. French Canadians were generally far less supportive of the war than English Canadians.

kilometres away. More than once, the teenager overextended his stay, which cost him dearly. "When I had money I slipped to London without a pass, and was always caught ... and taken back to my camp and sentenced to from five to fourteen days imprisonment, without pay and all the dirty work to do. Being young, I did not see the seriousness of the offence, but I was soon to learn plenty…"

Shortly after arriving in France, O'Brien and two other young soldiers were pulled aside because of their looks. "We were lined up ... for closer scrutiny as to our age. He [the officer conducting the inspection] was going to send us back to England, insisting we were not of age. One boy was fourteen years and I was fourteen and a half, and the other boy was fifteen. We lied as to our ages, swore we were eighteen ... and finally convinced him and got his consent to go up the line with the regiment. The other two boys were killed [in action]… I often think it was a bad move convincing the General we were eighteen, but after all I have had a priceless experience."

The wartime "experience" got a lot more serious for O'Brien and many others in a sector of the front that was considered "quiet" by battlefield standards. During O'Brien's first visit to the trenches, near Messines, he was nearly killed while hauling bags of rations. "I will never forget hearing the shellfire. We marched in single file, it was a very black night, the bullets were hitting very close, knocking a man down at intervals — sometime a machine gun would get seven or eight men at one time," he remembered, noting that in addition to ration bags he carried full equipment and many rounds of ammunition.

While picking their way forward along the shallow, exposed trench, O'Brien and the rest of the ration party tried to stay low, but for some there was no ducking the enemy fire, which targeted the locations where rations were picked up and dropped off. "I was badly frightened with seeing men killed and wounded all around me. At times when a German machine gun opened fire I ducked and tried to get my head in a hole a peanut would not fit in."

The sight of the young soldier trying to bury his head like an ostrich was too much for some of the more experienced men, who, despite being fired upon, found a moment to practise the dark art of trench humour. One of them grabbed some mud and threw it at O'Brien, striking the nervous greenhorn in the back. "I thought the German army had landed on me and I yelled loud enough to be heard for quite a distance. By this time I was just about speechless, as we were getting closer to the front-line trenches."[3]

As O'Brien moved cautiously forward, others were not so lucky or so careful and paid a price. For one man, the horrific sights and sounds of trench warfare were too much. "Although it [the front-line trench] was being raked with shell and rifle fire, it felt good to be down in the trench, instead of walking up exposed to everything fired at us," recalled O'Brien. "One man ... lost his nerve completely and shot himself."[4]

O'Brien's 4th CMR was part of 3rd Canadian Division, authorized on Christmas Day 1915 under Major-General Malcolm Mercer. The division's 7th Infantry Brigade, led by Brigadier-General Archie Macdonnell, contained the Royal Canadian Regiment, the Patricia's (transferred from the British), plus the 42nd (Royal Highlanders of Canada) and 49th (Edmonton Regiment) Battalions. Brigadier-General Victor Williams commanded 8th Infantry Brigade, which, in addition to O'Brien's battalion, comprised the other now-permanently dismounted troopers of the CMR's 1st (Saskatchewan), 2nd (British Columbia), and 5th (Quebec) Battalions. Both brigades were conducting operations on the Western Front before the end of 1915. The division's 9th Brigade, which was not formed until late February, was led by Brigadier-General Frederick Hill. It consisted of the 43rd (Cameron Highlanders of Canada), 52nd (New Ontario), 58th (Central Ontario), and 60th (Victoria Rifles of Canada) Battalions.

Although the journey across the English Channel lasted less than a day, the swell beneath the troopship on February 21, 1916, reminded Private David Waldron and the other men of the 58th Battalion of their uncomfortable Atlantic crossing. It had taken roughly ten days to cross from Halifax to Plymouth on board the overcrowded SS *Saxonia* back in November. Conditions on board deteriorated as food rotted and body odour grew from bad to worse. Men tried not to dwell on it, but throughout the voyage they could taste the fear of being torpedoed and lost in the frigid waters of the North Atlantic. They knew that a transport ship loaded with horses had been sunk not far from their route.

Born in the United States, Waldron was sixteen when he enrolled with a few neighbourhood chums from Toronto's east

David Waldron (far left of seated row) poses with the other members of the 58th (Central Ontario) Battalion signals section at Camp Niagara, 1915.

end. Instead of wearing shorts, the typical attire for boys his age, Waldron donned a pair of long trousers to look older to the recruiting sergeant. The ploy worked: in the wardrobe of deception, trousers were right up there with oversized shoes, bowler hats, and jackets with wide shoulders. From Toronto, the recruits headed southwest to Niagara-on-the-Lake. There the training regimen, punctuated by parades and long route marches, lasted until the end of October, culminating in a gruelling 112-kilometre march to Toronto. From there, the railway took them to Montreal, then to Halifax for embarkation.

The comparatively quick journey across the Channel to Le Havre began at Southampton after the troops arrived en masse from Bramshott. In France, the battalion travelled by train to Godersvelde, Belgium, a journey noted in Waldron's wartime diary as being completed in a boxcar loaded with twelve men and three horses — with the body heat from the animals keeping men warm as they stared at their own breath.

In mid-March, Waldron and the rest of the 58th were introduced to trench warfare at Vierstraat, south of Ypres, where much time was spent repairing crumbling trenches, pumping out water, and killing rats using bayonets baited with scraps of cheese. The young soldier was nearly killed while retrieving rations, saved only by the acquired sudden reflex of hitting the ground hard and then lying perfectly still between the rails of a tramway as bullets pierced the air above and ricocheted off the rails beside him.[5]

Seventeen-year-old Private Albert Fallon of the 52nd Battalion also arrived in late February 1916. He had enrolled at Fort William, Ontario, in April 1915, and before moving into the front lines shared a tent pitched in the snow at Le Havre. Staring down at the hard wooden floor, the 125-pound soldier, who had a history of respiratory illness, could not imagine how he could find any warmth while curled up on a rubber groundsheet beneath a single blanket. The body heat from the other lads would help, but he did not want to think about that. He figured he was the "youngest kid" in the unit at the time, but was determined not to show it. Instead, he would carry on and not complain — no matter what.

After moving closer to the sound of the guns near the Ypres Salient, the inexperienced battalions were "coached" in the art of trench warfare by more experienced units. Fallon went into the line with a work party from the 49th Battalion. Opposite them, the Germans occupied the high ground, which drained steadily into the trench where the Canadians stood shivering in muddy, contaminated water up to their knees. "I hope to God I can stand this," mumbled Fallon, while stubbornly hanging on to a "profound sense of responsibility" to do what he could for king and country.

"I would have hated like hell to have cracked up as a kid and been sent back due to my ill health," he recalled.

While preparing to fire on the enemy for the first time, Fallon was warned by his "coach" to never shoot from the same place twice because German snipers were constantly looking for green-horns to make that fatal mistake. As his first rifle shot rang out across no man's land beneath the whitish glow of the Very lights, the noise startled the young private, causing him to pitch forward and smack his face against the half-frozen parapet. Seconds later he was on his back, flailing away in the cold, stinking water. The unholy baptism soaked Fallon to the skin and sent piercing shivers up his spine, but he got up, brushed off the slush, and promised to do better next time.

The following night Fallon was assigned a more dangerous task, when he joined two experienced men en route to a listening post in no man's land. Crawling on his belly through snow and mud with his 49th Battalion mentors, he appreciated being in good company. The men had solid experience, having spent three or four months — on and off — at the front. "You were damn lucky to last that long," he remembered. Before embarking on the perilous journey, Fallon had been warned to stand absolutely still the moment a flare went up. For the greenhorn this was easier said than done because of the proximity of the opposing trenches, which he remembered as being only a hundred metres apart, in places. When one did go up, trying as best he could not to shake while facing the prospect of being ripped to shreds by shell or machine-gun fire, Fallon followed the advice and concentrated every ounce of energy on being part of the soggy ground on which he stood.

Seconds seemed like hours as the bright light fizzed and arced across the sky, bathing the grotesque landscape and causing shadows to jump and shift.

When darkness finally returned, the men waited a few moments until their eyes readjusted to their surroundings. Then they reached a creek where the more experienced men crossed on a half-submerged timber. Fallon, however, missed it and was in icy water again. For the next three hours he fought the damp chill while helping out at the listening post. It was a long night, but all three made it back, and Fallon was handed his first rum ration of the war. It burned his throat but took away the chill and settled his frayed nerves.

Somewhere else deep inside, he felt the pride and relief of having survived something many soldiers did not: the first trip into no man's land.[6]

In keeping with the generals' desire to maintain an offensive spirit along the Western Front, night patrolling continued in no man's land, and trench raids — an activity at which the Canadians soon became masters — were carried out.

To the south, as the French were being "bled white" by the Germans during the monumental struggle at Verdun, 2nd Division's introduction to combat was one of the most confused and frustrating battles of the war. In an attempt to straighten a five-hundred-metre section five kilometres south of Ypres at Saint-Eloi, where German trenches protruded into the Allied line from slightly higher ground, the British detonated six massive mines on March 27. The explosions sent geysers of earth, human remains, and other debris several metres into the air, obliterating trenches and landmarks and adding six huge craters to an existing seventh. Each of the four largest craters in the centre was roughly fifteen metres deep, fifty metres across, and surrounded by a fifty-metre-wide lip of muddy, churned-up earth that rose six metres above the ground, creating a barrier to movement and visibility.

When the 27th (City of Winnipeg) and 31st (Alberta) Battalions of Ketchen's 6th Infantry Brigade relieved the British on April 4, 1916, the few existing front-line trenches were simply water-filled indentations in the mud. At daybreak the Canadians were in full view of German artillery observers and heavy shelling followed. The Winnipeggers' sector, which was only a short line on a map, stretched the length of the craters and, because of the widespread destruction of the landscape, the line on the map did not accurately reflect the situation on the ground. Other locations were also mapped incorrectly — with disastrous results. By noon on April 4, the 27th was still hanging on, despite over half the soldiers in the forward companies becoming casualties. Finally, on the night of April 5–6, the much-depleted battalion was pulled back and replaced by the 29th (Vancouver) Battalion. However, before the relief was complete, the Germans attacked in force.

Just five days after arriving at the front, Private Keith Crosby, who had been sent over to help reinforce the 24th (Victoria Rifles of Canada) Battalion, went missing and was later reported killed on April 11.[7] The seventeen-year-old labourer from Hectanooga, Nova Scotia, had enrolled in August 1915 with the 40th Battalion, telling recruiters he was eighteen. From Valcartier he wrote home at least twice prior to being shipped to England.[8] In one of the letters, to his father that winter, Crosby noted "we have been drilling all day in the mud and water and it is still stormy" and so "we are sitting in the tent … playing cards." He also wrote that "a good many tents got flooded, but we got through all right." The teen also felt sure he would embark for England from Halifax, but was unsure whether he would spend the rest of the winter in camp on the east coast or at Valcartier.

By early January 1916, Crosby was at Bramshott, enduring a tough training regimen, punctuated by trips to London. "They certainly are putting the drill to us now — a route march most every day… I am going [back to London] again if I can before we move. I think there is a chance of us moving soon and hope there is." While overseas, Crosby did what a lot of good soldiers did while on leave: he had his portrait taken for the folks back home. The young soldier's last message, on April 7, 1916, was scrawled on the back of a YMCA postcard. "Well, we have arrived here at last," he reported. "We had a fairly good trip across [the English Channel]. Will write more later. Yours, Keith."

That was the last anyone back home heard of Private Crosby, who had put on a brave face to the end.[9]

As the fighting at Saint-Eloi continued, there was little the Canadians could do to conduct a coordinated defence against the enemy onslaught. Within three hours the Germans captured the four largest craters. The 24th Battalion went on to fight a vicious battle on the night of April 14, putting a halt to a German bombing party intent on recapturing Craters 6 and 7.[10] At one point the battalion was cut off from its commanders in the rear and had to rely on a carrier pigeon to inform headquarters that it had suffered many casualties but still held the position.

While the battle raged for another two weeks, confusion over the craters' exact location led the 31st Battalion to claim it occupied Craters 4 and 5 in the centre. In fact, the 31st was in the much smaller Craters 6 and 7, a mistake that took a week to clarify and led to more misunderstandings. By the time further attempts to take the craters were called off on April 16, Turner's 2nd Division had suffered 1,373 casualties. Its introduction to battle damaged the entire CEF's reputation. Looking for scapegoats, the British wanted to relieve Turner and Ketchen.

In the end Canadian sensibilities prevailed and the corps commander, General Alderson, was removed and replaced by Lieutenant-General Sir Julian Byng, another Briton.

On the night of April 26–27 the mud was flying again as the Germans exploded two mines along the centre of the corps front occupied by 1st Division. Opposite the 1st and 2nd Division sectors the enemy launched an infantry attack with strong artillery support, but the Canadians held their ground and beat back the attackers. A threatened attack against 3rd Division on the left of the corps front never materialized. Prior to that failed attack, the deadly exchanges in the centre and to the left of the corps front involved patrols and harassing fire — periodic sniping and shelling — as both sides worked to strengthen their positions.[11]

Seventeen-year-old Private Hubert Mills of Hamilton, Ontario, was killed in action on the 26th.[12] He had left school to enrol and had never been away from home before the war. "Mother, if you don't want me to go, I won't," he said before following in the footsteps of two brothers — one even younger than him — already in the army.

"I couldn't keep him back when his two brothers had gone," his mother told the *Hamilton Spectator* on May 11, just hours after she and her husband received word of their son's death. The newspaper described the Mills as one of the "most patriotic families in the west end." It noted that Hubert was born on King Street, attended Sunday school at the Gospel Tabernacle, and had joined the 36th Battalion before being transferred to the 1st (Western Ontario) Battalion. "He had been at the front for many months, and his mother received his last letter a week ago. It was written three days before he was killed and spoke of the constant danger from the bursting shells. He also said that the trenches were in awful condition from lice and rats, but looked forward to the time when he should return again."

The newspaper stated that Hubert's two brothers, Norman, who enrolled in November 1914, and Harold, who joined about a month before Hubert, were in France when their brother was killed, and that a sister, Pearl, was working as a nurse in nearby Guelph, Ontario. "Harold was only sixteen years of age last month, and yet he has been in the trenches for the past eight months. His mother has not heard from him for the past eight weeks, and as he was a regular writer she has entertained grave fears for his safety, and has sent to his commanding officer for news for him." Harold was two inches shorter than Hubert and had put down "rivet heating" as his trade, and 1896 as the year of his birth. And like his older brother Norman, who worked as a painter, Harold sported a large tattoo on his right forearm, displaying his loyalty to Buffalo Bill. His big brother had him beat though, with a flag on his right arm, an eagle on his left, and "lady of liberty" on his right shoulder.

For the parents, the pain of losing one son and not knowing the whereabouts of a second boy was paralyzing. "Mr. Mills is totally prostrated with grief over his bereavement," the Hamilton newspaper concluded.[13]

After Saint-Eloi, the Canadian sector remained quiet until June 2, when the Germans launched a devastating attack against 3rd Division, occupying a 2,225-metre front around Mount Sorrel and northwards, at the most easterly point of the Ypres Salient. It started with a fierce artillery bombardment while Major-General Mercer and Brigadier-General Williams were forward inspecting 4th CMR's positions. Shrapnel killed the already-wounded division commander and seriously wounded the brigade commander, who was later captured.[14] The shelling also nearly annihilated the 4th CMR. Only 76 of its 702 men survived. The Germans, meanwhile, had continued their advance, rolling over the CMR trenches and occupying Mount Sorrel and two other small prominences to the north, Hills 61 and 62.

Gunner James Drummond from Gananoque, Ontario, had been serving in the Ypres Salient since the spring of 1915, and though he survived the June 1916 fighting at Mount Sorrel, it was not as a free man. The teen was among more than five hundred Canadians captured by the advancing German infantry on June 2–3, and he spent the next thirty months as a prisoner of war.

Drummond was one example of the many orphaned children who served while in their teens. He and his two orphaned brothers were all underage when they enrolled between September 1914 and May 1916. While James, Robert, and David shared similar experiences during their early years, their paths to war were separate. Born in Dunfermline, County Fife, Scotland, the boys had two older sisters, Christina and Frances. A third sister, Annie, died at age two. Their father, David, toiled as a sawyer while their mother, Annie, kept house and cared for the children. James, born June 13, 1897, was the oldest boy, followed by Robert and David, born June 10, 1899, and August 6, 1901, respectively. Tragedy struck in 1904 when Annie, the mother, died of cancer. James was only seven at the time, while Robert and David were aged five and three. Christina and the other older children took on more household chores, but tragedy struck again when their father died in 1910, also of cancer.

That left the entire family in the hands of nineteen-year-old Christina.[15]

Two years later Christina got married, and that same year — on March 30, 1912 — the three boys, then aged fourteen, twelve, and ten, boarded the steamer *Scotian* at Glasgow for the long voyage to Halifax. All three arrived in Canada with the Quarrier Home Children, which operated a large orphanage far up the St. Lawrence River at Brockville, Ontario. From the orphanage the three boys were dispatched as unpaid child labour to different homes or farms throughout eastern Ontario.[16]

James, who had been employed as a farmer and a butcher, was the first of his brothers to enrol and head overseas, joining the local militia artillery unit in Gananoque on September 19, 1914, at age seventeen.[17] Before making it to Valcartier, the five-foot-six-inch lad injured himself in a riding accident, causing a four-day delay in the signing of his attestation paper, which provides a fabricated birth date of June 13, 1896. Robert — the second-oldest boy — enrolled in Ottawa with the 59th Battalion on July 3, 1915, at age sixteen. Unlike James and David, Robert, who served overseas with the 2nd (Eastern Ontario) Battalion, would be killed in action a little more than a year after James was taken prisoner. David, who enrolled at Kingston, Ontario, at age fourteen in May 1916, survived the war and died in Kingston in 1956.[18]

James's postwar life, however, was more fleeting. After returning home he was released from the artillery in September 1919 as medically unfit for duty. Within a year he died of complications from a disease few people talked about with any sympathy. Venereal disease caused tremendous physical and emotional grief and controversy during the war. Soldiers who contracted it were treated, but labelled as outcasts and docked pay. The epidemic began soon after the war started and by the fall of 1918 the CEF had registered 66,346 cases of syphilis and gonorrhoea.[19] Salvarsan, which produced terrible side effects, was used to fight syphilis. Gonorrhoea, meanwhile, had no known cure, but could only be treated with disinfectants. James had contracted the former in January 1915, and all attempts to cure him failed. It remained with him in battle and during his years of captivity. On top of that, in the summer of 1919, before heading back to Canada, he severely injured his knee and ankle playing football in England.

Just over a year later — on August 21, 1920 — James died at Sydenham hospital near Kingston, Ontario, not far from where he had enrolled. His death certificate gives the primary cause of death as syphilis and the contributory cause as "hypostatic pneumonia."[20]

The German assault at Mount Sorrel, where James Drummond was captured, was stopped only by a dogged stand by the Princess Patricia's Canadian Light Infantry in Sanctuary Wood, north of Hills 61 and 62, and 5th CMR in Maple Copse, to the rear of the position (see Map V).

Meanwhile, David O'Brien, the young 4th CMR private who convinced authorities he was four years older than his actual age, was lucky to escape death. He had witnessed the sudden loss of close friends on the battlefield and the violent deaths of strangers who piloted the flying machines above the scarred landscape.

"Day after day it was the same. Men killed and wounded — towns and villages blown up. Aeroplane battles overhead [and] every little while an aeroplane would crash to earth, with some

The Princess Patricia's Canadian Light Infantry determined defence of Sanctuary Wood on June 2, 1916, stopped the German advance at Mount Sorrel.

of the crew dead before they crashed. The war pilots with their crews were heroes supreme." O'Brien had also experienced "a real hot spot" near Ypres where "there was always a steady stream of stretchers carrying wounded men out to emergency hospitals." Even more sickening was how the constant, indiscriminate shelling robbed the dead. "We were fighting in a graveyard and very often even the dead would be blown out of their graves..."[21]

The teenager's time on the battlefield came to an end on June 2 — almost a year to the day after he enrolled — when he was wounded in the side and left leg. He went down, joining dozens of other Canadian casualties strewn across the battlefield. When enemy soldiers found him he was breathing, but about to enter a new life as a prisoner of war. "The Germans surrounded us... The wounded prisoners were dragged and kicked over to the German trenches. We were kept overnight in a church about three miles behind the German front line."

As the hours of his first night in captivity passed, O'Brien witnessed brutal treatment of captured men. Years later, in

Lance-carrying German cavalry, known as uhlans, *escort Canadian and British prisoners of war to the rear to face years in captivity.*

his memoir, he described German officers ordering men to be kicked or struck with rifle butts if they did not give up information concerning the strength and movement of Allied forces. He also recalled how the prisoners were ordered to get up and start marching to Germany.

"One boy from Toronto who was wounded in the head dropped to his knees from loss of blood. The German officer tried to kick him to his feet, but the man was too weak to get up again, so the officer simply shot him."[22]

O'Brien wrote that he also witnessed the death of a Belgian woman who had come out to toss a loaf of bread at the prisoners as they arrived at a railway siding. "The guard immediately rushed at her and drove a lance into her stomach, killing her almost instantly." The prisoners were ordered into boxcars, where they remained until the train stopped, two miles from Dulman, Germany. Those who could still breathe were marched at bayonet point into the Westphalian prison camp. For O'Brien and other Canadians it was the beginning of months of captivity during which he would witness cold-blooded murder, torture, hunger, and disease, and be put to work in a brick factory where he was forced to function with very little food. "I was wheeling about twenty five bricks on a wheelbarrow from the machines to the drying racks," he remembered. "I was hardly able to do the work [but] we had to keep moving..."[23]

Such recollections echo other accounts of cold-blooded abuse, but it is also true that the deplorable camp conditions that existed in the early months of the war were eventually rectified. Neutral inspections of German and Allied POW camps also served to reduce the worst forms of abuse and to limit the number of exaggerations of abuse.[24]

In response to the German advance that had swept hundreds of men into captivity or eternity, Byng, who had just experienced his first battle as the Canadians' commander, was determined to recapture lost ground. He ordered immediate counterattacks, all of which ended in failure. He then directed Currie to conduct a deliberate counterattack with 1st Division. The British cooperated by providing every gun in the Ypres Salient in support, which allowed Currie to adopt the German tactic of using massive artillery fire to destroy the enemy before the infantry assault. The counterattack bore many hallmarks associated with Currie's later operations: thorough planning; detailed reconnaissance, including aerial photography; registration of artillery targets; and methodical rehearsals. The Germans were bombarded for ten hours before the counterattack was launched at 1:30 a.m. on June 13, in heavy rain and under cover of a thick smokescreen. Within an hour, the

This sketch of Nursing Sister Blanche Lavallée was done while she was serving at No. 4 Canadian Stationary Hospital (French Canadian), near Paris.

attacking battalions regained the former Canadian line. It was the first large-scale counterattack by the Canadians.

As was to prove increasingly true, the cost of victory was not cheap. During the first two weeks of June, the corps lost 9,624 men, including many in their adolescent years.

Nothing, however, would compare to the carnage visited in the months ahead.

CHAPTER 6

"DEAD MEN CAN ADVANCE NO FURTHER."

The Newfoundland Regiment at Gallipoli and the Somme, August 1914 – October 1916

Jack Chaplin did not die a soldier's death.

The freckled, ginger-haired student was among the first to join the Newfoundland Regiment after the war broke out. When he enrolled in St. John's on September 22, 1914, he was only seventeen, although he claimed to be nineteen, the minimum age for joining the unit.

Chaplin became the first member of his unit to die overseas; not in battle, but in garrison. He died clutching his stomach in pain on New Year's Day 1915 at Fort George, Scotland, where the Newfoundlanders were undergoing training. Although various records state Chaplin died of an "abdominal illness," the official cause of death was listed somewhat cryptically as "Abdominal Newgrowth (liver)."[1] The popular young lad was buried with full military honours in the parish churchyard at the nearby village of Ardersier. As an expression of the high regard in which the youth was held, his platoon sergeant composed a poem in remembrance of him and had it printed on silk.[2]

Shortly afterwards, Chaplin's distraught father wrote to Newfoundland Governor Sir Walter Davidson to ask if his son's body could be shipped home. In reply he was told it was not British policy to repatriate the remains of soldiers who died overseas during wartime.[3]

When the First World War broke out, Newfoundland was not yet a part of Canada but a separate dominion of about 242,000 people. When the last British soldiers departed in 1870, the Newfoundland government had not seen fit to establish any armed forces of its own — even a militia — a decision partially driven by financial concerns. In 1902, a Royal Naval Reserve of six hundred sailors was created to augment the Royal Navy when required, but a 1907 proposal to establish a similar land element never came to fruition. The only men and boys in Newfoundland with at least some form of military training were the members of the various cadet corps sponsored by the major religious denominations, the Legion of Frontiersmen (an empire-wide civilian organization of marksmen), and the St. John's Rifle Club.

When word of the war arrived on August 4, Newfoundland was essentially defenceless. Mobilization of the Royal Naval Reserve could produce only seventy trained sailors initially, because the rest were away fishing. Newfoundlanders clearly wanted to contribute to the war effort, though, so government officials and various volunteer organizations swung into action. Britain quickly accepted an offer of five hundred men for land service abroad and an increase of the naval reserve to a thousand sailors.

On August 17, interested citizens formed the Patriotic Association of Newfoundland with Governor Davidson as chairman. The association recruited, equipped, transported, and administered the contingents raised in Newfoundland — with generally

The Church Lads' Brigade Armoury at St. John's, Newfoundland.

good results — until a Department of Militia was formed in late 1917. Recruiting started on August 21 at the Church Lads' Brigade Armoury, and the results were immediate.[4] The Newfoundland Regiment was formed, eventually another two thousand men joined the Royal Naval Reserve, and several hundred enrolled in the Newfoundland Forestry Corps. Although the government originally intended to provide only five hundred men for the regiment, by the end of the war more than six thousand had served in its ranks.[5] In total, some twelve thousand Newfoundlanders enrolled in the forces, with almost as many again volunteering but being rejected.

Before the first contingent departed, war fever gripped St. John's and there was broad support for the recruiting drive. As the various church-based cadet corps played such a prominent part in the life of many youths, it was inevitable that boys under the minimum age of nineteen would get caught up in the excitement, and several succeeded in joining. Initially recruiting was centred on the island's capital and St. John's provided the majority of the men. Recruiting later spread to the outports and interior communities, although none of these towns and villages succeeded in rivalling the support found in St. John's, with the possible exception of Grand Falls.[6]

As the great armada carrying the first Canadian contingent passed the south coast of Newfoundland on October 4, 1914, the SS *Florizel* was outward bound off Cape Race. With 538 soldiers of the Newfoundland Regiment on board, the Bowring Brothers flagship and seasonal sealing vessel was the last troopship to join the United Kingdom–bound convoy. After enduring seven weeks of rain on Salisbury Plain, the regiment spent the next few months training in Scotland before moving south in late summer to Aldershot — the home of the British army. Then, on August 20, 1915, the Newfoundlanders embarked for the eastern Mediterranean, destined to fight the Turks at Gallipoli.[7]

The Allied High Command decided to attack the Turks in the hopes of opening the Dardanelles, the narrow, sixty-five-kilometre strait that partially divides Turkey in Europe from Turkey in Asia. Control of the Dardanelles would allow the Allies to use the strait as a route for supplies to Russia through the Black Sea. It might even knock Turkey out of the war and convince some of the Balkan states to join the Allies. It did not achieve either aim. After a failed naval attempt to force the Dardanelles in March, a seventy-eight-thousand-man force of British, Australian, New Zealand, and French troops landed at Gallipoli in late April 1915, but never succeeded in advancing very far from the beachheads. The area soon resembled the Western Front, with the opposing forces dug in and engaging in vicious trench warfare.[8] Reinforcements followed for both sides, and soon fourteen Allied divisions faced twenty-two Turkish ones.

The Newfoundlanders' first taste of war was at Gallipoli. They landed at Suvla Bay, on the western side of the Gallipoli Peninsula, on the night of September 19–20. There they joined the veteran 88th Brigade of the 29th Division, British formations with which they were to serve until the last six months of the war. The Newfoundlanders walked into the middle of a sandstorm — and a maelstrom. From the commanding heights overlooking the shallow beachheads, the Turks poured down continuous artillery, machine-gun, and rifle fire into unit lines, causing many casualties.[9]

One of the first to fall was sixteen-year-old Bill Morgan, a plumber's apprentice from St. John's. Morgan had enrolled in January 1915 and sailed overseas in March. While in Britain, the young soldier was punished for a few disciplinary incidents, which may have resulted from either youthful exuberance or an inability to adjust to regimented life. A week after landing at Suvla Bay he was wounded by a bullet in the left shoulder. On September 29, he was evacuated to No. 5 Canadian Stationary Hospital (one of four sent to the eastern Mediterranean[10]) on the outskirts of Cairo. After a week in hospital, Morgan returned to duty and landed at Gallipoli for the second time on October 25.[11]

Bill Hardy and his younger brother, Ed, from St. John's, were both at Gallipoli. Twenty-one-year-old Bill, a fisherman, was one of the first to join the unit in 1914 and was assigned regimental number 179 on September 13. He went overseas with the First Five Hundred, the name given to the first group of Newfoundland volunteers to go. Ed, a dry goods clerk, joined after Bill, on December 15. He claimed to be nineteen, although he was only sixteen or seventeen at the time. Ed sailed to Britain with the second Newfoundland contingent on February 3, 1915, which went directly to Edinburgh. Two days after arrival, on February 19, he was reunited with his older brother when the remainder of the unit arrived from Fort George.[12]

The two brothers landed at Suvla Bay together. Three days later a Turkish sniper got Bill in his sights and fired. The bullet went through Bill's chest, killing him quickly.

He was only the second Newfoundlander to die in action.[13]

When the boys' mother learned of the "sad blow indeed" of Bill's death, she sent a poignant letter to the unit paymaster, Captain Timewell, asking that the parcel she had recently sent Bill be redirected to Ed. At the bottom she noted, "I would have wrote before but trouble prevented me." In response, the paymaster replied that her parcel had been redirected and expressed his "sincere sympathy in the deep sorrow of a mother's tribute to the great struggle."[14]

At Gallipoli, resupply was difficult, and rations often ran short. Drinking water was frequently limited to half a pint per day. Plagues of flies tormented the soldiers, bringing with them cholera, dysentery, and typhus, while body lice were a constant nuisance. Disease caused more casualties than the Turks.[15] Ron Dunn, a Bonavista fisherman, was seventeen when he enrolled in December 1914. In an interview conducted for Veterans Affairs decades later, he provided some first-hand comments about the conditions at Gallipoli: "We [were in] bad, bad, shape, dysentery." Insects were a particular problem. "We had blackflies, little ones, millions. We had crawlers on the bodies, swarming, eating us up."

Water had to be brought in from Egypt in five-gallon cans that had been used previously for other liquids, making the water taste like "pure poison" in Dunn's opinion, but "they were only glad to get it." Food was as problematic. "There was bread. Sometimes we'd get a potato. And more times, we had to do without anything." Much of the bread had bugs in it, but "we had to eat it." Some of the bread delivered in the morning had to be saved, in case "we didn't get nothing for our dinner." The soldiers stored it in their helmets; otherwise, "the rats would have it . . . Great big fellows." These harsh conditions also took their toll on young Ed Hardy, and he got severe diarrhoea — dysentery — which required his evacuation to Egypt. On November 5, he was admitted to No.

5 Canadian Stationary Hospital, where he remained for the rest of the month to recuperate.[16]

In November the weather replaced the Turks as the main enemy.

Dunn noted that at first "it didn't rain a lot, but after that … down it'd come, oh it'd come down in showers and showers and it come down, the real flood. And our trenches burst loose and went on down and swept everything down … everything all out." If that was not bad enough, temperatures fell below zero, and a severe blizzard struck. Many soldiers suffered frozen feet and hands.[17] By early December, the regiment was at a quarter of its strength, largely because of sickness.[18]

Although Dunn was sent to England to recover from dysentery, at least two boy soldiers were afflicted with frostbite and had to be evacuated.

Privates Norm Coultas and Steve Fallon had joined in early 1915 and went overseas aboard the *Florizel*'s sister ship, the SS *Stephano*: Coultas in March and Fallon the next month. The diminutive, blue-eyed Coultas, a former clerk from St. John's, had claimed to be nineteen on enrolment, while Fallon, a wiry fisherman from the small Conception Bay village of Harbour Grace, about forty-five kilometres northwest of St. John's, stated he was eighteen. In fact, both were seventeen.

The two teenagers followed the same evacuation chain after their injuries. Both went to 29th Casualty Clearing Station (CCS) and then to a hospital at Lemnos, Egypt, or to Malta. From there they were invalided to 3rd London General Hospital in Wandsworth, England, where many wounded Newfoundlanders were treated. Coultas was the first to be affected, on November 30. His frostbite turned out to be fairly serious, and he was invalided to Britain on Boxing Day aboard the Cunard liner RMS *Aquitania*, which had been pressed into service, initially as a troopship before being converted into a hospital ship for the Dardanelles campaign.

After treatment both Coultas and Fallon were released on furlough for recuperation at the regimental depot at Ayr, Scotland, before finally being returned to the front. They must have enjoyed the freedom these new arrangements offered, but Coultas lingered too long off-base on one occasion in February and was charged for "overstaying furlough" until 9 p.m. His disciplinary difficulties did not end there. The next month he was in trouble again for refusing to obey an order from a non-commissioned officer and being absent from morning parade. Fallon followed Coultas's medical — and disciplinary — journey closely. Invalided to England with Coultas, he also got into trouble while attached to the regimental depot. On one occasion he was charged with being absent for four days.[19]

At Gallipoli even the indomitable British had had enough by now and decided to withdraw. The last of the Newfoundlanders left Suvla Bay on December 20 and moved to Cape Helles, the one remaining beachhead, at the southern tip of the peninsula. There they assisted in the British withdrawal until January 9 and were among the very last troops to depart.[20] Although young Ed Hardy had returned to Gallipoli from hospital in Egypt at the end of November, he did not rejoin his unit until January 26 because the situation was so confused.[21]

The Newfoundlanders' losses in the Dardanelles were thirty-five killed or died of wounds and ten who succumbed to disease.[22] After the withdrawal from Gallipoli, those still fit to fight — less than five hundred all ranks — sailed back to Egypt and crossed the Nile delta by train to encamp at Suez. The regiment had a period of recuperation in Egypt before heading for France on March 14, 1916, where it would shortly be tested at one of the most infamous battles in history — the bloody first day on the Somme.[23]

As the Cunarder SS *Alaunia* chugged toward the French port of Marseilles with the Newfoundland Regiment aboard, Bill

Dugouts of the Newfoundland Regiment at Cape Helles sometime between December 22, 1915, and January 9, 1916, when the last of the Newfoundlanders left Gallipoli.

Morgan, still feeling the effects of his wounded shoulder, got in trouble again. Two days before the ship docked he was caught smoking below decks and paraded before his new commanding officer, Lieutenant-Colonel Arthur Hadow. The CO, a stickler for discipline — many considered him a martinet — was not amused and sentenced Morgan to three days' Field Punishment Number 1.[24] FP No.1 was a particularly humiliating form of punishment, which could be awarded only on active service. It consisted of the convicted soldier being shackled in fetters and handcuffs or tied with rope restraints and attached to a fixed object — such as a wagon wheel — for up to two hours per day, while standing.[25]

On July 1, 1916, a largely volunteer British army attacked a well-trained and well-entrenched German force. It was the blackest day in British military history. By its end, more casualties had been suffered than on any day before or since — a shocking thirty thousand in the first hour, and another twenty-eight thousand by nightfall. The simple phrase "First Day on the Somme" has come to symbolize the horrors of the First World War.

The main assault would be carried out by Lieutenant-General Sir Henry Rawlinson's Fourth Army, with supporting attacks from Third Army to the north and the French to the south. But Rawlinson lacked confidence in his so-called New Army battalions — inexperienced men who had enrolled in response to Lord Kitchener's call to beef up Britain's small regular army at the start of the war. He felt they could not be controlled in rushing German trenches and ordered a massive five-day artillery barrage to destroy the enemy. This would allow his troops to then simply advance in close formation across the battlefield, wiping up any pockets of resistance that survived, at a stipulated pace of ninety-one metres per minute with one-minute intervals between successive battalions.

In anticipation of the big push on the Somme, the Newfoundland Regiment was reinforced. After recovering from his frostbite, Steve Fallon, the former fisherman from Harbour Grace, returned to his unit — and promptly got into more trouble. He lost his gas helmet while in billets at Louvencourt and had to pay to replace it. The diminutive Norm Coultas had also recovered from frostbite and rejoined his unit in early April, only to be plagued by additional medical problems. In mid-May he was admitted to a CCS with "incontinence of urine" and was promptly sent to No. 1 Stationary Hospital in Rouen, where he underwent surgery for appendicitis. He was

Soldiers of the Newfoundland Regiment in St. John's Road support trench, July 1, 1916, before the start of the ill-fated attack that decimated the unit.

able to rejoin his unit once again on June 20, just in time for the fateful attack.[26]

In the pre-dawn hours of July 1, the assaulting infantry of fourteen British divisions moved toward their assembly areas, each man struggling under a thirty-two-kilogram burden. Rifle, bayonet, 220 rounds of ammunition, rations, water, gas helmet, wound dressings, two hand grenades, flares, a spade, and two empty sandbags were a typical load. Many men carried more: machine-gun ammunition, mortar bombs, wire pickets, or signalling equipment. To the south, twelve French divisions carried out similar preparations. The axis of advance was the old Roman road that ran in a straight line from Albert to Bapaume, nineteen kilometres to the northeast. The assault commenced at 7:30 a.m., when it was light enough to check the accuracy of the final

Mary Riter Hamilton's painting The Sadness of the Somme/La mélancholie de la Somme *depicts the lifeless landscape that the Somme region had become.*

bombardment. It was also light enough to let the Germans clearly see their attackers. In the last few minutes before zero hour, the British detonated seventeen mines.[27]

Among the assault battalions was the reinforced Newfoundland Regiment.

Just after 2 a.m. on July 1, eight hundred Newfoundlanders arrived at the front-line support trenches as part of the second wave. They were to pass through the first wave of two British battalions, and then advance to their final objective some three kilometres further on. At 7:35 a.m., the British attacked. It was over in forty minutes. German soldiers enfiladed the attacking troops and decimated them with machine-gun fire. That first attack ground to a halt as bodies piled up at gaps in the wire.

Now it was the Newfoundlanders who faced a daunting task. The soldiers, including teenagers, set off at 9:15 a.m. with A and B companies leading, followed by C and D. The latter two companies had a higher proportion of young soldiers going into action for the first time than the others.

Under deadly enemy shelling and machine-gun fire, the Newfoundlanders began crossing their own front-line trenches and the wire that separated them from no man's land. Many were killed before they reached the trenches. Those who managed to scramble past the dead and wounded were caught in a hailstorm of bullets. Incredibly, those still on their feet pushed on, down the bare slope, in an attempt to cross 550 metres of no man's land. In the face of overwhelming fire and without proper support, some Newfoundlanders made it to the German wire, but to no avail.

By 9:45 a.m., the battle was over.

Inside half an hour, the proud Newfoundland Regiment had virtually ceased to exist. Every officer who walked into that maelstrom became a casualty: fourteen killed and twelve wounded. Of the soldiers, 219 were killed and 374 wounded, with another 91 missing. Only 68 of those who went into action were uninjured.[28] D Company had three young casualties. Bill Morgan and Steve Fallon were killed in the storm of fire, while Norm Coultas was reported missing. His death was not confirmed until November, after it was ascertained that he was not a prisoner of the Germans. None of their bodies were found.[29]

Newfoundlanders trapped in no man's land suffered terribly in the blazing sun; the wounded bleeding and in pain, the injured and uninjured alike thirsty and unable to move because of German fire. They lay there all day. At nightfall those who could crawled back to the British lines, between German flares lighting up the battlefield, while stretcher-bearers recovered the wounded. Ron Dunn, the young Bonavista fisherman who was evacuated from Gallipoli with dysentery, was one of the injured who had been left in no man's land. Hit by rifle fire in his right

A front-line dugout (which she called a "shelter trench") on the Somme painted by Mary Riter Hamilton.

thigh, he tried to bandage his wounds, but "the wound was too far away. The bandages was not big, not long." Throwing up blood, he started to crawl until German snipers saw the movement and fired at him. By then, Dunn was desperate for water and had "lost a lot of blood, I don't know how much blood I lost, but everything was running out of me and I couldn't move."

The teenager somehow managed to crawl into a shell hole, where he stayed until dark.

That night, Dunn slowly probed in both directions, unsure which were Newfoundland lines and which were German. Finally, he made it to what he thought was the wire on his side, crawled through, and stayed there, hoping someone would find him. But he lay there all night "and there wasn't a soul came handy to me … and all the fellas around me was dead then." As

A wounded Newfoundland soldier is helped to the rear during the fighting at Beaumont Hamel.

he drifted in and out of consciousness, he thought of home "like everyone else" and "thought me mother was there but I couldn't see her, and I thought I was talking to her... I didn't hear her but I'm sure she was there. I had a feeling."

Dunn awoke before dawn to the sounds of German artillery shelling the Allied lines, as they were "afraid the British would attack again." As he lay there, "A shell [probably a piece of shrapnel] came down around an inch and a half ... and hit me right on the chest. Bango! I put my hand down and picked it up. Just warm it twas... I threw it away." Dunn lapsed into unconsciousness again and was finally picked up, although he remembered "no more about it, no more about nothing."

For Dunn the war was over. He received a medical discharge in October 1917, returned home, married, raised three children, and became president of the Bonavista Branch of the Great War Veterans' Association. He died in 1994 at age ninety-seven.[30]

Remarkably, Dunn was not the last Newfoundlander to escape alive from no man's land. On July 5, a soldier crawled in from no

Mary Riter Hamilton's painting portrays poppies blooming in the post-war remains of trenches dug into the white chalk of the Somme.

man's land, where he had survived for four days. He must have wondered what he had gotten himself into; he had arrived with a new draft only hours before the attack and missed all the preparatory training for it. After the attack, the division commander General de Lisle wrote to Newfoundland's prime minister about the battle. "It was a magnificent display of trained and disciplined valour," he declared, "and its assault only failed because dead men can advance no further."

After its decimation on the Somme the Newfoundland Regiment was withdrawn for a period of rebuilding. It did not last very long, and the Newfoundlanders returned to the front lines in mid-July 1916, long before they were ready to fight again. They moved north to the Ypres Salient, where they spent some of their time manning front-line trenches. In early October, the regiment left the salient and entrained for the south, back to the Somme — and back into combat. In the Newfoundlanders' absence, General Douglas Haig's planned breakthrough had not occurred, and the Somme battle was reduced to an agonizing war of attrition; but by October a few successes had been achieved, so Haig decided to renew his offensive.

The regiment's role was to capture German positions north of the village of Gueudecourt. The Newfoundlanders went into the trenches on the night of October 10 and manned a five-hundred-metre firing line on the northern outskirts of Gueudecourt by the next morning.[31] Among the soldiers who moved up that night was young Ed Hardy, whose older brother had been killed by a sniper at Gallipoli. Ed had been admitted to hospital with an ulcerated leg in mid-June and discharged three days later. Still not fit enough to fight, he did not rejoin his unit until July 4 and so avoided the murderous Somme assault of July 1.[32]

The regiment advanced at Gueudecourt at 2:05 p.m. on October 12, attacking with two companies in the lead and two more following. The Newfoundlanders soon reached their first objective, a German trench about 365 metres away. After some hand-to-hand fighting it was in their possession by 2:30 p.m. The soldiers quickly reorganized and began their advance toward the second objective, another 365 metres further on. They soon came under concentrated enemy fire and were forced to fall back. Ignoring orders to retire to Gueudecourt, the Newfoundlanders held on through repeated German counterattacks until they were relieved in the pre-dawn hours of the next day. Their two days at Gueudecourt resulted in 239 casualties, 120 of them fatal.[33]

Hardy had survived most of Gallipoli and missed Beaumont-Hamel due to injuries, but fate finally caught up with him and he was reported missing at Gueudecourt. When his body was found he was listed as "killed in action or died of wounds on or shortly after 12-10-16 (and buried)." In 1920, his remains were removed from their hasty battlefield burial site and re-interred "carefully and reverently" at Bancourt British Cemetery near Bapaume. His

parents and the next of kin of all Newfoundland soldiers who
died during the war received an official — and standard — letter of condolence from Newfoundland's colonial secretary, John
Bennett. After expressing sympathy over the loss the letters go on
to state, in the somewhat flowery language of the time:

> "… it will, no doubt, be some consolation to you
> to think that your son willingly answered the call of
> King and Country, did his part nobly, and fell, facing
> the foe, in defence of the principles of Righteous-
> ness, Truth and Liberty. Though he has laid down the
> earthly weapons of warfare, he now wears the Soldier's
> Crown of Victory, and his name will be inscribed upon
> the glorious Roll of Honour and be held in fragrant
> memory by all his fellow-countrymen. When the vic-
> tory is won and Peace again reigns upon the earth, it
> will be a comforting thought to you that in this glori-
> ous achievement he bore no small part. I trust that you
> may have the grace and consolation of the Great Father
> of us all at this time."[34]

In fact, such letters did mean a lot to the bereaved families.
Along with a memorial plaque and a scroll containing the king's
message — as well as any medals to which the soldier was entitled
and even a photograph of his gravesite — the letters brought
some closure and a sense of pride to the relatives of the fallen.
Many parents of boy soldiers even sent simple yet poignant letters to the authorities to thank them for these expressions of
sympathy. "Thank you and the Government for your very kind
sympathy," one mother wrote. "Our loss is indeed great but that
he died nobly we are proud."[35]

MAP I

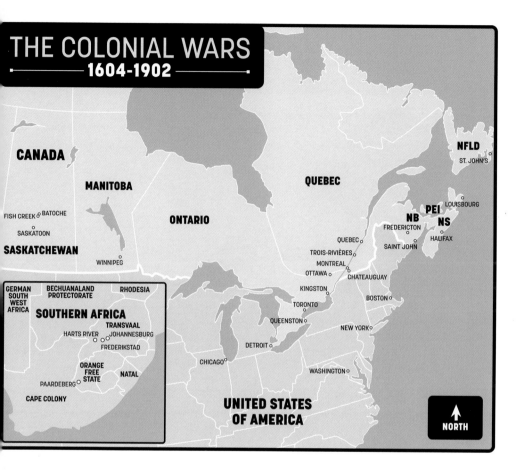

THE COLONIAL WARS
1604-1902

CANADA

NFLD
ST. JOHN'S

MANITOBA

QUEBEC

FISH CREEK & BATOCHE
SASKATOON

ONTARIO

LOUISBOURG
NB PEI NS
FREDERICTON
HALIFAX

SASKATCHEWAN

WINNIPEG

QUEBEC
TROIS-RIVIÈRES
SAINT JOHN
MONTREAL
OTTAWA
CHATEAUGUAY

GERMAN
SOUTH
WEST
AFRICA

BECHUANALAND
PROTECTORATE

RHODESIA

KINGSTON

TORONTO

BOSTON

SOUTHERN AFRICA

QUEENSTON

TRANSVAAL
HARTS RIVER JOHANNESBURG

NEW YORK

FREDERIKSTAD

DETROIT

ORANGE
FREE
STATE

NATAL

CHICAGO

PAARDEBERG

WASHINGTON

CAPE COLONY

UNITED STATES
OF AMERICA

NORTH

MAP II

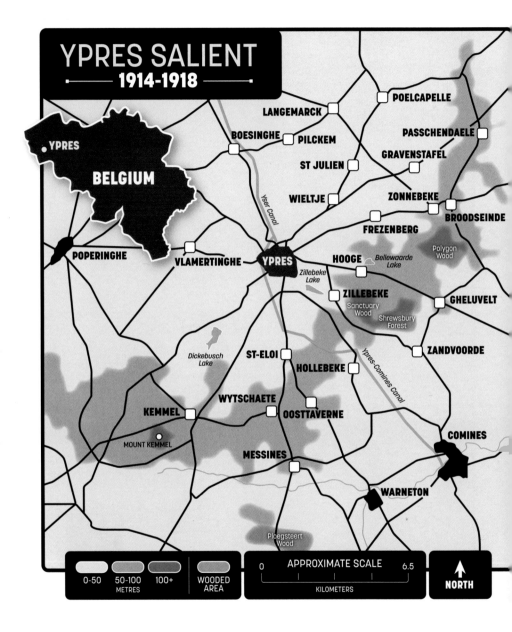

YPRES SALIENT
1914-1918

BELGIUM

YPRES

POELCAPELLE

LANGEMARCK

BOESINGHE   PILCKEM

PASSCHENDAELE

GRAVENSTAFEL

ST JULIEN

Yser Canal

WIELTJE

ZONNEBEKE

BROODSEINDE

FREZENBERG

Polygon Wood

POPERINGHE

VLAMERTINGHE   YPRES

HOOGE   Bellewaarde Lake

Zillebeke Lake

ZILLEBEKE

GHELUVELT

Sanctuary Wood

Shrewsbury Forest

Dickebusch Lake

ST-ELOI

HOLLEBEKE

ZANDVOORDE

Ypres-Comines Canal

WYTSCHAETE

KEMMEL

OOSTTAVERNE

COMINES

MOUNT KEMMEL

MESSINES

WARNETON

Ploegsteert Wood

0-50   50-100   100+   WOODED AREA   METRES

APPROXIMATE SCALE

0   6.5

KILOMETERS

NORTH

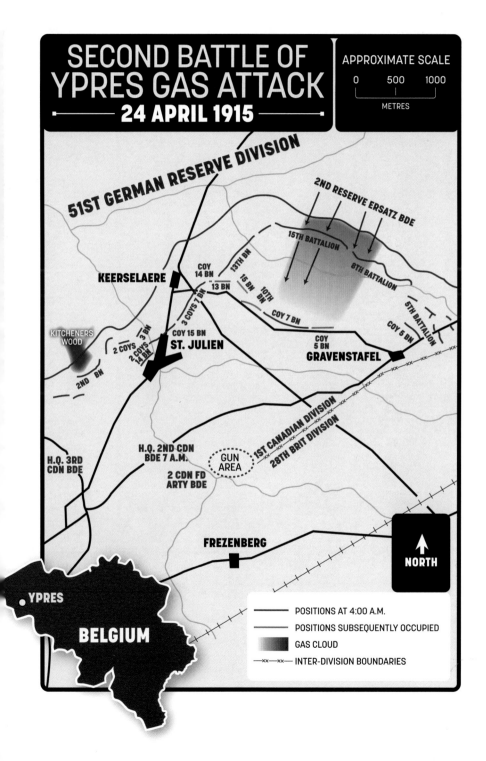

MAP III

SECOND BATTLE OF YPRES GAS ATTACK
- 24 APRIL 1915 -

APPROXIMATE SCALE

0   500   1000

METRES

51ST GERMAN RESERVE DIVISION

2ND RESERVE ERSATZ BDE

15TH BATTALION

8TH BATTALION

5TH BATTALION

KEERSELAERE

COY 14 BN

13TH BN

15 BN

13 BN

10TH BN

3 COYS 7 BN

COY 7 BN

COY 5 BN

KITCHENERS WOOD

2 COYS 14 BN

3 BN

COY 15 BN

ST. JULIEN

COY 5 BN

GRAVENSTAFEL

2ND BN

H.Q. 3RD CDN BDE

H.Q. 2ND CDN BDE 7 A.M.

GUN AREA

1ST CANADIAN DIVISION

28TH BRIT DIVISION

2 CDN FD ARTY BDE

FREZENBERG

NORTH

YPRES

BELGIUM

POSITIONS AT 4:00 A.M.

POSITIONS SUBSEQUENTLY OCCUPIED

GAS CLOUD

—xx—xx— INTER-DIVISION BOUNDARIES

MAP IV

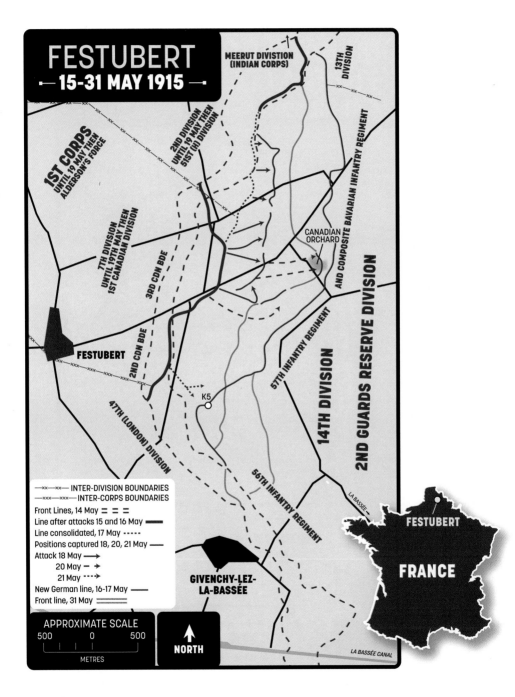

FESTUBERT
15-31 MAY 1915

MEERUT DIVISION
(INDIAN CORPS)

13TH DIVISION

1ST CORPS
UNTIL 19 MAY THEN
ALDERSON'S FORCE

2ND DIVISION
UNTIL 19 MAY THEN
51ST (H) DIVISION

AND COMPOSITE BAVARIAN INFANTRY REGIMENT

7TH DIVISION
UNTIL 19TH MAY THEN
1ST CANADIAN DIVISION

CANADIAN
ORCHARD

3RD CDN BDE

2ND CDN BDE

FESTUBERT

57TH INFANTRY REGIMENT

14TH DIVISION

2ND GUARDS RESERVE DIVISION

K5

47TH (LONDON) DIVISION

56TH INFANTRY REGIMENT

LA BASSÉE

INTER-DIVISION BOUNDARIES
INTER-CORPS BOUNDARIES
Front Lines, 14 May
Line after attacks 15 and 16 May
Line consolidated, 17 May
Positions captured 18, 20, 21 May
Attack 18 May
20 May
21 May
New German line, 16-17 May
Front line, 31 May

GIVENCHY-LEZ-
LA-BASSÉE

APPROXIMATE SCALE
500   0   500
METRES

NORTH

LA BASSÉE CANAL

FESTUBERT

FRANCE

MAP V

THE BATTLE OF MOUNT SORREL
—— 2-13 JUNE 1916 ——

2 JUNE · **3 JUNE** · **13 JUNE**

METRES: 0-40 · 40-50 · 50-60 · 60+ — WOODED AREA

—×—×— INTER-DIVISION BOUNDARIES

NORTH

APPROXIMATE SCALE
500 400 300 200 100 0 500
METRES

BELGIUM
MOUNT SORREL

Labels: 117TH DIVISION, HOOGE, SANCTUARY WOOD, 26TH (WÜRTTEMBERG) DIV, OBSERVATORY RIDGE, HILL 62, HILL 61, ARMAGH WOOD, 27TH (WÜRTTEMBERG) DIV, MOUNT SORREL, SQUARE WOOD, ZWARTELEEN, MAPLE COPSE, 6TH CDN INF BDE, 9TH CDN INF BDE, 3RD CDN INF BDE, 2ND CDN INF BDE, 7TH CDN INF BDE, 8TH CDN INF BDE

MAP VI

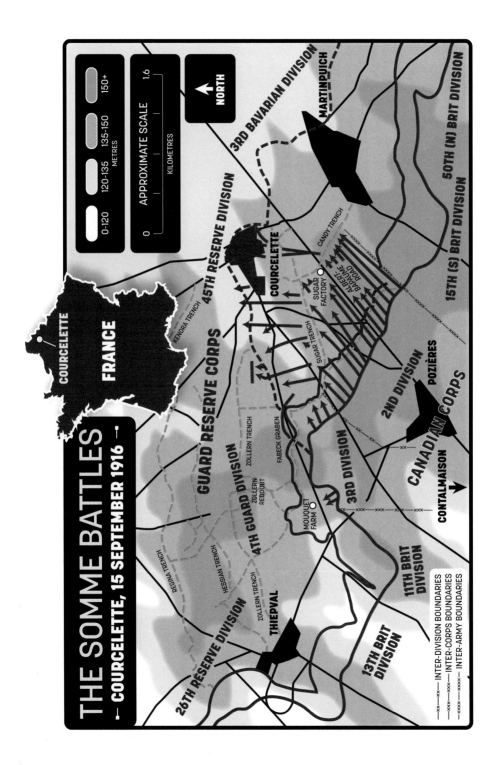

THE SOMME BATTLES
— COURCELETTE, 15 SEPTEMBER 1916 —

FRANCE
COURCELETTE

METRES
0-120   120-135   135-150   150+

APPROXIMATE SCALE
0   1.6
KILOMETRES

NORTH

3RD BAVARIAN DIVISION
MARTINPUICH
50TH (N) BRIT DIVISION
45TH RESERVE DIVISION
COURCELETTE
CANDY TRENCH
SUGAR FACTORY
ALBERT-BAPAUME BN ROAD
15TH (S) BRIT DIVISION
KENORA TRENCH
GUARD RESERVE CORPS
SUGAR TRENCH
POZIÈRES
2ND DIVISION
CANADIAN CORPS
ZOLLERN TRENCH
4TH GUARD DIVISION
ZOLLERN REDOUBT
FABECK GRABEN
3RD DIVISION
CONTALMAISON
REGINA TRENCH
MOUQUET FARM
HESSIAN TRENCH
26TH RESERVE DIVISION
ZOLLERN TRENCH
THIEPVAL
11TH BRIT DIVISION
13TH BRIT DIVISION

——×××—— INTER-DIVISION BOUNDARIES
——××××—— INTER-CORPS BOUNDARIES
——×××××—— INTER-ARMY BOUNDARIES

MAP VII

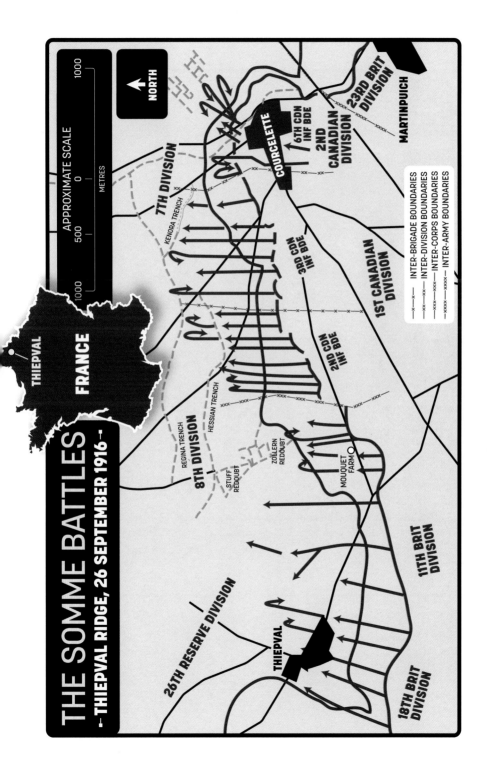

THE SOMME BATTLES
– THIEPVAL RIDGE, 26 SEPTEMBER 1916 –

FRANCE

THIEPVAL

APPROXIMATE SCALE

1000   0   1000

METRES

NORTH

INTER-BRIGADE BOUNDARIES
INTER-DIVISION BOUNDARIES
INTER-CORPS BOUNDARIES
INTER-ARMY BOUNDARIES

23RD BRIT DIVISION

MARTINPUICH

6TH CDN INF BDE

2ND CANADIAN DIVISION

COURCELETTE

7TH DIVISION

KENORA TRENCH

3RD CDN INF BDE

1ST CANADIAN DIVISION

2ND CDN INF BDE

REGINA TRENCH

HESSIAN TRENCH

8TH DIVISION

STUFF REDOUBT

ZOLLERN REDOUBT

MOUQUET FARM

11TH BRIT DIVISION

26TH RESERVE DIVISION

THIEPVAL

18TH BRIT DIVISION

MAP VIII

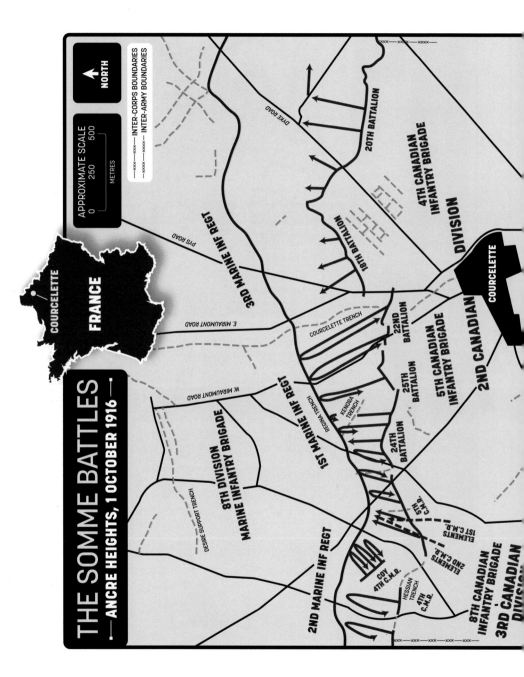

THE SOMME BATTLES
— ANCRE HEIGHTS, 1 OCTOBER 1916 —

FRANCE

COURCELETTE

APPROXIMATE SCALE

0   250   500

METRES

NORTH

XXXX — INTER-CORPS BOUNDARIES
XXXX — INTER-ARMY BOUNDARIES

DYKE ROAD

20TH BATTALION

4TH CANADIAN
INFANTRY BRIGADE

DIVISION

18TH BATTALION

COURCELETTE

2ND CANADIAN

3RD MARINE INF REGT

PYS ROAD

E. MIRAUMONT ROAD

COURCELETTE TRENCH

22ND
BATTALION

25TH
BATTALION

5TH CANADIAN
INFANTRY BRIGADE

W. MIRAUMONT ROAD

KENORA
TRENCH

REGINA TRENCH

1ST MARINE INF REGT

24TH
BATTALION

8TH DIVISION
MARINE INFANTRY BRIGADE

DESIRE SUPPORT TRENCH

5TH
C.M.R.

ELEMENTS
1ST C.M.R.

ELEMENTS
2ND C.M.R.

COY
4TH C.M.R.

4TH
C.M.R.

HESSIAN
TRENCH

2ND MARINE INF REGT

8TH CANADIAN
INFANTRY BRIGADE

3RD CANADIAN
DIVISION

MAP IX

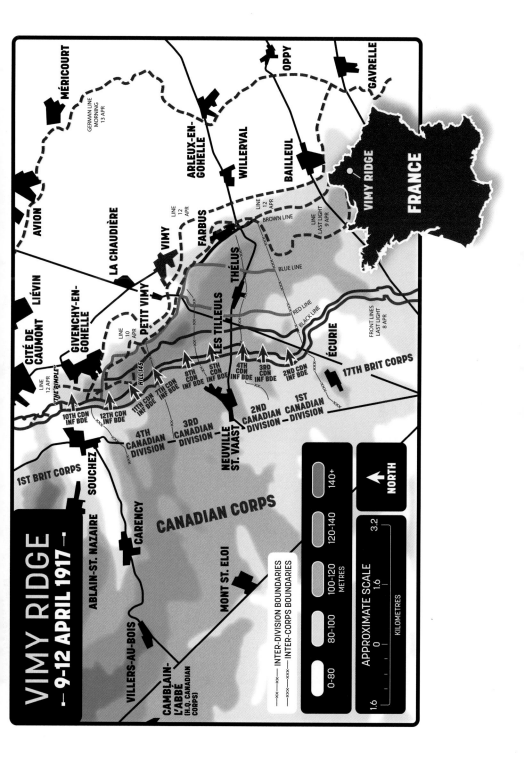

VIMY RIDGE
9-12 APRIL 1917

MÉRICOURT

GERMAN LINE
MORNING
13 APR

OPPY

GAVRELLE

ARLEUX-EN-GOHELLE

WILLERVAL

BAILLEUL

VIMY RIDGE

FRANCE

AVION

LA CHAUDIÈRE

LINE
12 APR

FARBUS

LINE
12 APR

BROWN LINE

LINE
LAST LIGHT
9 APR

VIMY

THÉLUS

BLUE LINE

LIÉVIN

CITÉ DE CAUMONT

GIVENCHY-EN-GOHELLE

PETIT VIMY

LINE
10 APR

LES TILLEULS

RED LINE

BLACK LINE

ÉCURIE

FRONT LINES
LAST LIGHT
8 APR

LINE
12 APR

THE PIMPLE

HILL 145

8TH CDN INF BDE

5TH CDN INF BDE

4TH CDN INF BDE

3RD CDN INF BDE

2ND CDN INF BDE

17TH BRIT CORPS

10TH CDN INF BDE

12TH CDN INF BDE

11TH CDN INF BDE

7TH CDN INF BDE

3RD CANADIAN DIVISION

2ND CANADIAN DIVISION

1ST CANADIAN DIVISION

4TH CANADIAN DIVISION

NEUVILLE ST. VAAST

1ST BRIT CORPS

SOUCHEZ

CARENCY

CANADIAN CORPS

140+

120-140

100-120

METRES

80-100

0-80

NORTH

ABLAIN-ST. NAZAIRE

MONT ST. ELOI

APPROXIMATE SCALE

3.2

1.6

0

KILOMETRES

1.6

VILLERS-AU-BOIS

CAMBLAIN-L'ABBÉ
(H.Q. CANADIAN CORPS)

—xx—xx— INTER-DIVISION BOUNDARIES
—xxx—xxx— INTER-CORPS BOUNDARIES

MAP X

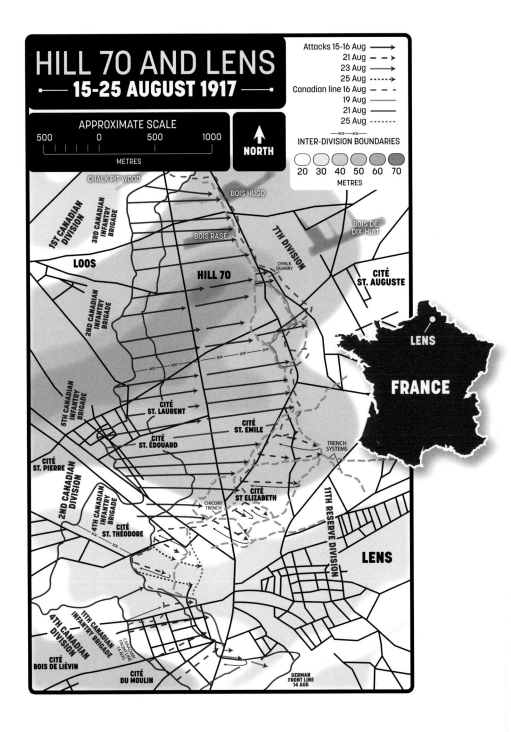

HILL 70 AND LENS
— 15-25 AUGUST 1917 —

APPROXIMATE SCALE

500   0   500   1000

METRES

NORTH

Attacks 15-16 Aug
21 Aug
23 Aug
25 Aug
Canadian line 16 Aug
19 Aug
21 Aug
25 Aug

INTER-DIVISION BOUNDARIES

20 30 40 50 60 70
METRES

CHALK PIT WOOD

BOIS HUGO

1ST CANADIAN DIVISION

3RD CANADIAN INFANTRY BRIGADE

BOIS RASÉ

7TH DIVISION

BOIS DE DIX-HUIT

LOOS

HILL 70

CHALK QUARRY

CITÉ ST. AUGUSTE

2ND CANADIAN INFANTRY BRIGADE

LENS

FRANCE

5TH CANADIAN INFANTRY BRIGADE

CITÉ ST. LAURENT

CITÉ ST. EMILE

CITÉ ST. ÉDOUARD

TRENCH SYSTEMS

CITÉ ST. PIERRE

2ND CANADIAN DIVISION

4TH CANADIAN INFANTRY BRIGADE

CHICORY TRENCH

CITÉ ST ELIZABETH

CITÉ ST. THÉODORE

11TH RESERVE DIVISION

LENS

11TH CANADIAN INFANTRY BRIGADE

4TH CANADIAN DIVISION

CANADIAN FRONT LINE 14 AUG

CITÉ BOIS DE LIÈVIN

CITÉ DU MOULIN

GERMAN FRONT LINE 14 AUG

MAP XI

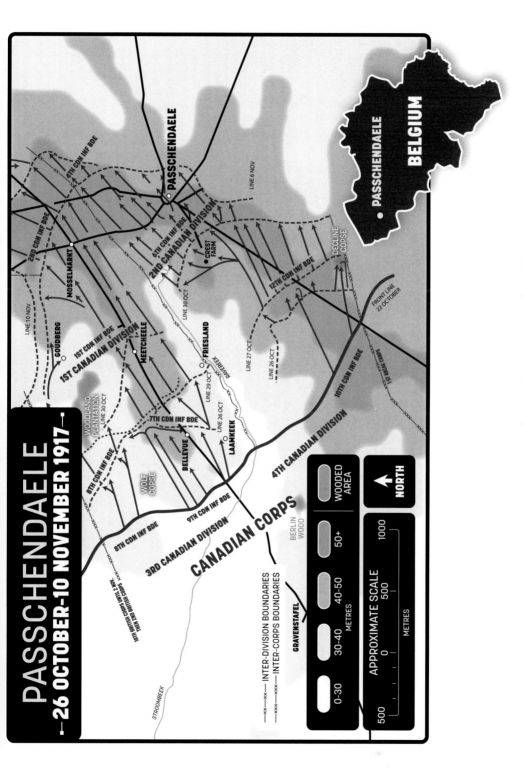

PASSCHENDAELE
—26 OCTOBER–10 NOVEMBER 1917—

BELGIUM

PASSCHENDAELE

PASSCHENDAELE

4TH CDN INF BDE

2ND CDN INF BDE

MOSSELMARKT

LINE 6 NOV

5TH CDN INF BDE

2ND CANADIAN DIVISION

CREST FARM

DECLINE COPSE

12TH CDN INF BDE

FRONT LINE 22 OCTOBER

LINE 10 NOV

GOUDBERG

1ST CDN INF BDE

1ST CANADIAN DIVISION

MEETCHEELE

LINE 30 OCT

FRIESLAND

RAVEBEEK

LINE 29 OCT

LINE 30 OCT

LINE 26 OCT

LINE 27 OCT

LINE 26 OCT

10TH CDN INF BDE

1ST ANZAC CORPS

WOODLAND PLANTATION

7TH CDN INF BDE

LAAMKEEK

8TH CDN INF BDE

BELLEVUE

WOLF COPSE

4TH CANADIAN DIVISION

9TH CDN INF BDE

8TH CDN INF BDE

3RD CANADIAN DIVISION

CANADIAN CORPS

BERLIN WOOD

10TH BRITISH CORPS UNTIL 2 NOV.
THEN 2ND BRITISH CORPS

GRAVENSTAFEL

STROOMBEEK

NORTH

WOODED AREA

50+

40-50

30-40

0-30

METRES

APPROXIMATE SCALE

500   0   500   1000

METRES

—xx—xx— INTER-DIVISION BOUNDARIES
—xxx—xxx— INTER-CORPS BOUNDARIES

MAP XII

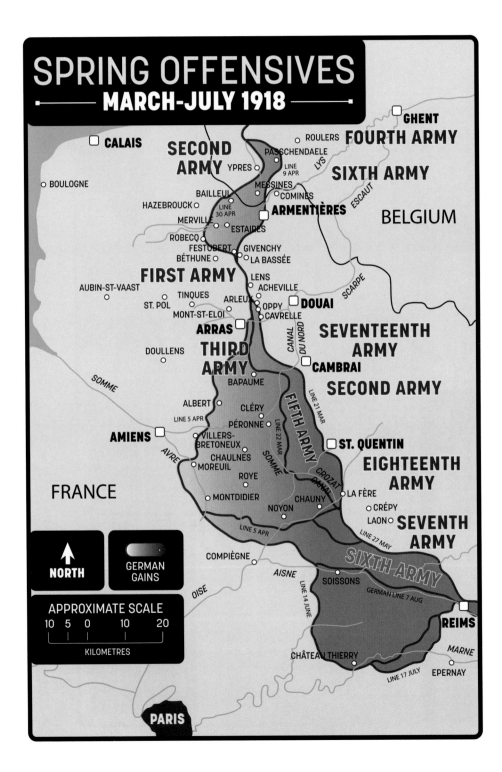

SPRING OFFENSIVES
— MARCH–JULY 1918 —

GHENT

CALAIS

ROULERS **FOURTH ARMY**

SECOND ARMY

PASSCHENDAELE

YPRES LINE 9 APR

SIXTH ARMY

BOULOGNE

MESSINES

LYS

BAILLEUL COMINES

HAZEBROUCK LINE 30 APR **ARMENTIÈRES**

ESCAUT

MERVILLE ESTAIRES

BELGIUM

ROBECQ

FESTUBERT GIVENCHY

BÉTHUNE LA BASSÉE

FIRST ARMY

LENS

AUBIN-ST-VAAST

ACHEVILLE

TINQUES ARLEUX

SCARPE

ST. POL OPPY **DOUAI**

MONT-ST-ELOI CAVRELLE

ARRAS

CANAL DU NORD

SEVENTEENTH ARMY

DOULLENS **THIRD ARMY**

BAPAUME

CAMBRAI

LINE 21 MAR

SECOND ARMY

SOMME

ALBERT

CLÉRY

LINE 5 APR PÉRONNE

FIFTH ARMY

LINE 22 MAR

ST. QUENTIN

AMIENS VILLERS-BRETONEUX

AVRE CHAULNES SOMME

EIGHTEENTH ARMY

MOREUIL

ROYE

CROZAT CANAL

FRANCE

MONTDIDIER CHAUNY

LA FÈRE

NOYON

CRÉPY

LAON **SEVENTH ARMY**

LINE 5 APR

LINE 27 MAY

COMPIÈGNE

SIXTH ARMY

NORTH

GERMAN GAINS

AISNE SOISSONS

GERMAN LINE 7 AUG

OISE LINE 14 JUNE

APPROXIMATE SCALE

10 5 0 10 20

KILOMETRES

REIMS

MARNE

CHÂTEAU THIERRY LINE 17 JULY EPERNAY

PARIS

MAP XIII

AMIENS
— 8-18 AUGUST 1918 —

CHAULNES

TRENCH SYSTEMS

HATTENCOURT

FRANSART

LA CHAVATTE

FRESNOY-LES-ROYE

GOYENCOURT

17 AUG

16 AUG

2ND CDN DIV

1ST CDN DIV

15 AUG

LINIONS

MAUCOURT

10 AUG

9 AUG

4TH CDN DIV

13 AUG

AMBUSE

3RD CDN DIV

11 AUG

ROSIÈRES-EN-SANTERRE

MEHARICOURT

WARVILLERS

ROUVROY-SANTE

32ND BRIT DIV

9 AUG

BOUCHOIR

BLUE DOTTED LINE

VRÉLY

HATCHET WOOD

BEAUFORT

FOLIES

ARVILLERS

RED LINE

2ND CDN DIV

1ST CDN DIV

8 AUG

3RD DIV

CAIX

LE QUESNEL

HARBONNIÈRES

HANGEST-EN-SANTERRE

AUSTRALIAN CORPS

GUILLAUCOURT

CAYEUX

CAYEUX WOOD

4TH CDN DIV

MÉZIÈRES

FRESNOY-EN-SANTERRE

WIENCOURT

PIEURET WOOD

GREEN LINE

BEAUCOURT-EN-SANTERRE

3RD CAVALRY DIV

IGNAUCOURT

HILL 102

MARCELCAVE

AUBERCOURT

COURCEL

DEMUIN

RIFLE WOOD

MORGEMONT WOOD

HANGARD

HAMON WOOD

HANGARD WOOD

MOREUIL

HOURGES

GENTELLES

CANADIAN CORPS

3RD CDN DIV

1ST CDN DIV

2ND CDN DIV

AMIENS

NORTH

GERMAN TRENCH SYSTEMS

WOODED AREA

0-40 40-60 60-80 80-100 100+

METRES

——xxx—— INTER-DIVISION BOUNDARIES

——xxxx—— INTER-CORPS BOUNDARIES

APPROXIMATE SCALE

2   1   0   1   2

KILOMETRES

FRANCE

AMIENS

MAP XIV

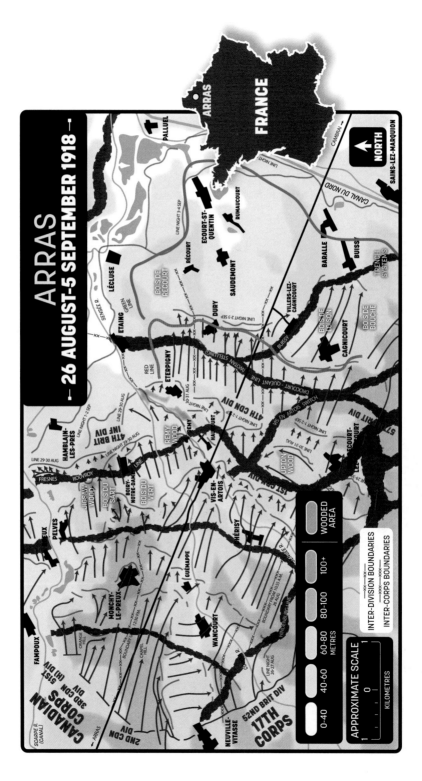

MAP XV

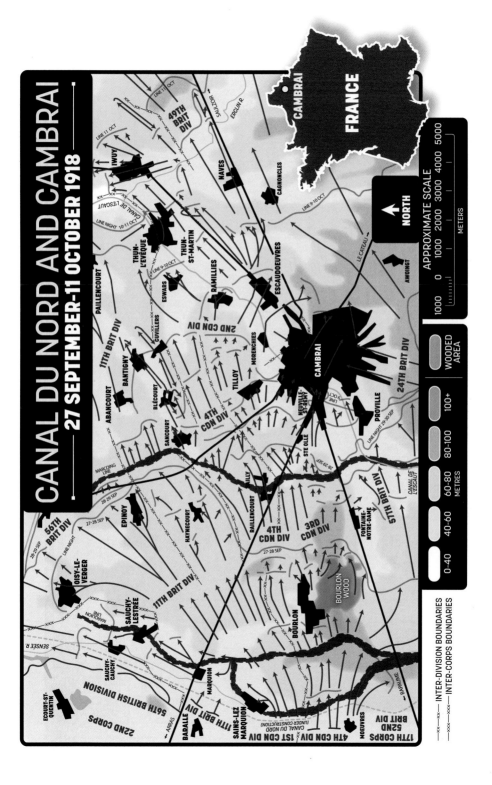

CANAL DU NORD AND CAMBRAI
27 SEPTEMBER–11 OCTOBER 1918

FRANCE

CAMBRAI

NORTH

APPROXIMATE SCALE

1000 0 1000 2000 3000 4000 5000
METERS

WOODED AREA

0-40 40-60 60-80 80-100 100+
METRES

—xx— INTER-DIVISION BOUNDARIES
—xxx— INTER-CORPS BOUNDARIES

MAP XVI

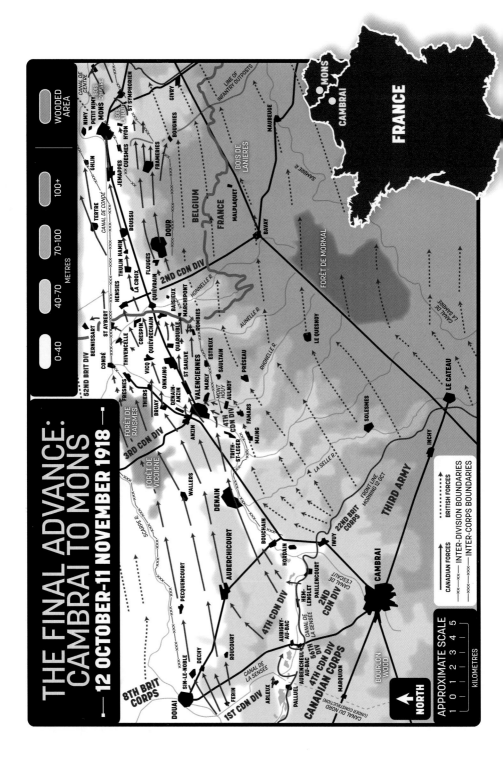

THE FINAL ADVANCE: CAMBRAI TO MONS
— 12 OCTOBER–11 NOVEMBER 1918 —

WOODED AREA

METRES
0-40 | 40-70 | 70-100 | 100+

52ND BRIT DIV

2ND CDN DIV

3RD CDN DIV

4TH CDN DIV

FORÊT DE RAISMES

FORÊT DE VICOIGNE

FORÊT DE MORMAL

BELGIUM

FRANCE

BOIS DE LANIÈRES

LINE OF INFANTRY OUTPOSTS

CANAL DE CENTRE

CANAL DE CONDÉ

SAMBRE R.

CANAL DE LA SAMBRE

MONS
PETIT NIMY
MINY
BOIS D'HAVRÉ
ST SYMPHORIEN
HYON
GIVRY
GHLIN
JEMAPPES
CUESMES
BOUGNIES
FRAMERIES
DOUR
FLOUGES
ELOUGES
BOUSSU
TERTRE
HAMIN
THULIN
HENSIES
LA CROIX
QUIÉVRECHAIN
QUÉVRECHAIN
CRESPIN
ST AYBERT
BERNISSART
CONDÉ
THIVENCELLE
FRESNES
THIERS
BRUAY
ONNAING
VICQ
QUAROUBLE
BAISIEUX
MARCHIPONT
ROMBIES
HONNELLE R.
AUNELLE R.
RHONELLE R.
MAPLAQUET
BAVAY
LE QUESNOY
MAUBEUGE
SAULTAIN
ESTREUX
PRÉSEAU
MARLY
VALENCIENNES
ST SAULVE
DENAIN-ANZIN
AULNOY
MONT HOUY
FAMARS
MAING
TRITH-ST-LEGER
ANZIN
SOLESMES
LA SELLE R.
WALLERS
DENAIN
AUBERCHICOURT
BOUCHAIN
HORDAIN
IWUY
INCHY
LE CATEAU

SCARPE R.

CANAL DE L'ESCAUT

CANAL DE LA SENSÉE

CANAL DE LA SENSÉE

CANAL DU NORD (UNDER CONSTRUCTION)

8TH BRIT CORPS

1ST CDN DIV

CANADIAN CORPS

4TH CDN DIV

56TH DIV

4TH CDN DIV

2ND CDN DIV

22ND BRIT CORPS

THIRD ARMY

FRONT LINE MORNING 2 OCT

DOUAI
SIN-LE-NOBLE
DECHY
PECQUENCOURT
ROUCOURT
FERIN
ARLEUX
PALLUEL
MARQUION
AUBENCHEUL-AU-BAC
AUBIGNY-AU-BAC
HEM-LENGLET
PAILLENCOURT
CAMBRAI
BOURLON WOOD

APPROXIMATE SCALE
0 1 2 3 4 5
KILOMETRES

NORTH

CANADIAN FORCES
BRITISH FORCES
—xxx— INTER-DIVISION BOUNDARIES
—xxx— INTER-CORPS BOUNDARIES

FRANCE
MONS
CAMBRAI

CHAPTER 7

"YOU WON'T BE ABLE TO GET ME BACK BECAUSE BUGLERS ARE NEEDED FOR THE GAS ATTACKS!"

Canadians on the Somme, August-November 1916

Private Willie Dailey was fourteen when he joined the army at Barriefield, Ontario, on August 2, 1915, making him one of the youngest Commonwealth soldiers to enrol in the First World War. Primed for adventure halfway through his summer break from school, Dailey packed up what he thought would be useful and left home in Gananoque, Ontario — for good.[1] Five-foot-six with a solid chest measurement, Dailey's size easily fit the bill, but one glance at his face could have called into question the 1898 birth date scrawled on his attestation paper — a year that still put him below minimum age. His actual birth date was November 12, 1900, but that did not matter to him because he was determined to fight. Now as a bugler with the 4th (Central Ontario) Battalion — participating in one of the bloodiest battles in the history of mankind, the Battle of the Somme — Dailey was busy trying to stay alive in the battered trenches near Pozières, France. It was September 7, 1916, and the day would not go according to plan.

Fourteen-year-old Willie Dailey wearing the cap badge of the 59th Battalion, his first unit. Could any recruiting sergeant have honestly mistaken him for eighteen?

Bright and responsible, Dailey was a good son, writing often to his mother, Florence, asking how things were back home. The handsome and energetic teen had also exchanged letters with a Miss Leona Hepburn of Lindsay, Ontario, anxiously reading what she sent to him and describing for her the journey overseas with the 59th Battalion and his training at Shorncliffe on the south coast of England. The unbearable part for Florence and Leona — and for thousands of others waiting at home — was the long silence between letters; not knowing for weeks — sometimes months — where their loved ones were, let alone how they were doing. Staying busy helped pass the time and provide temporary relief against such stress, but there was no cure for the nightmares and debilitating fear.

Outside her home near the St. Lawrence River, Florence noticed in March that winter's hold on the waterfront community was letting go. Soon the ice would be gone from the river, and the tourists would return. There would be picnics and boat rides to the islands, and maybe — just maybe — the war would end and everybody could get on with their lives. Florence's soldier son had gotten to know the islands and bays by name, and she was glad he had mentioned these happy connections to home in his letters. She understood why he had wanted to go, but blamed herself for not standing in the way. That would haunt her more each day, even after she began writing to authorities in an attempt to gain his release.

For young Dailey on the Somme, so much had changed since he had written to his mother in March, when he described the move to Shorncliffe and what he saw there. "The Zepps ["Zeppelins," German air ships] come around here quite often, but we are used to them by now. The air is covered with British arrow planes [*sic*], airships, seaplanes and all kinds of others are around here all the time," he wrote, on YMCA stationery. "I heard the guns over in France from here yesterday and today ... and sometimes [it sounds like] there are bigger battles than other [times.]" Dailey also noted it was only "twenty-one miles to France" from Shorncliffe, adding — with some exaggeration — that it was "about as far as Sugar and Grindstone Islands from Gananoque."

Dailey described the Kentish uplands as a "big line of mountains" with an aerial station on the other side. "Two airships are after us now [but] there are four [of our] monoplanes coming toward us too." A shorter letter in mid-June included a weather report, details of a YMCA concert, and some awkward lines describing a surprise visit from a female acquaintance. "She had come all the way up to the camp to see me and then we had a chewing match and she went home," he wrote before suddenly switching to more urgent matters. "Say, you can send me something to eat and some socks. They near starve us over here..."[2]

When not parading or drilling, Dailey used a pencil to sketch out his knowledge of semaphore. Other times he just drew what he saw or imagined: a couple of planes targeting a Zeppelin, a country inn or ramshackle cottage, weather-beaten ships, and even a surfaced U-boat plying the Strait of Dover. "Saw three subs today," he wrote on June 15.

With summer came more thoughts of home. "I ... was awful glad to hear from home," he wrote on the night of June 25, suspecting that the campers had returned to the Thousand Islands. "I received to [*sic*] letters from Leona... [She] writes every week and I write to her [and] you would be surprised if you heard some of the conversations between her and I…" Like many others swept up by war, Dailey and his girlfriend were in a long-distance relationship that could easily be ended by events beyond their control. The two had met while he was training in Canada. His mother did not seem to mind that most of his letters spoke of the girl. "I wish you would hurry up with her picture and something to eat," he wrote, adding "it has been very hot these last couple of days, but will rain [again] soon… Leona says we must have a hard job cleaning our boots. Well, we never clean them [and] we are certainly a tuff [sic] looking bunch. We are used to the mud now. I don't mind going out and getting soaking wet or walking in the mud up to our boot tops."

Florence could see her son talking to her when she read his letters. She could picture him "over there," impatient for better food and a few more comforts, but her priority was to do more than send socks and sweets; she desired — more than ever — to get him home before he was killed. But her appeals to the authorities were getting nowhere. Dailey, on the other hand, did nothing to encourage his mother, explaining that the "brass band and the bugle band are all that's left of the 59th, except 18 men in A Coy," the others having been transferred to other units in England or France. "You can't get me back now until the war is over," he added, showing some frustration. "You aren't the only one who wishes the war was over." He wrote again the day he was transferred from the 59th to the 39th Battalion, noting how quickly he could load a rifle. "I am the fastest clip loader in the bugle band. I put 14 in, in 1 minute. That is 70 bullets." Before closing he asked his mother again to stop trying to gain his release, although in the same breath admitting — perhaps for the first time — that he would be willing to return home if he could soldier all day at the local armouries, which would put him closer to Leona. "I would take it if they would give it to me," he wrote, adding that Leona is "trying to

A recruiting poster asking for men to join Montreal's Black Watch, which uniquely maintained three battalions in the CEF for much of the war.

do all she can [in her letters] to make me feel happy. I guess she will give me a good time if I ever see her again."

On July 17, still only fifteen, Dailey volunteered for the 4th Battalion, which was already on the Western Front. Days before linking up with the unit he wrote home again. "I am going to the trenches tonight as a bugler… I suppose I will see some great sights over there. I didn't have to go … but I volunteered. My kit is already to move away in a few minutes. They are using buglers for gas attacks now. Be sure to tell Leona if I get killed. I told her you would. Good-bye. Yours lovingly, Willie."

In late August, after being pulled out of the stench-filled Ypres Salient and conducting advanced battlefield training within fifty kilometres of the English Channel at Saint-Omer, the Canadian

Corps headed southeast toward the Somme, summoned there by Haig. When the Canadians arrived near the end of August, most of the German second line had been captured. But the third line was intact.

The world that greeted Dailey and the other reinforcements was a rat- and vermin-infested hellhole swirling with the smell of death. From the more experienced men they had heard about the June bloodletting at Mount Sorrel and the July massacres on the Somme. Dailey had written again to his mother, reporting that his uncle Walter had been killed in action. The war was no longer what it was cracked up to be, but while he would have accepted a transfer out, Dailey was prepared to carry on. "I wish you would send me some cedar oil to kill some of the 'elephants' (lice) on me... It is very hard to keep your clothes clean. Out here, the tuffer [sic] you look, the better you are."[3]

On September 4, men from 4th Battalion began falling seconds after leaving their start line along the south side of the Albert-Bapaume road, between Pozières and the smaller hamlet of Contalmaison. After dark on September 6 a work party of 127 men was sent forward to extend the newly occupied trenches toward the German lines, which were roughly a hundred metres away. Armed with picks and shovels — and with beads of sweat trickling down their smudged faces — the soldiers toiled until 3 a.m., each man acutely aware that he could be picked off by a sniper, blown to bits by a shell, or — if counterattacked — impaled on the end of a bayonet. There was no good way to die on the Western Front. The most anyone could hope for was a fast way.

It was September 7, and Dailey had a lot to live for. He would get home, see Leona, and take her out to the islands. All he had to do was survive this place. But it was not to be. He was killed instantly just north of the village of Contalmaison by a sniper's bullet — fired by a German soldier who for a split second saw just another soldier in his sights. Blasting through skin and bone

The ruins of a church rise above the destroyed town of Albert in this painting by Mary Riter Hamilton.

and slicing into vital organs, the bullet achieved its purpose.

In this case it was the life of a fifteen-year old that bled out on the ground amid the wider slaughter.

"I am sorry to say that young Dailey was killed … in no man's land and the men gave him a decent burial in the cemetery nearby," were the careful words Private Tom Haig used to try to comfort a grieving mother. "We all miss Bill very much," bugler James McGee told Florence. "He was always smiling and willing to do anyone a good turn. He met with his casualty on his second or third trip into the trenches, and we were very badly cut up."

That same day, young David Waldron of Toronto, who had been engaged in scout and reconnaissance training with the Australians, rejoined his unit — the 58th (Central Ontario) Battalion — just as it left for the Somme. Waldron, who had arrived in France that February, was by then battle tested. Moving by foot,

David Waldron, looking experienced beyond his seventeen years, had this photograph taken to record his arrival in France with the 58th Battalion in February 1916.

by truck, and by train — he and the rest of his battalion journeyed on aching feet and empty stomachs until they arrived behind the lines between Albert and Pozières on September 15.[4] Just ahead — crammed into the beaten-up jumping-off trenches — were the leading assault brigades of 2nd and 3rd Canadian Divisions, ready to move as part of the next major action. The front of the entire battle area stretched for sixteen kilometres and took in several villages, including Courcelette with its three chateaus and sugar refinery. Second Division's 4th and 6th Brigades were to go in astride the Albert-Bapaume road, which skirted the village's south side. Their objectives were the fortified ruins of the refinery and two intersecting trenches named Sugar and Candy, which crossed roughly eight hundred metres in front of the village. About to be tested in combat for the first time were two new concepts: the tank, which had arrived from Britain in great secrecy to provide direct fire support for the infantry;[5] and the "rolling barrage," which would allow the infantry to advance from their trenches behind a moving curtain of shellfire (see Map VI).

Private Lance Cattermole was seventeen when he arrived in France that May to help reinforce the 21st (Eastern Ontario) Battalion. Now in the trenches northeast of Pozières he could feel the lump of fear in his throat. Some of his mates had taken to calling him Cattie. These were the lads who had known him since August 1915, when they joined the Simcoe Foresters and later enrolled and sailed overseas with the 76th Battalion. Although only five-foot-three, Cattie was a tough kid and — like Dailey — loved to draw, a talent traced to his grandfather George, who, before his death in 1868, was a prominent watercolour and oil painter whose illustrations appeared in books by Charles Dickens. Born in England on July 19, 1898, Cattie attended both preparatory and grammar school before moving to Canada in October 1914, aiming to farm.[6]

Zero hour was set for 6:20 a.m. and in the final seconds everyone rechecked his kit. Cattie's battalion, which had just arrived in the trench after a long march through darkness and heavy ground mist, would attack the refinery, which served as a bastion for the village. It would also go after a section of Candy Trench to the left. To the battalion's right, the 20th (Central Ontario) and 18th (Western Ontario) Battalions would storm into the same trench, to the right of the refinery. Thankfully, their "fighting kit" was a lot less cumbersome than what had formerly been worn into battle. It included a haversack worn on the left side over the bayonet scabbard, and "We carried an extra issue of ammunition in a cotton bandolier, and a spare Mills bomb in each side pocket," remembered Cattie, whose "iron ration" included a tin of bully beef, hardtack, and cheese. He also recalled the bright, triangular patch men wore on their backs so they could be seen by friendly spotter planes, but most of all he remembered the strict orders to take no prisoners until the objective was met.

While readjusting his equipment, Cattie leaned his rifle against the side of the trench. Within seconds it disappeared, taken by someone who had mistaken it for his own. With no time to gripe, Cattie grabbed another rifle minutes before his platoon, part of the third and final wave of the advance, began moving.

The capture of Courcelette on September 15, 1916, in the Canadians' first major offensive operation, was recognized as a great feat of arms (detail).

With a "terrific crash" the artillery barrage began at zero hour. "The air over our heads was suddenly filled with the soughing and sighing, whining and screaming of thousands of shells … making it impossible to hear anything." When he turned around, facing west, he saw a "sheet of flame" as "far as the eye could see" from "hundreds of guns lined up almost wheel to wheel."

Seconds later a shell landed just in front of the platoon, spraying the men with loose earth and other debris. It was a dud, but the force of the earth flung Cattie onto his back, filling his mouth with dirt. He got up, spat, and then quickened his pace through shell holes and nervous laughter. In the mist and smoke he came upon Private John Robb, on his knees with helmet off and arms at his sides. "His face was turned to the sky. There was on his face a look of most joyous astonishment," recalled Cattie who also remembered shouting to his friend, wondering why in hell he had stopped to kneel at such a time. "As I moved around in front of him to his other side, I saw the blood gushing from his neck... I knew he was finished ... there was nothing I could do." Confessing after the battle that he was not a religious man, Cattie said he would "give a lot to know what that young soldier saw in the sky as his life blood ebbed away."

Arriving at the section of battered trench to the left of the refinery, Cattie noticed "little columns of steam" rising in the cool air "either from the hot blood or from the urine" of the Germans who lay there. The battle was still on, and in keeping with the "take-no-prisoners" edict two Canadians stood over the trench killing more Germans as they emerged from their dugouts. One young German with wire-rimmed spectacles dodged between the Canadians, screaming for his life. "He pulled out from his breast pocket a handful of photographs and tried to show them to us in an effort to gain sympathy. It was all to no avail. As the bullets smacked into him he fell to the ground motionless, the pathetic little photographs fluttering down to earth around him."

It remains difficult to understand the brutal killing of unarmed combatants, but on the battlefield soldiers had witnessed the death of close comrades at the hands of prisoners who had picked up a discarded weapon and turned it on their friends. Eliminating this threat entailed "mopping up" the trenches and buildings they overran. Sometimes just pure vengeance took over, especially if it was a close friend or brother who had been killed.

Near the smashed refinery, an enemy shell nearly wiped out Cattie, who had been walking with two other lads. It burst to their left, sending shrapnel in all directions. A small, jagged piece skimmed above the heads of the shorter men before finding the left shoulder of the tallest. Cattie helped remove the wounded soldier's equipment, and used a knife to slice through the left sleeve

The thick strokes of The Sunken Road *by Fred Varley, a future Group of Seven artist, blend bodies and rubble into an amorphous mass.*

up to the shoulder where he found the smouldering object half buried in the deltoid muscle. "It was very hot, but we ... eased it out ... and poured a liberal dose of iodine" on the wound. "Kelly went very white, but took it splendidly."

During the night, Cattie's bloodied battalion was told it would be going over the top in the morning to attack a place known as Sunken Road between Courcelette and the Albert-Bapaume Road. At 6 a.m. the whistle sounded and the men attacked. Within seconds they were met by enemy machine-gun fire aimed a little higher than Cattie's head. "They were picking off the taller chaps, who went down one after the other." One man near Cattie was hit five times.

Scrambling into Sugar Trench, the Canadians located a wounded German in a funk hole. "He had been hit in the head. One eye bounced about on a cord below his chin and the other socket was empty." The Canadians bandaged him up and then delivered him to the rear, and soon Cattie's platoon was spread out along a mist-shrouded road. A small group of wounded enemy appeared, led by "a young German who could not have been more than seventeen." The lad was wearing a large grey helmet and carried a homemade Red Cross flag. It "was a piece of white sheeting with a red cross … dabbed in blood." The Canadians allowed the walking wounded to pass, and in the mud and rain around midnight they were finally relieved. Tired, wet, hungry, and sore, they stumbled back

A confident-looking David Waldron adopts a somewhat stiff formal pose in this studio portrait.

along Sugar Trench with the rain hitting their faces. "There were only about twelve of us left out of the twenty who had gone forward to … Sunken Road." The men were treated to a double ration of rum and generous servings of bacon, bread, and tea. They then entered their dugouts and "slept like logs."

Courcelette became the first of more than 250 villages and towns captured by the Canadians during the war. First Division passed through Courcelette and attacked the heights beyond the village, but made only minimal progress. Third Division's objective would be the next line of German defences, Zollern Graben, and a strongpoint at its western end, Zollern Redoubt. On the evening of the 16th it launched a hasty attack toward Zollern Graben, but the effort failed. There was some success when units of 7th Brigade captured the last 250-metre section of the trench.

Additional attacks were made, including one against Zollern Graben on the morning of the 20th, involving the 58th and 43rd (Cameron Highlanders of Canada) Battalions. Planned as a surprise, it too failed when the men ran into an enemy trench block. German heavy machine guns picked off several men caught with nowhere to run. Young David Waldron survived and was confident enough to record an opinion on why the attack failed. He stated it was because the 58th Battalion attacked an hour after the two flanking battalions, and blamed the divisional commander for the mistake.[7] By September 22, the battle was over; Zollern Graben remained in enemy hands.

Four days later the Canadians entered the Battle of Thiepval Ridge. The objective was Hessian Trench, in the corps' left sector, and Kenora Trench, a spur running toward Courcelette. After three days of bombardment the infantry attack began at 12:35 p.m., September 26. Soldiers from 1st Division's 2nd and 3rd Brigades were cut to pieces by shrapnel and machine-gun fire. On the left, 2nd Brigade's 5th (Western Cavalry) and 8th (90th Winnipeg Rifles) Battalions, each with a company from the 10th (Calgary-Winnipeg) Battalion attached, managed to fight their way through Zollern Graben and just short of Hessian Trench. Some soldiers from the 5th Battalion even penetrated beyond Hessian to the next German line, Regina Trench (see Map VII).

The enemy launched immediate counterattacks, but somehow 5th Battalion retained a foothold in Hessian Trench. On the division's right, 3rd Brigade's 14th (Royal Montreal Regiment) and 15th (48th Highlanders of Canada) Battalions, with elements of the 16th (Canadian Scottish) attached, were also on the move. Charging forward with the 15th Battalion was Private James Owen, one of three boys from the same family — all underage. Owen, like Dailey, was fifteen when he got to the trenches for the first time. His twin brothers, Cecil and Iorwerth — also in the 15th — were not much older, at seventeen. Born at Llanfair,

Wales, the Owen brothers had moved with their parents to Canada in 1909, settling in the farming and lumber district of North Cooking Lake, approximately thirty kilometres southeast of Edmonton. All three enrolled with the 51st Battalion on August 21, 1915. James got in by saying he was born June 17, 1897. His real birth date was June 17, 1900.[8]

Now weaving and ducking across the tangled, cratered mess of no man's land, James hoped enemy fire would not find him. A lot of lads had kicked themselves before going into battle for not writing home more often. James, however, could take comfort that he had written to his mother at least half a dozen times, promising her sixteen dollars from his monthly pay as well as describing the trip to Halifax and a visit with relatives in England. Beneath his feet the ground rolled and bounced as if struck by a gigantic sledgehammer. All around him men fell, some torn to pieces by shrapnel and others picked off by small-arms fire. The wounded screamed, but there was no time to stop. Anyone who slowed to help became an easier target. In the middle of it all James witnessed a comrade bayonet a German who had first attacked him before attempting to surrender. The scene would haunt him for years — the sight of the German trying to use his bare hands to fend off several inches of steel jabbed repeatedly into his body. "He was screaming for mercy. Oh God, it was brutal!"

Moments later, James ran into two Germans in a trench. Both had their hands up, hoping to be taken alive. A second Canadian raised his rifle and fired, barely missing their heads. The Germans scattered, and James jumped into the trench in search of more enemy. He found a group of them firing on the Canadian advance, and quickly killed several. The enemy soon abandoned that section of trench, leaving behind the dead, the dying, and the soon-to-be captured. James and his buddies immediately went to work, amid screams and groans and the ear-splitting screech of shellfire. They had to hurry and fortify the trench against counterattack, and the first priority was to relocate the fire step to the rear of the trench, where it would be more useful. However, a mountain of sandbags on the parados quickly eliminated that option. While they were figuring out their next move, an exploding shell wiped out the man next to James, splattering James's face and tunic with blood and tissue. Shrapnel from the same shell ripped into James's leg, knocking him to the ground. With blood streaming from his torn thigh, the teenager struggled to his feet and joined the attack as it swept deeper into the enemy trench system. More men fell, but the remainder pushed on. When a German suddenly appeared, James — weakened by loss of blood — raised his rife and fired. The bullet found its mark. "I should have given him a chance to surrender," he recalled years later. "I've felt sorry about it ever since. However, we had always been told to shoot first and talk afterwards, and life was extremely cheap that day."

Somehow, in the midst of chaos, a lucky twist of fate could find a man, even in a trench littered with dead and smouldering debris. James looked up and stared into the face of his slightly older brother, Cecil. The two embraced, and then Cecil began bandaging his brother's leg. Both expected the Germans to counterattack any second, but when a nearby officer realized the two were brothers, he ordered the wounded one to the rear. James politely refused, but the no-nonsense officer would have none of it. Before hobbling away, James said goodbye to Cecil, and in a final glance each realized that he would probably never see the other again.

By mid-afternoon, soldiers from the 14th Battalion got into Kenora Trench and held out against counterattacks until the next evening, but by then they were down to seventy-five men and had to withdraw. The grim nature of the trench warfare involving James' twelve-man section was confirmed at roll call next day. The teenager was one of two who made it back alive. Cecil survived the counterattack, but his twin Iorwerth died of horrific

Canadian gunners fire a 6-inch howitzer in support of an attack on Thiepval during the Battle of the Somme.

wounds three days later.

On September 28, 3rd Division attempted to advance on Regina Trench but was stopped by uncut wire entanglements. Many men of the 24th (Victoria Rifles of Canada) and 25th (Nova Scotia Rifles) Battalions were cut down by machine-gun fire. Although the Canadians had advanced their line by roughly a thousand metres and taken part of the German trench system, it was hardly victory. The fight for Thiepval Ridge petered out.

The Canadian Corps' next part in the bloodbath entailed several attacks on one of the most formidable defensive positions on the Somme, Regina Trench. The first assault was made by units from 4th, 5th, and 8th Brigades on October 1, only a few days after the depleted units had secured Hessian Trench. When the day ended, more than half of the attackers were dead or wounded, without any gain to show for it — and the bloodletting was still far from over (see Map VIII).

Private David Low of the 43rd Battalion was one of lucky ones. Employed as a runner — delivering messages between the front line and headquarters — he came to rely on his instincts and knowledge to reduce the risk of being shot or blown to pieces. On the night before another attack on Regina Trench on October 8, Low, who enrolled in Winnipeg on his sixteenth birthday, watched in amazement as his unit's padre got up on a soap box and tried to get the men to sing. "He didn't get much enthusiasm — so [the effort] sort of died out." Low and fellow runner Dick Barlow were soon ordered to lead D Company into position, but all hell broke loose the moment they arrived at the assigned location. "Our 9.2s started to open up and they were falling short... We had to pull the company back into the shell holes till they got the range lengthened."

The next morning the Canadians were again confronted by an awful reality. Artillery fire had failed to destroy or create gaps in the German barbed wire, and the results were catastrophic. More than 1,360 men were wounded or killed on October 8, many left hanging on the wire. Hundreds of others died trying to defend the front in the short days after the attack.[9] "It was a real slaughter," recalled Low. "We finally had to drop back to our jumping-off trench." Low and Barlow were sent back to battalion headquarters with the news. No sooner had they delivered it to the colonel and found safety in a cubbyhole when a German shell landed. It killed some men and wounded more, including the colonel, who died when another shell hit the horse ambulance he was being hauled out on.[10]

Meanwhile a young greenhorn named Morris Searle could not help noticing how brave the men were around him. He enrolled under age in the armouries at Toronto — with the 124th Battalion — and after two months in England was sent over as part of a reinforcement draft to the 18th Battalion. "You had men around you who were some of the greatest — some of the most courageous individuals you could find anywhere," he recalled. "Those fellows maintained your morale and kept you going." The private's curiosity outweighed his fear during his first few days, but this spirit of adventure quickly gave way to the thought that his next trip into the line could be his last. Searle survived the war, but only after a narrow escape in the months ahead near Vimy Ridge.[11]

In mid-October, 4th Canadian Division, under Major-General David Watson, arrived on the Somme. In France since mid-August, it would take part in three more attacks on Regina Trench as part of II British Corps. Among the ranks in the 46th (South Saskatchewan) Battalion was Private Vic Syrett of Regina, who at age sixteen was anxious to follow in the footsteps of two older brothers. While working as a bricklayer in the fall of 1914, Syrett discovered he could enrol if he could play the bugle. The fact he had no idea how to play the instrument was — in his view — a mere bump on the road to overseas service. Standing just above five-foot-eight, Syrett joined the 95th Saskatchewan Rifles and soon had a bugle in hand. By Christmas he could sound more than a few good notes. Days later his request for a transfer to the next overseas contingent was approved. It was a proud moment; not only was he upholding the family's tradition of service, he had learned a skill that would prove useful on the battlefield.

Authorized in February 1915, the 46th Battalion would become one of the most bloodied Canadian units on the Western Front. Its own men would refer to it as the "Suicide Battalion" for the engagements it fought and the number of times it nearly ceased to exist. While that reputation was a long way from being forged, history was made in May when an initial draft of the battalion was ordered overseas. A few weeks later the main body of men, including Syrett, boarded a train that dropped them at a camp on the sandy and windswept Manitoba prairie. Five months later, after inhaling copious amounts of grit, the men of the 46th and 44th (Manitoba) Battalions left for Halifax, where on October 23 they boarded the SS *Lapland* and crossed to Plymouth. On August 10, 1916 — a year and a half after the battalion was authorized — the men embarked on a creaky side-wheeler for France.

Mud-spattered soldiers of 4th Division return from front-line trenches for a much-needed rest in the rear during the Battle of the Somme, October 1916.

By early October, Syrett, who had been assigned to B Company, had seen enough mud for one life. "Our transport lines had weigh scales, and it was found that a man's clothing became so coated with half-frozen mud that together with his boots and puttees they weighed in the neighbourhood of 120 pounds ..." But there were worst things than mud. While making his way forward to the company trenches in pitch darkness, the bugler-turned-runner was nearly killed by enemy artillery. Sharp, bright flashes turned night to day, but Syrett kept his head down while racing for cover. "It was throwing dirt all over me, and of course steel was flying everywhere. I jumped into a shell hole ... and put my hand squarely into a dead German's face. He had been there for some time, and I didn't enjoy his company, but better there than in the open, even if the hole was half full of water."[12]

On October 21, 4th Division met its baptism of fire as the 87th (Canadian Grenadier Guards) and 102nd (North British Columbians) Battalions followed a creeping barrage into a six-hundred-metre section of Regina Trench. A second, smaller attack on October 25 by the 44th Battalion against a part of the line further to the east failed, partly because of inadequate artillery support. A third and final attack went in after midnight on November 11 against the only portion of the trench still in enemy hands.[13] In just over two hours the division consolidated its positions in the whole of Regina Trench.

Canadians manned positions on the Somme well into November and, while the major fighting was drawing down, life remained cheap. Syrett was nearly killed while carrying a message forward. The sniper "was up on the hill above us, somewhere in the outskirts of the village of Pys. His first shot went through my neck, between the windpipe and the jugular. He took off the end of my nose with a second shot before I gained the shelter of our front line."[14]

The bloody battering-ram battle of the Somme was over. For the exhausted Allied and German troops it marked the end of major fighting in France for 1916. Not much had been accomplished by the effort, although it did succeed in drawing Germans off the French at Verdun, and revealed the potential of the creeping barrage and the tank, both used with varying degrees of success. Still, it was a heavy price to pay for an advance of some nine kilometres on a thirty-two kilometre front. No gap had been opened, no breakthrough exploited. And the numbers of killed and wounded reached previously unheard-of heights: 432,000 British Empire, 204,000 French[15] and more than 650,000 Germans; a shocking million-and-a-quarter men. Such a waste of manpower in battles of attrition could not continue; a means had to be found to restore the seemingly forgotten principle of fire and movement to the battlefield. On the Allied side it would be the exhausted and bloodied Canadian Corps that would lead the way.

CHAPTER 8

"I AM ONLY A MERE BOY, BUT I THOUGHT I WAS A MAN . . ."
Winter in the Trenches, November 1916 – March 1917

Trudging north from the Somme in the fall of 1916, the hungry and exhausted remnants of the Canadian Corps were less interested in their "next big show" than in where their next hot meal would come from.

Dry socks and an extra ration of overproof rum would also work nicely for the cold, mud-spattered soldiers, including Private Fred Claydon of the 43rd (Cameron Highlanders of Canada) Battalion, who arrived in France shortly after his seventeenth birthday.[1] Although still a teenager, the former ranch hand from Elkhorn, Manitoba, was no rookie. From an early age he was physically and mentally tough: first scarred at the hands of a belt-swinging father, and then hardened to the bones by long days of manual labour on the harsh Canadian prairie.

Claydon was two weeks shy of turning eighteen when the corps began moving toward the quieter and drier Artois region on October 17, 1916. By then he had escaped death several times

Private Donald McKinnon, 73rd (Royal Highlanders of Canada) Battalion, exemplifies the resilience of Canadian soldiers as he returns from the front lines, March 1917.

on the Western Front, including a near-miss when enemy fire killed a chum huddled in the mud next to him. The bullet had struck the soldier in the neck, releasing a fountain of blood that spewed onto Claydon's kilt. More close calls occurred near Courcelette when a bullet ricocheted off his helmet, and in the town of Albert while he was gazing up at the partially destroyed basilica.

Even for the tough-minded Claydon it was hard not to be impressed by the statue of Mary there, leaning over the bell tower as if caught in the throes of a suicidal plunge. A shell fired earlier in the war had knocked the statue into a horizontal position, but Mary, with the help of some engineers, had held on to the crumbling tower and to the baby in her outstretched arms.[2] Claydon had heard the war would end when the Leaning Virgin fell, but was quick to dismiss it as superstitious nonsense right up to the moment *his* war almost ended. "I was right underneath her when a bloody shell came over" and exploded on the cobblestone road next to the basilica, he remembered. Sparks, bits of stone, and searing metal flew in every direction,

and a small piece of metal pierced one of his ankles. "I never got operated on. It

Both the British and Canadian armies attempted to recruit their citizens living in the United States by appealing to their loyalty to their adopted country.

just buggered up some meat down there. They looked me over … then chased me out… I didn't miss any trips up the line."

Claydon had learned early that life held no guarantees, and the loss of many good men on the Somme reinforced his belief. Like a lot of enlisted men he knew, no matter how careful or competent you were, it was mostly luck that determined whether you lived or died on the Western Front. Why a bullet or searing piece of shrapnel would cut down a man who seldom stuck his head up or took unnecessary chances, instead of a man who regularly volunteered

Before the war, Canada tried to recruit men living in the United States for the more peaceful cause of the annual western harvest.

and exposed himself to danger, is a question only fate could answer. It just happened, and Claydon — for one — did not dwell on it. It helped that his mind was free of everything. The young soldier had no one to bother with — no family, although he had an Uncle Jim back in Elkhorn who was more of a father to him than his real one.[3]

The final toll from the Battle of the Somme was not known among the soldiers then, but they knew how widespread and ugly the violence had been. Private David Waldron was among those travelling north, burdened by a heavy pack and the stark memories of how his unit, the 58th (Central Ontario) Battalion, had been "cut up" during the October 8 major attack on Regina Trench. In his diary, which he kept throughout the war, Waldron noted how 3rd Division was used as the "sacrifice division" in that unsuccessful and costly bid.[4] Just a teenager when he enrolled at Toronto, he had arrived in France with his unit in February and over the last several months had proven to be a good, dependable soldier in battle. In June, he even had been recommended for a Military Medal; but it all had been hell, and some of his more dangerous moments had come while delivering important messages or supplies to the front.

It was from that unprecedented battle of attrition on the Somme that the survivors emerged with a mixture of grief and pessimism, although many were looking forward to drier digs and more time out of the line.[5] Still, the Artois region they were headed for, which included Vimy Ridge, did have a nasty reputation. While the trenches in front of the ridge were in better shape for the time being, the battlefield was a shell-pocked slope, honeycombed with tunnels and caves, and bloated with the corpses of thousands of French and German soldiers killed in earlier fighting. Additionally the Canadian units coming off the Somme were in desperate need of rest and replenishment. They would get more rest than they had been used to, but rugged, battle-tested reinforcements were in short supply and this — combined with the sickening, rat-infested environment and the approaching winter — caused many to wonder if the war would ever end.[6]

It was also tough for men like Claydon to place much trust in the greenhorns who had just joined the ranks. For many veterans it hardly made sense to get to know the new men, whose survival would depend not so much on their training as on how fast they could adapt in the line.

Private Percival Moore of the 38th (Ottawa) Battalion was among the boy soldiers trying to quietly fit in. He would discover that, when it came to hard work, age made no difference in the trenches, where every soldier was expected to "buck up" and do his duty. Born in England, Moore had moved with his family to the eastern-Ontario town of Carleton Place, a farming community that straddles the copper-coloured waters of the Mississippi River southwest of Ottawa. The dark-haired, 125-pound lad worked as a factory hand before joining the 130th Battalion on January 4, 1916, at age fifteen, swept up by the patriotism and masculine chest thumping he had surely witnessed in other lads anxious to "do their bit." Indeed, it had been impossible for Moore to sit back, bury his pride, and watch other boys join the colours.[7] He got in by claiming he was eighteen, and was quite capable of handling himself. Boys, after all, were used to being away from home, engaged in rugged, manly work — seeking adventure where they could.

Moore was a good, obedient soldier; but, like those of a lot of men, his days on the Western Front were numbered.

By Christmas the men in the trenches on the western side of Vimy Ridge were familiar with the escarpment that to some resembled the back of an enormous whale. To others it looked like a large ocean swell, frozen just as it began curling toward the east. From their places in the line the Canadians faced an open, treeless land-scape that rose gradually until it dropped off more dramatically. Just more than eleven kilometres long and rising to 145 metres above sea level, the ridge afforded an unmatched view of central France's important logistical hub, one that included the coal-rich area around Lens. Advancing across an open slope and wresting it away from the dug-in Germans would be a daunting task, but at least there would be a three-month break before preparations were complete.[8]

It was in the line near the destroyed town of Neuville-Saint-Vaast where good fortune paid Claydon another visit. An enemy shell sailed right over him and blew up the doorway of a half-completed dugout into which he and another man had scrambled. The resulting avalanche of wet, heavy earth, steaming splinters of wood, and chunks of shrapnel did not kill the men; it just buried them alive. The explosion blew the doorway in, and the steps down into the dugout vanished. "We were down in the bottom of it, covered in dirt and wood, and blocked off from the trench. We couldn't [immediately] get out," reported Claydon.

The five-foot-seven ranch hand was sixteen when he joined the 79th Battalion in October 1915 and only a year older when he headed overseas and was assigned to the 43rd. Claydon lied about his age, like thousands of other lads; but for him, enrolling was not a noble, selfless act of patriotism. It was more of a way to get off the ranch and on to something new. He remained straight-faced when he told recruiters he had been born on October 29, 1896. The month and day were correct, but the year was two years early.

If anyone had bothered to check they might have discovered his actual age and learned the lad standing before them had come to Canada without his parents when he was three, that he had made the journey across the Atlantic and out to the Prairies with his teenage brother, John, and that the two had settled in a sod shanty on their grandparents' ranch in the upper Assiniboine Valley. "I don't know why we came to Canada," he remembered. "I think it was on account of our grandparents — they were kind of lonesome."

Claydon believed the move was also because his working-class parents had eight children to feed and clothe at a time when unemployment was rampant. In total, he only spent about a year with his mother and father, and one of his most painful memories from that time was his father's leather belt. "It had this buckle or thistle on it and when it hit you, that thistle would come up on your ass."

Most of Claydon's brief childhood in London was spent with his grandparents, and when they emigrated to Canada they immediately sent for the boys. Elkhorn was just a few shacks along a wide dirt road, with a couple of hotels, a stockyard, and a livery. "Some of us used to bed down in the livery because we couldn't afford the hotel. It was cold, but I got used to sleeping anywhere." That kind of personal detail was never offered nor sought at the Brandon recruiting centre, although Claydon was glad when the sergeant sitting across from him learned of his previous militia experience with the 12th Manitoba Dragoons.

Shortly after arriving in England Claydon was surprised to be contacted by his mother, who broke the news that one of his older brothers had been seriously wounded and was not expected to live. She urged him to come to London and visit his dying sibling. Claydon was granted leave and during his short time in the city also met his father again for the first time since he left for Canada. His father told him that under no circumstance was he going to allow another son of his to go to France and end up the same way. Claydon quickly challenged his father's assumption, explaining he had no right telling him what to do for the simple reason that his father was no longer part of his life.

Claydon's third stroke of luck that day below Vimy Ridge came when he felt around in the damp, smothering darkness after the shell burst and found a hole in one corner of the dug-out. Such unpredictable moments help explain why soldiers carried matches and, in Claydon's case, a candle stub. With hot wax sticking to his fingers, he was able to see that the hole led to a lower tunnel running parallel to the ridge. The tunnel was about a metre and a half high, quite level, and was floored with sandbags. Digging like moles, the two soldiers created an opening large enough to drop through, and then — with the flickering candlelight casting shadows against the shaft's dripping ceiling and walls — groped their way along until they rounded a corner and met a curious sight. There was a man down there. He had tubes in his ears and was listening against the chalky walls of the tunnel. "Oh Christ was he surprised to see us. He said, 'Where the hell did you men come from?'"[9]

Working for one of the tunnelling companies that had helped take the war underground, the sapper was using a geophone to detect enemy mining activity.[10] Intelligence from this cold, lonely work was used to destroy an enemy gallery before it could be packed with explosives and devastate an Allied position above or below ground.[11] The intricacies of such work — however important to the cause — did not concern Claydon and his chum. They just wanted to get out of the darkness and back to their post. The sapper quietly pointed them in the right direction.

In their billets behind the lines, they shared some "starvation rations" — eight men to a loaf of bread. "We had all kinds of bloody cheese. It was good, but we got sick of eating cheese," remembered Claydon, who had grown wise to the ways of scrounging, even if it meant lowering one's standards. French beer, for example, "tasted like horse piss" — but not always. The keg he and some other lads liberated from the cellar of an *estaminet* during their hike up from the Somme was a case in point. After hauling it up the warped and rickety wooden steps of the musty establishment, they took turns rolling the smelly barrel about a kilometre through muddy, pot-holed streets, around piles of debris, and finally into the barn where they were billeted. Alone with their treasure, the men filled their metal dixies, held their noses, and swallowed. Surprisingly, it was not half bad.[12]

Such moments helped strengthen the bonds between men, and any lad who excelled at scrounging and was open to sharing would automatically hold an advantage when calling up a favour. One night, after escorting a work party into the line to repair a damaged trench, the newly-promoted Lance Corporal Claydon turned to the sixteen hungry and exhausted men huddled around him to announce that he and another man would leave and return with enough grub for everybody. With food in such short supply, it was easy for the men holding the picks and shovels to be skeptical as the two men slipped quietly into the darkness.

Time passed slowly but it was worth the wait; Claydon and his assistant somehow found a way to collect at least double the amount of rations, including two water bottles full of rum.

Canadian impressionist artist James Morrice painted this composition of Canadian troops trudging along a snowy, muddy road, while British fighter aircraft fly overhead.

When reports of drunkenness reached company headquarters Claydon was immediately busted down to private, although the captain who had him on the carpet also observed that Claydon would make a fine scout — a man he and the rest of the company could depend on. Claydon accepted that job, but only after it was agreed — with a handshake — that he would take his orders from the captain — "and no bloody NCO."

The weather by then was turning colder, causing the foul water in the trenches to freeze. Men shivered under greatcoats while their feet and fingers went numb, and the mush in their mess tins solidified. The main feast was enjoyed by the lice that crawled out from behind buttons or from dark seams in kilts and tunics where they laid their eggs.[13]

Conditions dropped from bad to worse as France entered one

of its coldest winters on record. Making matters even more disgusting were the obese rats that continued to gorge themselves on battlefield remains, often trying to take bites out of those still breathing. As a scout, Claydon preferred lying low on the grey, shell-pocked expanse of no man's land to taking his chances in the deplorable and well-marked trenches. Snipers were a constant concern, but it was easy for the young soldier to blend in and even to get some sleep.

Part way up Vimy Ridge — northeast of Neuville-Saint-Vaast — seventeen-year-old Private Walter Scott was making a name for himself and his unit, the Princess Patricia's Canadian Light Infantry (PPCLI). The location was dubbed the Crater Line, after the British, in the spring of that year, blew a series of holes along the front in an effort to edge the line forward and provide more cover. The combatants were less than seventy metres apart, shooting, swearing, and tossing bombs at each other from opposite sides of the line. Because the chalky depressions were now part of the front, each one was given a code name. The crater on the northern edge of the PPCLI position was Broadmarsh, while the one on the southern extremity was Devon. In between were four others: Durand, Duffield, Common, and Tidza.

Privately raised by Hamilton Gault, the wealthy heir of a cotton-mill magnate, the PPCLI was the first Canadian unit to enter the trenches of the Western Front. Initially composed mostly of university-aged men and experienced British soldiers, the PPCLI had arrived in France in late December 1914 and between early January and March 23, 1915, served in the Saint-Eloi sector. During May 1915, at Frezenberg Ridge, the Patricia's again proved their mettle. While desperately short of men and ammunition, the battalion held out against severe enemy bombardments and infantry attacks. The situation was so bad that Gault, who had taken over command of the regiment on May 5, ordered signallers, pioneers, orderlies, and even batmen forward to the support trenches.[14] The battalion — at least what was left of it — was resupplied before being relieved by a British unit, but its losses were enormous; nearly seven hundred killed, wounded, or missing in action. At the end of that fighting, the Germans had gained roughly nine hundred metres, but the new British line held.

The teenager Scott, who had developed a knack for getting into trouble after too much rum, was under open arrest when — on December 19 — engineers blew charges on either side of Tidza. The explosions blew at least one new hole and expanded the outer edges of the existing crater, making it easier for the men to find cover and defend. After braving enemy fire, young Scott was the first Patricia to reach the opposite edge of the new crater, and when he returned to his unit he carried with him three bloodstained German helmets. The charge against him was soon forgotten, and the hole became known as Patricia Crater.[15] Nestled with his head below the western lip of the depression, Scott was perhaps too excited at first to notice anything but his souvenirs. To the west was the ridge's pulverized lower slope and the plain stretching off beneath smoke and mist toward the old ruins atop Mont-Saint-Eloi.

The ground beneath the teenager contained a grim history. The ridge had fallen to the Germans in October 1914. Two months later the French failed to recover it. A second attack by the French in the summer of 1915 was more successful but ended badly, resulting in tens of thousands of casualties. The Allies attacked the ridge again in September, and nearly succeeded. In all, some 300,000 German, French, and British troops had been killed or maimed in the battles at Vimy.[16]

Soldiers were constantly reminded of all this, especially when the frost heaved corpses of long-dead French soldiers to the surface or when trench walls came crashing down under the weight of snow or rain. While heading into the line, the Canadians in

A temporary British cemetery lies in a small valley below the ruins of the Abbey of Mont-Saint-Eloi.

one section of trench paused to shake hands with a French soldier whose skeleton arm had been unearthed during trench construction. Such grim discoveries were common throughout the war, and soldiers learned to take them in stride — even to laugh about them as parts of the Western Front's strange theatre of the macabre. Even the non-superstitious Claydon accepted the notion that it was good luck to greet the Frenchman.[17]

By late December 1916, soldiers were quite familiar with the Lewis gun and the popular No. 5 Mills bomb, an egg-shaped grenade that weighed about half a kilogram and had a serrated exterior to maximize fragmentation. Both weapons were introduced in 1915, although the Mills bomb was not available in large quantities before the middle of that year. "They [the grenades] used to come up in boxes, and I would say they were a handy thing, although there was a lot of complaining about them at first," remembered Claydon. "Prior to that we made our own explosives — jam-tin bombs — made out of jam tins and pork and bean cans. We used to stick a bayonet through the top of the can, make an X across it, and then bang back the four corners from the centre. We would then take a piece of sandbag (burlap) and stuff a chunk of gun cotton in there with a detonator and a fuse. You had to guess at how long a fuse you needed. We used to sit all bloody day making those bombs, placing them aside for nighttime. We filled them with rocks, glass and nails — anything that could do damage. They were very effective."

As temperatures continued to drop, soldiers worked hard to stay warm and — above all else — keep their feet dry, but such efforts ultimately failed amid the collapsing trench walls and the brown icy slush beneath duckboards or in the bottoms of craters. One day, after being relieved from outpost duty, Private Gordon Lawson and seven other men were crossing a shell hole with mud halfway to their knees when Lawson, who had enrolled at age seventeen at Winnipeg, got a surprise. He and the other men had been careful to feel their way along a sunken duckboard that could not be seen on account of the muck. "The man ahead of me shouted 'broken mat.' I was slogging along ... both hands in greatcoat pockets, rifle cradled on right pocket, when I heard this, so I halted until I thought he was over the broken mat and started on. He wasn't over it, he was just at the far end and the mat came up and hit me in the pit of the stomach, sending me headlong into the mud. With both hands in my pockets, I could only kick. The fellow behind me just used me as a mat, putting one foot on my buttocks and the other between my shoulders."

The next soldier in line was more obliging; he caught hold of the teenager's flailing feet and pulled him out. Then, while wiping globs of mud off of Lawson's face, the soldier asked "me why in hell I was trying to swim with all my clothes on."[18] Drenched, and with exposed pores clogged with slime, the young Lawson just carried on until he and the others made it back to the relative safety of their trench.

In a letter home, Private J. D. Thomson, who had enrolled at sixteen and was experienced in trench warfare by seventeen, described the cold, grimy existence the majority of men endured.

"My mate and I walked all over the place looking for a place to sleep and to get out of the rain, which was now falling. At eleven o'clock we had run onto one of our field kitchens where we got some tea in a cigarette case and some biscuits. As we were walking back from our fine supper I noticed a hole in the ground, and looking more closely we found it was, or had been, a dugout, so we went in, and lighted a little bit of a candle ... the water was dropping through in places and the mud in the bottom was two inches deep but it had to do."

Thomson and his buddy grabbed a few sandbags and plopped them in the slush, and on top of that placed a rubber groundsheet. "We used our packs for pillows, lay down, and put the two blankets over us with our coats on top and before we went to sleep my chum said, 'Will you ever forget this Christmas Eve?'"

Thomson finished his letter by writing: "I am only seventeen... I am only a mere boy, but I thought I was a man, and now I know I have to stick to it." He signed his letter with the words "Not a Hero."[19]

Staying awake — especially for teenage boys — was not easy, but the consequences of catching some unauthorized shuteye ranged from being shot and killed by a sniper to being hauled out by an angry officer or sergeant.

At the very least, falling asleep while on duty could ruin the tough, manly image many boy soldiers actively sought.

Rarely were soldiers cut the kind of slack underage Private Roy Henley of the 42nd (Royal Highlanders of Canada) Battalion received much later in the war when he nodded off. "One night I had my head down — right on the parapet — and the gun was right alongside me. I was sound asleep and he (Major Beresford Topp) just shook me gently and said, 'Wake up son. I know you are tired. We are all tired, but try to keep awake and I will get another man up to relieve you as soon as I can.' That was it. Normally, you'd have been in a lot of trouble."[20]

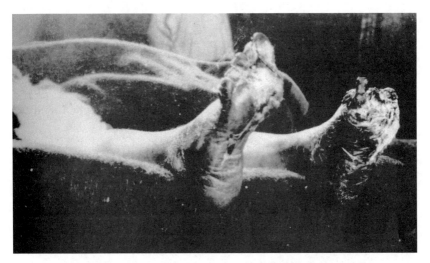

A severe case of trench foot suffered by an unidentified Canadian soldier.

Topping the list of common miseries, though, was trench foot. "You took your bloody shoes off and the skin came off with the mud and shit," remembered Claydon, who helped pack a man out with the crippling inflammation that could lead to amputation or death.[21] The prospect of sitting or standing for hours in smelly, icy water caused many men to volunteer for patrols or raids. By then, raiding had become a key component of fighting on the Western Front, used regularly to test tactics, collect intelligence, gain more fighting experience, or just to keep the enemy on edge. Indeed, Canadians were the acknowledged masters of the trench raid and developed many of the techniques and weapons involved.

While boy soldiers regularly fulfilled dangerous duties in the front lines and volunteered for patrols and raids, they were often held back by officers who found somewhat safer tasks for them to perform, like hauling water or ammunition up from the rear. Still, soldiers of any age did live or die in raids, that ranged from small probes to large incursions. The Canadian Corps launched sixty raids between November 1916 and the end of March 1917.

Nearly fifty of them reached German trenches, and many drew casualties.[22] Enemy snipers, mortars, and counterattacks also continued to claim lives of all ages.

In mid-January, young David Waldron came close to "going west," the common euphemism used by soldiers to take the sting out of the words "killed" or "dead."

While participating in one of several night patrols, Waldron and close friend Lorne Craig were nearly killed when they were accidentally bombed by their own men. These dangerous forays into no man's land — shared by Waldron and Craig and others in their unit — were interspersed among hours of trench maintenance, usually done under cover of darkness, although the risk of being picked off by a sniper was never completely gone, especially if the assignment involved crawling out in front of the trench to repair the wire. During such times soldiers depended on their own training, but they also placed great trust in those who would most likely risk their lives to extricate them from bad situations. The friendship between Waldron and Craig was typical of the camaraderie that existed between enlisted men, and theirs was a trust that grew stronger by the day.

It was during that same cold and dangerous winter that Claydon found a little comfort while away from the front. Out on a two-day pass, he decided it was time to call in a favour from a good friend — an old cowpuncher from Calgary. Claydon had bumped into a very attractive woman who asked him up to her house. "She was real pretty, but I had no money. I went out and found old Dick Richards… He gave me the money, and I told him I'd pay him back next pay… I went back and stayed in that house all night and the next day. It was one of those places right close to the street. As soon as you walked out the front door, you were on the sidewalk. I had just stepped out when who was walking by but Dick Richards. He stopped, looked at me and said, 'You son of a bitch! That's my girl!' Boy, did I beat it out of there."[23]

While men lucky enough to get leave could stop and enjoy a variety of simple pleasures behind the lines, the war crashed on, exacting ever-higher tolls from both sides. In front of Vimy Ridge, trench raiding continued unabated, adding lustre to the Canadian Corps' fierce reputation and causing some battalions to compete for the best results. The days ahead would bring both great victories and unmitigated disasters.

CHAPTER 9

"I WAS JUST A YOUNG BOY. BUT WE KNEW WHAT WE HAD TO DO SO WE JUST WENT AHEAD AND DID IT."

Preparing for Vimy, January-March 1917

On January 17, 2nd Division's 4th Brigade launched one of the war's most successful raids, although it is among the lesser-known. The aim was a series of heavily fortified enemy trenches along the Lens-Béthune railway, northeast of the town of Calonne. Assigned were 860 specially trained soldiers from the 20th (Central Ontario) and 21st (Eastern Ontario) Battalions, supported by machine-gun units and engineers from the 4th (Montreal) Field Company.

As the evolving masters of the trench raid, Canadians were constantly experimenting with new techniques and use of weaponry. The 20th and 21st Battalions were divided into five operational companies or storming parties. Each had four platoons, and two engineers from 4th Field accompanied each platoon. In addition, platoons formed separate raiding parties with bombers, riflemen, stretcher-bearers, and wire-cutters. To prevent the infantry from being slowed down by obstacles that could change the course and pace of the raid, some soldiers would carry long, canvas-covered boards to lay over barbed wire and trenches. Bringing up the rear would be others armed with light machine guns. Engineers would target dugouts and bunkers while perilously armed with phosphorous grenades stuck to a container of gasoline and a few kilograms of ammonal.

The Germans' battle tactics had also evolved. No longer were they standing closely side-by-side in the trenches; they were spaced further apart, in firing positions that could support each other.[1]

Preparing for the raid in the wee hours of January 17 was a former bookkeeper named Arthur Esdon of Bainsville, Ontario. The young private had joined the army in Kingston, Ontario, on November 4, 1914, two months after his seventeenth birthday. He told recruiters he was born in 1895, but his actual birth date was September 6, 1897. This, however, did not seem to matter; Canada was at war and "men" were needed overseas.

Six months after enrolling — on May 6, 1915 — Esdon hauled himself and his kit aboard the troopship *Metagama* at Montreal, and was soon steaming down the St. Lawrence River past Quebec toward the Atlantic and the "great cause" beyond. He arrived in France a few days after his eighteenth birthday, eventually joining the 21st Battalion at Bully-Grenay. "Seen the old year out and the new one in," he scribbled in his notebook.

On January 3, Esdon's unit was ordered into the front line to relieve the 19th (Central Ontario) Battalion. His entry for January 6 does not speak of fear, nor does it suggest he had anything to prove while trying to kill the enemy. It just coolly describes how he stuck it out by automatically doing his duty — just like his older mates. "Stood to for early part of the night and fired 12 magazines from the front line."[2]

Younger than Esdon — and also serving with the 21st Battalion — was sixteen-year-old Private Charlie Hyderman. Born

Seven Canadian soldiers leave an advanced listening post to go on a night raid across no man's land and into the enemy's front-line trenches.

July 25, 1900, at Deseronto, Ontario, he had worked as a labourer before enrolling at age fifteen on January 17, 1916. The war, he reasoned, would earn him recognition and the much-needed regular pay, and so he told the recruiting sergeant he was born in 1897.

Predeceased by his father, Hyderman asked that twenty-five dollars a month be taken off his pay to support his mother, Eva. From his home just north of Lake Ontario he travelled by train to Halifax, where he boarded the steamer *Northland* on October 18, 1916. Ten days later the crowded and weather-beaten troopship reached Liverpool, and not long afterwards Hyderman was in France. There is no hard evidence that Hyderman was part of the Calonne raid, but at the very least he was there for the preparations. Those selected were served a hot meal at 4 a.m. and within forty-five minutes the first, then second, and third waves of troops moved out of Bully-Grenay to take up positions in the front line and communications and support trenches.[3]

In the dark chill of morning on the 17th, Esdon, who had been in reserve January 8 to 16, finished his meal and moved off to the trench opposite no man's land. For nearly thirty minutes he and the other attackers shivered in cold silence while snow accumulated on their equipment and uniforms. Opposite them German sentries, who perceived no immediate threat in the morning calm, were going about their daily rituals after stand down. They too were busy wiping snow and freezing mud off their kit, stopping once in a while to expel warm breath over icy hands.[4]

At 7:45 a.m., Allied shells shattered the calm. From the enemy's perspective chaos intensified when they noticed Canadians advancing on their right. But this was only a diversion by the 18th (Western Ontario) and 19th Battalions, operating to the left of where the 20th Battalion would go in behind a smoke screen.[5]

With speed and purpose, accompanied by the familiar knot of fear in their stomachs, the first wave of Canadians scrambled out of their trench and stormed into no man's land. Within minutes they were rushing through the gaps in the wire as German machine guns opened up. The raiders from the 20th and 21st Battalions raced into enemy trenches already severely damaged by shelling. German soldiers in the front-line dugouts were either killed or captured, while Lewis gunners quickly checked the counterattack by taking up positions on the high ground. Troops in the first wave wreaked havoc in the enemy's front line and secured the flanks, while soldiers in the second and third waves passed through to assault objectives further on. Armed with their highly flammable bunker bombs, the engineers were close behind.

In less than an hour, the raiding force of which young Esdon was a part blew up more than forty dugouts, exploded three ammunition dumps, captured two machine guns and two trench

A Canadian soldier bayonets a German during a trench fight as other Canadians join the battle.

mortars and destroyed several others, and took approximately a hundred prisoners.[6] The enemy suffered a large number of casualties, most of them burned or buried alive. Canadian casualties amounted to 135 wounded and 40 killed. The 21st suffered one officer wounded, eleven other ranks killed, and sixty-one wounded.

Seeking out and killing the enemy while concentrating on self-defence and situational awareness were physically and mentally draining. Soldiers, including the younger ones, drew energy and excitement from victories, but raids were exhausting. This helps explain why Esdon's diary entry for January 17 is so short. His brevity is also perhaps a sign of a maturing soldier getting used to the fighting and the carnage. "Made a raid on enemy trenches on 300 yd front; penetrated to near 3rd line; 99 prisoners and one officer, also 2 Machine Guns and Fishtail machines. Prisoners mostly 22nd German Bn. All emplacements and dugouts burned."[7]

Within weeks, John Hyderman's time on the Western Front would be cut short, not by bullet or bomb but by a suspicious and concerned officer who discovered his true age. Once sent to the rear as a minor, Hyderman's fate was decided: he was first shipped to England, then to Canada.[8]

If Canadians back home were concerned about underage soldiers making it to France they certainly remained quiet on the subject, although the question did come up a second time in the House of Commons on February 1, 1917, when the government was asked about boy soldier Noel Gazelle, who enrolled at sixteen but lied saying he was eighteen. A. E. Kemp, in charge of the Department of Militia and Defence, replied that because the young soldier had lied in a "legally-binding" document (his attestation paper) he was, in effect, trapped in the CEF. The matter was quietly dropped.[9]

The German army, meanwhile, was focusing on orders from the kaiser for a deliberate withdrawal to the Hindenburg Line, a strategically intelligent move that not only changed the complexion of the front but freed up thirteen German divisions and many artillery units. The planned retreat also gave the German army time to replenish supplies, specifically guns and shells, which had fallen perilously short of expectations.[10] The withdrawal, however, in no way signalled German abandonment of the Chemin des Dames Ridge, the sector in front of Arras, or Vimy Ridge.

It had been known since late 1916 that the Canadian Corps would attack the ridge. What was not known — until nearly the end of January 1917 — was that the corps would be doing it

alone.[11] Failure was not an option, as that would seriously jeop-
ardize the British attack along the Scarpe River from Arras. The
primary Canadian task, therefore, was to form a tough defensive
flank for the British effort. But taking the ridge was important
for another reason. It was considered the key that could unlock
the defences linking the new Hindenburg system to the main
German lines leading north from Hill 70 to the Belgian coast.

German defences on the ridge included approximately 34,000
metres of fire trenches and some 14,900 metres of communication trenches, all protected by thickly layered barbed wire,
enormous dugouts, and bomb-proofed caves supplied with water
and electricity. In the event of an infantry attack, machine-gun
posts were sited to ensure overlapping fields of fire. The high
ground also gave the Germans the advantage of directing shellfire
with such accuracy that it denied safe daylight movement to any
Allied troops that might amass in front of the ridge.[12]

Facing the ridge from the west — and fighting together for
the first time — the four divisions of the Canadian Corps were
arranged in numerical order from south to north.[13] To win the
battle, the Canadians in 1st and 2nd Divisions — anchoring the
right — the south side of the attack — would have to cross nearly
four thousand metres of undulating ground studded with a variety of strongpoints. On the left flank of the Canadian front, 3rd
and 4th Divisions would come up against the ridge's two highest,
most formidable positions: Hill 145, which was quite familiar to
4th Division, and a feature to the north dubbed the Pimple. These
too were heavily fortified with men and barbed wire, and inter-
woven with trenches, dugouts, machine-gun and sniper posts.[14]

Failures by other Allied forces on the Western Front had shown
that vast numbers of infantry alone would not spell success.
Instead, the key to winning the ridge would be the application
of new infantry and artillery tactics; aerial reconnaissance; and,
especially, the successful delivery of supplies, including guns and

The ruins of St. Nazarius's Church in the small farming village of Ablain-Saint-Nazaire, near Vimy Ridge.

ammunition. Men in large quantity were essential, but trained men and specialists — at all levels — would decide who would win and who would lose.

Underage Signaller Thomas Rowlett was exactly the type of man needed. From late February to the end of March, the lad from Centreville, Nova Scotia, had worked his way by train and by foot from Le Havre to the Canadian lines in front of the ridge — a distance of some two hundred kilometres. He had travelled there with a group of signallers whose skills would be used to help maintain more than 4,025 kilometres of vital communication cable buried below the surface. After getting off the train at Aubigny, Rowlett's party hiked seventeen kilometres to Mont-Saint-Eloi. "We each had our dinner with us and started off. It was a bright sunny day, but it was rough country — no trees or houses. When we stopped for dinner we could hear guns roaring and shells bursting in the distance. In the middle of the afternoon we were getting close to Mont-Saint-Eloi when we saw a shell burst in one of the towers of the convent."[15]

Rowlett was to meet up with the 25th (Nova Scotia Rifles) Battalion, but the unit had moved the day before to Maisnil-Bouché, approximately twelve kilometres west of the ridge. The road was being shelled and so Rowlett and his crew were forced to find a cross-country route. He remembered slogging "through some horse lines with mud up to our knees" before arriving at their destination well after dark. "Hungry and tired we slept on a wire netting bed with one blanket between two. The next morning we got up and cleaned the mud off our clothes and reported to the Orderly Room and then the stores where we got our badges changed and drew our PH helmet (gas mask) and goggles for tear gas, and picked up our mail. We were then sorted out; some went to the various company signal sections. I stayed with the battalion headquarters section." Rowlett became a linesman and "quite enjoyed it although it was exciting at times as we got on a line that was exposed to sniper and machine-gun fire."

A large replica of the ridge, which employed coloured tapes to mark specific locations and objectives, was built behind the Canadian lines. Rehearsals were held to ensure all soldiers knew their jobs, including where to go, so they could take control of matters should their leader be knocked out of battle, although Fred Claydon, years later, could not recall receiving any such detailed instruction. "I was in the bloody line the whole time and no one told me — never got told a fucking thing."[16]

Rowlett had a much different take. He reported that "as the battle ... was shaping up the whole section and battalion too went over the tapes... A plot of the area was taken by the Royal Flying Corps and after being developed and enlarged a spot was picked out behind the lines where the terrain was similar to where we were going to attack." Rowlett recalled the coloured tapes representing terrain, objects, and even expected actions.[17] Seventeen-year-old Cyril Smith with the 54th (Kootenay) Battalion assigned to 4th Division was simply told where he was, where the Germans were, and what ground they were to win. "They told us, 'You are here. The Germans are there and there's this bump in between, and you are to take it.'"[18] Those instructions were clear enough for Smith who, before enrolling on April 27, 1916, had learned how to fend for himself while ranching along the Fraser River at Port Hammond, British Columbia. Growing up on the farm was tough, and Smith had at least one scar — on his left ankle — to prove it.

During the lead-up to the big battle, many kilometres of roads, water pipelines, reservoirs, light railways, field kitchens, casualty dressing stations, and additional tunnels were built under enemy sniper and shell fire. At night ammunition was delivered and carefully stockpiled; gun pits were dug, and communication cable buried or strung. Water — enough to satisfy a daily requirement of 2.7 million litres — and field rations were hauled in and distributed.[19]

Hundreds of mules and horses carried or pulled ammunition and other supplies and, like the men who rode or drove them, the animals paid a terrible price crossing uneven, muddy terrain deep enough to swallow man or beast. Some of the animals would be whipped until they either moved or dropped. Others would be killed by bursting shells or have to be mercifully destroyed with a bullet to the head after falling victim to the mud or a broken leg — or sheer exhaustion. Fatigue, death, disease, and injury also greeted the thousands of labourers who performed the back-breaking work that would give the infantry protection from artillery fire as well as closer jumping-off positions.

The artillery planning was as thorough, incorporating aerial observations and an advanced system of sound-ranging that

The Canadian Overseas Railway Construction Corps built railways to be oper-
ated by battalions of the Canadian Railway Troops. All served outside the
Canadian Corps.

helped gunners target enemy gun positions with great accuracy.
And this was not just a Canadian effort. British and South African guns of all calibres were also lined up nearly wheel-to-wheel.
More than a million shells would be fired at the enemy, including
shells with new fuses that allowed the explosive to detonate in the
air just before hitting the ground, to cut through barbed wire.[20]

As the day of the battle loomed, the dangerous work of stock-
piling shells went on unabated. "The artillery had working parties
from the infantry piling shells and one of our signallers helped too
and was piling shells when a German shell came along and stopped
between his legs," reported Rowlett. "He waited a few minutes and
nothing happened so he went on piling shells on top of it."

The preliminary artillery bombardment of German positions
began in earnest March 20, and lasted thirteen deafening days.[21]
It was massive, but still incorporated only about half of the gun

Canadian troops unpack artillery ammunition from boxes and load it into limbers for delivery to the gun positions.

batteries. One week before the attack, all of the guns opened up, and the results were catastrophic for the defenders. They labelled it their Week of Suffering. The maelstrom of fire was unabated, easing only within hours of the start of the attack — which created among some Germans a false sense of security.

The infantry, meanwhile, was ready with a system of attack very different from the 1916 British battle doctrine. Instead of attacking in long lines across an open landscape, waves of infantry

The massive preliminary artillery bombardment of German positions on Vimy Ridge continued for a total of eighteen days.

would follow a rolling barrage, while platoons of thirty or forty men with specialists — some armed with Lewis light machine guns or rifle grenades — would try to eliminate enemy resistance.

The overall plan of attack identified by colour four primary objectives, all of which had to be reached by a specific time. From first to last or west to east, they were the Black, Red, Blue, and Brown lines. Both 1st and 2nd Divisions would have to reach all four, while 3rd and 4th Divisions would fight to the Black and Red lines only. The Black Line, which was beyond the enemy's thick front-line defences and observation posts, included the powerful Zwolfer Stellung line in the south as well as the intersecting Zwischen Stellung line that meandered north past the hamlet of Les Tilleuls and along the crest of Hill 145.

Further east the Red Line included a section of the Zwischen Stellung that ran for more than a mile in a southeasterly direction from where it linked up with Zwolfer Stellung. From there it swung north between Les Tilleuls and the smashed but strongly held village of Thélus, and included the heavily fortified Turko Graben Line. The distance between the Black and Red lines varied from four hundred to nearly a thousand metres.

More than nine hundred metres to the east — beyond Thélus — was the Blue Line. Counted among the many objectives there were strongpoints in the village itself, Hill 140, and most of the Bois du Goulot. The final objective — the Brown Line — skirted past the east side of Farbus Wood and the southwest side of the village of Farbus, where it headed in a northwesterly direction past the southwest side of the village of Vimy, where it joined the Red Line which ended southwest of Givenchy-en-Gohelle.

The attackers would have thirty-five minutes from zero hour at 5:30 a.m. to capture the Black Line. This would be followed by a forty-minute delay to dig in as fresh attackers pushed past them. Twenty minutes after the pause the Red Line was to be taken. A longer break — lasting two and a half hours — would follow for 1st and 2nd Divisions, after which the Blue Line was to fall in seventy-five minutes. The advance to the Brown Line would start at 12:26 p.m., and infantry would be given fifty-two minutes to capture it. From start to finish, the attack on Vimy Ridge was — as envisaged by its planners — to last a scant seven hours, forty-eight minutes.[22]

Waiting it out in the relative safety of a dugout in the chalk pits below the ridge, Corporal David Moir of Winnipeg was not complaining. He had joined the army at seventeen and was now part of a machine-gun company attached to 3rd Division. "We were 25 feet underground with electric lights, bunks to sleep in and various other amenities not usual in a soldier's life."

But even underground sudden death was never far away. A sergeant walking past the gun crew next to Moir's was accidentally shot in the head. "It was customary after cleaning and oiling [the machine gun] to half cock it and then press the trigger to release the pressure on the spring. The gun was then half-loaded and with one more pull on the lever it would be fully loaded and ready to fire." The responsibility to prepare the gun rested with the number one man on the gun crew — nobody else. The sergeant died because the number two man on the crew assumed the gun had not been cocked and, when he pressed the trigger to release the pressure on the spring, it fired.

Above or below ground, the fear was palpable as each dissolving second brought soldiers closer to zero hour. The more experienced men, including Claydon, thought about the little things that had gotten them through previous scraps — like when and where to move against traversing machine-gun fire, when to duck or dive for cover. Wide-eyed and working hard to swallow the fear in their stomachs, the younger lads nervously watched the more experienced men, but understood that luck was the best for which one could hope.

At 3 a.m. Moir and his crew began picking their way along a tunnel toward the front line, "not an easy feat burdened as we were with guns, tripods, spare parts and ammunition boxes ... and especially difficult by the PPCLI men stretched out on the floor of the tunnel trying to get some sleep" before they had to move.[23] He accidentally woke one man who began swearing at him until both men realized they were from Winnipeg. Exiting the tunnel, Moir stared up at an overcast sky. There was a steady wind from the west and sleet was pelting his back and the top of his steel helmet.

Silently, Moir and his crew were guided into no man's land, where they took cover for the rest of the night in watery shell holes. Then, slowly raising his head by just a couple of centimetres, Moir looked back toward his own front line and heard the distant burst of machine-gun fire. He then watched as "the whole sky lit up with an orange flare as ... guns and innumerable machine guns opened up on the same second and all hell broke

Canadians dug deep tunnels and dugouts at Vimy Ridge for protection, to hide their preparations, and to cover their forward movement prior to the attack.

loose." It was 5:30 a.m., Easter Monday, 1917. All around and beneath Moir and his crew the earth shook violently from the massive bombardment.

The pounding from nearly a thousand guns was relentlessly mind-numbing, even to those deep underground or at slightly safer distances above ground. Signaller Jack Fitsell of Barrie, Ontario, had been busy laying telephone cable when he heard what sounded like a "gigantic rolling thunderstorm." With teeth chattering and knees shaking from vibration and fear, the short but muscular teenager just kept his head down and soldiered on. "You could hardly hear yourself think. I was just a young boy... But we knew what we had to do, so we just went ahead and did it."[24]

Fitsell had joined when he was seventeen, enrolling with the 157th Battalion on December 4, 1915. Now into his fifth month on the Western Front, he had learned how best to survive, even while performing duties that left him exposed to enemy fire. It helped that he got along well with his trench mates and enjoyed the trench humour and funny little ditties sung by the boys. One of his favourites was "The Moustache Song," which he heard for the first time at Camp Borden, Ontario, in 1916.

> *You've got to let your moustache grow,*
> *For the orders are out, you know.*
> *You don't have to shave*
> *Your upper lip, you see*
> *For if you do you get "CB"*
> *Some look fine, some look swell*
> *But some of us look like hell*
> *The order says you must obey*
> *You've got to let your moustache grow!*

Besides his love of verse, Fitsell had strong hands and a solid work ethic — developed before the war when he both worked on the farm and logged ten- and twelve-hour days, mostly kneading and rolling dough, at a popular bakery. Life had been busy, but good — so very different from what it had been just years before. After bidding farewell to his beloved auntie, who had raised him following his mother's death, Fitsell moved with his father Benjamin — a Boer War veteran — from Hastings, England, to Canada in 1912. Life on the central Ontario farm came with fresh milk and an abundance of produce; a nice switch from the smelly fish he ate in England while working in his father's fish and chip shop. Like a lot of lads, Fitsell's education was limited to the early grades in a small, country school where he sometimes demonstrated his shooting skills with an elastic band fired at a flock of stuffed birds hanging above the teacher's desk.[25]

Fitsell treasured those memories, and he would be lucky enough to carry them for years past the "giant thunderstorm" that devastated the enemy and shook him and many others to the core. It seemed that a man could easily die or go insane just listening to the noise, but for Fitsell the calculated mayhem was just one more thing to overcome in the fight for Vimy Ridge.

CHAPTER 10

"IT WILL BE ONE OF THE BIGGEST THINGS IN CANADIAN HISTORY."
Vimy Ridge, April 1917

Sixteen-year-old Johnny Jenken of London, Ontario was not the only one to feel the weight of fear against his chest during the early hours of April 9, 1917. And the longer the young private with the 15th (48th Highlanders of Canada) Battalion stood waiting in the crowded forward trench opposite the German line, the more difficult it was to breathe.

Loaded down with rifle and bayonet, 120 rounds of ammunition, Mills bombs, rations, a small box respirator, sandbags, water bottle, and groundsheet, it seemed — at least to the less experienced men — that it would be a victory just to climb out of the slippery trench, let alone fight across no man's land to 1st Division's initial objectives. The air here was certainly fresher than it had been in the winding tunnels that led to the jumping-off positions. Like 3rd Brigade's other three units, the 15th was battle-tested and ready to prove itself once more.[1]

That opportunity came at zero hour, when — all at once

across the front — more than 12,500 men from twenty-one Canadian leading assault battalions emerged from their frozen forward trenches and tunnels and, with a strong wind at their backs, followed the rolling barrage into no man's land and up Vimy Ridge. The ridge's defenders emerged from their dugouts dazed and deafened by the violent pounding, but many were prepared to fight to the end while staring blindly into sleet and snow. "The day sentries all bawled, 'Get out! Here come the British! [sic]. We leapt up, all tiredness forgotten, then it was a life or death fight for the Fatherland," remembered German Grenadier Otto Schroder of the 12th Company Reserve Infantry Regiment 262 (see Map IX).

"Suddenly, in the early dawn, thousands of British guns opened up as one, pouring their thunderous ball of iron on our positions. For the regiment a bombardment of such violence was totally unprecedented. In all directions an endless dense series of fountains of clay shot upwards. Rocks were reduced to dark dust and tiles into red dust clouds," German officer Paul Radschun, of the 261 Infantry Regiment, recalled.[2]

On the southwestern slope Jenken's 15th stormed onward beside the 10th (Calgary-Winnipeg) Battalion, which formed the left flank of 1st Division's 2nd Brigade. The 10th had advanced against severe small arms fire over ground ripped open by the barrage and into occupied trenches where vicious, close-quarter fighting with bombs and bayonets ensued.

Only five-foot-five, with blue eyes and brown hair, Jenken had already been treated in hospital for a wound suffered months earlier on the Somme, more than a year after he enrolled at age fifteen with the 33rd Overseas Battalion. While with the 15th, Jenken had learned to survive as best he could. But on this day — not long after going over the top — his luck ran out. Though caught momentarily by friendly fire his battalion surged forward, attacking and destroying enemy positions, but paying a heavy price between the Black and Red Lines. By mid-morning, approximately sixty of its men had been killed in action, many others critically wounded and near death.

Young Jenken was among the dead.[3]

Fighting with the division next to Jenken's was Lance Corporal Frank Davern, who was only a few months past his seventeenth birthday when he enrolled in April 1915.[4] The Napanee, Ontario, youth's 21st (Eastern Ontario) Battalion, which was part of 4th Brigade, 2nd Division, followed the 18th (Western Ontario) and 19th (Central Ontario) Battalions and attacked toward the town of Thélus. The former high school student had boarded the RMS *Metagama* at Montreal on May 6, 1915, and spent only four months in England before heading to France in September 1915. The following April he was promoted to lance corporal.

In December the natural tendencies of a teenager introduced him to gonorrhoea, for which he was treated at No. 6 Canadian Field Ambulance before being transferred to No. 22 Casualty Clearing Station. It was not all bad, though: while being moved Davern had been honoured for earlier bravery and awarded the Military Medal. The following February he rejoined his unit near the front.

On the day of the battle — shortly before 7 a.m. — Davern and the rest of the 21st Battalion rushed forward, eventually passing through the two lead battalions behind the barrage to the Red Line east of Les Tilleuls.

Davern lived long enough to write briefly about his time at Vimy. In a May 1, 1917, letter to a buddy back home he played down the seriousness of the advances made through April. "Of course you will see by all the papers that we have been very busy lately taking Vimy Ridge and several other places. Things have been very lively of late and we have had lots of excitement pursuing our machinations against the hated Hun. The only thing disagreeable is that we lost a lot of sleep and the weather for about a week or so of the advance was very damp and a considerable amount of snow fell."

Youthful bravado was perhaps used here to relate a story that starts out much brighter than most accounts. "It was a joke going over — fellows stopping to light cigarettes and everybody acting as if they were walking down the Strand — of course we had it all our own way as our artillery put up a terrible barrage which put all the [Germans] out ... or drove them into their deep dugouts and when our men came up the Germans would throw up their hands and there was nothing to it," he wrote, adding that the battalion did not suffer nearly as badly as it had on the Somme.

The 21st would lose a third of its strength before securing the Red Line. Private Archie Barrow was among those who got as far as the outskirts of Les Tilleuls, a destroyed village on the old road between Neuville-Saint-Vaast, on the ridge's western slope, and Thélus, less than a kilometre to the east. The second youngest of eleven children born to Charles and Mary Barrow of Ingersoll, Ontario, the gregarious Barrow had spent his childhood in the western Ontario town before enrolling with the 168th Battalion on January 20, 1916, two months after his sixteenth birthday.

Standing as tall as his five-foot-six-inch frame would allow, Barrow, the son of a respected tailor, gave 1898 as the year of his birth, and listed himself as "an unmarried labourer."[5] With those simple words and a few other short statements he became a member of a battalion known simply as "Oxford's Own." It was a proud moment for the young man who would, in less than two months, face the difficult loss of his father at age sixty-one. From Ingersoll, Barrow's earliest army adventures took him to Camp Borden, where he trained, and then to Halifax in the fall of 1916 for the trip overseas in the steamer *Lapland*. When his battalion was broken up in England, Barrow and the other lads from the Oxford's Own were switched to various reserve units before crossing the Channel. In France, he became a tough and reliable soldier, as proven by his fatal efforts to reach the battalion's objective that Easter Monday.

Barrow was the first Ingersoll boy of the Oxford's Own to be killed in action. The headline over his tiny obituary acknowledged that he "Made [the] Supreme Sacrifice on April 9th." Below that it read: "He was well and favourably known to the young people of the town."

Maintaining an accurate rolling barrage in 2nd Division's sector was a challenge because of the irregular width and curved shape of the area of attack. Drawing enemy fire from ahead and to their left, 5th Brigade's 26th (New Brunswick) Battalion — with the 24th (Victoria Rifles of Canada) Battalion on their right — pushed on to capture a number of trenches and hidden fortifications en route to the Black Line.

In the thick of it, Private Percy McClare of the 24th Battalion kept his head down while fighting across the cratered, machine-gun-swept landscape. McClare had enrolled six weeks after his seventeenth birthday, but only after begging his mother to sign the consent form. Although born at Boston, Massachusetts, he was the first of eight children raised by Canadian-born parents who moved back to Canada. By early 1914 the family had settled on a farm at Mount Uniacke, Nova Scotia. McClare had just turned sixteen when his father purchased the farm, which he later named Mapledale. Tucked among the rolling hills in the lake district northwest of Halifax, the town and its environs offered plenty to do, but much of McClare's time was spent helping on the farm or attending school with his sister, Helen, in nearby Hillsvale. Telling recruiters he was eighteen, McClare joined the 63rd Regiment Halifax Rifles on April 26, 1915. He trained on McNabs Island, where he was pleased to have the company of two enrolled cousins from America. By the middle of July 1916 all three boys were part of a draft that boarded the *Empress of Britain* bound for England, where — much to the lads' great disappointment — they were separated into different units. In France since February 1917, McClare entered the trenches for the first time one day before the April battle.

During the attack, the young soldier was focused on survival, but in the back of his mind that stormy Easter Monday was the letter he had recently written to his mother, Gertrude, describing the French farmhouse he had been billeted in and the thunderous noise of the guns. "It is not very far and maybe tomorrow or the next day I will be nearer to it," he managed to write before darkness fell. He ended his letter by stating he had not received any mail, and would "be mighty glad to get it."

McClare's battalion moved from Maisnil-Bouché to Bois des Alleux, where — after a brief rest — it was issued bombs, ground flares, sandbags, rations, and rifle grenades. That evening the men fell in again and marched to the assembly trenches in front of Neuville-Saint-Vaast. From there they journeyed to the front, hampered en route by the rough condition of the communication trenches. Arriving around 1 a.m., wiring parties were sent out to cut gaps in the Canadian wire for the infantry to advance through. In the meantime, the drenched and exhausted men, including the rookie McClare, shivered away the seconds before zero hour.

Hidden from view, but in the midst of the muddy, torn up ground, was the entrance to the Volker Tunnel, its massive depths packed with Germans armed with machine guns and patiently waiting for the initial waves of Canadian infantry to pass over before popping up and attacking them from behind. Advancing with the third wave of infantry, McClare and his buddies in A Company helped destroy these determined soldiers, but the young private was soon hit by shrapnel.

By 6:14 a.m. the lead company in the battalion's attack had fought to the Black Line. Half an hour later the 25th Battalion passed through as planned and with two pipers leading drove

Percy "Winnie" McClare of the 24th (Victoria Rifles of Canada) Battalion kept up a steady wartime correspondence with his mother, other relatives, and friends.

against the German positions in the Red Line, capturing the position. "More than 200 prisoners were passed back. Two officers of the 24th were killed and four wounded. Approximately 230 other ranks were killed or wounded. All day on April 9 and all during that stormy night, and for three days thereafter, the 24th stayed in the captured Black Line."[6]

McClare, who was known as Winnie, survived the battle: not bad for a soldier with limited experience. Six days later he would celebrate the arrival of twenty-one letters and a parcel of gum. On April 16, he sat down in the mud to write a reply. "My Dear Mother: I can only write a short letter this time, but hope I will be able to [write a longer letter] soon... I have been in the trenches for nine days and it is impossible to write up there. You have no doubt heard before this of the big advance of the Canadians and the capture of Vimy Ridge. I was in the whole of that battle and it was Hell. I got a small splinter of shrapnel through the fleshy part of my shoulder. It was very slight... It was some battle and I am glad to say that I was through it, as it will be one of the biggest things in Canadian history." Before closing, McClare asked for some socks and anything else "in the line of eats," but "please fix the parcel up good."[7]

Nineteen days later, on May 5, McClare was killed in action. The grim news reached his home on May 17.

To the north, in 3rd Division's sector, Fred Claydon, the young Manitoba ranch hand who had enrolled at age sixteen, was painfully biding his time. He and the rest of the 43rd (Cameron Highlanders of Canada) Battalion were in reserve, ready to follow the lead battalions onto the ridge. The young scout was nursing some broken bones in his face, the result of a nighttime accident while crossing a railway bridge in the days leading up to the big attack. "I went right through and the side of my face hit the bloody rail."

Besides smashing bones, the fall caused one of Claydon's eyes to swell and close, but that did not stop those in charge from assigning him additional scout duties. Making matters worse, he developed a cold in his good eye. "I couldn't see a goddamn thing. I was bloody blind. It lasted through the winter — hell of a bloody thing."

Four days prior to the April battle Claydon was "bayonet man" on a sixty-man raid. His job was to keep the area clear while two other men threw bombs and others fired light machine guns. "You got used to the bloody bayonet. We came out of that raid without losing any men." Now about to lead his men up onto the ridge in support of the initial waves, Claydon told himself to remain sharp — to maintain a keen eye for snipers and pockets of hidden resistance. A wily veteran with a strong sense of danger, Claydon was a careful scout who never downplayed the skill of the enemy.[8]

Further up on the ridge — in the relative shelter of the crater to which they had been led — Corporal David Moir's machine-gun crew watched intently as members of the Royal Canadian Regiment (RCR) ran toward them. Moir, who had enrolled at Winnipeg at age seventeen on May 20, 1915, had transferred to the 7th Brigade Machine Gun Company in June 1916.[9] He remembered that as soon as the RCR "passed through we grabbed our guns and equipment and followed." In front and to the sides,

Carefully preserve this letter

France
April 16. 1917

My Dear Mother.

I can only write a short letter this time, but hope I will be able to do so soon. I have not written a letter for over a week an a half as I have been in the trenches for 8 days, and it is impossible to write up there.

You have no doubt heard before this of the big advance of the Canadians and the capture of Vimy Ridge.

I was in the whole of that battle and it was Hell. I got a small splinter of shrapnel through the fleshy part of my shoulder. It was very slight and I went thro it all with it.

It was some battle and I am glad to say that I was through it, as it will be one of the biggest things in Canadian history.

We are out for a few days rest and believe me we need it. I don't know how Roy and Lyle came through it. I have not seen them yet, but expect to soon. Well Mother if you can, please send me some socks when you can and any thing else you care to send in the line of eats.

In a letter to his mother one week after Vimy Ridge, Winnie McClare wrote "it will be one of the biggest things in Canadian history.

The telegram that every family dreaded receiving. Five weeks after he survived Vimy, Winnie McClare was reported killed in action.

Moir saw gruesome scenes and widespread destruction. German barbed wire and trenches were smashed; wounded men and shattered bodies appeared out of the smoke. The former clerk came across "one poor RCR who looked as if a shell had made a direct hit. He was sitting there on what was left of his legs, calmly smoking a cigarette."

Advancing further, the five-foot-nine, 140-pound Moir and two others in his gun crew jumped into a crater to escape German machine-gun fire that was tearing into their left flank. Moir leaned over close to his buddies and told them there was no point in all three of them getting knocked off with one shell — that it would be better if he took off and joined a fellow named Walker whom he had spotted in another hole roughly ten metres away. "Walker was a new man with our unit, just out from England.

The night before his mail had caught up to him but he hadn't had a chance to read it. When I crawled over to him he looked quite natural sitting in his hole with a letter in his hand as if he was reading it, but on speaking to him I got no answer." Taking a closer look, Moir saw that a machine-gun bullet had entered Walker's head just below his steel helmet.

On into the battle, Moir and his buddies found themselves waiting for an infantry counterattack that never came. Later he watched as an enemy shell scored a direct hit on one of the company's newly established gun positions. A split second after that he noticed an object "spinning over and over" through the air until it landed upright about six metres behind his gun position. It was the head and upper torso of a man named Scotty Henderson. "I remember him because he had a little wispy moustache, a twinkle in his eye, and always a crooked grin on his face as if he was laughing at the world and our foolish ways."[10]

As the morning unfolded, Claydon's 43rd Battalion came across dozens of dead Germans, many killed by artillery fire. At La Folie Farm, beyond the Black Line, he stumbled upon a scene he would never forget. "The bricks from the [farm building's] foundation formed a little hill of broken bricks, and laying right alongside of it was this young Heine. He was just a young fella. I looked at him. He had got killed by a machine-gun. He had packed two sacks. One sack full of rye bread, which was a little old by this date. The other ... was full of sausage, tied up. He was packing these rations up when he got killed."[11]

Further back, fifteen-year-old private Harold A. Carter had a rather unceremonious start to his journey into no man's land. While scrambling out of the trench he lost his footing in the muck and fell back on two other members of his Lewis light machine-gun crew. Now serving in 3rd Division with the 5th Canadian Mounted Rifles, Carter had told recruiters in February 1916 that he had been born on December 23, 1899, a date that would have made him only sixteen. However, recruiters followed up and noted in his file the date on his birth certificate: December 23, 1901. Carter, therefore, was only fourteen when he left home in Saint John, New Brunswick, and joined the 140th Battalion, listing teamster as his trade, and his married sister, Eva Jamieson, as next-of-kin. On his attestation form the army was careful, however, to note his apparent age as seventeen.

As snow began to accumulate on Carter's muddy face and uniform, he was grabbed and either pulled or pushed out of the trench. But even before he got his bearings, Carter was handed four canvas bags of ammunition. Tall for his age, Carter had arrived in England the previous fall and was bounced between units before being sent to France to join the CMR, even though a medical board had concluded he was "underage — only 15" and "very immature and underdeveloped." And although it did not stick, the board had recommended he be "discharged as permanently unfit."[12]

Loaded down with the ammunition, plus 120 rounds for his rifle, a knapsack, water bottle, and bayonet, Carter did not get far before enemy fire tore into the ground around him. Taking cover in a low, watery crater, he remained partially submerged as globs of mud — ripped up by machine-gun fire — splattered on top of him. Those trying to kill him were soon distracted by an Allied observation balloon, and when the firing stopped, the "permanently unfit" Carter took a deep breath and made a dash for it.

Having survived his awkward and muddy encounter with the broken trench mat, Private Gordon Lawson was busy helping to chase the enemy from the edge of La Folie Wood, where some of the trees remained upright. Searching for a field of fire the young sniper climbed one of the larger trees left standing and found a firing position a few metres above ground. Thirty minutes later he saw a German soldier rise from the ground in front of him, quite intent on joining his retreating comrades. "I knew he had

War artist Richard Jack shows walking wounded moving toward the rear, while Canadian gunners continue to batter Vimy Ridge with their 18-pounder field guns.

information as to where we were digging in, so I up and fired point blank at him, right between the shoulders. He threw both hands in the air and fell forward."

Lawson noticed more movement, but before he could reload and fire again, he felt a sudden surge of pain. The enemy sniper had missed his kill shot, but the single bullet smashed Lawson's collar bone and shoulder blade. After slugging back a mouthful of rum offered to him from his officer's water bottle, Lawson joined the walking wounded until he was stopped by a medical officer who dressed his wound.[13]

To the northwest the leading shock troops of 4th Division were struggling with the battle's toughest objectives. The landscape here was much steeper, and it included the well-fortified summit of Hill 145. Waiting his turn as part of a reserve unit attached to the 12th Infantry Brigade, young Eddy Forrest could — at certain moments — hear the sound of his own heart beating between the heavy pounding that assaulted his senses and reverberated along the walls of the cave he was in. The generous tot of rum issued shortly after 4 a.m. had dropped like a hot stone into his gut. Looking around he noticed other men nervously writing letters or scratching their initials into the walls of the cave. Forrest used the time to check each item he would carry into battle, which — because of his large size — included a shovel. Waiting was the hardest part. New to battle he had listened to a few stories about men who, taking a direct hit, were turned into pink vapour, and about others whose lifeless bodies showed no outward sign of concussion, but whose bones were pulverized.

While 4th Division had less ground to cross, its infantry would have to run, climb, and fight through deep mud and water-filled craters — all while under intense fire — to reach the flat plateau known as Hill 145. Forrest's 78th (Winnipeg Grenadiers) Battalion would go over the top in support of the 38th (Ottawa) Battalion, the unit spearheading the right flank of 12th Brigade's attack.[14] Four lines of defence, bristling with wire and machine guns, ringed the hilltop. Carved into its reverse slope were deep dugouts untouched by artillery. Making matters worse was the Pimple, just to the north. From there the Germans could easily target the left flank of the attack.

Forrest's unit had been in France since August 1916, but few of the originals were left by the time he arrived. Just months before, he had been a sixteen-year-old patient in a Toronto tuberculosis sanatorium, where he anxiously followed the news from overseas, paying particular attention to the casualty lists. Humid weather had done nothing to make life comfortable in the san, so when he learned that the doctor who had sent him there was doing the enrolment medicals in Toronto, he quietly checked himself out and headed to Hamilton, where he joined the CMR.

All before he turned seventeen.

The anxious lad had passed through weeks of foot and rifle drill before boarding a troop train to Quebec City. By then he

had cleaned stables, learned to ride, and spent hours shining buttons, boots, belts, and saddles. At Quebec City, Forrest boarded
the *Mauritania* for what would turn out to be a rough crossing
to Liverpool. From there the recruits travelled by train to Shorncliffe, where Forrest was transferred to the infantry from the
cavalry. Suddenly there were no more horses to groom or feed or
saddles to buff, but there were training trenches to dig and "long
marches on bleeding feet."[15]

At the ridge, Forrest's feet were still sore and wet at zero hour
when mines were exploded along the front, creating gaps in the
German lines. The initial waves of infantry got bogged down in
the mud, which sucked the boots off soldiers' feet, but the front
lines were quickly overrun behind the barrage. The deeper mud
and water-filled craters between it and the second line of objectives stopped men in their tracks. Some were sucked in up to their
waists, where they could do nothing but face the possibility of
being picked off by a sniper or blown away by a shell.

The terrain also slowed the 38th Battalion's advance, eventually forcing its men to attack without the protection of the
barrage, which had moved on without them. Caught in the open,
men were ripped apart by machine-gun and mortar fire. Others
drowned after stumbling or sliding hopelessly into craters, where
chocolate-coloured water turned crimson. In the mad dash forward, enemy positions were missed and became pockets of deadly
resistance for the next wave of attackers. Mud jammed rifles and
machine guns, and on several occasions a soldier's life hung in
the balance for the time it took to clean his weapon, take aim, and
fire. It was on this hellish ground that sixteen-year-old Private
Percival Moore of Carleton Place, Ontario, went missing and was
later presumed dead.[16]

Forrest's 78th eventually passed through the line established by the 38th and 72nd (Seaforth Highlanders of Canada)
Battalions, and reached its objective twelve hundred metres

ATTENTION!

EIGHTY-SEVENTH
OVERSEAS
BATTALION

CANADIAN
GRENADIER
GUARDS

NOW
RECRUITING
———
HEADQUARTERS:
Grenadier Guards Armoury
Esplanade Avenue - - Montreal.

A recruiting poster for Montreal's Canadian Grenadier Guards, which formed the 87th Battalion of the CEF and fought as part of 11th Brigade, 4th Division.

from the start line, where they were assaulted by gunfire on three sides. Snipers showed no mercy, picking off runners and stretcher-bearers. Forrest ran on as comrades disappeared into shell holes. The ground was covered with dying men, some crying out for their mothers — others silent. The toughest part for Forrest was witnessing the moment a comrade was hit — seeing men suddenly clutch themselves, "some with a cry and others with faces frozen in agony."

At one point the 78th was ahead of its barrage and exposed to German machine-gun and sniper fire. It was then that Forrest — three months shy of his eighteenth birthday — collapsed onto the frozen, blood-spattered ridge.[17] With mud, sweat, and smoke stinging the corners of his eyes, he stared through the blowing snow, tossed eastward into the faces of the enemy. Nearby was the village of Givenchy-en-Gohelle. He could smell the cordite rising from the shell holes and hear the cries of men. "A counterattack came in and I was wounded in the foot and could go no further," he recalled years later. "My war was over. I would fight no more."[18]

To the right of 12th Brigade, 11th Brigade was busy attacking four lines of defence to take Hill 145. The initial assault by the 102nd (North British Columbians) and 87th (Canadian

Grenadier Guards) Battalions, was followed closely by the 54th (Kootenay) and 75th (Mississauga) Battalions. Small-arms fire decimated the Canadians, but they pressed on. When the 54th passed through the 102nd it came under fire from three sides. The 87th also suffered grievous losses because of an enemy trench that had either been purposely left off the artillery's list of targets for the barrage or simply overlooked.[19]

Immediately after "going over the top," Cyril Smith, the young rancher from Port Hammond, British Columbia, was blasted in the face by freezing rain. Flares and explosions lit the sky as shells rained down in front of him, leaving craters "large enough to swallow a house." When Smith made it to the first German line, he noticed soldiers "pouring out of their fortifications like a swarm of hornets. I had a sack of grenades and I was popping them off as fast as I could. This young fellow next to me kept saying 'Shoot some more … shoot some more!' I looked around and it was just him and me there. By then I had only three grenades left, so I said to him: Let's get out of here… We took off, but we hadn't got far when — boom — I was wounded." Exhausted and hungry, Smith hobbled back toward his trench with a hole in his back. He remembered thinking at the time: "By golly, I think I am going to make it to England."[20]

The fighting continued, but by late in the day on April 9 the Canadians had captured more ground, more prisoners, and more equipment in one day than in any previous British offensive in two-and-a-half years. Few of the blood- and mud-spattered soldiers were in any mood to celebrate, however. Too many chums had been killed or wounded during those first hours.

And a lot more would die before the entire ridge was in Canadian hands.

On April 10, it fell to the raw 85th (Nova Scotia Highlanders) Battalion to take Hill 145. The task handed to the highlanders came as a surprise. Up to then they had been engaged as a

A lone soldier makes his way over the crest of Vimy Ridge sometime after the momentous battle.

work party, relying mostly on shovels and picks — not rifles and bombs. Nevertheless, they were rushed to the front, where bayonets were fixed in anticipation of the lead-off artillery barrage. The barrage never came. But the daring attack went in anyway, and after much vicious hand-to-hand fighting the hill was captured with only parts of the eastern slope remaining in enemy hands. That courageous achievement, forged in a firestorm of bullets and bombs, brought the Canadians significantly closer to winning the entire ridge.[21]

Two days later the last high strongpoint — the Pimple — fell, and the Battle of Vimy Ridge was over.

One boy soldier who has been written into the story of Vimy Ridge is Private Roy Edward Henley. He certainly fought and was wounded in the First World War, but whether he participated in the Battle of Vimy Ridge is complicated by conflicting information. While two popular histories place Henley on the ridge during the battle, his wartime service records at Library and Archives Canada contain nothing to indicate he was there.[22] It is clear, however, that he enrolled in Canada more than once and made it to England more than once. The first time he was discharged to Canada from Hastings in late December 1916, presumably on account of being underage. He had also been treated at Shorncliffe military hospital for a bronchial cough. Henley's second attempt to get to France was more successful. His troopship — the SS *Welshman* — left Montreal and arrived in England on May 21, 1917. There is no sailing list for the *Welshman*'s journey, but the departure and arrival dates correspond with what is found in Henley's record of service.[23]

Roy Henley poses in an American uniform. Does the twinkle in his eyes hint at a sense of humour?

Many years after the war — in 1982 — Henley was interviewed about his wartime experiences. A lengthy oral history, which is part of the Reginald Roy Collection at the University of Victoria, features him talking about his military service and how he came to be wounded in battle.[24] His service file clearly shows he made it to France on January 12, 1918, and was wounded in the face and neck on August 29, 1918, while serving with the 42nd (Royal Highlanders of Canada) Battalion.[25]

Decades after the capture of Vimy Ridge, Canadians continue to proudly point to it as an epic battle that turned a large, but relatively remote colony into a modern nation. Winning the ridge was one of the few bright moments for the Allies on the Western Front that year, and the soldiers of the Canadian Corps instantly became the darlings of the British press, firmly establishing their reputation as elite "storm troops." Indeed, it was a spectacular military achievement, but one that should be remembered more for the way in which Canadians fought and died during those four bloody days.

Counted among the seven thousand wounded and 3,598 dead are dozens of boy soldiers, many of whom proved capable and courageous under fire.

This poster for Victory Bonds, based on an actual photograph, shows victorious Canadian soldiers returning from the capture of Vimy Ridge.

CHAPTER 11

"HE SEEMS TO WANT TO GO . . . HIS MOTHER AND I WILL BE WILLING TO LET HIM."

The Newfoundland Regiment, October 1916 – October 1917

"One year's Imperial hard labour."

As the stern-faced president of the field general court martial read out his sentence, Private Sam Reid felt himself go weak at the knees. Officially his offence was "receiving, knowing them to be stolen, goods, the property of a comrade." Reid never imagined that buying a few items of kit that a buddy had "liberated" from a French soldier could have such disastrous consequences.

As it turned out, he never got to serve his sentence.

Reid's time in the army had gotten off to a decidedly rocky start. The sixteen-year-old fisherman from Heart's Delight, a small coastal community on picturesque Trinity Bay, west of St. John's, joined the Newfoundland Regiment at the end of March 1916, claiming to be twenty-one. He sailed to England that July on the SS *Sicilian* and underwent further training at the regimental depot at Ayr. Shortly after arrival in Scotland he had several brushes with authority. In August, Reid was charged with insubordination and sentenced to seven days confinement to barracks (CB). On the second last day of CB he failed to appear at several defaulters' parades — a standard condition of CB that required the soldier undergoing the punishment (the defaulter) to appear at specified times, usually wearing battle order and frequently carrying additional items that had been shined, blancoed (treated with a khaki-coloured compound), pressed, or otherwise maintained. A punishment of forty-eight hours detention ensured Reid would not miss the next defaulters' parades.

Reid joined his unit in France in mid-October, one of the replacements for the losses incurred in the Battle of Gueudecourt. Then in quick succession in late November came the theft, his arrest, and court martial. While undergoing his sentence at a military prison in France, Reid was admitted to No. 12 General Hospital at Rouen on January 3, "dangerously ill of some abdominal trouble the nature of which had not then been diagnosed." He died two days later of bronchial pneumonia.

Like underaged soldier Jack Chaplin almost two years earlier, to the day, Reid was the first casualty of another new year for the Newfoundland Regiment.[1]

While Reid was undergoing his court martial for receiving stolen goods, the exhausted commanding officer of the Newfoundland Regiment, Lieutenant-Colonel Arthur Hadow, was invalided home, not to return until May 1917. Hadow's second-in-command, British Major James Forbes-Robertson, replaced him and was made acting lieutenant-colonel. Under Forbes-Robertson, the regiment spent its third Christmas overseas, thankfully out of the line.

But that was soon to change.

The Newfoundlanders re-entered the trenches in mid-January and occupied a new section of line the British had taken over from the French at Sailly-Saillisel, about twenty kilometres due east of Albert. The British held the western, Sailly, part of the village; the Germans occupied the smaller eastern, Saillisel. Use of the word "line" was a bit of a misnomer, as the regiment initially held a series of eighteen posts where there was no actual continuous trench line. On January 27, a new British offensive began, ostensibly with the aim of convincing the Germans that the Battle of the Somme was recommencing. The Newfoundlanders were not one of the assault battalions but supported the 87th Brigade bombardment with their trench mortars.

In addition, C Company had been assigned the tasks of helping to bring in 87th Brigade's wounded and carry forward the necessary supplies to consolidate any new positions. In their eagerness to get into action a few soldiers in other companies, tired of being mere spectators, went over the top to become more directly involved in the battle. In providing this support — both official and unofficial — several Newfoundlanders were wounded and seven were killed.[2] One of the wounded was Private Gordon Lewis of St. John's.

Lewis, a steward, had enrolled in March the previous year as a drummer in the regimental band. He claimed to be eighteen years and five months old, although he was only sixteen. Like many other boy soldiers, Lewis retained his actual date and month of birth to be able to answer quickly in case he was ever asked for it. He sailed with Sam Reid and was part of the same replacement draft, with one notable exception. When the *Sicilian* departed St. John's he was aboard — but as a stowaway, so keen was he to get into action. In Newfoundland, Lewis was initially reported as missing until authorities got wind of what had happened. A short telegram from the regimental depot at Ayr confirmed suspicions: "All well. Lewis with us."

But things were not well for long, as the injuries Lewis received at Sailly-Saillisel were serious enough to require his evacuation to 89th Field Ambulance.

He died of his wounds the next day.[3]

"The Men Who Saved Monchy" were all that stood between the Germans and the town of Monchy.

After a brief respite from front-line duties the Newfound-landers returned to Sailly-Saillisel at the beginning of March, took part in an 86th Brigade attack, and were withdrawn for a rest and training period. The instruction included something new — the start of "training for open warfare." They would need it; the regiment was about to participate in Haig's great 1917 spring offensive, launched on a twenty-two kilometre front east of Arras on Easter Monday, April 9 — the same day the Canadian Corps successfully stormed Vimy Ridge.[4] Its part in the battle would result in heavy losses, exceeded only by those at Beaumont Hamel.

And a handful of Newfoundlanders would save the day.

At 5:30 a.m. on April 14, the Newfoundland Regiment, with the 1st Essex on their left — and an open, unprotected right flank — advanced behind a rolling barrage from the salient around the town of Monchy-le-Preux, which was perched on a conical hill. The soldiers moved toward their first objective of the enemy's front line at Shrapnel Trench, followed by the second objective of Infantry Hill, about seven hundred metres to the rear. Forbes-Robertson, who had established his headquarters in the centre of town, received revised orders at 3 a.m. and briefed his company commanders only at 4:45 a.m., just behind the front line.

As they advanced, the Newfoundlanders were raked by intense machine-gun fire, but made it to the front-line enemy trenches. On Infantry Hill, a fresh German battalion met them, immediately followed by two more. Under pressure and counterattacks from three sides, the regiment quickly disintegrated into little knots of men, desperately fighting on until they were killed or captured. By ten o'clock there was not a single unwounded Newfoundlander east of Monchy, and less than five hundred metres away were roughly 250 Germans advancing on the village.[5]

Seven boy soldiers are known to have been killed in the onslaught or to have died later of wounds.

Office clerk Joe Vaughan was only fifteen when he walked into the Church Lads' Brigade Armoury in St. John's just before Christmas 1914, wearing the clothes of an older brother and claiming to be nineteen. Even then his ruse did not work and the recruiting officer sent him home to get his parents' written consent. Vaughan returned a few days later with a letter from his father, which stated, "He seems to want to go, under those circumstances, if you find him fit, his mother and I will be willing to let him go." The five-foot-six, 120-pound Vaughan sailed to Britain on the SS *Dominion* on February 3, 1915.

Vaughan's youthfulness may have been the reason for three disciplinary incidents in May, June, and July at the regiment's tented camp near Hawick, Scotland: smoking in the ranks after being warned to stop, smoking on picket duty, and talking in the ranks while at attention on parade. The standard punishments of confinement to barracks or confinement to camp were the result. Vaughan arrived in time to participate in the Dardanelles mis-

*The next of kin of all
soldiers of the New-
foundland Regiment who
were killed in the war
received a death certifi-
cate like this one.*

adventure and sailed to the Middle East in August. Like many of
his comrades, a case of frostbite at Gallipoli required his evacuation to No. 3 General Hospital at Wandsworth. The Boxing Day
voyage aboard the luxury Cunard liner *Aquitania* was undoubtedly much more pleasant than the conditions his comrades left
behind faced from the weather and the Turks.

The teenager was sent to rejoin his unit, which by now was in
France, on April 13, 1916. Before he made it there he was admitted to No. 6 General Hospital at Rouen a few days later with
"inflamed glands." It turned out that the inflammation was on the
foreskin and head of his penis, which was diagnosed as *balantitis*,
a condition usually caused by poor hygiene in uncircumcised
males. Although not considered a sexually transmitted disease

today, Vaughan was listed as having a venereal disease, which required admission to two more military hospitals before he was discharged on June 12. Venereal diseases (and alcoholism) also triggered a stoppage of pay for the length of time a soldier was considered to be incapacitated, but for some reason Vaughan only lost one day's pay.

Vaughan returned to his unit in time for the fateful first day on the Somme on July 1. Miraculously, he was one of the few to survive the inferno, but he did not come through unscathed. He suffered gunshot wounds to both legs and was evacuated once again to the military hospital at Wandsworth. After treatment and convalescence he rejoined his regiment on March 6. Now seventeen he was initially reported as missing at Monchy on April 14.

Vaughan was never seen alive again; his body was never found.[6]

The Vaughans were one of many Newfoundland families devastated by the war. The parents, Harry and Ellen, were both sixty-three when the war ended and they were left impoverished. In their declining years, they could no longer rely on any support from their sons who served. In addition to losing young Joe, the Vaughans were bereaved by the wartime deaths of two older sons. A fourth son was wounded in the same battle that killed Joe. He was taken prisoner but repatriated, possibly because of his wounds. He returned home and was demobilized in 1919.

Bill Adams and Alf Cake joined in the spring of 1916 and sailed together on the SS *Sicilian* to Britain on July 18 as part of a five-hundred-man reinforcement draft. Adams, a slightly built fisherman from the tiny hamlet of Arnold's Cove on Placentia Bay at the base of the Avalon Peninsula, claimed to be eighteen although he was fifteen or sixteen at the time. He joined the regiment in France on October 14, immediately after it withdrew to the rear following the fighting at Gueudecourt. Four days later he was part of a 250-man stretcher-bearer party tasked to support an attack by two other battalions in the brigade. During this operation, Adams received a gunshot wound to the left leg and was evacuated to No. 11 Stationary Hospital in Rouen. The tough, wiry lad recovered and rejoined his unit on November 17, only to be admitted to 88th Field Ambulance with influenza at the end of December 1916.

After the attack at Monchy, Adams was declared missing in action. Like Joe Vaughan's, his body was never recovered. Adams was presumed dead for official purposes in November 1917.[7]

Adding four years to his true age was not a problem for Alf Cake, a fourteen-year-old grocery clerk from St. John's. He had hardly stepped into his uniform when he had his first run-in with authorities. On July 2, he was charged with disobedience and insolence to an NCO. In Scotland, two incidents in quick succession in August were perhaps more a reflection of his age than anything else. "Throwing food around dining room" and "messing up tent" are probably two of the most obscure charges ever to appear on a soldier's conduct sheet. Both charges resulted in a few days CB. Although difficult to handle at times, Cake got to France and entered the fray until suddenly, on April 14, he was reported missing in action. Back home in St. John's, his family held out hope that he might be a prisoner of war, until a letter arrived from Private Charlie Wiseman, one of 150 Newfoundlanders taken prisoner at Monchy. In it, Wiseman stated that he was in the same shell hole with Cake when the boy was killed.[8]

Another lad who sailed on the same troopship as Adams and Cake also died as a result of the fighting that April. Sixteen-year-old Harold Jacobs was a 137-pound, five-foot-six-inch fisherman from Northern Bay South near Bay de Verde on Conception Bay. On enrolment he side-stepped his true age by claiming to be over eighteen. Months later on the Western Front, veracity about his age did not concern him as much as the stark reality that surrounded him. Shot through the left kidney, spinal cord, and liver, Jacobs was captured by the Germans, who put him in the civilian St. Clotilda Hospital in Douai. Jacobs died a painful death five days later and was buried in the Douai Communal Cemetery.

Jacobs's story is one that demonstrates how slowly news travelled between soldiers at the front and loved ones back home. Parents could easily believe their boy was still alive for weeks or even months after he was reported missing. After Jacobs's death, there was a British War Office extract from a Red Cross postcard addressed to Miss Alice Tessier in St. John's. It stated, "I am quite well. Prisoner."[9]

Harold Jacobs was the youngest Newfoundlander to die as a prisoner of war.

While the regiment was being decimated at Monchy, Forbes-Robertson quickly collected sixteen available men from his headquarters and led them to a trench on the edge of the village, collecting weapons and ammunition from dead and wounded soldiers along the way. As they ran, they came under enemy fire. By the time they got to the trench, there were only ten of them left. In desperation, they opened up with rapid-fire rifle bursts on the advancing Germans. The enemy went to ground, assuming they were facing a strong defending force. For the next four hours, in the words of the British Official History, the ten determined Newfoundlanders were "all that stood between the Germans and Monchy, one of the most vital positions on the whole battlefield." The actions of the "men who saved Monchy" were decisive, but the regiment's losses totalled 460 casualties (including prisoners).[10] Today, a Newfoundland caribou stands on top of the ruins of a German pillbox on the eastern edge of Monchy. It gazes from the now-quiet little farming village toward Infantry Hill.

The last-stand action at Monchy marked the second time the Newfoundland Regiment had been practically wiped out since arriving in France.

Troops enter Ypres at dawn over the canal on the road from Elverdinge.

On May 5, 1917, Lieutenant-Colonel Hadow returned to the regiment from sick leave and James Forbes-Robertson reverted to second-in-command. Shortly afterwards he returned to the British army to command a battalion.[11] By the end of the month, the regiment was down to 221 all ranks and a period of rest, recuperation, and rebuilding was necessary. Reinforcement drafts totalling five hundred men arrived in June and July to bring the regiment up to fighting strength. One of them contained a young soldier named Tommy Ricketts, who would later achieve the empire's highest award for valour. Soon after his arrival at the front, Ricketts saw his first action at Langemarck, twenty-five hundred metres northwest of the Belgian village of Saint-Julien, where the Canadian Division had distinguished itself at the Second Battle of Ypres in April 1915.

Haig's latest Flanders offensive had started on June 7 with a rapid victory at Messines Ridge, but this initial success was not followed up until July 31. By then, stiffening German resistance and several counterattacks, coupled with seemingly ceaseless rain, halted the British advance. The enemy took advantage of this pause to reorganize their defence and bring up reinforcements, while the British relieved their forward divisions. On August 16, the Newfoundland Regiment was part of a renewed British attack that came up against something new in the German defences: circular shelters of reinforced concrete, placed above ground because of the water table. They were quickly nicknamed "pillboxes." Surrounded by barbed wire, these fortifications dotted the landscape in a checkerboard pattern to provide supporting fire. Their thick walls and roofs and narrow firing portals presented formidable obstacles, but in time the Allies would discover a weak spot. Courageous soldiers eventually learned to creep up on them — outflank them — and toss in a grenade. As part of 29th Division on August 28, the Newfoundland Regiment moved into the lines in front of Langemarck. The terrain over which the soldiers had to fight was a vast, sodden, and muddy wasteland, characterized by stagnant pools, overflowing "beeks" (drainage ditches), and streams that became long stretches of bog.

Ypres quickly came to epitomize the very worst of the appalling conditions under which Allied soldiers had to live and fight during the war.

After a month's pause, Haig renewed his offensive on September 20. The rainy weather in the salient continued unabated, turning the low ground into an impassible morass, while shell holes and craters on higher ground produced a similar effect. Despite these difficulties, Haig continued the attack to keep German forces from redeploying to counter a planned British assault against Cambrai. On October 9, the Newfoundland Regiment was initially in support for an attack against the northern end of Passchendaele Ridge, centred on Poelcappelle. Once the first two objective lines were captured, the Newfoundlanders moved through to seize the final line. Although rough terrain, stiff

*Unidentified soldiers from the Newfoundland Regiment pose for a group photo-
graph. Will we ever know their names?*

enemy resistance, heavy casualties, and the movement of flanking units stopped the regiment's attack short of its objective, by
nightfall Poelcappelle was in Allied hands.[12]

During the fighting for Poelcappelle, Herb Adams decided
he simply could not take it any longer. The deafening rattle of
machine guns, the powerful concussions from artillery shells, the
stinging smell of cordite, the gritty taste of earth, and the bloody
sight of his buddies falling dead or wounded around him was
more than the boy could bear. He dropped his rifle and scrambled up out of the trench, heading for the rear.

He had to get away from the madness.

Otto Herbert Adams, a St. John's farmer, had joined the
regiment two years earlier on August 11, 1915, claiming to be
eighteen years and three months old. In fact, he was only sixteen.
Herb could neither read nor write and marked his attestation

form with an "X." Times were hard for many Newfoundland families, and after he left home his father became ill and could not work. If things were bad at home, they were even worse for young Adams overseas. Before he joined the regiment in the field he had three run-ins with authority, including a serious one of refusing to obey the order of an NCO.

As the Newfoundland Regiment moved to France after its grim introduction to warfare at Gallipoli, Adams was moving to join the unit. He was part of a reinforcement draft of sixty-six soldiers that arrived on June 30, the day before the debacle at Beaumont Hamel. These new soldiers had missed the preparations and rehearsals for July 1, as they were originally scheduled to join the unit two days after the battle commenced. Yet despite their lack of training and experience, the new arrivals were absorbed immediately into the front-line companies. Remarkably, Adams was one of the few to survive, but the memory of that bloody slaughter affected him deeply.

His record remained clear until the spring of 1917, when he was awarded seven days Field Punishment No. 1 on April 10, just before the fierce battle at Monchy-le-Preux. If Adams thought his actions and the resulting punishment would keep him out of battle — a common misconception among soldiers — he was mistaken. Regulations specifically stated that if F.P. No. 1 would keep a soldier from his unit during an attack, the punishment was suspended and he would participate. At Monchy, Adams was still suffering the effects of witnessing the carnage at Beaumont Hamel — what today is known as post-traumatic stress disorder — and "left the trenches while under shell fire." The seventeen-year-old was charged with desertion, tried at a field general court martial, found guilty, and sentenced "to suffer death by being shot" on May 18. Fortunately the sentence was overturned by Third Army commander Lieutenant-General "Bull" Allenby on May 31 and commuted to ten years penal servitude at a military prison.

At about the same time, Adams's mother, Fanny, had written to the authorities as she had "never got no reply from himself yet," but asked them to write or telegram him to write as soon as possible as his family was "awfully anxious to hear from him." She asked that, if the query could not be done without charge, then to "let me know and I will send you the cost. I am only a poor woman but I don't mind what it costs as long as I can hear a word from my poor boy he is only seventeen (17) and he is to [sic] young to be out."

In response, a letter from an officer informed her that, "it would appear that your son ... is well and is still serving with his Unit." In fact, by that time her son was sitting in prison waiting for a decision on his disposition, having just had his death sentence commuted one week earlier.

When the officer in question learned of Adams's true fate, he sent a letter to the authorities in Newfoundland, suggesting that "the subject is one that can perhaps be better dealt with verbally in St. John's... The results of attempting to explain this to his Mother in writing might cause unnecessary pain and misunderstanding." He suggested that they "may be good enough to direct that an Officer ask Mrs. Adams to call on him and that he should explain the case as he thinks fit." The outcome of this meeting — if it ever occurred — is unknown, but it is instructive to note that even for such a delicate and unsettling duty, the suggestion was for Adams's mother to call on an officer and not the other way around.

Shortly afterwards, Adams was released to his unit pending review of his case, initially scheduled for August 31, later changed to November 30. The pressures on the small colony to keep the regiment up to strength in the field may have influenced the decision to return the young lad to duty. Whatever the reason, Herb Adams became a fighting soldier once again. On October 9, after the attack on German positions near Poelcappelle,

A poster exhorts civilians to back up the men at the front by buying Victory Bonds.

he was reported missing in action. Later that same day his status was changed to died of wounds or killed in action.

Over the course of several battles in the Ypres Salient, the mud of Flanders swallowed the remains of thousands of other soldiers who were killed or wounded, never to be recovered. Against the odds, Adams's partially buried remains were discovered two months later, but it was too dangerous to attempt to recover them as a battle raged nearby. When a burial party returned the next day, the ground had been churned up by artillery fire and his remains had disappeared. To compound the misfortune, the personal effects recovered by the burial party and sent home to his mother in a kit bag were actually those of another soldier.

In response Mrs. Adams wanted to know ". . . if those things were taken from my sons person or from his kit bag out of the depot or station." She did "not believe that the belt is his because the last report I received in July he was not on the ambulance service."

In a letter to Fanny Adams the unit records officer attempted to explain the realities of modern warfare: "So great is the confusion wrought in a big battle in these times," he wrote, "that months can often lapse before the bodies of the fallen soldiers can be recovered from the battlefield… In due course it is hoped that the exact site of Pte Adams' grave will be known and a cross will be erected... While it is hard, I know, to assuage a Mother's grief, will you allow me to say this, that Pte Adams laid down his life in the noblest manner, dying himself that others might live in Freedom and Lawfulness."

A grief-stricken Fanny refused to believe her son was dead and in a letter to the authorities on January 16, 1918, angrily stated:

How can they report him killed except they have found his body... My mind is always wondering ... if he is captured by the enemy or did he get lost in what we call Bogs of Rivers... I cannot see how they could send out a poor boy that was so badly shell shocked has lots of the boys that's returned home told me he was. I call this War on out rages [outrageous] murder from the beginning. I would like for you if its possible to try and hunt the Hospitals as much as you can if its in your power and the Salvation Army Huts as you know some where back of the fighting line. My poor dear boy is not able to write himself has you know this is a great hinderance to him... I have been speaking to returned soldiers that have been reported killed for seven or eight months and their friends in mourning for them and today they are walking the streets of St. John's, so you see that I can't give up hopes until the body is found and the tokens that on him sent back to me. The tokens I means is his brother's photo, and a girl's photo also the girl's ring and his wrist watch... My mind tells me that he is still alive some where, he was a boy that had a wonderful roving mind... Please answer this for I would more than like for you to answer before I dies... please try and do your best for a poor broken hearted Mother...

In June, Adams's kit bag was found and sent home, but it was small solace to Fanny, who now had to fight for the wages that were due to him. "My poor dear son would have been a good help now if he had been left home to me," she wrote. "A poor boy enlisted and he was only 16 and 6 months old, so you see it was a terrible thing to take away a poor child, away from his home. Dear friend, please do your best for me, as I am very sick ... no money to pay the Dr.'s bills... My poor child's blood money."

To add to the distraught woman's misfortune, in February 1919, her husband, Thomas, died from "asthma and tumours." Yet in a letter acknowledging receipt of her son's memorial scroll and letter from the king, she apologized for her tardiness. "Owing to the seriousness of my husband's illness which ended fatally," she explained, "I am sorry to have delayed in thanking you ... trusting you will excuse this as the cause for the delay." Fourteen months later — and thirty months after her son was killed — a cheque for $438 was sent to Fanny as her son's War Service Gratuity. A confirmation letter, dated April 20, 1920, is the final entry in his file.

In the end Herb Adams's remains were never found; his sacrifice is commemorated on the Newfoundland Caribou Memorial at Beaumont Hamel.[13]

CHAPTER 12

"WELL, THEY MIGHT HAVE AT LEAST GIVEN YOU A NEW UNIFORM."

Arleux and Hill 70, April–August, 1917

When the call for recruits blew across the Alberta prairie, sixteen-year-old Walter King was not much older than the children he taught.

For a year the young schoolteacher had watched and waited, reading news and listening to questions from his students or anyone else seeking an educated take on the war. In the classroom, King took his grades 6 to 8 students very seriously, but how could he teach them what they really needed to know about the war if he were to remain in Wainwright? The answer was simple: he would enrol and see it for himself. And so on December 7, 1915 — at the age of seventeen — he stood in line to enrol with his father, Henry, and older brother, Arthur.

Sixteen months later he was still "the young teacher," although he had become something more while serving with the 5th (Western Cavalry) Battalion. He was now a battle-tested soldier, a survivor of the Battle of Vimy Ridge, but still a teenager who had fought next to men five, ten — even fifteen or twenty years — his senior. He also had plenty to tell his students and his family about the ugly, indiscriminate nature of war. "We had quite a few casualties, but nothing compared to the German losses," he wrote in an April 16, 1917, letter to his mother. "When the fight was over the street was lined with hospital transports waiting to get into the hospital. I was helping to carry the stretchers in for a while. The German wounded were mixed right in with ours, and were treated alike. What surprises me most is the number of them that can speak English."[1]

Although named after the governor general's wife, the 199th (Duchess of Connaught's Own Irish Rangers) Battalion was absorbed into a reserve battalion after arrival in England.

King told his mother about a major who had two fingers blown off his left hand, one off his right, and was shot in the left thigh and foot with shrapnel. He was "sniped at in the right knee as he was being carried out on the stretcher … and … he is still smiling." While hauling ammunition and water supplies King witnessed dozens of walking wounded and other stretcher cases. There were men from both sides with blackened faces, shattered or missing limbs, and ugly lacerations. Many took long, desperate drags off broken cigarettes, while others stood shaking with glassy eyes and mournful expressions.

Sent forward as part of a burying party, the young man was

horrified by what he found and had to do. "We buried 72 5th Batt. men, but the dead Fritzes lying around was a terror. Nearly every dug-out was piled up with them."

Assigned to the 78th (Winnipeg Grenadiers) Battalion and arriving just after the battle, Archie Brown — still a teenager — was in awe of the tunnels that had turned Vimy Ridge into an underground city. He was attending normal school in Manitou, Manitoba, when a fellow student showed up in uniform. Within a day Brown and four other classmates were newly minted members of the 184th Battalion.

Bright and bursting with energy, the sixteen-year-old did not have his mother's permission to enrol, but that did not matter. When asked to prove his age, the confident youth explained that students had to be eighteen to attend normal school in Manitoba. He, therefore, had to be eighteen. The short explanation conveniently skipped over the fact that he had gotten into normal school by adding two years to his age.

During the next few weeks Brown's main concern was keeping his enrolment a secret from his parents. "I hadn't told my mother... About two weeks before the normal class finished, this lady from Manitou knew my sister in Winnipeg and she told her I was in uniform. I was afraid my sister would spring it on my mother, so I asked for special leave and went home."

Brown's mother resided in the south-central community of Macdonald and her modest house was set back ninety metres from the gate. While walking up the long laneway, Brown, who was in uniform, noticed his sister and mother at the window, watching him. After going inside and kissing his mother on the cheek, Brown found himself at the receiving end of a long, uncomfortable stare. "She said, 'Well, they might have at least given you a new uniform.'" The growing teen's uniform had been new when he got it, but he had lived in it for three months.

At Camp Hughes, near Shilo, Brown drilled and learned to

assemble, disassemble, and operate a machine gun, a skill that would save his life at Passchendaele.

In England, his age finally caught up to him when a doctor — conducting a physical exam — suggested he was only fifteen, let alone sixteen. Brown's chest measurement of twenty-nine inches did not help, either; enlisted men were supposed to have at least thirty-two inches. But all of that did not seem to matter to those making the final decisions. Instead of sending him back to Canada they made him a bugler — even though he never did blow a bugle.

Brown was first sent to the Young Soldiers Battalion, where he remained until he was shipped to France to join 4th Canadian Division just after Vimy. The impressionable youth would never forget the little stream running through the Zouave valley and the many potholes and shell holes red with the blood of men who had been wounded or killed.[2] But while the grisly landscape brought him face-to-face with the darkest side of war, his indoctrination — even at such a young age — had taught him some valuable lessons on how to survive.

Assigned to B Company of the 78th, Brown was in close reserve on top of the ridge when he found an abandoned German trench and a small stockpile of stick bombs. It was a brief opportunity to be a playful kid again — and to sharpen his bombing skills. "I was having quite a time throwing these out and exploding them around there," he recalled years later in an interview with the CBC. The fun ended when a German battery began lobbing shells in his direction. "The fourth [shell] came within a hundred yards … so I got out of there."

Hiking back through the muck, Brown discovered how easy it was for the war to affect a man personally. Spring rain had washed the dirt off the white faces of the dead, and for a few seconds they appeared to be blooming above their shallow graves. "They weren't ravished at all, but there was this one particular case —

one of the boys who had been in the machine gun section of the 184th, and here his face had been washed out in the open. It was the first time the war was actually brought home to me … what it was … what could happen … and what could happen to me."

In time, Brown would be toughened by the constant horror, but he would never get used to it — just as he would never get used to ignoring the one horror that for him was worse than death. "It wasn't fear of the enemy, it was fear of myself, that I would show fear in front of somebody else."

Meanwhile, it was business as usual for the Canadian Corps. The Germans had retreated east, but their strong, layered-defence included machine-gun nests, hidden outposts, rows of barbed wire, and supporting trench lines. Around the time King drafted his letter and Brown made his grisly discovery, the Canadians were inching their way down the ridge's eastern slope onto the Douai Plain. Further east, the infantry probed a darkened, treeless landscape in search of enemy outposts, which were systematically attacked and destroyed in a hail of gunfire. The advancing Canadians found abandoned guns and stockpiles of ammunition, which they turned around and used on the enemy.

Young Fred Claydon, the former sheep herder from Elkhorn, Manitoba, was leading a nighttime patrol with another scout when his instincts caused him to stop. "He [the other scout] was on the left. I was on the right. I had a bloody hunch something wasn't right. Just then a flare went up and oh my I could see a whole bunch of Heine digging a trench just in front of us. We could see their bloody tin hats. We all froze and I don't think any of us took a breath. We just stayed there in the grass waiting for the bloody light to go out."

If the Germans had noticed anything — a flash of metal or a muffled cough — all hell would have broken loose. When darkness returned, Claydon exhaled and everyone slowly moved back toward their lines. During such times bottled-up anger could explode like a Mills bomb. One soldier in Claydon's group decided it was time to settle an old score with an officer he despised. "A rifle — one of ours — went off," remembered Claydon, who was anything but naïve; he knew it was no accident. Instead of killing the officer the bullet pinged off his helmet, "just above the brim."

"You could kill a guy out there and nobody would know," Claydon remembered.[3]

Teenager Walter King, meanwhile, remained busy. "We went up the line, past our old front-line trenches, over no-man's land, and right into the old German support lines. Our artillery was firing over our heads all the time. Fritz shelled us a little, but our artillery was so active that he thought best to quit."

Travelling by foot — especially across open ground — was nearly hopeless. King described the land as "an awful mess" with "not a yard of level ground left, for it is just one mass of shell holes and huge mine craters. We were out until half past one in the morning collecting waste ammunition and carrying up water to the trenches. We had some time getting home in the dark and went quite a long way round, tripping over wire entanglements and slipping in shell holes and trenches full of water. My puttees are pretty well ripped to pieces."

Two days later King's battalion was at it again. "It is about 7 or 8 miles from here so the walk there and back was quite a stunt," he wrote. "We started at 5:30 in the morning and got back about 9:30. We were off at the same time the next day and got back about five o'clock. At 6 the same day we got orders to pack up and move out again. We went about a mile and waited there for further orders which were to come, but never did. So we had to go back and sleep on the floor of the town hall."

It is no wonder King ended his letter to his mother with a small request: "A good pair of socks would be appreciated."

On April 23, Haig ordered a new attack, which became known

as the Second Battle of the Scarpe. The Canadians, however, would sit this out as the British Third Army advanced roughly two kilometres in five days of vicious fighting. Hit by machine-gun fire and shelled by long-range German guns, the British suffered thousands of casualties. The advance ground to a halt against a thick band of barbed wire. A new phase, involving the Canadians as major participants, was launched on April 28 when four battalions — the 5th, 8th (90th Winnipeg Rifles), and 10th (Calgary-Winnipeg), supported by the 25th (Nova Scotia Rifles) further to the north — attacked the heavily fortified village of Arleux-en-Gohelle. Located on the Douai Plain a few kilometres off the southeastern tip of Vimy Ridge, the village sat behind rows of barbed wire and featured an unusually high number of machine guns pointed directly at the Canadian line. Less than a thousand metres to the east, the red-roofed village of Fresnoy gave the Germans a perfect location from which to launch a counterattack.

Gritting their teeth, the Canadians rose from their shallow jumping-off trenches at 4:25 a.m. and followed a creeping barrage into no man's land. According to plan, they had six minutes — the time allotted for the barrage — to cross the cratered ground and attack the Arleux Loop, a spur just west of the village. Falling behind and losing the protection of the curtain of steel was not an option for those who wanted to live.

Only fifteen years old, Private Frank MacMackin of Turtle Creek, New Brunswick, was ready to fight to the end alongside his buddies in the 10th Battalion.

While B and C Companies found gaps in the wire, Mac-Mackin's D Company had no such luck. Men fell while searching frantically for a place to squeeze through. One of the first casualties was company commander Captain Wilfred Romeril. Stepping up to take his place was Lieutenant Francis Costello, who organized an attack on two enemy machine guns. The courageous and cool-headed MacMackin helped Costello deal with the machine guns and get men through the wire.

An after-battle report noted that when the No. 1 man on the Lewis gun was killed, MacMackin "engaged the enemy gun with his Lewis gun, and when it jammed, he used a rifle, and succeeded in keeping the enemy gunners' heads down, while they were outflanked and killed." MacMackin was wounded, but refused to be evacuated. Instead, the teenager fought on and his actions and the bravery of others helped expel the Germans from Arleux and defend it against counterattack. For MacMackin the morning resulted in the awarding of a Military Medal and promotion to lance corporal — not bad for a fifteen-year-old boy raised by deaf mute parents in rural New Brunswick.[4]

Growing up in "the old days," MacMackin did not have time for school. It was a lot easier to skip class than join in. His parents, Murray and Florence, had to leave it up to the grandparents to teach the three children how to speak. MacMackin's older brother, Grant, died in 1913, followed by his mother in March 1916. A month later some older friends pressured him into joining the army. He was only fourteen, but looked nineteen.

Half an inch shy of six feet, it had been easy for MacMackin to add four years to his age when he stood in front of the recruiting sergeant at Moncton on April 5, 1916.

Following initial training, MacMackin boarded the SS *Tuscania* on September 25 and arrived in Liverpool on October 6. Two months later he was in France, joining the "Fighting Tenth." An unknown illness took him out of the line in February 1917, and while he had rejoined his unit during the final preparations for Vimy, he was left out of that battle. The action at Arleux was the teenager's first, but not his last, major engagement.

By early May the Canadians were focused on the red-roofed hamlet of Fresnoy, roughly nine hundred metres east of Arleux. Showing little damage, Fresnoy sat behind the well-wired trenches of the enemy's Oppy-Mericourt Line. In that sector the Germans had established a number of strongpoints along the western outskirts of the hamlet, and in the woods to the north and south. After losing Arleux, the enemy was ready for an attempt on Fresnoy, and in the bright moonlight of May 3 they noticed the Canadians making final preparations to cross the plain in front of the village and to the north. A powerful rolling barrage led the Canadian attack, but the enemy retaliated by dropping artillery fire into the rear waves of 1st Brigade. Lead elements of the brigade, meanwhile, were caught in a machine-gun crossfire. The thick wire in front of the hamlet had been cut, but the gaps were hard to find in the dark. Men fell, but others carried on to clear the southern woods, seize the German front trench, and clear pockets of resistance within the hamlet.

On the right, the lead company of the 27th (City of Winnipeg) Battalion reached and overran the German front trench. The Germans counterattacked throughout the day, but their assaults were smashed. When it was over the two Canadian brigades had suffered more than a thousand casualties, but had captured Fresnoy and more than five hundred prisoners. On May 5, the Germans launched a successful attack to recapture the hamlet. In just a few days the right flank of 2nd Division was pushed back almost in line with Arleux.[5]

Private Eric Parlee's 24th (Victoria Rifles of Canada) Battalion did not participate in the main attack on Fresnoy, but the young soldier had remained busy until wounded on May 5. Parlee had been on the Western Front since October and was very proud of his battalion's achievements and the fact that he could toe the line just like the older lads. But unlike fellow teenager and New Brunswicker Frank MacMackin, Parlee would die of wounds on May 8, 1917, at No. 6 Casualty Clearing Station.[6]

Just two months past his fifteenth birthday when he enrolled in Saint John with the 115th Battalion on December 17, 1915, Parlee

Many Canadian soldiers, like Eric Par-lee, had a formal studio portrait taken in England to send to relatives back home before they deployed to France.

had spent much of his youth dreaming about becoming a soldier.

When the opportunity arose, Parlee's parents, Henry and Lily May, were not around to stop him. His mother died when he was five, his father in 1914. After that, his Uncle William stepped in to help. "...I came over to do my little bit and [I am] going to do it like a man if I can," Parlee told his uncle in a letter from France. He asked his uncle if he managed to "cut the hay on the hill," noting that he wished he were home to help. "I thought of home a good many times the first day I was in the trenches, but don't mind it now." In another letter, the five-foot-five, 134-pound soldier mentioned the rain, the mud, and the constant sniping. "I had a few shots fired at me once or twice, but they could not hit me. I guess I can't be big enough yet."[7]

Another teenager, Private Morris Searle of Toronto, did not experience such luck after emerging from a trench on May 28. Searle had matured considerably since arriving in October to help reinforce the 18th (Western Ontario) Battalion. In April he helped ensure the delivery of ammunition that fed the guns firing on Vimy Ridge, and prior to that he was busy working in the tunnels beneath it. Bending over to pick up a cartridge belt that had fallen on the ground above his trench, Searle heard the sound of a plane and, just as he turned his head to look up, he heard another sound that was much closer. Whatever it was, it walloped him on the back. He sat down and within seconds a buddy was asking him if he had been hit. Searle thought he had been struck by shrapnel, but he did not feel much pain. His friend noticed a hole in the back of his tunic, and asked him to take it off. The friend then saw that the hole also went through his braces and his shirt. "He said, 'Morris, you are hit!' When it got dark I went down to the dressing station and then back out to the field ambulance on the crest of Vimy Ridge."

Searle got a tetanus shot and was shipped further behind the lines to a hospital where he spent part of his time helping the nursing sisters clean the ward. "The doctor came round one day and looked at me and said, 'How do you feel, Canada?' I told him I felt fine — other than I had something in my back. 'Sure,' he said, 'you've got something in your back … let me have a look.'" The doctor gave Searle a local anaesthetic and worked on him for half an hour. When he was through, he handed Searle a German bullet, which had missed his spine by "a fraction of a hairsbreadth."

Shrugging it off as a minor wound, Searle rejoined his battalion.[8]

Later that summer, while still nursing a parched throat near the front line at Fresnoy, Private William Woods of the 1st (Western Ontario) Battalion consoled an underage soldier who had "come through with two cans of water." The boy was "crying because his mate [also underage] had been killed on the way in. Crossing that space they would have been targets for machine guns or artillery fire." At the time, Woods could not contain the frustration he felt over such a senseless loss. After all, a general order had just been issued that no man under nineteen years was to be sent into the front line. "Some lads who were under age had been held back at the horse lines … but someone ordered two of these boys to carry water up to us ... without thinking there would be no communication trenches through the previous no-man's land."[9]

Woods was not the only older soldier to feel such frustration. Stupid mistakes — whether made higher up the chain of command or closer to the bottom — claimed many lives in the war. Underage soldiers — especially the greener ones — were often given safer jobs behind the front lines, but could still be put in harm's way through direct orders or because the boys themselves refused to accept the notion they were too young to fight or incapable of taking on riskier work at the front.

But even if they were held back from greater risk in jobs behind the front lines, boy soldiers — like their older mates — could fall to disease, be killed, or be horribly maimed through enemy shelling or accident.

Sadly, the tragic consequences of immaturity or the inability to recognize danger also claimed the lives of teenagers.

Private Thomas Davy of Amherst Island, Ontario, was lucky enough to survive and tell his own story. It was May 26 and members of his unit, D Company of 4th Canadian Mounted Rifles, were playing baseball when a young lad picked up what he may have thought was a blind shell. It exploded, killing the soldier and eight others. A spray of shrapnel ripped into Davy's left leg, right arm, and shoulder, and at least nine other men were wounded. Davy was seventeen when he enrolled just after Christmas in 1915. Only five-foot-three and 125 pounds, he was a tough farmhand when he volunteered with the 146th Battalion. In France since December, he survived the "big scrap" at Vimy, but not what amounted to a momentary lapse in judgment on the part of another young soldier.

Shrapnel from the same blast caught Private Shurley Asselstine in the chest and smashed his left femur. He, too, was only seventeen when he enrolled. Asselstine made it out to No. 6 Casualty

Clearing Station, but died the next day. He had been wounded earlier in the year near Vimy, although he was able to rejoin his unit the next day. Two months later he fought alongside Davy and the rest of the battalion as it stormed up the ridge. Like many others, he cheated death on April 9 and even bounced back later from a minor case of trench fever.[10] With so many ways to die on the Western Front, it was tough for any soldier or his family to realize that death could come in such a form, but it happened.

More terrible still was losing more than one son to war. Sadly, the vicious fighting throughout the summer of 1917 would deal this fate to many.

In Toronto, the family of Garnet and Walter Skimin were among the households rocked by such heart-wrenching news. Sixteen-year-old Garnet, who was working in a hardware store and as a chocolate dipper when he enrolled, was a year older when he was killed while serving with the 20th (Central Ontario) Battalion on July 15. His slightly older brother Walter had been killed in action at Ypres in April 1915, and the boys' father, Walter Sr., had been serving with a pioneer battalion when he was invalided home three months before Garnet's death.

Heartbroken over the loss of her first son, shaken by the illness of her husband, and only recently hearing about a minor wound suffered by Garnet, Florence Skimin was anxious to secure Garnet's release from the army. She was asked to forward a birth certificate, which she did right away, and her son appears to have been chomping at the bit to return home. By the time the lad's proof of age reached authorities, however, it was too late. "Hurry that certificate along," was the message in Garnet's last letter. In her terrible grief, Florence told the *Toronto Star* newspaper that, "our people were all soldiers. I suppose that's why they went so young."[11]

When Sir Julian Byng was promoted to command the British Third Army, his successor at the head of the Canadian Corps was

Arthur Currie, the former commander of 1st Canadian Division. It marked the first time a Canadian had ever commanded such a large formation. On July 7, Currie was ordered to attack the French coal-mining city of Lens to draw the Germans' attention from Haig's latest Flanders offensive and to prevent enemy reserves from moving north. The British wanted a direct assault on the city, but after a personal reconnaissance of the area, Currie — always mindful of the tremendous infantry casualties that a frontal attack would entail — proposed an alternate plan. Lens was dominated by two enemy-held features: Hill 70, situated roughly two thousand metres north of the city, and Sallaumines Hill to the southeast. Instead of a large-scale frontal assault on well-entrenched Germans in the ruins of Lens, Currie proposed attacking Hill 70. This assault contained the element of surprise, and capturing the hill would give the Canadians high ground overlooking the enemy, as well as strongpoints against expected enemy counterattacks.

Soldiers rehearsed the attack and thoroughly familiarized themselves with the ground where the operation was to take place. An artillery bombardment before the attack would knock out machine guns, cut wire, and neutralize German batteries. A rolling artillery barrage during the assault would keep slightly ahead of the advancing Canadians, forcing the Germans to shelter in their trenches and dugouts.

At 4:25 a.m. on August 15, about seven thousand men in ten assault battalions of 1st and 2nd Divisions rose out of their jumping-off positions and advanced on a four-thousand-metre front behind a rolling barrage, while other guns hit trenches and strongpoints. At the same time, engineers fired five hundred barrels of burning oil, creating a thick smokescreen to conceal the Canadians' real objectives. Within twenty minutes, the leading wave of infantry had captured the first objective — the crest of Hill 70. Twenty minutes later the 18th and 21st (Eastern Ontario)

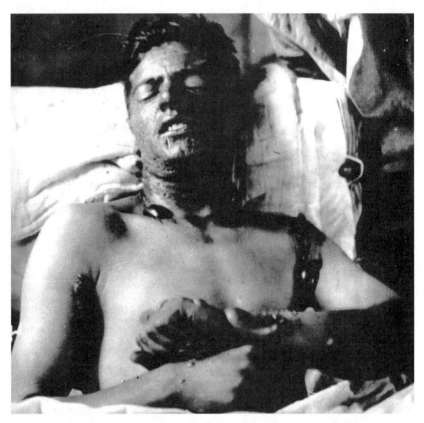

A young Canadian soldier suffers from the terrible blistering caused by mustard gas.

Battalions reached Chicory Trench, a defensive flank facing the northern edge of Lens (see Map X).

By six o'clock that morning most of the final objective, including the base of the hill on the enemy side, was reached. Only in the centre at a well-fortified trench and a chalk quarry in 2nd Brigade's sector did the Germans put up a spirited defence. Here the 7th (1st British Columbia) and 8th Battalions had a tough fight before reaching the quarry, only to be pushed off it later that afternoon. The next day, the 5th and 10th Battalions succeeded in finally capturing the two objectives, but at great cost.

As expected, the Germans counterattacked in force. For two more days the fearsome onslaught continued, using new weapons: flame-throwers and mustard gas. The blistering liquid caused many casualties, even in the artillery gun lines. The Canadians countered with devastating artillery and machine-gun fire — controlled for the first time by wireless radio communications. The Germans counterattacked twenty-one times, but the Canadians defiantly held their ground even when some Germans broke through to the Canadian lines and vicious hand-to-hand fighting followed.

Lance Corporal Frank MacMackin, the decorated boy soldier from Turtle Creek, New Brunswick, who had enrolled just over a year earlier at age fourteen, was once again in the thick of it. It would be his last fight. Enemy fire caught the 10th Battalion soldier in the right forearm and left calf on August 15, and he was soon pulled off the battlefield and evacuated to England, where someone discovered his true age. Despite his strong protests, the now-sixteen-year-old combat veteran did not rejoin his unit. He was posted to the Alberta Regimental Depot at Bramshott before being shipped home in mid-May 1918. MacMackin spent the rest of the war in uniform, wondering about his buddies overseas while working as a clerk in Fredericton.

Amazingly, MacMackin was promoted to corporal and then to sergeant before he was discharged on October 31 — for being underage.[12]

By August 18, the Germans had suffered nearly twenty thousand casualties and gave up trying to recapture Hill 70. Fighting continued on the outskirts of Lens until August 25. Ten days of combat cost the Canadians 9,198 casualties, one-third of them fatal.

William Ogilvie, who had enrolled underage in 1916, had been in France only a month when he and a fellow signaller were ordered to go forward in search of German telephone equipment

A. Y. Jackson painted a night-time gas attack that he had witnessed.

at Hill 70. The Lakefield, Ontario, teen and his buddy hiked nine kilometres before arriving at the first line of trenches. "Although the gun fire had greatly abated there were a few shells dropping here and there," he wrote in a memoir years after the war. "We must have been gawking like babes in the wood when we were accosted by a major who asked us what the hell we were doing up at the front."

As the two signallers stood there taking in the battered landscape and walking wounded, stretcher parties began emerging from the trenches. That's when the major ordered the two young greenhorns to pick up a stretcher and help out. "I don't recall how many trips we made, three or four at least."[13]

Six soldiers received Victoria Crosses for their courage at Hill 70. Currie described it as "altogether the hardest battle in

Stretcher-bearers from the 43rd (Cameron Highlanders of Canada) Battalion carry a wounded comrade to the rear, followed by walking wounded.

which the Corps has participated,"[14] while the British Official History of the war noted that the fighting on the slopes and summit of Hill 70 had been "as bitter as any experienced by the Canadian Corps."

CHAPTER 13

"I SAW A MAN STUCK IN THE MUD UP TO HIS WAIST AND THERE WAS NOTHING WE COULD DO FOR HIM."

Passchendaele, October – November 1917

By the fall of 1917, torrential rain had turned the low-lying Flanders plain around the town of Passchendaele into a sea of mud. Three years of artillery barrages had destroyed the region's normal drainage system, and large pools of standing water mingled with soil and clay. The result was a gooey, clinging, waist-deep morass that slowed all movement and dragged heavily laden or wounded soldiers to their deaths as they struggled across the stinking ooze. "We had sacks and sandbags tied around our legs and ... boots ... to keep us from sinking in the mud. If we ever got off the duckboards, we had it," recalled Private Jack MacKenzie of the 72nd (Seaforth Highlanders of Canada) Battalion, who enrolled in Vancouver at age seventeen after quitting his job as a bank clerk.[1]

MacKenzie's journey into the quagmire began in mid-October 1917 after Haig summoned the Canadian Corps to capture Passchendaele Ridge, east of the Ypres Salient. The Canadians were not the first to be thrown onto the nearly impassable

War artist Maurice Cullen painted this macabre scene of a dead horse and its rider in a trench.

landscape. Since the end of July, British formations, including the Newfoundland Regiment, had been fed continuously into Haig's grand offensive, which aimed at breaking out of the salient and clearing the Belgian channel ports. Sadly, this monumental struggle continued long after any hope of achieving the original objectives had disappeared. In mid-August alone the British lost more than sixty-eight thousand men, while gaining just over four thousand metres of wasteland.[2] The utter futility of the fighting, coupled with plummeting morale and the possibility of widespread mutiny, forced a change of plans, but Haig did not quite abandon the idea of capturing the ridge and what was left of the town on top of it. A new attack in September saw British and Anzac troops push beyond nearby Gravenstafel Ridge where they were stopped cold near the flooded banks of Stroombeek Creek. By then, the British Expeditionary Force had suffered more than two hundred thousand casualties for a gain of less than ten kilometres.[3] It was then up to the Canadians — arriving from the Vimy area — to enter the fray and seize the crescent-shaped ridge and the narrow but heavily fortified spurs that reached out into the surrounding swamp.

While passing through Ypres in the lead-up to the battle, Archie Brown, the young private with the 78th (Winnipeg Grenadiers) Battalion who had dropped out of normal school to enrol, was shocked by the extent of the damage. It was "blown to pieces," he recalled.[4] Another young man with the same last name, seventeen-year-old Private Gordon Brown of Redvers, Saskatchewan, was entering the line for the first time. Picking his way through the town past heaps of broken brick and twisted timber with D Company of the 46th (South Saskatchewan) Battalion, Brown heard the screams of incoming shells as they plunged down on a busy intersection. One of them hit a man on horseback who was less than twenty metres from the former farmhand. It caught the rider "square in the head and the horse too."[5]

The biggest shock for Brown was the deep, sucking mud, which trapped men in midstride or left them sliding without their boots. The putrid ooze, which included pulverized human remains and the poisonous remnants of gas shells, got into mouths, eyes, ears, and noses. It clung like globs of heavy, wet cement to boots, clothes, and equipment. Worst of all, pockets of the liquefied earth swallowed men and beasts whole. Others would slip in and "go down up to the neck," Brown remembered.

"There was no trenches. Just shell holes," recalled Fred Claydon, the young 43rd (Cameron Highlanders of Canada) Battalion scout from Elkhorn, Manitoba, who, like his fellow highlanders, felt like a drowned rat. "You couldn't dig a bloody trench [on account of the high water table] ... so you stayed up on the bank of a shell hole, just out of the water... Sandbags would get wet and your bread would be in the sandbags. It was a real miserable life. It was cold."[6]

Sir Douglas Haig and Lieutenant-General Sir Arthur Currie discuss the course of the war with French President Raymond Poincaré as staff officers look on.

After viewing the battlefield, Currie objected vigorously to Haig over what he considered a useless mission. And although he was overruled the Canadian Corps commander advised Haig that in his estimation the final advance of twenty-five hundred metres would cost sixteen thousand men. In fact, he confided in his diary, "Passchendaele is not worth one drop of blood."

Currie was right; by the time the battle ended in early November his corps had suffered 15,654 casualties.[7]

The Canadians started taking over the sector on October 18. Faced with the inevitable, Currie made detailed preparations — as he had at Vimy, while in command of 1st Division, and later at Hill 70 — to destroy enemy artillery before the infantry assault. He also developed methods to overcome the mud, both to get the guns and their ammunition forward and to ensure the infantry's mobility. Part of that involved moving the infantry into the front lines early so they would be rested prior to the attack, and not arrive exhausted from hours of wading through the porridge-like bog. Thousands of board feet of lumber were used to lay roads and pathways —"duckboards," or "bathmats" — and build gun platforms over the mud. Morris Searle, the teenager who came within a hairsbreadth of having his spine severed by a bullet at the end of May, remembered the bathmats, which often floated away like rafts. "I have never seen any place where you can see as far as you can see with shell craters lip to lip and the majority filled or half-filled with water."[8]

Currie's plan also hinged greatly on the men who risked their lives maintaining the communication lines and transport links, hauling the guns forward and delivering stockpiles of ammunition. Curled up on a rubber groundsheet beneath the teetering ruins of the Ypres insane asylum, Will Ogilvie, the young signaller from Lakefield, Ontario, stared up at the open sky and tried not to think about the next twenty-four hours.

Assigned since mid-August to an ammunition column, Ogilvie was tired of the work and frustrated by the men with whom he travelled. He noticed that some of the drivers were more frightened than other soldiers because they could not get used to the shelling during their short visits to the forward gun positions. The young signaller did have a soft spot for the horses, and was happy to have their company, but hoped to get back to what he knew best — operating telephones and maintaining communication lines. Just before bedding down on the cold floor of the rat-infested ruins, Ogilvie learned that he and the other men would be up early to deliver artillery shells to the guns. After only a few hours rest, the young signaller was watering and feeding the horses before a hazardous journey to an ammunition dump southwest of Passchendaele.[9]

Toiling in the damp misty gloom, the men slipped 18-pounder shells into canvas sacks draped over the backs of their horses. It was tough, dangerous work and, no matter how hard he tried,

Signaller Will Ogilvie was temporarily diverted from his normal duties to load artillery ammunition onto pack horses like the ones seen here and deliver it to the gun lines.

Ogilvie could not keep up. He was soon forced to fend for himself. He led his horse along a shattered road, past blackened trees that had been smashed or stripped of their branches. He saw the remains of an ambulance, flipped on its side and half-submerged in a water-filled crater. "Dead horses lay along the roadside. Broken guns and limbers lay where they had been hurriedly shoved out of the way by the work crews whose nightmare jobs kept them busy filling up shell holes…"

Ogilvie delivered his supply of shells and made it back to his cold and musty quarters in the asylum, but not before experiencing other roadside horrors, including corpses that remained where they fell, along with dead horses and mules, to be ceaselessly pounded by shelling. He would remember the landscape as "an inhuman repository of the dead." Sore, hungry, and exhausted, he spread out his rubber groundsheet and curled up on the floor again, conscious of how far removed he was from the days in Lakefield where he canoed the Otonabee and sometimes escaped the heat by diving for the porcelain doorknobs he and his pals took turns throwing into the river.[10]

Next morning the grim, chaotic reality of war returned when he learned that thirty horses — tethered on the other side of the wall from where he had been sleeping — had been ripped to pieces by a German shell. Now that there were fewer horses, Ogilvie drew a shorter straw and was given a mule to deliver his next load of shells. The mule was sure-footed enough, but while coming out along a narrow, rain-slicked path between two water-filled craters, the tired beast lost its footing and after a short, futile struggle slipped beneath the surface of the murky water. "Just a few bubbles marked his departure and then the pool resumed its mirror-like surface and I was left standing there in a state of help-less frustration."

Further east, the Germans were employing a new tactic, known as defence in depth. At Passchendaele this defence included the strategic placement of pillboxes. After giving much consideration to these and other important realities on the battlefield, Currie planned the assault in three main phases, with lengthy pauses between each to resupply, as well as to reinforce or replace, the attacking battalions. The first phase was the hardest as the ground it would cover was the most heavily waterlogged, including a five-hundred-metre-wide flooded area in the Ravebeek Valley, which separated the attacking divisions.

Hunkered down in the slime on the north side of the swamp, Fred Claydon could not believe his bad luck. He had just returned from leave in London to rejoin his highland unit in "the field." Some field. Not a blade of grass could be found — just churned-up mud, smashed tree stumps, and the half-submerged, pale dead left to rot in the craters.

It was worlds apart from where he had just been. In England, Claydon made a surprise visit to his parents, the same people who years before shipped him to Canada with his older brother. "They hadn't known I was coming home on leave." It was two or three in the morning — "dark as a fiddler's bitch" — when he

Fred Varley painted this sombre scene of German prisoners walking along a muddy road past shattered trees, scattered debris, and dead bodies.

arrived at the small house and knocked on the heavy front door, waking up his younger sister who slept in the room above. "She stuck her head out the window and yelled, 'Moma! Moma! It's Fred! It's Fred!' I had no idea how she knew it was me." Claydon took his "old man" out on a pub crawl, during which they swapped stories. "He knew all the pubs because he had delivered beer to them — with a team of horses."

The two got along, but there was distance between them. Claydon was a lot younger, but he had seen more of the world than his father, and it was soon time for him to move on.

Before heading back to war, Claydon and a buddy enjoyed the sights and sounds of London's Piccadilly Circus, where an "old major" introduced them to two women — one in her thirties, the other in her fifties. Before departing, the major promised the boys the women would take good care of them. Such intimate liaisons appealed to many soldiers on leave — boys who just wanted to live a little before returning to the front and possibly to their deaths. Even quick, abrupt encounters provided a welcome release — and besides, many young men held the view that if they did not follow through they might never get the opportunity again. "We come out of there, had a mug-up in some bloody local restaurant ... and I got stuck with this old lady. She had an apartment and as soon as I gets in bed with her she asks if I had a rubber. I said no. So she dug one up."

After putting the condom on, Claydon found that he had to urinate. Reaching down and heading to the loo, he pulled at the rubber and got most of it off before relieving himself and climbing back into bed. The next morning the young soldier was in terrible pain. He was sure the woman had given him a dose. Claydon told his buddy about it, and the other man bravely volunteered an examination. He discovered part of last night's condom, still tight around the base of his friend's penis. It was cutting off the circulation.

"It was all right once the feeling came back," recalled Claydon.[11]

On October 25, Claydon was staring out at a landscape that defied description. "Oh, it was a bastard," he said years later, flashing back to the names and faces of men who never made it out of Passchendaele. "We were in a shell hole — that was company headquarters — a great big shell hole [near Stroombeek Creek]... It was right in front of this other hill. We were supposed to take three bloody pillboxes on the top of it." As a scout, Claydon was instructed to go forward with another man to locate a patrol that had not reported in. "We got near the top of this bloody hill when I happened to look back and saw this bloody shell land right down in this Stroombeek Creek, and I said [to the other soldier] 'that's one of our own bloody shells!' I said, 'Let's get the hell out of here... ' We dangled back, and never did find the platoon that night. But the next day we found them up on the back of this [other] creek above the water. They were all right."

Further behind the lines, but closer than he had ever been to the action at Passchendaele, Will Ogilvie was no longer delivering ammunition. He had gotten a transfer to the 21st Howitzer Battery, Canadian Field Artillery. The unit's guns had been moved forward into the ruins of the Zonnebeke church, where Ogilvie was introduced to other signallers who spoke in tight, raspy voices: they had been lightly exposed to mustard gas. In addition to manning the telephone, which was connected to the wagon lines, brigade headquarters, and three other brigade batteries, Ogilvie took his turn as a linesman. These unsung heroes went out — usually at night — to locate and repair breaks in the telephone wire. "Three or four breaks in the line were not unusual when there was heavy shelling. Groping through or around the shell holes, letting the foul slime-covered wire slip through your hand, trying not to lose your footing in the dark was a nightmare and you swore that this was a job not fit for humans."[12]

At 5:40 a.m. on October 26, the Canadian artillery began firing a massive barrage aimed at destroying the enemy's batteries. Attacking behind the rolling barrage, several thousand Canadians moved across the shell-torn quagmire toward the German lines along the slight rise that commanded the battlefield. As 3rd Division attacked to the north of the morass, 4th Division's attack to the south was squeezed into a one-battalion front. Despite the obstacles, the assaulting troops made surprisingly good progress. In 3rd Division's area, the 4th (Central Ontario) Battalion Canadian Mounted Rifles (CMR) went over the top on the far left flank of the front. It was raining lightly and the men found it hard to spot the Germans, who had both a strongpoint at Wolf Copse and several pillboxes. Although supported by the barrage and machine-gun fire, the CMR met strong resistance. Some men were picked off by snipers, while others fell to the enemy's counter-barrage. One CMR company was annihilated by a storm

In Canadian Gunners in the Mud, Passchendaele, 1917 *Alfred Bastien depicted a group of artillerymen trying to free their gun limber from the mud.*

of Canadian shells that fell short. Still, the CMR advanced, led by the example of brave men like nineteen-year-old Private Thomas Holmes, who had quit his job on an Owen Sound, Ontario, chicken farm to enrol at seventeen on December 12, 1915 (see Map XI).[13]

Born in Montreal, Holmes moved with his family to Owen Sound in 1903. Always somewhat of a risk-taker, Holmes had a boyish grin, but his forthrightness and solid work ethic impressed many. His confidence helped convince local military authorities he was eighteen — old enough to fight. Arriving in France in early 1917 as part of a draft for 4th CMR, Holmes fought at Vimy Ridge and was wounded in the arm on April 11. After recovering in England, he returned in time for Passchendaele. It is hard to say what drives men forward under dire circumstances. The young and confident soldier from Owen Sound displayed great courage while the CMR were pinned down by withering machine-gun fire. Cool and quick as the wind that blew through his hometown on Georgian Bay, Holmes dashed forward, somehow avoiding the hail of steel. He threw two bombs, which killed and wounded the crews of two machine guns. He then ran back, grabbed another bomb, rushed forward again, and tossed it into a pillbox, forcing the surrender of nineteen men. Holmes was awarded the Victoria Cross for his bravery, and when he returned home it was to a hero's welcome.

Sadly, his VC medal was stolen from his Toronto home in 1935. While he was working as a chauffeur for the Toronto Harbour Commission, Holmes's wartime experience caught up to him. He contracted tuberculosis — an illness that plagued many veterans — and cancer took his life on January 4, 1950.

Staying alive and killing the enemy were Fred Claydon's priorities, but each step brought more peril. With shells and bullets smacking into the mud around him, he struggled to remain on his feet as he dashed forward, sliding from crater to crater. Occasionally, a shell buried deep in the muck would rumble and explode, exhaling a foul-smelling gaseous spray that saturated men's faces and clothes. The 43rd Battalion's job was to clear the enemy pillboxes on the approaches to Bellevue Spur, a tactically important piece of higher ground. When German artillery fire slowed the advance, the 52nd (New Ontario) Battalion, on the left flank of the 43rd Battalion, managed to work its way forward and secure much of the spur that afternoon. The intensity of the enemy's artillery and machine-gun fire did not let up.

"There was one fellow from the 58th Battalion [off to our right]. I was talking to him when a fucking shell came along and landed [in the mud] right between us. It sank and exploded," Claydon said. He was temporarily stunned by the force of the blast, which knocked his helmet off. Shrapnel cut both sleeves and his shoelaces, and riddled his respirator. He picked up his helmet, dumped out the mud, and kept going, not knowing where the fellow from the other battalion ended up. "I was going down the hill when the feeling started to come back. I wasn't badly hurt, but my gas mask was all shot up." Claydon eventually made it into a trench on the other side of the spur.[14]

On 4th Division's front, the 46th Battalion came under heavy fire from the start and lost several men before reaching its objective. German counterattacks forced the remnants back, but nearby companies from the 47th (British Columbia) and 50th (Calgary) Battalions rallied to the 46th and recaptured much of the lost ground. Well before the attack of which they were a part, Gordon Brown and Vic Syrett — the two young soldiers with the 46th — were overwhelmed by the preparations. Huge work parties manhandled the guns into position, only to have them sink with the recoil after each shell was fired. Everything from timbers to bully-beef cans got shoved under the gun wheels to slow the inevitable, and to keep the shells from falling short. It was painful, dirty work and sometimes guns had to be abandoned. "The infantry became so exhausted — not a good way to be when it was your turn to take over the front line," recalled Syrett.[15]

Punching forward at zero hour, Gordon Brown had only taken a few steps when a shell fragment caught him on the back of the head, knocking him cold. After regaining consciousness, the seventeen-year-old felt the back of his head and then counted his lucky stars. He figured the fragment had come from an Allied shell that had fallen short. Finding his balance, Brown rejoined the attack near the basement of a destroyed building where the platoon used a Mills bomb to rout the enemy within. "One poor devil came out with his guts in his hands — a fragment had ripped him right across the stomach." Moments later an enemy machine gunner hidden in the swamp to the left began picking off the men. Brown and a few others helped another young soldier armed with a rifle grenade get into range for the kill shot. "I

Canadian stretcher-bearers carry a wounded soldier through mud and water-filled craters to an aid post during the Battle of Passchendaele.

watched that grenade go up in the air, turn, and come straight down beside the enemy gunner."[16]

The first phase of the battle ended that night, with the Canadians having advanced 725 metres at a cost of half the strength of the assaulting battalions. As stretcher-bearers attempted to collect the injured, several of the walking wounded heading to the rear slipped off duckboards and were lost forever in the mud. Others suffered slow, agonizing deaths while waiting to be rescued by stretcher-bearers who diligently fought through waist-deep goo to save those they could find. Locating a man was hard enough, getting him onto a stretcher while under fire and then hauling him out to the nearest medical unit — while still under fire — was tougher still, often taking several exhausting hours.

Along the way, stretcher-bearers and survivors encountered

grisly scenes too bizarre to comprehend. When Private W. A. Crouse of the 102nd (North British Columbians) Battalion entered a pillbox he found several other Canadians sitting upright, all dead. The eighteen-year-old, who had enrolled when he was sixteen, was amazed to find that none had outward signs of being harmed in any way. They had died instantly, not from the fragments of a bursting shell, but from the powerful concussion of a shell that exploded on, but did not penetrate, the thick concrete roof of the pillbox.

The blast wave was so powerful it had ruptured the men's internal organs.[17]

On the evening of October 29, Private Jack MacKenzie, the teenager from the 72nd Battalion, was cautiously making his way forward over the broken duckboards on the south side of the flooded Ravebeek Valley. "We had our overcoats, our blankets, our packs and a stretcher." MacKenzie also carried ammunition and a shovel. He and the other men assembled on the reverse slope of a hill behind the front line. By 10 p.m., everyone was dug in. Zero hour was set for 5:50 a.m. "Our objective was Crest Farm [roughly 450 metres southwest of Passchendaele village]. C Company, which I belonged to, was taking the southwest corner. It [the farm] kind of came up on a bit of a hill, and then down into a valley."[18] The Germans, meanwhile, were dug in deep at the farm. They had at least a dozen machine guns and a dozen more scattered around a small lake.

To the right of the 72nd, Private Archie Brown of the 78th was crowded into a shallow trench. "We planned it so we would go over the top in sections and not in a straight line." With tension building and the last seconds evaporating before zero hour, the men swallowed and tried to conceal their fear. Some were successful, some not — and many thought about the folks back home. The rum issue — delivered to Brown's 7th Platoon in a mess tin — helped take the edge off. "Each man was told to drink what he considered his rum issue out of the mess tin." There were roughly thirty men in the platoon at the time, and when the mess tin came back after making a full round it was a quarter full. Brown was impressed by the way fellow soldiers — even as they faced death —consumed only what they saw as their single ration.[19]

On the left, MacKenzie and the rest of the 72nd Battalion lurched forward at zero hour, supported by the barrage and machine-gun fire. "The shell fire we had was absolutely intensive. We got our own shells and the German shells. We were caught in between. However, we went forward, our boys falling here and there… "

Moments before zero hour, Archie Brown, who was a section commander, slithered out of his shallow trench to await the signal. It was just daylight when he looked back and noticed a familiar face among the smudge of men ready to attack. There, big as can be, was an underage soldier he had met while with the Young Soldiers Battalion in England. "He was fat, round-faced, chubby and very serious. I looked back and we both grinned at each other…" Just as he got above the lip of the trench, a shell — fired from an Allied gun further back — caught Brown's young friend in the back.

"He just more or less disintegrated."

All six battalions leading the charge that morning were met by heavy fire. On the far left — well north of the Ravebeek — the 5th (Quebec) Battalion CMR fought across the most difficult ground, yet achieved the best advance of the day. In the centre, approaching the hamlet of Meetcheele, devastating enemy fire decimated the 49th (Edmonton Regiment) Battalion and the Princess Patricia's Canadian Light Infantry (PPCLI). In their weakened state, the PPCLI could advance no further, dug in, and held on against several counterattacks until reinforced by the Royal Canadian Regiment.

On the right flank of the Canadian front, the battalions of 4th

Division made difficult progress. The 72nd, 78th, and 85th (Nova Scotia Highlanders) Battalions continued to suffer extensive casualties in the opening minutes, but fought on to their objectives. After swinging left across the pulverized bog, the main force of the 72nd took Crest Farm on top of the ridge before sliding into the small valley on the other side. The rest of the unit plunged straight ahead along the north side of the heavily damaged road into Passchendaele. With shells flying above their heads and others ripping into the mud, MacKenzie and several others dug themselves into a shell hole opposite a destroyed pillbox. Inside the dripping ruins they found a dead German captain, who had maps showing where the Allies would attack, including arrows indicating where the Seaforths would advance. "We were in there for four days — until November 4," recalled MacKenzie, noting that shelling came from both sides. One shell ripped the equipment off the back of a young private named Walter Bloom, who had enrolled just two weeks after his eighteenth birthday. "It [the shell] took the flesh off his shoulder right down to his elbow. We bandaged him up as best we could, and covered him in a ground sheet." Bloom remained there for two days because there was no way to safely evacuate him — and, of course, no one could take a step without sinking.

Six German prisoners hauled Bloom out, but one of them got shot through the helmet by a sniper as he stepped out of a hole. The bullet made a mess, but did not kill him. MacKenzie recalled that a seventh prisoner — a boy of about seventeen — was "split right from the knees down, from a shell." The severely wounded lad was placed in a hole dug for his protection, but during the night an exploding shell ripped him to pieces and smothered MacKenzie and two other men in poisoned muck. Eventually they crawled out of it.[20]

Following an artillery barrage across the ridge toward their objective roughly 570 metres to the east, the surviving men of the 78th Battalion knew they could be vaporized by a shell from either side. Archie Brown got forty-five metres from the shallow jumping-off trench when something exploded next to him. When he regained consciousness he was in a shell hole, covered in dirt, with one of his legs up over his neck. He untangled himself and noticed that his bomb bag, which contained No. 5s, was shredded, his coat was torn, and there was a hole through his steel helmet. He could feel blood running down his face from a gash in his forehead. "Otherwise, I was intact. I figured it was safer to go ahead than back."

By then, Brown was more or less in charge of the platoon. He helped set up a defensive position on the ridge and waited for the counterattack. Within seconds, the Germans began advancing. "They were getting closer and our machine guns had all been knocked out." Without a workable gun, the situation was desperate until Brown's training kicked in — dating back to lessons learned on the Manitoba prairie, where he had become an expert at tearing down and reassembling a machine gun. With the enemy closing in, the young soldier got one of the guns to work, and it was used to great effect by another man. Brown and his comrades endured an anxious night of random artillery fire before they were relieved and sent back toward Ypres. He was recommended for a commission, but his outflow of pride had more to do with his mother than with fighting the Hun.

"I wasn't pleased for myself. It didn't make any difference … but I was proud because I thought my mother would be proud of me," because "I was only seventeen [when I joined]."[21]

During the week-long pause before the last phases of the operation, 1st and 2nd Divisions relieved 3rd and 4th Divisions while guns, ammunition, and supplies moved forward. In anticipation of the attack the Germans strengthened their defences and laid down artillery harassing fire on the Canadians as they assembled. "We were sent up to this so-called frontline to help carry out the

This recruiting poster used Will Ogilvie's job of signaller to
emphasize the need for more men at the front.

wounded," recalled Morris Searle, who was quite appreciative of
the thick mist that settled over the battlefield. While awaiting further instructions, the small party of men noticed the pale outline
of a timber hut. Peering inside they discovered a mound of German bodies — all cold and still except one. "He was a kid. I don't
believe he could have been more than fifteen or sixteen years
old, and he had a wound in the ankle." When one of the men

picked up a discarded enemy bayonet, the young German panicked and started to yell, thinking the Canadian was going to run him through. Searle calmed the prisoner down. "I stayed around that kid. He couldn't have weighed more than ninety pounds. I thought he would be a good one to carry back."[22]

At 6 a.m. on November 6, a bombardment by hundreds of shells crashed down on the Germans, followed two minutes later by six assault battalions' charging forward. The enemy appeared to have been caught unawares, and by 7:45 the village of Passchendaele and the whole of the Canadian objective line was captured.

A final attack was made on November 10, in driving rain, against the last part of the ridge still in enemy hands. Within an hour, the Canadians had taken most of their objectives. The costly twelve-day battle succeeded in capturing the ridge — but it was ground that served no tactical purpose.

The horror at Passchendaele became a watchword for the useless waste of lives.

Over the course of the battle, Canadian bravery in the most appalling conditions imaginable earned nine VCs, two of them posthumously. The cost, however, was enormous. Of the 15,654 Canadian casualties, more than twenty-six hundred died in what will forever be remembered as a bloody quagmire — a battle that conjures up the most horrific images of the entire war. In less than three and a half months, more than 250,000 Allied soldiers were killed, wounded, or reported missing. And although the advance proved insignificant to the overall outcome of the war, Canadian soldiers earned a victory few thought possible. Their determination and courage added to an already solid Canadian reputation.[23]

Many men survived the nightmare, including Brown, Claydon, Holmes, MacKenzie, and Syrett, but few could ever escape the memories of the poisonous and impassable landscape that swal-

A.Y. Jackson's picture of the remains of a shattered copse is regarded as the most significant of all his wartime paintings.

lowed their friends. Claydon remembered talking to one young man just before the battle. "He showed me a ring he had gotten from his mother on his birthday. He looked at me and said, 'Fred, I'm not coming out this time.' I said to him, 'Oh, bullshit. Stop that nonsense.' I told him that because what he said was something you didn't want to hear yourself. But he said, 'Yeah, I think I've had it.'" Roughly three hundred metres from Bellevue Spur, the young man with the ring was hit. The "bullet killed him cold, and he dropped," said Claydon; but the sudden miseries of war did not stop a fellow soldier from pulling the ring off the dead man's finger and returning it to his mother.[24]

CHAPTER 14

"WE ARE ANXIOUS TO KNOW WHETHER HE IS LIVING OR NOT."

Cambrai, November– December 1917 and German Offensives, March–April 1918

Confusion reigned.

Rifle, machine-gun, and artillery fire suddenly poured down on the Newfoundlanders from several directions as they advanced toward the Saint-Quentin Canal. Pockets of enemy soldiers, bypassed by the leading divisions, were firing on them from cleverly concealed hiding places and deep dugouts. For seventeen-year-old Chesley Bennett, his first battle was a frightening, noisy, nightmarish experience as he moved across the open landscape, trying to keep up with his mates and resisting an almost overpowering urge to fling himself to the ground.

The short, sharp fight to gain a bridgehead across the canal on November 20, 1917, was marked by chaos as the men fought off German defenders on all sides.

After the battle, the Newfoundlanders counted their casualties; Bennett was nowhere in sight.

No one knew whether he had been killed, captured, or left

buried alive and unconscious. The young fisherman from the north-central Newfoundland town of Lewisporte had been in France less than a week before he was plunged into combat and then reported as missing.

Seven months earlier — on March 6 — the anxious boy had bamboozled his way into the military by adding a year and several months to his actual age. Two months later he was in Halifax, where he spent several restless days waiting to board a troopship for Britain. By November 14 he was with the regiment in France, facing the biggest test of his life.

Bennett's parents did not learn of their son's status until January 8, when a telegram arrived from the Minister of Militia informing them Chesley had been reported missing on November 20. On April 23, Bennett's mother, Alice, wrote to the minister asking if he had made "further inquiries" as well as, "What information have you obtained?" as "We are anxious to know whether he is living or not." No reply came until June 18, when another telegram arrived, addressed to "Methodist Minister or School Teacher, Lewisporte."

It stated that Bennett was now presumed dead.

Like many other parents whose sons were initially reported as missing, Bennett's mother and father refused to accept that their boy was dead. In a letter sent the day the Armistice was signed, James, his father, asked the Minister of Militia for more information. "Our neighbours here who have had sons killed," he wrote, "have received fully official statements re the death, burial etc and because of this we are very anxious to ascertain all particulars regarding him."

Any answer to this plaintive request — if there was one — remains unrecorded.[1]

After the slaughter at Passchendaele in the fall of 1917, for so little gain, the normal course of action for an army would have been to settle into winter quarters to rest, recuperate, reinforce, and resupply. But before Field Marshal Haig could do that, he had to relieve some of the German pressure against Passchendaele Ridge. Because of the state of his troops, he needed an objective where a surprise attack would be assured of quick success to restore morale. Haig chose the French city of Cambrai, an important rail hub used as a rest area by German soldiers from the Ypres Salient.

The original plans for a large-scale raid blossomed into an all-out attack by General Sir Julian Byng's Third Army, using 378 fighting tanks and five infantry divisions. Once these troops smashed through the formidable defences of the Hindenburg Line, five divisions of the Cavalry Corps would pour through a secured gap — the Holy Grail for the cavalry — and capture large areas behind Cambrai.

Leading the 5th Cavalry Division on the right was the Canadian Cavalry Brigade under British Brigadier-General Jack Seely. The attack began at dawn on November 20 and took the German defenders by surprise. The tanks advanced swiftly at first and by evening had breached the forward defences of the Hindenburg Line to a depth of six kilometres along a ten-kilometre front. Church bells rang out in Britain in celebration; prematurely, as it turned out.[2]

While the cavalry was moving forward, young Chesley Bennett and the rest of the Newfoundland Regiment were advancing on the Saint-Quentin Canal west of the village of Masnières, about six kilometres short of Cambrai. Their division, the 29th, was in reserve. Once the leading divisions seized the main Hindenburg Line and Hindenburg Support Line, the 29th was to move through and establish a line on the other side of the canal, which would allow the cavalry to follow safely. The Newfoundlanders were to cross the canal on a lock between Marcoing and

Hessian screening was used along roadways by both sides to mask the movement of troops and supplies, as painted here by A. Y. Jackson.

Masnières and establish a bridgehead with the other battalions of 88th Brigade.

At 6:20 a.m. the unprecedented and awe-inspiring sight of a massed assault by tanks caused many German defenders to surrender immediately. Once the leading elements moved on, the Newfoundlanders advanced in attack formation toward their objectives. They encountered enemy resistance almost immediately, but were able to overcome it with minimal losses and carry on toward Marcoing Copse, from which they were to launch their attack on the canal.[3]

As the Newfoundlanders fought across the canal, the Cavalry Brigade was in the long single street leading up to the bridge over the canal in Masnières. Under artillery, machine-gun, and sniper fire, the troopers were told to await orders to gallop forward to capture various objectives. Unknown to the Canadian horsemen, the British advance at Masnières had been stopped by a strong German defence. To compound the problem, just before noon the only bridge over the canal at Masnières — already half destroyed by the Germans — had collapsed under the weight of a tank. In response, Seely ordered his machine-gun squadron to work on improvising a crossing at a narrow and dilapidated canal lock a thousand metres east of the village. Shortly after 3 p.m., a primitive plank bridge was ready for the horses. Seely thought the British attack had broken through and ordered the Fort Garry Horse to cross the canal as the brigade's advance guard. But realizing that the overall attack was failing to go as planned, 5th Cavalry Division Headquarters ordered the horsemen back.

The order came too late; B Squadron of the Garrys had already crossed and was out of touch. Although B Squadron had started the day at full strength, several horses slipped off the wet wooden planks thrown up across the canal, while German snipers shot a few more riders and their mounts. Once across the canal, the squadron galloped off to the northeast to capture a German corps headquarters on the outskirts of Cambrai, but before they went very far the squadron commander was killed. Lieutenant Harcus Strachan took over and, as the Garrys crested the next ridge, saw a cavalryman's dream. There, spread out before him, was an unprotected battery of four 77-mm guns with their crews nearby.

The German gunners scrambled to fire a few rounds, but did not inflict any casualties as the massed horsemen came galloping down the hill toward them.

Private John Gould, who had enrolled at age seventeen, rode though the guns along with his mates, swept up in the excitement and exhilaration of a cavalry charge. As their horses surged forward, Gould and the others slashed left and right with their heavy cavalry sabres, killing and wounding enemy artillerymen who made no attempt to fight back but instead tried to run away.

To the right, a group of about 150 Germans stood up with their arms raised in surrender, four machine guns on the ground in front of them. Strachan ignored them and led his squadron forward, assuming the two other Garry squadrons were following and would sweep up the enemy infantry.

It was a serious mistake that cost many lives.

As soon as B Squadron rode by, the Germans began firing at them from the rear with rifles and machine guns. Strachan led his weakened squadron into the protection of a sunken road eight hundred metres away and counted his losses. He had forty-three men left. Several of the wounded died there. Only a few horses were not wounded.

Gould fell after the cavalry charge.

He had enrolled underage on March 30, 1915. A farmer from the uniquely named tiny hamlet of Steam Mill Village in Nova Scotia's fruit-growing Annapolis Valley, Gould did not take well to military life. After arrival in England in July, he had a string of run-ins with authorities for various offences, which continued after his arrival in France. Gould was also unwell on several occasions and received treatment for mumps, tonsillitis, influenza, and endocarditis. He was treated for that last ailment at Moore Barracks Hospital in Shorncliffe, Kent, where he also complained of chest pain, coughing, headaches, constipation, and poor appetite. After ten days' leave in England, Gould returned to the Garrys on October 8, 1917. He was killed six weeks later.[4]

His body was never identified.

As the battle wore on, the Royal Canadian Dragoons and Lord Strathcona's Horse were dismounted and occupied defensive positions west of the canal. At times, the entire cavalry brigade was called on to help hold off German counterattacks. On the last day of the battle, December 7, Strathcona Private John Wilson suffered a gunshot wound to the head that resulted in a compound fracture to his skull and evacuation to No. 10 General Hospital at Rouen.

Lieutenant Harcus Strachan leads his Fort Garry Horse squadron near the Cambrai battlefield, where he had earned a Victoria Cross a few days earlier.

Wilson, a member of the first contingent, had enrolled directly into the Strathconas at Valcartier on September 22, 1914, claiming to be twenty when he was only seventeen. A mystery surrounds Wilson's early life. Although he was born in Port of Spain, Trinidad, the son of George Hector Wilson and Rosa Cadiz, he listed his next of kin on his attestation form as Mrs. Co Smith in Salmon Arm, British Columbia, where he worked as a rancher and served for a month in the British Columbia Horse before joining at Valcartier. His father, who died in 1914, is listed in an online site for Burke's Peerage, but shows as his only offspring William Orde Wilson, born in 1905.[5]

Why John Wilson is not listed is unknown. Did his parents disown him for some reason? Could he have been born out of wedlock and sent to Canada from Trinidad because of family embarrassment? If so, did he harbour feelings of resentment as a result? This is one possible explanation for his subsequent — and serious — run-ins with military authority.

While overseas, Wilson was charged several times; once in England and the rest in France. The punishments were generally severe, either Field Punishment No. 1 or No. 2, because the charges against him were serious, including refusing, failing, or hesitating to obey orders; insolence to a non-commissioned officer; absence from work; and being late for parade. After ten days' leave in England in August and September 1917, Wilson spent a brief period in 5th Cavalry Division's pioneer battalion before rejoining the Strathconas on November 18. Two days after he was wounded, Wilson died of his injuries in hospital at Rouen.[6] He was buried in the nearby Saint-Sever Cemetery Extension, where the cemetery registry lists George Hector and Rosa as his parents.

Eventually, the battle to establish a bridgehead across the Saint-Quentin Canal ended in a stalemate on December 7. By then, the Newfoundland Regiment had been fighting in the area for two weeks and had taken heavy casualties. Like the Canadian horsemen, the Newfoundlanders had also beaten off repeated German counterattacks. As the only non-regular unit in a division made up of regular army battalions, the Newfoundlanders received a rare distinction. On December 17 King George V granted the title "Royal" to the regiment in recognition of its heroic actions both at Masnières and, earlier, at Ypres.

It marked the only time this distinction was awarded to any British Empire unit during the First World War.[7]

About this time, the British government began to deliberately withhold reinforcements from Haig to overcome his propensity for wasting men in battles of attrition. This simple expedient prevented the British commander-in-chief from undertaking any new offensives and saved countless lives. Suddenly, the French and British began to talk of merely holding out during 1918, until sufficient numbers of fresh American soldiers arrived. In Canada, war weariness had already translated into a sharp reduction in the number of men volunteering. Immediate replacements came from the large number of Canadian infantry battalions in

England, but that could not continue indefinitely.

After attending the first Imperial War Conference in London and visiting the Canadian Corps in France in the spring of 1917, Prime Minister Sir Robert Borden returned home convinced conscription was necessary for Canada to continue to support the war. When the *Military Service Act* became law on August 29 it split political parties and the nation, sparked riots, and laid the groundwork for future national divisiveness. In the general election that November, Borden's Unionists won a majority — partly because of the soldiers' vote — and brought conscription into force in January 1918. Although it was intended that conscription would produce one hundred thousand reinforcements, only some twenty-four thousand conscripts eventually reached France, beginning in late summer 1918.[8]

The Germans, fully aware that their numerical advantage was only temporary, planned what they hoped would be their final offensive. It was not long in coming. Deputy chief of the general staff, General Erich Ludendorff organized a series of five offensives to achieve a decisive victory. Despite numerical superiority, the Germans were not strong enough to mount a general offensive along the entire front. Instead, Ludendorff conceived a succession of coordinated, massive attacks. The British were chosen over the French as the object of these attacks, on the assumption the British had less room to manoeuvre in northern France than the French did further south, leaving them open to defeat in detail.

During preparations for these attacks the Germans carried on with a vigorous policy of raids and other offensive actions. One raid on the morning of March 4 was against Aloof Trench, held by the 21st (Eastern Ontario) Battalion in relatively quiet front lines near Lens.[9] The main part of the raid fell on D Company, in which Lance Corporal Howard Salisbury was serving in 13th Platoon.

Salisbury had joined at Kingston, Ontario, on December 22,

1914, claiming he was eighteen. In fact, the former wood turner had been born on August 17, 1899, making him fifteen years old on enrolment.

Salisbury sailed overseas in May 1915 with his battalion on the RMS *Metagama* and crossed the Channel to France in September, in what happened to be the first time a unit had made the crossing during daylight. In a letter from home his sister, who had viewed some demonstration trenches at Camp Barriefield in Kingston, asked him why she had seen so much lumber there. In his reply of December 1915, Salisbury noted,

"Why the lumber is for to build dugouts, fix up the trenches also for the sappers so that they can tunnel through to the enemy's line. The other night we had to carry twenty foot beams up to the front line from the reserve which is about 3/4 mile walk and I can say it certainly was some job. We couldn't go by the communications trenches as the beams wouldn't take the corners so we went by the overland route. First the hail started and it would cut your face then you would fall in about every shell hole you could find, fall and about break your shoulder when you popped down every time a flare went up. When you came to an old trench you would put your plank down, walk across and then pick your plank up again and all the time the bullets were whistling unpleasantly close to our ears. We were certainly some sorry sights when we got back to our dugouts. But still I like this life. In fact, I'm thriving on it as I have gained a good many pounds since I left Canada."

Salisbury had spent a considerable amount of time in various hospitals or undergoing punishment for military offences, including absences, but overall he excelled in the field. He was appointed lance corporal in September 1916, having just turned seventeen; an appointment reinstated a year later after he lost it for six weeks. During the March 4, 1918, German raid his actions during the fierce battle that ensued resulted in a recommendation for a Distinguished Conduct Medal. But, in fact, Salisbury should not even have been in France.

In June 1917, he had been returned to England as a minor, to be discharged. While waiting to sail, Salisbury was employed as an assistant gas instructor in the 6th Reserve Battalion at Seaford. In July, Brigadier-General W. S. Hughes (who had been his commanding officer in the 21st Battalion for twenty-one months), recommended him for commissioning, noting he found Salisbury to be "a good soldier, trustworthy and capable." At Seaford his last AWOL took place on February 19, 1918. From leave in London, Salisbury somehow managed to make it back to the 21st Battalion in France just before the March 4 German raid.

When his officers back in England discovered his absence from the 6th Reserve Battalion, he was returned to England and charged again. His punishment of loss of thirty days' pay would probably have been more severe if his company commander, Captain A. W. Black, had not written a letter to the authorities in England, noting that his conduct during the raid "was a fine example to his comrades and at all times he has proved most capable in carrying out his duties." This letter, cosigned by the CO, probably resulted in the relatively lighter sentence. Unfortunately, the AWOL incident likely still led to the denial of the Distinguished Conduct Medal, although no such decision is recorded. In October 1918 Salisbury returned to Canada, where he worked at the Belleville, Ontario, armouries until he was discharged two weeks after the signing of the Armistice.

Salisbury lived to be one of the last survivors of the 21st Battalion and was one of only four veterans to attend the unit's final reunion in 1985.[10]

For the first German offensive — codenamed "Michael," after his country's patron saint — Ludendorff chose the old Somme battlefield that stretched south from Arras. At 4:40 a.m. on March 21, more than six thousand German guns began a

Soldiers of the Canadian Motor Machine Gun Brigade prepare their lightly armoured cars and machine guns for battle.

six-hour bombardment with high-explosive and gas shells — described as the fiercest of the war to date — along a hundred kilometres of the southern part of the British lines, held by Third and Fifth Armies (see Map XII).

Confusion reigned again.

The main weight of the attack initially fell on Saint-Quentin. All British reserves — and some French units — were rushed forward to plug the gaps. Although the Canadian Corps was in First Army to the north of the German advance and largely unaffected by it, some Canadian units were committed to battle.[11]

On March 22, the Canadian Motor Machine Gun Brigade and the Canadian Cavalry Brigade were deployed to assist the beleaguered British. Each of the five batteries of Canadian machine-gunners had eight Vickers machine guns, mounted in open-topped, lightly-armoured cars or trucks. These vehicles were able to move quickly about the battlefield and played a key role in delaying the advancing Germans. The Canadian Cavalry Brigade, meanwhile, operated in the southern part of Fifth Army's sector, where it was employed in several diverse roles, both mounted and dismounted.

To more effectively coordinate their efforts — and in desperation — the Allies appointed Marshal Ferdinand Foch commander-in-chief on the Western Front on March 26.[12] Meanwhile, the German spearhead was pressing toward the important rail junction of Amiens, roughly along the line of the boundary between the British and French armies. Early on the morning of March 30, German battalions began to occupy Moreuil Wood on a commanding ridge on the right bank of the Avre River, only twenty kilometres upstream from Amiens. The Canadian Cavalry Brigade was sent to recapture the triangular wood, with its fifteen hundred-metre-long sides.

Seely ordered mounted thrusts by three squadrons of Royal Canadian Dragoons into the wood, followed by two dismounted attacks by squadrons of Lord Strathcona's Horse, while the third Strathcona's squadron would gallop around the northeast corner to disperse any Germans trying to move into the trees. The machine-gun squadron would provide covering fire on the flanks while the Fort Garry Horse would remain in reserve.

An intense battle soon raged among the trees, as mounted dragoons fell upon the defending Saxon infantrymen, cutting and thrusting with their swords. The desperate fight seesawed, in and out of the trees, as men and horses struggled to gain the upper hand.[13]

Private Frank Daly was the youngest in a family of five brothers and two sisters. Born in the small village of Bancroft, in a rural part of Ontario's Hastings County, he was living in Toronto with his parents, John and Louise, by 1917. Three of Daly's older brothers, Mark, Bob, and Elvan, were already serving, and

Lieutenant Gordon Muriel Flowerdew and the soldiers of C Squadron, Lord Strathcona's Horse, painted minutes before their fateful charge at Moreuil Wood, March 30, 1918.

young Frank had been anxiously waiting the day when he turned eighteen so he also could join. While he laboured at his day job of munitions worker, he had even enrolled in the city's famed Queen's Own Rifles militia regiment six months earlier to get some military experience on evenings and weekends. Finally he could wait no longer and, on April 1, 1917, just four days before his eighteenth birthday, he strode into a recruiting centre, fudged his birthday by a year, and claimed he was eighteen. It worked, and despite weighing only 123 pounds, authorities noted his apparent age as eighteen years and eleven months and enrolled him in the Royal Canadian Dragoons.

Events in Daly's new life then moved forward at a rapid pace. On April 29 he sailed overseas on *Titanic's* sister ship, the SS *Olympic*, and arrived in England a week later. He was assigned to the Canadian Reserve Cavalry Regiment at Shorncliffe on the English Channel coast for training, proceeded to France at the

Lieutenant Gordon Flowerdew leads his squadron in a charge against the Germans lines at Moreuil Wood in this somewhat fanciful composition by Alfred Munnings.

end of October, and joined the Dragoons in the field on November 11. Sometime during the confusing ebb and flow of the vicious hand-to-hand fighting in Moreuil Wood, Daly fell, mortally wounded. His body was never found.

Frank's brothers survived, although all had close calls. At the time of Frank's death Mark had been wounded but returned to the front, Bob had been gassed, and Elvan was convalescing from injuries in Kingston's Queen Street Military Hospital.[14]

Daly's and the Dragoons' desperate fight succeeded in driving about three hundred Germans to the eastern edge of the wood. Meanwhile, Lieutenant Gordon Flowerdew galloped toward the northeast corner of the wood at the head of the Strathcona's C Squadron. Rounding the wood, the mounted troopers ran into the enemy, who had deployed in two lines in the open, supported by an artillery battery and a machine-gun company.

Many Allied soldiers' smiles would be dimmed forever during the Germans' last major advance, three months after this edition of The Maple Leaf *was published.*

The Strathconas galloped bravely forward, sabres drawn. More than 70 per cent became casualties.

For his gallantry in leading one of the last great cavalry charges in history, Flowerdew was posthumously awarded the Victoria Cross.

By April 5 the Allies brought the German advance to a standstill and Ludendorff halted Operation Michael. Despite making several tactical gains and literally destroying Fifth Army, the Germans failed to achieve their strategic goal and lost a high proportion of their elite assault troops.[15]

The second of the German 1918 spring offensives was originally code-named "George," but by the time it began, Ludendorff had reduced it in scope due to heavy losses during Operation

Michael and renamed it "Georgette." The scaled-back assault was launched in Flanders, on a narrow twenty-kilometre front that ran roughly along the valley of the River Lys. By nightfall on April 9, the Germans had torn a fifteen-kilometre-wide gap in the British line and penetrated to a depth of eight kilometres. In desperation, Haig called on two British divisions in the Ypres area for assistance. One of them was 29th Division, which contained the Newfoundlanders in its 88th Brigade.

At the time, the Newfoundlanders were finishing a four-day tour in the front lines near Passchendaele. As the regiment made its way south, enemy shells fell near it in support of the second day of the offensive, which was initiated by fresh German divisions at 5:15 a.m. When the Newfoundlanders reached the town of Bailleul on the afternoon of April 10, they were immediately deployed about two-and-a-half kilometres to the east. Their mission was to prevent the Germans from outflanking Armentières in a pincer movement before the British could withdraw safely. About 5 p.m. on April 13 a particularly determined assault penetrated a section of the British line and the Germans carried on astride a road. An hour-and-a-half later, they came up against the Newfoundlanders in D Company, which included seventeen-year-old Fred Bugden in its ranks. As the Germans advanced, Bugden and his D Company comrades were able to pour devastating fire onto them and exacted a heavy toll. The rest of the regiment soon joined their comrades and succeeded in stopping the enemy, in one case less than twenty-five metres from the Newfoundland lines.[16]

Bugden was among several casualties that day. The former fisherman came from the tiny but scenic village of Epworth — formerly known as Spoon Cove — on Newfoundland's Burin Peninsula. He had enrolled in June 1917, claiming to be eighteen, and joined the regiment in France on February 15, 1918, where he was assigned to D Company. His time in France started off badly. Two days after arrival he was admitted to 89 Field Ambulance with "P.U.O." (pyrexia of unknown origin), a catch-all for unexplained high fever. This was followed on February 28 with admission to No. 7 Casualty Clearing Station with a more definite diagnosis — diarrhoea. The debilitating condition required hospitalization until March 14. A month later, east of Bailleul, Bugden was dead.

Such was the ferocity of the action during the last two days that the bodies of forty Newfoundlanders had to be left behind, among them young Bugden's.

After his family received its memorial plaque and scroll with the king's message sent to all bereaved families, Bugden's sister, Jennie, replied with a letter of thanks to the authorities on March 5, 1920. It illustrates the pride most families felt for their fallen:

"Thanks very much for "Memorial Scroll" and His Majesty's message in honour of our dear boy who so willingly laid down his young life for right and liberty.

"I may say that we as a family appreciate all the things which go to prove that the noble dead are not forgotten. We feel proud of our soldier lad, our father also died in Aug. 1919 and so once more on behalf of my widowed mother I thank you."[17]

Additional enemy attacks failed to break through and advance any further, helped considerably by the arrival of Allied reserves. After a smaller German attack on the Somme to the south, Ludendorff again turned his attention to his Flanders offensive during the last week of April, where he concentrated on the line of hills running south from Ypres. But the Allied line held firm. By now, the Germans had suffered terrific losses: this was their last attack. As with the earlier Operation Michael offensive to the south, the Germans had gained a considerable amount of territory at the tactical level, but at a terrible price in casualties and without achieving the desired strategic breakthrough.

Sometime in France during October 1917, the true age was

The Halifax Explosion devastated the city's naval dockyard and badly damaged HMCS Niobe, *making black smoke on the far right.*

discovered of Robert Clarence Thompson, the young lad who had managed to enrol twice in early 1916 when he was only fourteen. Now fifteen, Thompson was sent home to Hillier, Ontario, where he once again displayed the same perseverance as earlier and promptly re-enlisted, in Toronto, on November 22, claiming a birth date of December 12, 1898, and noting his occupation as "chauffeur." This time he was assigned to a reinforcement unit, the 1st Depot Battalion of the 1st Central Ontario Regiment.[18]

Only days after this enlistment, Thompson's unit was rushed by train to Halifax, Nova Scotia, to assist in the relief efforts after the Halifax Explosion. At 9:04:35 on the cold, clear morning of December 6, 1917, the reality of the First World War was driven home to the residents of Halifax. Twenty minutes earlier, the French munitions freighter *Mont Blanc* and the Belgian relief ship *Imo* collided in the narrowest part of Halifax harbour. Steel grating on steel caused sparks, igniting benzol stored on the French ship's deck, which seeped into the holds, where nearly three tons of picric acid, TNT, and guncotton were crammed together. The two ships slowly drifted toward the shore, *Imo* toward Dartmouth and *Mont Blanc*, engulfed in flames, toward Halifax's wooden Pier 6.

When *Mont Blanc*'s highly volatile mixture exploded, it blew pieces of the freighter sixteen hundred metres into the air and literally shredded the ship, while *Imo* was blown out of the water onto the Dartmouth shore. Haligonians had just experienced the largest man-made, non-nuclear explosion in history. The destruction was immense. The blast destroyed everything within eight hundred metres — including a massive sugar refinery and a dry dock — and damaged buildings within sixteen hundred metres — including several port facilities.

Within seconds, almost two thousand people were dead, nine thousand injured, and twenty-five thousand rendered homeless, all from a population of less than fifty thousand.

Stoves knocked over by the blast ignited shattered wooden houses. Soon blazes burned all over the city's north end, fed by coal stocked in coal sheds.

Then, the next day, one of the worst blizzards in recent memory hit the city, adding to the survivors' misery and hampering rescue efforts. Property damage amounted to $35 million.[19]

Military and civilian relief efforts began immediately, firstly from local resources — including sailors and soldiers in the city at the time — and then from further away, including the United States and other parts of Canada. When his work in the stricken city was done, Thompson returned to Toronto with his unit and was soon promoted sergeant-major. He was still only sixteen years old — and his time overseas was not yet over. Thompson went back to France, transferred to the Canadian Mounted Rifles, and took part in the final engagements of the war. After the Armistice, he returned to Canada, where he worked for his father in his cheese factory, eventually managing the Mildmay Creamery, a branch of the family business.

Thompson married in 1937 and died in 1950, still a young man.[20]

CHAPTER 15

"IT WAS A HUSH-HUSH PERFORMANCE."

Amiens and Drocourt-Quéant Line, August–September 1918

The bullet caught Private Fred Claydon square on the left kneecap.

It smashed through flesh and bone, the force knocking the young soldier's leg out from under him. The former ranch hand from Elkhorn, Manitoba, had survived the Somme (before his eighteenth birthday), Vimy Ridge, and the carnage at Passchendaele, but the fighting on August 8, 1918 — east of Amiens, France — was his last. Blood from the wound spattered his lower leg and the top of his boot. He did not know if he would bleed to death or be finished by another bullet. The pain was excruciating; it felt as though someone had rammed a hot poker through his knee into his thigh. Clinging to his Lee-Enfield rifle, Claydon struggled to remove the pull-through stored in the weapon's butt trap. He had used the narrow cord dozens of times to clean the barrel, but today it would become a tourniquet, cinched up with a bayonet around his lower thigh.

It had been a rough couple of days for the scout from the

43rd (Cameron Highlanders of Canada) Battalion. Earlier that morning — after penetrating thick fog over the Luce River toward Rifle Wood — a cornered German had slashed him in the arm with a bayonet. Claydon had approached the dugout from behind and surprised several Germans who were looking the other way over the sights of their machine guns. Too late they saw Claydon, who shot a few before another man lunged at him with his bayonet. The Canadian deflected the blade with his forearm, and the aggressive soldier was shot dead in front of his comrades who were promptly searched and taken prisoner. "Most of them wanted to quit," recalled Claydon. "I went through their pockets and told them where to go." Earlier, he had admonished two French soldiers for killing a wounded German.[1] "There was a French corporal and a private. They had him down on the ground and poked their bayonets in him. I bawled them out — asked them what the hell they were doing… The corporal just looked at me and said, 'We're not taking prisoners.'"

Now it was Claydon's turn to be stretched out helpless on the ground. There was not much he could do except bandage the wound and try to stay calm. The fog began to dissipate and he could hear machine-gun and rifle fire, and screaming men. It seemed like his head was spinning, and he felt nauseous.

Hours earlier — before heading into battle — a bizarre sequence of events had him earmarked for court martial. It began when military police foolishly put him in charge of a drunken private. "This guy — the private — was a hell of a good guy. There wasn't a mean bone in his body," he remembered. The inebriated soldier got away from Claydon, plowed through a column of men, and cold-cocked a colonel, knocking him down. As a lowly private, Claydon should not have been in charge of another private, but the military police were looking to offload their prisoner and had assigned him to the scout. Hauled before the colonel in the kitchen of a battered farmhouse, Claydon pleaded his case but was told he would be remanded to a court martial. Once out of the farmhouse, and while keeping an eye out for the MPs, Claydon received orders to guide some tanks as part of the major offensive.

It was the opening day of the Battle of Amiens — the day Fred Claydon caught one.[2]

By the time German General Erich Ludendorff called off the last of his spring offensives in July, he had lost five hundred thousand men in five months. Although the Allies lost a similar number, some three hundred thousand American soldiers a month were now replenishing them, while the Germans had used up all of their troops released from the east after the peace treaty with Russia. Ludendorff had couched his offensives in terms of total victory. When this was not achieved it had a greatly demoralizing effect on the Germans. Meanwhile, the morale of the Allies rose correspondingly. A turning point had been reached; the Allies had regained the strategic initiative, and they kept it to the end of the war.

Amiens was one of the key battles in snatching the initiative from the Germans. Renowned British historian J. F. C. Fuller called it "the most decisive battle of the First World War." During the first seven months of 1918, the Canadians had been largely kept out of major battles. Instead, they were built up and trained to spearhead what the Allied High Command hoped would be the beginning of the last assault against the enemy. The powerful and experienced Canadian Corps led the advance at Amiens, known as the start of The Hundred Days. The Germans' name for the initial attack, on August 8, was different.

They called it the Black Day of the German Army.[3]

With the main roles assigned to the Canadians and Australians,

An armoured car of the Canadian Motor Machine Gun Brigade advances down a road during the Battle of Amiens.

this massive assault was like no other the Allies had launched. Previously, uninspired tactics and strategy had resulted in a war of attrition, where the body count and number of metres of ground gained became measures of success. Amiens and afterwards changed all that. For the first time, operations began to resemble those that would occur over twenty years later during the Second World War, in such areas as command and control, indirect fire, mechanization, tactical air support, logistics, chemical weaponry, and electronic warfare.

The Germans recognized the Canadians as elite shock troops and viewed their positioning in any area as a precursor to an attack. As a result, the Allies resorted to a massive deception plan to fool the Germans into thinking the Canadians were headed somewhere else, and certainly not to Amiens, an important north-south railway hub between Boulogne on the Channel coast and Paris.[4] Two battalions plus two casualty clearing stations and a wireless signals section marched north to Flanders and simulated the presence of the entire Canadian Corps through radio message traffic, while the bulk of the corps — roughly one hundred thousand men — secretly headed south — by train, bus, and foot — on July 30–31. The final destination was unknown to the troops, who received security instructions before their marching orders. These were stenciled in their pay books under the heading "KEEP YOUR MOUTH SHUT."

"We moved mostly at night ... and we stayed under cover during the day," recalled Gordon Hamilton of the 58th (Central Ontario) Battalion, who noted how clear of traffic the roads were during the day, and how jammed bumper-to-bumper at night. By then it had been three years since the young scout enrolled, encouraged by the colourful military marching bands and patriotic gatherings; back in Toronto there was a lot to entice a fellow to join the army. Only seventeen, Hamilton got in by stating he was nineteen. He could have said eighteen, but figured it was safer to add two years instead of one. For him the army offered excitement and travel, but best of all there was gallantry and romance attached to a young man in uniform destined for overseas.[5]

Heading into Amiens, Hamilton was still proud of the uniform and prepared for whatever lay ahead. Since landing in France in 1916, he had participated in every major battle, including Sanctuary Wood, the Somme, Vimy Ridge, Lens, and Passchendaele. "I don't think I missed very much," he recalled, noting his work varied from guiding to observation to sniping. He understood how quickly a situation could change from bad to worse, as it had earlier that summer when he was gassed after stumbling into barbed wire. He had removed his respirator to see where he was caught when the shelling began. Within seconds he inhaled enough poison to cause permanent damage to his respiratory system.

Signaller Will Ogilvie, the Lakefield, Ontario, teenager who had

Not enough French Canadians joined the CEF, but that did not stop recruiting efforts like this one, which called upon the sons of Montcalm and Châteauguay.

spent summers enjoying the Otonabee River, was with the 21st Battery when it arrived at Boves Wood near Amiens on August 5. During the day the large oak trees kept the men cool and, more importantly, hid them from enemy observation. By then Ogilvie was still kicking himself for trading his horse for a bicycle on July 31, the day 4th Brigade, Canadian Field Artillery, and 4th Canadian Division received orders to head south. Under moonless skies and over dirt tracks and rough cobblestone roads it was stop-and-go for cyclists, who often had to wait for the gun and wagon teams to catch up. On several occasions the men walked their fully loaded bicycles through several inches of muck that stuck to the tires like tar. At Boves Wood, Ogilvie was glad to get his horse back, and he quickly thanked the animal by checking its hooves, patting it down, and washing the mud off its fetlocks. For the next two days man and beast delivered supplies, including rounds of ammunition, to the gun positions three kilometres away. Moving along in the dark, "great trees loomed up alongside, making the night seem darker. It was a hush-hush performance," save for the rumbling wagons and crash of shellfire.[6]

One common denominator then and throughout the war was the fear all soldiers faced.

It could hit them any time, as a hard lump in the throat or an intense pounding in the chest. It could also make men crack up

A tank advances down the Amiens-Roye Road during the Battle of Amiens, as German prisoners of war are pressed into service as stretcher-bearers.

completely. The trick was to learn how to manage it by accepting that there was no point talking about something you could not change and that everybody felt. Often the best antidote was a good shot of rum. "The greatest fear of all was the fear of being afraid," remembered Hamilton. "The last thing in the world you would want to do was show fear ... you just had to get on with the job."[7]

For the thousands of other Canadians primed and nervously waiting for zero hour, set for 4:20 a.m., it was time to think of loved ones or to make last-minute adjustments to equipment. At 4:08 the tanks rumbled forward, operating in second gear to reduce the noise of their engines. Their sound was also masked by the usual amount of artillery fire and by aircraft that buzzed the enemy's forward trenches. At zero hour a far more powerful artillery bombardment was accompanied by the sudden surge of several tanks, followed by the infantry. All across the 7,775-metre front east of Amiens, Canadian infantry supported by British armour advanced, wading or rumbling into the thick mist.

It was the most complete surprise attack of the war.

General Currie led with three divisions forward: 1st Division in the centre, 2nd on the left and 3rd on the right, with 4th Division in reserve. Each of the lead divisions had a battalion of forty-two fighting tanks (4th Division had thirty-six) to deal with the machine-gun posts and barbed wire, plus six supply tanks to maintain the momentum by delivering ammunition, water, and engineering equipment. The day's attack was in three phases, each marked by a colour-coded line. The initial objective was the Green Line, three kilometres behind the German front. The intermediate objective, the Red Line, was roughly two and a half kilometres further on. The final objective was the Blue Dotted Line, which 4th Division and the Calvary Corps, including the Canadian Cavalry Brigade, would seize. It was roughly twelve kilometres beyond the original front (see Map XIII).

Moving as fast as they could, the assaulting infantry skirted enemy strongpoints at every opportunity; focusing instead on their final objectives. It took roughly an hour for Claydon's 43rd Battalion — part of 3rd Division's 9th Brigade — to pass through a portion of Hamon Wood on the south side of the Amiens-Roye Road. Minutes later some of the battalion's men entered Rifle Wood just past the Green Line. By 7:30 a.m. this stubborn strongpoint was clear, but only after the 116th (Ontario County) Battalion destroyed enemy resistance north of the road and tanks dealt with enemy machine-gun posts. Grinding through the fog and operating without much ground reconnaissance, the nearly blind iron giants had a tough time plowing over tree stumps and through the marshy terrain, but the deed was done, and by then 9th Brigade had reached the Green Line.[8]

Inside the tight, noisy confines of a tank on 9th Brigade's left flank, Hamilton fed map references and other information to the officer in charge. It was hot and sweaty, and the engine fumes and lack of circulation in their limbs caused men to faint or vomit. "They were slow and cumbersome. I think the top speed was

Strathcona's Horse on the March *by Alfred Munnings, one of the finest equestrian artists of all time, who was attached to the Canadian Cavalry Brigade.*

about seven miles per hour," recalled Hamilton. "It was terribly hot, but they were quite powerful." The tanks were also prone to breaking down, and it was not long before the Germans brought more guns forward to deal with rolling or stalled armour. While this made it easier for the infantry to attack the enemy's guns, it was not good news for the tanks.[9] Those that suffered a direct hit often "brewed up," incinerating the crews where they sat and filling the air with black smoke and the sickening smell of burning flesh.

To the left — on the north side of the River Luce — the 1st (Saskatchewan) Battalion CMR got well ahead of its tanks — and within forty minutes captured its first objective, Cemetery Copse. Tanks helped clear the village of Hangard, and a bridgehead was established over the Luce on the northwest side of the hamlet of Demuin. There the 2nd (British Columbia) Battalion CMR passed through to complete 8th Brigade's part in the first stage. "It was foggy," remembered Private M. E. Parsons of the 2nd CMR. "We waded through that and then the fog lifted and it was the nicest feeling of all, we were just set free."

Raised on a farm by an uncle who did not want him in the war, Parsons ran away from home in 1915 to enrol at Winnipeg at age seventeen. He had no trouble getting in underage. "As long as you could breathe, you were able to get in." Parsons went in seeking excitement, but his adventure took an ugly turn soon after arriving — as part of a reinforcement draft — in the battered Ypres Salient in June 1916. The battle-weary men he met there had barely scraped through the horrendous bombardment at Mount Sorrel; all of them "looked grey and beaten." It got worse. His indoctrination in the salient resumed a few days later when a sniper's bullet killed a man who had replaced him on sentry duty. "I had just sat down when he got hit ... and his head was splashed all over me." Fortunately for Parsons, his instinctive company sergeant major reacted quickly. "He got hold of me right away and cleaned me up and gave me the biggest shot of rum I've ever drunk. He threw me into a funk hole and I was left there until I came to." Well after the war Parsons remained convinced the sergeant major's actions saved him from shell shock. Now, at Amiens he did not notice many Canadian casualties, just a lot of dead Germans.[10]

With the sun beating down, Parsons felt "kind of clean all over," a positive outlook that was mostly justified. By 8:15 a.m. on the 8th, 1st Division was on the Green Line. The attack was going well and supporting battalions were clearing out pockets of bypassed enemy, taking hundreds of prisoners in the process.

Meanwhile, on the right flank of the Canadian attack, Claydon was slipping into unconsciousness when he was discovered by a fellow scout. Soon others were on the scene, offering him rum, which he refused. "I knew if I took a swig of that I would heave up right away." Four German prisoners were assigned to carry him out along the main road under constant shelling. At a dressing station his wound was assessed, and from there Claydon was loaded into a crowded ambulance and taken to a field hospital. When he woke up it was in an amputation ward to the sound of an argument. "There was an Irishman on one side of me and another on the other. One was from the north (of Ireland), the other was from the south. One had a leg off, the other an arm — and they were fighting."

By then, Claydon knew his left leg was gone from above the knee, but decided he would still be able to carry on after the war by helping out on the ranch in Manitoba.

While bumping their way through the countryside and a diminishing haze of morphine toward the coast, Claydon and his fellow passengers were ready to strangle the heavy-footed ambulance driver who seemed bent on hitting every rut and pothole she could find. The young soldier got up and while balancing on one leg yelled through the small window behind the driver, urging her to slow down or "by God we'll finish you." Eventually the painful ride ended in the shadow of a hospital ship that took them to England.

For Fred Claydon, a prairie lad who had enrolled underage in 1915, survived many hard-fought battles, and earned the Military Medal, the war was over; left to return to Elkhorn with a twenty-four-centimetre stump where his left leg used to be and the stubborn will to carry on.[11]

August 8th's final objective, the Blue Dotted Line, was taken by evening. By then the Canadian Corps had advanced an unparalleled thirteen kilometres and captured 5,033 prisoners, 161 artillery pieces and an uncounted number of machine guns at the cost of 3,868 casualties, of which 1,036 were fatal. German losses were roughly twenty-seven thousand men. Crossing the battered countryside, 4th Canadian Division was following up on the success of 1st, 2nd, and 3rd Divisions.

Private Gordon Brown, the young farmhand from Redvers, Saskatchewan, was impressed by how quickly the lead attackers had steamrolled the enemy. His 46th (South Saskatchewan) Battalion, which called itself the Suicide Battalion because of the tough battles it had waged, was having an easy morning, stopping occasionally to check the dead or watch shells explode on the horizon. The battalion was part of 10th Brigade, which was the divisional reserve, and Brown was amazed by what he saw. Death and destruction lay everywhere, along with signs of hasty retreat. In one village he surmised that a group of enemy must have just sat down for breakfast. "Porridge and everything was there on the table — everything."[12]

Will Ogilvie, meanwhile, was on horseback, assigned to mounted liaison. Picking his way around shell holes, dead bodies, smashed vehicles and guns, he found his sombre mood not liberated by the sunshine. He was struck by the "futility of war and the stupid slaughter" of men. It was not the tableau of the dead that shook him; he had seen plenty of splayed and bloated corpses since the bloodletting at Hill 70 and Passchendaele. What bothered him most — then and afterwards — was the bigger picture; the failure of mankind to resolve problems before they turned into such carnage, and the silly belief you could wage war to end war.[13]

That same day — closer to the sharp end of the advance — Private Vic Syrett, the young bugler who had survived Passchendaele after being wounded on the Somme, was still hard at work as a runner. Sunshine had faded to dusk and he was returning to battalion headquarters after delivering a message to a tank crew near Le Quesnel. It was one of several he had delivered that day while operating on some hidden reserve of energy. The day's work was nearly done when a machine-gun burst ripped into his left arm.

Soldiers of the 13th (Royal Highlanders of Canada) Battalion pose with a German field gun they captured during the Battle of Amiens.

Syrett's days as a runner for the 46th Battalion were over. He was packed up and sent to England, where he recovered and moved on with a headful of memories.[14]

Young Parsons, meanwhile, was having a better evening. He and his battalion had stopped for the night, but before bedding down he decided to investigate a large orange glow in the sky. "We topped this rise and there were seventeen (Allied) tanks on fire"

Private Morris Searle, the young soldier who nearly had his spinal cord severed by an enemy bullet near Vimy, was also on the move, but his duty was not at the sharp end. He had come out of the mud at Passchendaele with a badly split toe that, not surprisingly, became seriously infected. After ten days' rest he returned to the 18th (Western Ontario) Battalion, but struggled to keep pace and was ordered to report to a field ambulance, which resulted in several more weeks of rest. Searle was still recuperating when the Germans launched their spring offensive, but instead of being returned to his old company he was assigned to "the bath staff," which transported and erected the mobile baths. "We were always within a mile or a mile and a half of a battalion. We put them up any place we could find the water. It was exciting because there was a considerable amount — or at least more than an ordinary element of danger," recalled Searle, remembering the enemy artillery that often targeted the baths and mobile kitchens.[15]

The speed of the offensive during Canada's Hundred Days meant that the baths, field kitchens, artillery batteries, and the various supply transports were — like the men — constantly on the move. A lot of men grumbled, but most accepted the heavy lifting and frantic pace as part of the success they were experiencing.

The tremendous gains of August 8 were followed by further moves the next day, against an enemy that was far from destroyed. By then the Germans had roughly three reserve divisions facing the Canadians with two more en route. The Allies also faced another problem. While the speed of the first day's advance would come to be regarded as the most successful of the war, at the time the achievement caused serious confusion at 4th Army Headquarters, which resulted in orders being sent down the line — only to be rescinded. Despite this, the Canadians gained another five kilometres before the Allied advance slowed. On August 10, three more kilometres were achieved; remarkable gains won by tough combat veterans.

Parsons, who still had the image of the burning tanks in his head, became part of an early-morning attack on Le Quesnoy, northeast of the main road. Three companies of the 2nd CMR pushed forward at 4:20 a.m. and by 6:30 captured the village, but were soon beating off counterattacks. Following on their heels, the 1st CMR entered the village and then occupied old trenches to the northeast. "There was no artillery and there were no tanks," recalled Parsons. "We went right into it," adding that the CMR "took that field like playing a game of football. A group would start firing and a group would move in behind and so on."[16]

After the battle Canadian casualties totalled almost twelve thousand, but the units had advanced twenty-two kilometres and captured ninety-three hundred prisoners, more than 750 machine guns, roughly two-hundred artillery pieces and many trench mortars.[17]

The success convinced the Allied High Command that further strategic offensives, rather than purely local operations, were warranted. This resulted in three converging attacks coming from the north, centre, and south. In the centre, the British objective was the Hindenburg Line, a great fortified zone consisting of a number of defensive belts, which the Germans had recently completed. As the last major position left to the Germans in France, they had fortified it with every means at their disposal, creating one of the strongest positions on the Western Front.

The Canadian Corps had to smash through the northern hinge, known as the Drocourt-Quéant Line.

The attack to break through the Hindenburg Line opened at 3 a.m. on August 26. It involved 2nd Canadian Division on the right, south of the Arras-Cambrai road; 3rd Canadian Division in the centre, between the road and the Scarpe River; and a British division, 51st Highland, on the left, north of the Scarpe. Dominating the battlefield facing the Canadians were three high features, all held by the Germans. These included Orange Hill, which rose eighteen metres above the countryside, Chapel Hill to the south, and the town of Monchy-le-Preux.[18] For the soldiers counting down the moments before zero hour, it was another anxious and uncomfortable wait. Drenched and shivering after a night of heavy rain, they could barely see what lay ahead until

James Kerr-Lawson's painting Arras, The Dead City *depicts the ruins of that city's cathedral as they appeared in 1917.*

the landscape was suddenly lit by a tremendous artillery and machine-gun barrage. Behind that creeping storm of fiery steel, the soldiers advanced (see Map XIV).

The 5th (Quebec) Battalion CMR attacked straight ahead in a bid to draw attention away from the 2nd and 4th (Central Ontario) Battalions CMR advancing to the north. While attacking Orange Hill with the 2nd CMR, Parsons was impressed by the number of Canadians he could see whenever the sky was lit with explosions. "We made a dash for it and got bumped around a bit. A group that was in the lead, I don't know which platoon it was, they got a bunch of wounded and when they got their stretchers loaded Jerry gave them a burst of machine-gun fire." Parsons never forgot one brave stretcher-bearer, a short kid from Toronto who served as a drummer. After returning to the dressing station with a stretcher case the lad was tapped on the shoulder by a sergeant who pointed to the holes in his tunic. Between breaths, the exhausted young stretcher-bearer looked up at the sergeant and told him the perfectly rounded holes were not caused by moths.[19]

Advancing in the open, between Orange and Chapel Hills, 5th CMR was hit hard by machine-gun and mortar fire, and by Allied fire falling short. Overall, it was a successful start, though; 3rd Division seized Monchy-le-Preux while 2nd Division captured the villages of Guémappe and Wancourt.

Corporal David Moir, the young machine-gunner who had enrolled at age seventeen in Winnipeg, was suddenly — and painfully — knocked out of action near Monchy. He had survived the fighting on the Somme, at Vimy Ridge, and Passchendaele, but here there was no escaping the shrapnel that sprayed toward him. The tiny, red-hot fragments sliced into his arms and legs, peppering flesh and bone. The deepest and most debilitating wound was near his right ankle, which began to balloon. From the Canadian Casualty Clearing Station in Arras, Moir was sent on August 27 to No. 2 Australian General Hospital at Boulogne.

By the end of the month he was in hospital in England, where he underwent more operations to remove shrapnel and repair tissue damage. While they treated him, doctors and nurses could not help noticing the Union Jack and the word CANADA tattooed on his right forearm. Left with superficial scarring and with pain in his right ankle, Moir was returned in January 1919 to Canada, where he underwent more treatment at the Manitoba Military Hospital in Winnipeg. There another piece of metal was removed from his right foot — several months after he was wounded on the battlefield.

On June 6, 1919, Moir was discharged as "medically unfit."[20]

He lived to be ninety-three, passing away in November 1989.[21]

South of Monchy, the 42nd (Royal Highlanders of Canada) Battalion was given the difficult task of dislodging stubborn enemy resistance from the deep and heavily wired trenches between the village and the Arras-Cambrai Road. Among the soldiers participating in that tough fight was Private Roy Henley, one of the youngest soldiers to enrol in the CEF. Born in 1902, he had enrolled twice, and made it overseas to England twice. The first time he was only thirteen years old and was sent home — in late 1916 — a few months after his fourteenth birthday. He persisted, though, and eventually landed in France in January 1918, where he joined the 42nd well before his sixteenth birthday. His service file at Library and Archives Canada includes more than one date of birth, but in an interview years after the war Henley stated he was born on September 21, 1902.[22]

On the battlefield the five-foot-four-inch soldier "was scared and stayed scared," but he also learned there was no point worrying about things he could not control, including whether the next bullet or bomb had his number on it. He remembered telling himself before going into a skirmish or battle that if he went in and came out without a scratch that was fine. On the other hand, if he went in and was slightly wounded he would get to go back to base for a rest. "If I'm wounded seriously I get to go to Blighty... If I'm wounded seriously enough I may get sent home. And if I'm killed I'm not going to know bugger all about it so ... what's the worry?"

While the teenaged soldier survived the fighting on August 26, he was not so lucky on the 28th when the battalion was at Jigsaw Wood and Boiry Trench northeast of Monchy. There, enemy fire caught him in the face and neck. The wounds, apparently, did not end his time in France. In his interview years after the war he described being wounded again in late September 1918 by "five potato mashers [long-handled German hand grenades] all tied to a stick. All I can remember is just a bloody flash." He recalled making his own way out of the line to a casualty clearing station, and that doctors eventually found a piece of metal lodged in his back, dangerously close to his spinal cord.

Henley returned to England later that year and was among many caught up in the rioting at Kinmel Park in 1919.[23] He was sentenced to jail time, but the sentence was later reduced, and he was soon on his way back to Canada, where he worked as a bus driver, married twice, and helped raise several children.

A self-educated man, Henley died in British Columbia nearly eighty years after the war.

To the east, the Canadian infantry pounded its way forward and by nightfall had advanced roughly six thousand metres. Met by stronger resistance at the Fresnes-Rouvroy Line, the men held on against counterattacks. Rain turned the battlefield into a mess, which delayed the start of the next phase. The enemy, meanwhile, brought in fresh divisions and more machine guns. When the attack resumed, the Canadians were registering smaller gains for a greater number of casualties because of the uncut barbed wire, trench lines, and the relentless machine-gun fire.

On August 28, units of 9th Brigade seized a portion of the line, but by then 2nd and 3rd Divisions were extremely tired, replaced in the line by 1st Canadian and 4th British Divisions.[24] It took three more bloody days to capture Fresnes-Rouvroy, and while that was a major achievement, an even stronger defensive system lay just two thousand metres ahead. The Drocourt-Quéant Line included a front line on the forward slope of a long, low ridge. Further back — on the far side of the ridge — was a support line. Making matters worse for the attackers were thick bands of barbed wire, concrete machine-gun posts set up for interlocking fire, and deep dugouts that shielded the infantry.

Believing the attack would be the most difficult task ever undertaken by the corps, Currie called a two-day pause to reposition the artillery and make other final preparations. The attack commenced at 5 a.m. on September 2 when the infantry — supported by tanks — surged forward behind a massive barrage. First

Canadian Division advanced on the right, while 4th Canadian Division moved southeast along the battered Cambrai Road.

Up ahead and slightly to the left, Private Gordon Brown of the 46th Battalion was with D Company when it entered the north-eastern end of Dury, making it as far as the enemy's support line. Earlier that morning, his unit had passed through the 47th (Western Ontario) and 50th (Calgary) Battalions, which helped breach the Drocourt-Quéant Line. During the 46th's advance on the village, resistance varied from light to difficult, especially near the southwest corner where there was intense machine-gun fire. A dozen men from A Company moved out under heavy fire and — after working their way along a sunken road — outflanked and attacked two machine-gun posts, taking more than a hundred prisoners. Brown and the rest of D Company, meanwhile, were hunkered down in their vulnerable posts east of Dury, expecting the inevitable German counterattack. When the Germans responded with heavy artillery and machine-gun fire, the men were forced to seek better shelter, zigzagging in pairs over open ground raked by machine guns. Brown was one of the last two to make it in. Despite suffering heavy casualties, the battalion was ordered to hang on to Dury and to recapture the lost outposts. It was a costly struggle, but the ground was retaken, although enemy shelling and machine-gun fire continued.[25]

On the evening of September 2, 1st Division continued the advance and captured another trench system roughly three kilometres further on. The day was hard, but more than six thousand prisoners had been captured. As the troops halted for the evening, Currie announced the advance would continue the next day. Once again the Canadians had the enemy on the run, but the day's carnage was not over. Heavy concentrations of German artillery and machine-gun fire claimed more lives as the forward troops — amid clouds of poison gas — stared through the dusty and sweaty goggles of their respirators,

Alfred Bastien's Over the Top, Neuville Vitasse 1918 *shows the 22nd (French Canadian) Battalion assaulting the Fresnes-Rouvroy Line on August 28, 1918.*

anticipating a counterattack. It never came.

During the night the Germans began withdrawing to positions behind the still-unfinished Canal du Nord, and in the morning the corps swept forward unopposed to the canal's west bank.[26] It was the infantry that shone brightest in a battle that had called for a combination of artillery, infantry, machine guns, tanks, and planes. The soldiers were the ones who faced the machine guns and shellfire and met the enemy up close in poisoned trenches — sometimes without proper artillery support — in kill-or-be-killed confrontations.

On September 4, Brown, who had escaped the intense counterattack on the 2nd, was out of action after being hit in the arm by shrapnel. For the young front-line soldier the wound presented a three-week interruption at a time when the momentum was clearly with the corps.[27] The Canadians were proud of the tremendous gains made at Amiens and Arras, but overall the experience was bittersweet as entire battalions had been decimated or pushed beyond exhaustion. The corps suffered nearly twenty-five thousand casualties, including good officers and seasoned soldiers.

Many of those who came out alive were disfigured or dismembered.

Others suffered deep psychological wounds that would last a lifetime.

Near Monchy, young Morris Searle was trying to keep things clean, but it was a losing battle. His mobile bath unit had found the perfect place to set up shop. There was a substantial well and some solid infrastructure abandoned by the enemy, and the baths were in use when the Germans "put a shell right in the middle of this confounded shelter." Fortunately, the baths themselves were not hit, but the occupants left in a hurry, "scampering down the streets in various modes of apparel." Studying the mess, Searle figured there must be some fight left in the Hun.[28]

CHAPTER 16

"MY ADVICE TO YOU IS, GO BACK HOME AND WAIT UNTIL YOU GROW UP!"
Hindenburg Line, September – October 1918

The rum and the nicotine found their marks. Both drifted into the bloodstream; coating the chill in men's hearts.

Within seconds, young Arthur MacKenzie would rise from the cold, slippery ground opposite the Canal du Nord. What he and the other men were about to do was calculated madness. But they were soldiers and it was their duty to follow the lead battalions and bring whatever hell they could to the enemy. The objective for the 85th (Nova Scotia Highlanders) Battalion was the French village of Bourlon, some three thousand metres to the east. Occupying the high ground to its south was the dark and gloomy, and heavily fortified, Bourlon Wood. To reach the village the highlanders would have to cross the canal, dodge enemy fire on the shattered battlefield beyond, pierce the heavily wired Marquion Line, and then pound through a reinforced trench in front of the village. It was just before 6 a.m., September 27, 1918, and the men were not in the best of moods after a miserable night of rain (see Map XV).

Tobacco was an important morale-booster during the war, and several patriotic groups organized contributions to Canada's Tobacco Fund for soldiers serving overseas.

Forty minutes earlier, the four lead battalions in the corps' attack — the 4th (Central Ontario), 14th (Royal Montreal Regiment), 44th (New Brunswick), and 46th (South Saskatchewan) — launched themselves at the enemy-held canal from behind a massive creeping barrage reinforced by Canadian heavy machine guns. On the German side, fountains of dirt mixed with splinters of wood, barbed wire, and body parts revealed the deadly weight and accuracy of the combined artillery of the Canadian Corps. The soldiers watched as the overcast sky rolled with black smoke and the red, orange, and violet blooms of exploding shells delivered by some 785 guns.[1] They had never seen nor heard anything so powerful; enough, it seemed, to put an end to all life caught beneath it. But even with this massive firepower, MacKenzie was experienced enough to know that death could come even before he took his first step toward the canal. He did not dwell on the possibilities, but if there was something with his name on it, he wanted it to be quick. The last thing anybody wanted was a slow, agonizing death — suffocated by gas or left on the battlefield with bleeding stumps where legs used to be or split down the middle like a fish in season. Pondering such outcomes served no useful purpose, and a fellow could survive with a bit of luck. The big question was how long would it take for the bloody war to end.

At the highest level on the Allied side, the General-in-Chief of the Allied Armies, French Marshal Ferdinand Foch, had one central goal: smash the enemy all along the front by deploying British, French, and American forces. He and Field Marshal Sir Douglas Haig believed the Germans were at — or close to — the breaking point and that one more massive offensive would bring them to their knees and possibly end the war before winter. Under this plan, the British would drive against the northern extension of the Hindenburg Line, toward Cambrai and Saint-Quentin. Haig ordered Third Army to advance on the former while First Army protected the left flank. The Canadian Corps, which was part of General Sir Henry Horne's First Army, was assigned a lead role in that attack.[2]

The Canadian front faced one of the most strongly held German sectors.[3] For MacKenzie and the thousands of others lined up for battle, the prospect of survival was dim. Even without the big picture, these fighting men knew the shocking level of platoon- and company-level casualties that had been the cost of recent victories. Many close friends — tough, brave fellows who had watched the backs of other men and survived fight after fight — were no longer with them; killed or maimed in the last "big show."

On the plus side, reinforcements were arriving in the form of conscripts, men drafted under the *Military Service Act* invoked by the Canadian government in August 1917.[4] Their greeting on the Western Front was a mixture of disdain and grudging acceptance. M. E. Parsons, the young soldier who had enrolled in Winnipeg in 1915 and survived Amiens and other battles with 2nd (British Columbia) Battalion CMR, remembered that "a good portion of our new draft was conscripts ... [and] they just followed those of us with experience. [Their] discipline was just like veterans'."[5] Like many other volunteers, Parsons quietly appreciated the new arrivals because he knew first-hand how understrength the fighting units were after the latest bloodletting. Instead of nine hundred to a thousand men, some battalions had shrunk to a total striking force of between three hundred and six hundred.[6] But battlefield veterans like Parsons could see also that many of the conscripts lacked solid training. Compounding the problem was the loss of so many good officers, non-commissioned officers, and men, leaving the army short of battlefield experience.

Currie's bold plan for crossing the canal had been cast well before MacKenzie and the thousands of other soldiers moved forward on the night of September 26 and hunkered down on the soggy ground just east of Inchy-en-Artois. The plan was risky because it involved placing a heavy concentration of infantry in a confined space that could easily be obliterated by enemy artillery. The Canadian point of attack was only twenty-six hundred metres wide, bordered by marshland the Germans had flooded and turned into a small lake.[7] Facing it was an unfinished section of canal, which Currie favoured for the crossing. The width of the ditch at the top was sixty to a hundred metres, but the bed — roughly forty metres across — was dry. The unfinished banks were sloped but relatively firm, although at least a metre and a half in height.

Cavalry and tanks advance near Arras during the Hundred Days. Although both played a role in harassing the retreating Germans, the tanks were more effective.

A larger concern was the open ground to the east, which sloped upwards into the mouth of the enemy. It was a perfect kill zone, dominated by well-sited German machine guns and other strong-points, and protected by numerous bands of barbed wire and other obstacles.

While the narrow corridor selected for the crossing was meant to surprise the enemy it was also the reason there were only four 1st and 4th Division infantry battalions in the first wave. Other battalions, including MacKenzie's, would follow on their heels, but that placed an even greater number of men within the perilous confines of the assembly area. Memories of other muddy battles haunted soldiers as they stared at the swamp and contemplated the canal, a key part of the enemy's last line of defence. Like sand in an hourglass, the men would have to squeeze through the gap, cross the canal, and then immediately fan out on the other side. From there the Canadians faced a powerful German defence system that stretched back over several kilometres, overseen by desperate commanders and occupied by soldiers — some as young as or younger than MacKenzie — ordered to fight to the death.

The Marquion Line — situated on a reverse slope, running parallel to the eastern side of the canal — was a major obstacle. So was Bourlon Wood. A veritable fortress, it overlooked the canal and the open ground. The Germans had filled the shaded areas beneath its ancient oak trees with machine-gun nests and artillery. If the Canadians could not quickly fan out across the canal and take that small forest, the move up the slope would be a bloodbath and the British advance to the south would stall. Further on, the Canadian objectives included the Marcoing Line and the biggest prize of all, Cambrai, roughly ten kilometres from the Canadian start line.

The massive artillery barrage began on time at 5:20 a.m. It was a work of genius, and solidly lethal. There was one 18-pounder gun for every fourteen metres of frontage, and the creeping barrage not only rolled forward but steamrolled backwards over enemy positions toward the Canadian advance, giving the shocked enemy the impression they were being hit by their own artillery. The firepower included high-explosives, shrapnel, and smoke — the latter meant to conceal the waves of infantry as they crossed the open ground.[8]

Will Ogilvie, the young signaller from Lakefield, Ontario, was in a forward observation post opposite his battery's gun position. Days earlier, while the enemy was retreating to the east side of the canal, he had met emaciated, but grateful, French civilians emerging from dark cellars. "It was a sad, heartrending sight to see these aged residents struggling to pull crude carts which carried their possessions along the road."[9]

The delivery of ammunition was a higher priority just then than was supplying the men with food, so when Ogilvie and several others had stumbled upon an abandoned turnip field they quickly pulled the vegetables out of the war-sullied ground and ate them raw, stuffing extras into their pockets. Ogilvie's group also went fishing with a box of grenades found in an abandoned building. "Taking my position behind a tree on the water's edge, I gingerly pulled out the pin and threw the bomb into the water. There was a muffled explosion and water shot high into the air" followed by a harvest of dead or nearly dead fish. For a hungry teenager, this was a delicious substitute for bully beef and hardtack.

Now equipped with field glasses and nestled into the forward observation post near the canal, Ogilvie and another signaller used an Aldis lamp in the dark — or flags in daylight — to receive and transmit signals. Conditions for communicating with the battery were poor, and the two soon realized that any serious message would have to be delivered by hand. It "turned chilly and rainy and there was a mist which totally obscured our gun position, making communication with them next to impossible."[10]

True to form, MacKenzie's unit — the 85th — crossed the canal at 6 a.m., the men breathing and sweating heavily through their respirators while trying to avoid the poison gas the enemy released. Staggering forward with eighty pounds of equipment, including sandbags, water bottles, and 220 rounds of ammunition, individual soldiers scanned the terrain for booby traps and hidden enemy. Pieces of the dead lay everywhere — in the debris-strewn canal, in smoking, gas-filled craters, in pulverized funk holes and dugouts, and splattered among piles of shredded equipment and barbed wire.

The Canal du Nord was a formidable obstacle to the Allied advance, but it had to be crossed before the attack on Cambrai could occur.

On the canal's east side the 85th advanced as they were trained to do; one platoon behind the other over the shell-pocked, bullet-swept ground toward the village. MacKenzie heard screaming shells and the unmistakable crack of bullets passing overhead. Fellow Highlanders fell, picked off by enemy soldiers who had survived the intense bombardment and the first waves of infantry that had rolled over their positions.

For the Nova Scotian teenager, no one back home in Hants County could ever come close to imagining such a savage landscape. It was so far removed from his boyhood days in the tiny farming community of Nine Mile River, where he had been born on June 15, 1898.

The fighting in Europe had been waging a full year and a half before MacKenzie — at age seventeen — decided to enrol. "The movement was on ... patriotism was rife in every direction. It was happening all around me. My friends — chaps I went to school with — were enlisting."

A local unit was recruiting, including boys eighteen, nineteen, and twenty, and MacKenzie figured he was "just as old."

His parents, Ben and Minnie, thought otherwise; the boy was too young — legally — and besides he had schooling, farm chores, and a future to think about. Quite simply, he was not joining up and going to war; surely the army had older men to recruit.

Stubborn and brimming with youthful enthusiasm, MacKenzie devised a plan to overcome the hard line drawn by his parents, although he knew a visit to the doctor did not guarantee success. During the physical, the curious doctor asked the five-foot, five-inch lad how old he was. Eighteen, he replied. Still unconvinced, the doctor asked MacKenzie when he would turn eighteen. Truthfully, MacKenzie reported his next birthday was in June, at which point the doctor looked at him and said: "My advice to you is, go back home and wait until you grow up."

Hedging his bets, MacKenzie sold the doctor on the idea of completing the physical and issuing a certificate, which, if signed by his parents over the weekend, would get him into the army by Monday. Pleased with himself, he took the certificate home, and on Friday night placed it on the middle of the living room table. "It stayed there all day Saturday, all day Sunday and nobody said a word. I didn't dare ask them to sign it, but when I came down Monday morning it was signed by both my parents."

The grateful MacKenzie thanked his mom and dad, promising he would do everything in his power to stay safe. He was a tough lad, having survived being kicked in the face by a horse when he was nine — and he had the scar on his right cheek to prove it

A DH9 bomber flown by Canadian Lieutenant W. J. Dalziel of 27 Squadron, RAF, bombs a German airfield at Cambrai in October 1918.

(not that he was especially proud of that).

Fully caught up in the cause, he did not think his age was such a big deal because he knew there were younger lads — only sixteen — getting in with him. "A friend was six months younger than I was. We were pals together right through the war and went to college together afterwards. He — along with another eight or ten [in our area] — were younger than I was."

MacKenzie weighed 136 pounds when he had packed his bags and left for Shubenacadie — roughly twenty kilometres away — and enrolled with the 193rd Battalion on March 31, 1916.

In late April he was sidelined with the measles, and then —

on October 12 — he got his wish and sailed to war from Halifax on *Titanic*'s sister ship, the massive RMS *Olympic,* arriving at Liverpool, England, on the 18th. By late January, MacKenzie was training with the 17th Reserve Battalion at Bramshott, but any chance of a fall trip to France was scrubbed by a football injury — a badly sprained left ankle — which had resulted in a plaster cast and several weeks in hospital.[11] On the home front, parents who witnessed the pain endured by neighbours who had lost loved ones quietly prayed for more such injuries to interrupt or end their own loved one's service, although most were careful not to share such thoughts outside the home.

On March 28, 1918, MacKenzie had crossed to France, where he joined the 85th. In August he was part of the vast but secretive movement to Amiens, where his battalion was in the wave that had leapt past the units that had taken the first objectives. The learning curve was steep, rapid, and deadly. Now — more than a month later — MacKenzie was facing the enemy again, on the pulverized slope leading up to the Marquion Line and Bourlon.

Dashing from crater to crater through smoke, around heaps of barbed wire, and into and out of abandoned excavations and dugouts, the Canadians found some shelter, and from their positions provided covering fire for others on the move. Besides being extremely dangerous, the work was physically exhausting. With bullets ripping into the ground around them and shells screaming overhead, the tired men had to stop to catch their breath and plan their next move, which in some cases ended violently in the blast of a shell or spray of bullets.

MacKenzie's unit breached the Marquion Line and followed the creeping barrage to Bourlon, where it encountered a heavily reinforced trench. "We were on the move… When we started that … morning we were all warned to travel at a certain rate [behind the barrage]." In front of Bourlon, the men were to wait outside the trench "until the barrage played on it for 15 to 20 minutes." But in the excitement of being under fire, and looking for cover, the men forgot to wait and "practically all of us went right on into the reinforced trench and we were in our own fire."

Some men tried to scramble back while others desperately searched for better cover. The options were limited: stay in the open or seek shelter in the same trench with the enemy, pummelled by your own artillery. A few, including MacKenzie, managed to get in front of the barrage — between it and the town — as the crash of fiery steel fell on the trench. "We couldn't find cover because every dugout was filled with Germans who had thrown their arms away, but were afraid to come out. We had to bomb them out. We had to use grenades to bomb them out — to make room inside for our own men in the dugouts."

MacKenzie never did find cover. He was between the trench and the town when an Allied shell got him. It was not a direct hit. The high explosive landed several metres away, but the concussion blew him into the air. Dazed and in tremendous pain from serious contusions to his arms, legs, back, and shoulders, he was extremely vulnerable to anything the enemy might throw his way. But he was found, packed up, and shipped out to hospital in England, where he recovered and was deemed fit for duty two months after the war ended.[12] Back in Nova Scotia, he married in 1926 — and again in 1935, following the death of his first wife. Remaining in the army, he rose to lieutenant-colonel; and between 1945 and 1956 he served as a Liberal in the Nova Scotia Legislative Assembly where he held two cabinet posts, one as minister of agriculture, the other as minister of lands and forests. He died in April 1986.[13]

Breathing hard through his respirator, Private John Cadenhead of the 102nd (North British Columbians) Battalion felt exposed the moment his unit jumped into battle from the Marquion Line. "You didn't have much cover there," he recalled, noting that he and the other men in his company had to settle for whatever they could find under the intense fire coming from the south side of the forest. "You also had to take your chances by running overland or doing whatever you could to get to wherever you wanted to go. It was nasty."

Cadenhead had been sixteen and an inch taller than his older brother, George, when he enrolled at Vancouver on February 21, 1916. Born in Aberdeen, Scotland, both lads had been living at home in Vancouver when they joined. Anxious to follow George, who had enrolled five months earlier with the 72nd (Seaforth Highlanders of Canada) Battalion, John had quit school early and earned "a few nickels here and there" before skipping off to a tent where the recruiting officer looked him over and told him he was too young, but could join the bugle band if his father agreed.

Like a lot of parents, George Cadenhead Sr. probably figured his underage son could not get into much trouble as a bugler. So he gave consent and within days John was training at Goose Spit on Vancouver Island. At first, army life was not what he imagined; instead of learning right away how to shoot a rifle or jab things with a bayonet he spent a lot of time tarpapering the roof of a movie house that served as temporary barracks. It had been hard work, but it toughened the teenager who also learned — for the first time — how to smoke and drink, like the older lads. "After we tarpapered the roof they gave us a shot of rum — first shot of rum I ever had ... pretty well knocked me cuckoo."

Cadenhead's time at Goose Spit had been short-lived. By June he was in Halifax, embarking for Liverpool on the *Empress of Britain*, which provided "three servings of stewed rabbit every day" during the crossing. Two months later he was in France, where many lads his age became company runners. During his baptism of fire he witnessed the sudden death of an officer. "He was just standing there, looking around the trench and something hit him. That was it. It was quite an experience. And when you are a young lad and you see something like that you realize how serious it was … but those things happened and you had to get used to it."

Cadenhead never did get used to it. "It [the chance of being suddenly killed] always preyed upon your mind. You were thinking of these things all the time. You felt every time you went near the line you were gambling."

While at Vimy, Cadenhead had learned that his brother was badly wounded. The news served as another wakeup call for the young runner who, although still a teenager, was growing wiser about ways to survive or at least to reduce the odds of being killed or maimed when delivering messages. "You just had to pick and choose the way you went — go up the trench a certain way and then you'd have to hop into shell holes, and get up the best way you could."

His breadth of experience in the lead-up to September 1918 included the vanishing of two fellow runners in an explosion. They had been with him well behind the line when they were "blown sky high. Never did find them until the show was over."[14] Such violence left indelible impressions on many young minds that had initially thought of war and their participation in it as something more glorious or romantic. But there was no glory in finding just a hole where a fellow soldier had been and it was sadder still if the missing lad was not yet out of his teens.

With casualties on the rise at Bourlon Wood, the attackers still on their feet carried on through the forest, seeking out, surrounding, and destroying machine-gun nests and gun positions, and then beating off repeated counterattacks. By midday, Cadenhead's battalion and the nearby 78th (Winnipeg Grenadiers) Battalion were so short of men they had to join forces. It was tough, bloody fighting, but by nightfall the woods were in Canadian hands. The war would end in less than seven weeks, but this was unknown to the battle-weary men in September. All swore that the fighting had become more vicious as the enemy

YOURS
not to do and die -
Yours but to go and
BUY
VICTORY
BONDS
1918

A poster urging the purchase of Victory Bonds in the war's last year compares the safe existence of civilians with the hazardous lives of soldiers.

became more desperate.

All across the front, the first day of the attack had been a major success. By nightfall the Canadians had advanced more than seven kilometres and were well on their way to the next big objective, the Marcoing Line. It was a stunning achievement, but the cost was high. The advances had also left the Canadians spread more thinly across a wider front. All around them German dead lay where they had fallen, many still clutching their weapons, while fellow soldiers — now prisoners of war — streamed by in shocked silence.

Anxious to exploit the day's success, Currie issued orders for the advance to continue that night and the next day. Cambrai was less than fifty-five hundred metres from the Canadian lines east of Bourlon Wood. Directly in front was the vaunted Marcoing Line trench system. In Currie's mind, it made sense to advance on the north side of the populated city and prevent the Germans from setting up a defensive line on its western approaches. This meant smashing through the trench system that ran on a north-south axis more than halfway between the Canal du Nord and Cambrai. Initially, Currie ordered 3rd Division to relieve 4th Division and capture the village of Fontaine-Notre-Dame, which straddled the Bapaume-Cambrai Road on the south flank of the Canadian attack.

As the night of September 27 wore on, it became obvious that 3rd Division would not be able to take its assigned position on the front line until Fontaine was captured. So instead of relieving 4th Division's 11th Brigade, 3rd Division — with 7th Brigade on the left and 9th Brigade on the right — launched a two-pronged attack at 6 a.m., September 28. By 8:50 a.m., 7th Brigade, led by the Royal Canadian Regiment, reported the capture of the Marcoing front line. From then on, however, German resistance stiffened enough to prevent the Canadians from capturing the Marcoing Support Line and crossing the Canal de l'Escaut in front of Cambrai, where, during the previous night, German Field Marshal von Hindenburg had ordered his soldiers to fight to the death.

With the RCR pinned down on the enemy's front line, the Princess Patricia's Canadian Light Infantry joined the action and by early afternoon the Marcoing position between the Arras and Bapaume roads was secure. To the south, the 9th Brigade was also making progress. With the 102nd Battalion — loaned from 4th Division — providing covering fire from the south side of Bourlon Wood, Private Fred Claydon's old battalion — the 43rd (Cameron Highlanders of Canada) — attacked Fontaine.

Private David Low, the Winnipeg teenager who had enrolled on his sixteenth birthday, had just returned to action after being treated for a wounded hand suffered near Vimy in 1917. Acutely aware of the large number of casualties the corps had suffered in the last two months, the young runner hoped the next bullet with his name on it would not cause any more damage than the first.

Low was young, but like other runners he trusted his instincts and his experience — especially the lessons from the Somme. A good sense of direction was sometimes just as or even more important than a weapon, because without it a soldier could easily get lost and end up in no man's land. His assigned trip that morning was more challenging than usual because he was carrying a crate of carrier pigeons, to be used to deliver messages between headquarters and front-line units when other means of communication were impractical or non-existent. While picking his way across the shattered landscape he could smell the birds and hear their gentle cooing, interrupted by gunfire.

As he stumbled forward in the morning light, it may have been the added burden of the crate, his disdain for the war, or his sympathy for the creatures that prompted Low to free the birds well before he reached his destination. "Luckily we didn't need them so there was no questions asked."[15]

Small gains were made throughout the 28th, and by evening the entire Marcoing Line was in Canadian hands. But the next three days were not so successful. Little progress was made north of Cambrai, where casualties were severe. With his men exhausted and losses high, Currie broke off the attack on the night of October 1.

The casualty index, however, continued to grow.

On October 3, Private Louis Albrecht of the 116th (Ontario County) Battalion helped bury two friends whose remains barely filled a mess tin. There was not much beyond a belt buckle and a boot at the bottom of the crater where Albrecht had been with his Lewis gun crew. Missing the tip of his right thumb and with sizzling shrapnel in his right arm, shoulder, right buttock, and left heel, Albrecht had picked himself up and vigorously sworn a half-crazed rant at the Germans. It was the second time the teenager had seen close friends vaporized while nearly being blown to bits himself.

Fluent in German and English, Albrecht had been working as a rubber-cutter in Berlin, Ontario, when he had brazenly walked into the armouries and used the birth information of a deceased older brother to enrol at the age of sixteen. Someone must have questioned the age of the tall, skinny kid, though, because there are two attestation papers on file, one signed in March, the other in September 1916.

Sent in to help reinforce the 116th in March 1918, Albrecht was a quiet, unassuming boy — whose temper could explode like lava. Those who knew him swore his brown eyes changed colour just before he blew.

On one occasion Albrecht nearly drove a bayonet through a pompous British officer who accused a group of tired soldiers of being "a bunch of malingerers." But Albrecht's passion and athleticism served him well both on the battlefield and before and after the war playing shinny on outdoor rinks and frozen ponds. In 1918, before he was hit near Cambrai, he had been popular as an interpreter, used often to obtain information from prisoners; including one who — amazingly enough — turned out to be a first cousin.

In England, doctors removed most of the shrapnel and saved his arm before he embarked for Canada in January on the *Olympic* and was demobilized in February. The trauma of war, including psychological wounds and the effects of poison gas, remained with him through postwar life. The best times were the fishing trips with a nephew — a fishing pole in one hand, a beer in the other, and a cigar between his teeth. The worst moments included the thrashing nightmares that woke him and his wife Lil. Night after night he could not escape the men and horses caught in barbed wire or being buried alive.

In the 1920s Albrecht worked as a municipal tax collector, but wound up in a correctional facility when he skimmed cash to fuel a gambling addiction. Relatives believe this was caused by shell shock and that the habit was somehow part of an adrenalin rush carried over from the war. When asked by a relative why he went to war, he replied "it was the thing to do. There was no god, king or country. It was just that when the shit hit the fan I wanted to be standing there."[16]

While the Canadians broke off their attack, the British, French, Belgians, and Americans continued to advance. Currie received

On the Edge of the Wood *by Alfred Munnings shows a trooper holding his horse and that of a comrade. Is the enemy nearby?*

orders on October 6 to renew his attack on Cambrai and to link up with Third Army, which had crossed the Canal de l'Escaut south of the city. At the time, the Canadian front was held by 2nd Division to the north of Cambrai with 3rd Division immediately to the west, while 1st and 4th Divisions were in reserve.

Parsons, the young farmer who had enrolled at Winnipeg, had already seen the outskirts of Cambrai. Because 2nd CMR was short of non-commissioned officers he had been ordered to establish outposts opposite the city. One night, prior to October 6, an officer had sought him out for a reconnaissance. "We went past the outpost and waded through the drainage canal of the main canal up to our waists. We slopped through there as quietly as we could and walked around for a while."

The setting sun and dense clouds of smoke produce a dramatic combination as Canadian troops enter Cambrai a few hours after its fall.

The young private and his captain then "quietly stumbled" upon two sleeping German sentries. "They were asleep at the switch and they are still asleep," he recalled years later. "We looked around some more and then headed back."[17]

When the Canadian attack resumed under darkness at 1:30 a.m. on the sixth, the Germans were busy withdrawing to the Hermann Line, a new defensive position several kilometres to the northeast near Valenciennes. Overwhelmed and surprised by the Canadians, the German rearguard in Cambrai was busy destroying installations, including the remaining bridges. That same morning, Cambrai was liberated.

Between August 22 and the fall of Cambrai, the Canadian Corps had advanced thirty-seven kilometres against strong and determined opposition. In the process the Canadians captured 18,585 prisoners, 371 guns, and nearly two thousand machine guns, and liberated fifty-four towns and villages in addition to the city of Cambrai. The cost, however, was paid in full with 30,806 Canadians killed or wounded. The Germans, meanwhile, knew they faced defeat. On October 4 the German chancellor contacted the United States' president to plead for armistice negotiations.[18]

The war, however, was not over.

CHAPTER 17

"THIS IS THE YOUNGEST VC IN MY ARMY."

The Royal Newfoundland Regiment, April-November 1918

Private Tommy Ricketts looked around and quickly took stock of the situation.

It was not good.

He and his small group of fellow Newfoundlanders were in an exposed and dangerous position. The operation had started well enough the previous evening, October 13, 1918, when the seventeen-year-old and his regiment crept forward under cover of darkness along the railway track stretching north from the Flemish village of Ledeghem. As they advanced, the soldiers came under German artillery fire, which had pre-registered the railway line as a target. But casualties were few and shortly after midnight the Newfoundlanders were in position; hunkered down next to the railway embankment, awaiting zero hour, 5:35 a.m. Catching their breath in the cool damp air, Ricketts and the other lads from the Rock did not dwell on the notion that the next few hours could be their last. Instead, they resolved to carry on as best they could.

Ricketts, however, would do a lot more than that. His heroic deeds would be worthy of the Empire's highest military award for valour — the Victoria Cross.

The last month and a half had been a busy time for the Newfoundlanders. During the summer the regiment had slowly rebuilt its strength as various drafts arrived to be trained and incorporated into the unit. By September it was ready for action once again, assigned to 28th Brigade, 9th (Scottish) Division for operations in Flanders. On September 20, the Newfoundlanders relieved a British battalion in the front-line trenches just east of Ypres, some eighteen hundred metres *behind* positions they had occupied two years earlier. In front of them stretched the long and battered semicircle of Passchendaele Ridge, for which thousands of soldiers had already given their lives.

A week later, on September 28, the Newfoundlanders — 50 per cent of whom had never been in action before — advanced in a drenching downpour in support behind two battalions of 28th Brigade, who attacked the ridge. One of the new soldiers was Alex Barter, a seventeen-year-old from St. John's who had arrived at the regiment only in July. The five-foot-seven-inch, 120-pound teenager claimed to be eighteen when he joined a year earlier and listed his occupation as "collector." Forward battalions overcame most of the minor resistance encountered, and by noon the Newfoundlanders were safely ensconced in Polygon Wood, having advanced nearly five kilometres. Then the sun came out, drying rain-soaked uniforms and boosting everyone's morale.

The Allied advance continued the next day. The Newfoundlanders led on their brigade's left flank, with Ricketts's B Company forward on the right. The regiment formed up on the western slope of Passchendaele Ridge and moved over the top

Until its destruction by repeated shelling and bombing during the war, the Ypres Cloth Hall was one of northern Europe's surviving wonders of medieval architecture.

shortly after 9 a.m. As soon as the unit cleared the crest it came under artillery fire, which caused several casualties. Nevertheless, the soldiers pressed on, often moving in short rushes by twos and threes, covering each other as they advanced. As they ascended the next feature, Keiberg Ridge, the soldiers came under direct fire from a 6-inch gun, which was protected on either side by a machine gun, making a frontal assault impossible. Ricketts's company commander, Captain Sydney Frost, quickly issued orders to one of his platoons to work around to the south. Under covering fire from the company's two Lewis guns, the platoon stormed the German position, clearing the way for the capture of Keiberg village by 10 a.m. The advance eastwards off Keiberg Ridge recommenced shortly, with Allied troops moving for the first time through country that had not been devastated. Ahead of the Newfoundlanders lay two successive German lines, the Flanders I and Flanders II Stellung, about four kilometres apart and based on a series of strongpoints centred on farmhouses behind thick belts of wire. In concert with flanking units the first position was taken by mid-afternoon. Recently arrived Alex Barter fell in the fighting. His death was witnessed by a buddy, Private L. P. Byrne, who was wounded in the same action.

From his hospital bed in No. 3 London General Hospital at Wandsworth, Byrne provided a vivid, first-hand account of his friend's death:

"I know that [Barter] was killed in action. He got a bullet wound in the throat. He only lived about three minutes. He is buried in Belgium (cannot remember the spot). Q[uarter]/ Master Sellers buried him and took a note from him to give to his mother. He wrote 'Tell my mother I died for a good cause.' Q/Master Sellers is since dead, killed by a shell. We were the best of pals since we left home together. His last words were of his mother. I made a will in his favour on my pay book, and he had done the same for me. I don't know where his pay book is and should be glad to know."

Byrne's statement was not made until March 1919. In the interim, Barter's parents attempted to find out what had happened to their son, who was initially reported as wounded and missing. A month after the battle, the military authorities in St. John's sent a telegram to the Newfoundland Pay and Record Office in London asking for particulars of the young soldier as "Parents in bad way." No additional information was received until April 1919, when his status was changed to presumed dead, based on Byrne's account.

On May 28, 1919, after attempting to visit Minister of Militia J. R. Bennett at his office in St. John's, only to find he was absent, Barter's mother, Annie, sent a long letter to him, pleading for financial assistance:

A Volunteers Aid Detachment poster congratulates wounded soldiers on a job "Well Done." At least thirty-eight Newfoundland women joined this organization, which assisted medical services overseas.

"… his father, as you know, is not well or strong and Alex was his only child and only help we had in our old age he was the only help we had to look to and now he has gone and left us alone. The way things are now we cannot get enough to live and pay out. If he is home sick one day his pay stopped and every holiday is stopped, and if anything should happen to him I am not strong enough to work for myself. The poor boy always said he went to protect his Mother and now he is gone from me. I would like to know what allowance is for me and what money am I his poor Mother to get. Aint my poor boy's life just as precious as any other boy's, as others got it that [have] other children, but I got no one.

"Please pardon for taking the liberty of writing you but I thought you were the only one that would take any interest in me as my heart is very weak and I am not strong enough to speak to any one on such a subject.

"Will you kindly answer and let me know what I am to do and will you oblige."

Barter's military estate, consisting of $22.48 remaining in his pay book, was paid to his family on April 24, 1920. Two months later, the Board of Pension Commissioners authorized the continuance of Barter's allotment of sixty cents a day to his mother "for a period of two years from date of death."

Barter's body was recovered from the battlefield and interred in Tyne Cot Cemetery, near where he fell. It is the largest Commonwealth War Graves Commission cemetery in the world. In May 1924, a "partly damaged Identity Disc taken from [his] body" was sent to his parents. It was one of the few mementoes that James and Annie had to remind them of their son.[1]

In Belgium, the Newfoundlanders' advance continued toward the second line as 9th Division pushed ahead of its flanking formations toward the Flanders II Stellung, centred on the town of Ledeghem. The line, however, was too strongly held for 9th Division to attack alone. Ricketts and his wet comrades, exhausted after forty-eight hours in battle without sleep, dug in for the night to await the arrival of flanking units. The next day, to their great delight, they were sent to the rear for some rest.

On October 2, Ricketts moved forward again with his regiment to the front line. By then, portions of the Flanders II Stellung had fallen to other brigades in the division. The Newfoundlanders took over the train station at Ledeghem and roughly 450 metres of track along the western edge of the town, where they dug in. The next day seventeen-year-old Charlie Bennett, a fisherman from the tiny coastal community of Seal Rocks, St. George's, just outside Stephenville on the island's west coast, was killed while serving in C Company. In January, at Hazeley Down Camp near Winchester, England, he had written to his mother while waiting to be sent to his unit in France.

His unsophisticated message is touching in its simplicity:

"Just a few lines to let you know that I am well hoaping you ar all well at home and is you getting my money whot I am sending home write and tell me if your ar getting it all write & when you writes tell me if you got them two letters that I wrote you in st Johns I never got no ancer yet but I spose you will ancer this one all write I would like hear from home now & when you write send me a copple of pears of socks and a cake & some tobacco &

tell me how all the girls is & a good fine coam and soote of inside cloase and we is getting good wrobe [grub] hear better & we was getting in scottland & give my love to all tell me all the news when you write good by from your son charley bennet."

Bennett's parents were informed of his death at the end of October, and in mid-1919 his father, Jim, wrote to authorities to ask if his son had any money "on his person or in safekeeping when he was killed at the front?" In response, he was advised that the balance of his son's estate, amounting to $59.90, would be forwarded shortly. Later that year, Charlie's mother, Maggie, also wrote to the authorities with a request:

"...I would like very much to get his clothes what is left and he had a good watch, it is the only son that we had and we would like to get his clothes for remembrance of my son, I heard the mothers of these sons had the clothes sent — so please try for me."

A formal reply from the Pay and Record Office in London pointed out that "in view of the lapse of time since his decease 3-10-18, it is not expected that any [effects] will now be received." The last entry on Bennett's file is a thank-you note from his mother, acknowledging receipt of a photograph of her son's grave.[2]

During the next four days at Ledeghem, the Newfoundlanders resisted German efforts to drive them out before being withdrawn on the night of October 6–7. They returned to the railway embankment near Ledeghem on October 13 in support of the next phase of the battle in Flanders. At 5:15, field guns located only 180 metres behind the infantry opened up with a barrage of shrapnel and smoke, soon joined by heavy machine guns firing over the heads of the troops. At zero hour the men rose out of their positions, with Ricketts's B Company leading on the right and D Company on the left. Success came quickly as three German pillboxes, each manned by fifteen to twenty soldiers, were

Mary Riter Hamilton's painting shows the interior of a reinforced dugout in Flanders.

outflanked and silenced. Suddenly, the battlefield was plunged into darkness. Artillery smoke had combined with a typical Flanders heavy ground mist to produce an almost impenetrable fog. With visibility reduced to less than a metre, soldiers could not even see their own feet. Split into small groups of two or three, the men kept in touch with each other by shouting.

While the Newfoundlanders could at least continue to grope forward, the effect on the Germans was worse. Deprived of their visibility, they were also denied use of their prime weapon in the defence, the deadly machine gun. Although Ricketts and the regiment continued to move forward, their advance was slowed by the murky gloom, numerous small streams that crossed their path, and several new wire entanglements. In the process, a large number of German prisoners were captured and escorted to the rear.

A newly promoted Sergeant Tommy Ricketts wears his Victoria Cross and French Croix de guerre avec étoile de vermeil. Ricketts generally shunned publicity all his life.

By mid-morning a breeze sprang up, strong enough to disperse the smoke and mist. It revealed the Wulfdambeek, a stream winding diagonally across the Newfoundlanders' axis of advance, nearly two metres deep in some places and too wide to jump. There was no choice but to cross it, in bright sunshine and in full view of the enemy. And so they did, some by swimming and some by wading, in the process sustaining heavy losses from artillery fire. Once across, Ricketts and his companions advanced another nine hundred metres to a farm on a ridge. There, direct enemy shelling from a battery on a feature known as Drie-Masten, about 550 metres away to the southeast, pinned them down. A call for artillery fire to deal with the Germans went unanswered; the regiment had outrun its own artillery support.

Casualties began to mount.

Ricketts volunteered to go forward with his platoon commander, Lieutenant Stanley Newman, and a small group of men with a Lewis gun to try to outflank the German position to the right. The soldiers advanced in quick rushes, under heavy enemy fire, until they were roughly 275 metres from the German battery. There, within point-blank range of the field guns and under fire from the battery's protective machine guns, they ran out of Lewis gun ammunition. At the same time, the Germans brought up horse teams in an attempt to get their guns away before the Newfoundlanders could assault their position.

Without hesitation, Ricketts dashed back ninety metres to the closest section of B Company, picked up some ammunition, and ran back to his Lewis gun, all under concerted machine-gun fire. With the additional ammunition, Ricketts, supported by some well-placed rifle fire from his section commander, Lance Corporal Matthew Brazil (the only other unwounded New- foundlander), forced the Germans back to some farm buildings. Ricketts's platoon then advanced on the enemy without sus- taining any more casualties. In the process, they captured four field guns, four machine guns, and eight prisoners, soon after- wards adding a fifth field gun to the tally.

With the battery out of the way, the regiment regrouped and continued its advance. But they were not to move much farther before they ran into a more heavily defended position roughly a kilometre and a half to the east. At dusk, the Newfoundlanders dug in for the night. It had been another successful day; they captured five hundred prisoners, ninety-four machine guns, eight field guns, and a large quantity of ammunition. As always, it came at a cost; and the next day the regiment mustered only three hundred rifles. Fortunately the end was near and the advance continued against sporadic opposition.

During the fighting after Ricketts's brave act, Private John Russell was killed in action on October 20. The Bay Roberts fisherman had enrolled earlier that year on February 28, joined the unit in the field on September 6, and was assigned to C Company. A big lad at five-feet-eleven-and-a-half inches and 160 pounds, Russell had no trouble convincing authorities he was eighteen years and one month old. In fact, he was only sixteen when he died, having served less than eight months.

Led by their commanding officer, Lieutenant-Colonel A. E. Barnard (right), and Captain Arthur Raley, the Royal Newfoundland Regiment crosses the Rhine, December 13, 1918.

Russell's body was never found; he is commemorated on the Beaumont-Hamel Memorial.

His parents received $23.75 as the balance of their son's estate.[3]

On October 26, the Newfoundlanders handed over their front-line positions for the last time and marched to the rear. In B Company, only Ricketts and forty-five others remained. After the Armistice of November 11, the Newfoundlanders became part of the British Army of Occupation and began a long move eastwards. They marched into Germany on December 4 and crossed the Rhine into their assigned bridgehead at Cologne on December 13. Two days before Christmas, the Newfoundlanders received the welcome news on a regimental parade that Ricketts was to receive the VC for his heroism at Drie-Masten.[4]

Like so many other young boys, Tommy Ricketts lied about his age to get into the army.

Born in Middle Arm, a small community on the Avalon Peninsula a few kilometres southwest of St. John's, on April 15, 1901, he was the son of John Ricketts, a fisherman, and Amelia Castle.[5] His mother died when he was young and Tommy's sister Rachel helped raised him for a few years. That — along with the fact his father was serving a prison sentence at the time — is likely the reason Tommy designated her as the recipient of the standard allotment of sixty cents a day from his pay, which most soldiers started on enlistment.[6] Tommy attended school in Middle Arm and enrolled in the Newfoundland Regiment on September 2, 1916, signing his attestation form with an "X." He gave his age as eighteen years and three months, much older than his real age of fifteen years and four months, and so was able to follow his older brother, George, who had joined more than a year before. While Ricketts was on guard duty at the regimental depot in St. John's before going overseas, the RSM discovered he had been drinking and charged him with being drunk on picket. Perhaps taking his youthfulness into account, Major Alexander Montgomerie, the officer commanding the depot, had let him off with an admonishment.[7]

On January 31, 1917, Ricketts sailed overseas on the SS *Florizel*, the same ship that carried the First Five Hundred to Britain, arriving in Ayr to begin training. In mid-June he had crossed the Channel to the Western Front, joined his regiment in France on July 2, and immediately went into the trenches. During the fighting to break through the heavily defended Marcoing Line near Cambrai on November 20, Ricketts was severely wounded in the right thigh by a rifle bullet. He was treated at 48th Casualty Clearing Station and admitted to 89th Field Ambulance the next

Wounded Newfoundland Regiment soldiers convalesce on the grounds of the Wandsworth Hospital, London, about 1916.

day, before being transferred to No. 1 Canadian General Hospital at Étaples (known to the soldiers as "eat-apples"). On November 28, he was admitted to No. 3 London General Hospital at Wandsworth, where many other Newfoundland soldiers were treated. While Tommy was there recovering from his injury, his brother was killed two weeks later in the same long battle in which Ricketts had been wounded. George has no known grave; his name is engraved on the Caribou Memorial at Beaumont-Hamel. Once his wound healed, in mid-December, Ricketts was attached to the regimental depot to recover. From there, he was eventually sent back to France and rejoined the regiment on April 30, having missed the heavy fighting at Masnières and Bailleul.

On the day before Ricketts got back to his unit, because of their heavy losses at Bailleul the Newfoundlanders had been withdrawn from the front line along with 29th Division — with which the regiment had served since Gallipoli — for rest and replacements near the base depot at Étaples. Ricketts's division commander,

Major-General D. E. Cayley, noted in his farewell tribute, "I wish to place on record my very great regret at their withdrawal from a division in which they have served so long and brilliantly . . . the battalion has shown itself to be, under all circumstances of good and bad fortune, a splendid fighting unit . . . they have consistently maintained the highest standard of fighting efficiency and determination."

When Ricketts rejoined his unit, the Newfoundlanders relieved 1st Battalion, the Honourable Artillery Company, in providing guards for Sir Douglas Haig's headquarters at nearby Montreuil. Soldiers were billeted a short distance away in the village of Écuires and those selected for guard duty paraded in the village square for inspection every morning. Ricketts's officers remembered him as "a good soldier — smartly turned out, obedient, efficient." About the same time as this duty came to an end in early September, Ricketts received a disconcerting message from the authorities in Newfoundland regarding the pay allotment of sixty cents a day he had assigned to his sister. His father, John, "an old man of 77 or 78 years of age" had just been released from the penitentiary "in a helpless and destitute state" after serving "something like four years." The elder Ricketts could not understand why he "cannot get the allotment that is sent to Rachel monthly," especially as she was "married to a young man with no family" and he (the father) "has not the means of buying a mouthful of food and unable to earn anything." Officials noted that it was entirely up to Ricketts to decide the beneficiary of his allotment.

Whatever dilemma this request may have caused Ricketts, he dutifully changed the allotment from his sister to his father.[8]

Tommy Ricketts's Victoria Cross investiture was held on January 21, 1919, at Sandringham, the country estate of King George V. Sergeant James Dunphy accompanied the young hero. Because the king and queen were in mourning for Prince John, their youngest son, who had died only the day before, the ceremony was a private one. John afterwards was referred to as the Lost Prince, because he was kept in seclusion for most of his life due to epilepsy and the Royal Family's embarrassment over it. Rather than delay Ricketts's early return to Newfoundland and demobilization, the king agreed to a special investiture on the estate at York Cottage, where Prince John had been born thirteen years earlier.

Dressed in civilian clothes, the king read aloud the citation for the award as published in the *London Gazette* just two weeks earlier. He then pinned the VC on Ricketts's chest and, turning to the small group in attendance, remarked, "This is the youngest VC in my army." Coincidentally, the second-oldest living VC recipient was also there. General Sir Dighton Probyn, comptroller to Queen Alexandra, was eighty-five and had earned his VC during the Indian Mutiny more than sixty years earlier. The next day the king wrote in his diary, "Yesterday I gave the VC to Private Ricketts, Newfoundland Regiment, who is only 17½ now, a splendid boy."

Ricketts was the youngest soldier from Canada (or a territory that eventually became part of Canada) to receive the VC, as well as the youngest army recipient in a combatant role in the history of the medal.[9]

After the simple ceremony, Queen Mary suggested a walk in Sandringham's gardens, and she, the king, and Princess Mary (who forty-four years later became the Royal Newfoundland Regiment's colonel-in-chief) took their guests outside. In the garden, the queen plucked a white rose and gave it to the young hero. Then it was off by car to the train station. As they drove slowly down the gravelled drive, one by one the soldiers comprising the Royal Guard who lined the driveway came smartly to attention as the car passed — a mark of respect for Ricketts's achievement. The next day, the *Daily Mirror* (London) interviewed the "fresh-faced, fair-haired young soldier." The normally reticent Ricketts — years later Dunphy recalled that "he wasn't a man of few words, he was a man of no words at all" — was quoted as saying that he was quite nervous, but the king's "kind manner soon put me at my ease."[10]

In addition to the award of the VC, the army promoted Ricketts to sergeant on January 29. In early February, he returned to St. John's on the SS *Corsican*, a few months before the regiment arrived. One of the first people to greet him was a young reporter from the *Evening Telegram* who rowed out to the troopship as it rode at anchor in the harbour overnight before disembarking its passengers the next morning. Ricketts was his normal shy and retiring self, but the reporter managed to get the story of his exploit out of him, including a rough map of the area where the action occurred. The reporter spent the rest of the night writing it up. The next day the story appeared under the largest banner headlines possible: "DEED THAT WON THE EMPIRE! HOW RICKETTS WON THE VC. THE HERO INTERVIEWED BY THE TELEGRAM."

The reporter was a man who was to become a celebrity himself in future years as Newfoundland's most famous son — Joey Smallwood.

When Ricketts came ashore, the citizens of St. John's gave him a tumultuous reception. He was carried from the Furness-Withy Pier up to Water Street, where a sleigh and pair of horses met him to take him to various receptions throughout the city. A number of spectators did not feel this was an appropriate welcome, so they unhitched the horses and pulled the sleigh themselves through the city streets behind several marching bands as the citizenry cheered. At one of the receptions, Ricketts received an illuminated address.[11]

In 1920, Newfoundland's governor general presented Ricketts with $500 on behalf of G. W. B. Ayre, who in December 1915 promised that amount to the Newfoundland soldier and sailor who earned the highest award during the war and survived.[12] That same year Ricketts returned to school, entering Bishop Feild College, then Memorial University College. On graduation he was employed at McMurdo's Drugstore, where he passed his pharmacy exams. He eventually opened his own drugstore on Water Street at the corner of Job, where his daughter, Dolda, also a trained pharmacist, worked with him for nearly two years. In August 1923, the British War Office somewhat belatedly advised Ricketts that he had been granted a ten pound annual allowance (awarded to all Victoria Cross recipients), backdated to the date of his heroic act.[13]

A modest, quiet, and introverted individual before the war, he became even more so afterwards — probably because of his wartime experience. Ricketts continued to shun publicity and seemed to draw further into a protective shell. He refused to give interviews, have his photograph taken, or appear in public. He did however, travel to London in 1929 to attend a reunion dinner given by the British Legion in the House of Lords for VC recipients. While there, he laid a wreath of poppies at the Cenotaph in Whitehall on behalf of the Great War Veterans' Association of Newfoundland. His refusal to make public appearances extended even to royal visits. He politely declined invitations to functions during the visit of then Princess Elizabeth in 1951, and then again during the first official visit of Princess Mary as his regiment's new colonel-in-chief in 1964.

Ricketts was not a well man and had a serious heart attack in his mid-forties. He was in pain much of the time and his wife Edna used to drive him to his drugstore daily. On February 10, 1967, Edna had just checked on him when, about an hour later, he collapsed on the floor of the store and died of a sudden heart attack.

The war hero who had survived two years of fighting on

the Western Front was two months shy of his sixty-sixth birthday.

The young reporter who interviewed the returning soldier forty-eight years earlier was now premier of Newfoundland. Joey Smallwood and his government decreed a full state funeral to honour Ricketts, with the lieutenant-governor, premier, Supreme Court judges, and other dignitaries in attendance. After lying in state and a funeral at St. Thomas's Church, Ricketts's coffin was placed on a gun carriage and escorted to the Anglican Cemetery on Forest Road, where he was buried. His headstone notes he was "awarded the Victoria Cross in action with the Royal Newfoundland Regiment."

A rare photograph of Tommy Ricketts taken in his drugstore in 1957. He collapsed and died of a sudden heart attack there ten years later.

For many years Ricketts's VC and other medals remained the property of his family and were on display in the Newfoundland Naval and Military Museum in the Confederation Building. Throughout his lifetime, Ricketts insisted his medals were never to be sold for profit. On October 22, 2003, his ninety-year-old widow, son Thomas, and daughter Dolda Clarke, donated his VC and other medals to the Canadian War Museum, almost eighty-five years to the day after the act that earned Ricketts the prestigious award.

There are a number of tributes to Ricketts in Newfoundland.

Schools and other public buildings in the Middle Arm area were named after him, but the village has been deserted since the late 1940s. There was also an ice rink in Baie Verte named in his honour. In 1972, the mayor of St. John's unveiled a plaque on the site of his Water Street drugstore, which had been torn down in the late 1960s. It commemorates Ricketts as "Soldier – Pharmacist – Citizen." But perhaps the best testimony to Tommy Ricketts is the quotation engraved at the foot of his black granite headstone, which also bears an etching of the Victoria Cross. It is the motto of the Church Lads' Brigade to which he had belonged all those years ago: "Fight the Good Fight."

That he did.

CHAPTER 18

"THERE WAS SOME JUMPING AROUND AND THINGS LIKE THAT ... BUT I WAS KIND OF FED UP, GLAD IT WAS OVER."

The End of the War, November 1918 – June 1919

Private David Low was taking a breather.

Beneath the thinning clouds of war, the young soldier — who had enrolled in Winnipeg on his sixteenth birthday — entered a little house along the main street of Valenciennes. Inside, he and a few buddies discovered a closet full of ladies' dresses. Drinking beer from a liberated barrel, which they had rolled into the house, some of the soldiers paused long enough to pull the colourful dresses over their oily heads and unwashed bodies. Raw jokes, lyrics, and laughter filled the room as they bowed to each other and took up the dance while another man played piano.[1]

🍁

After the fall of Cambrai in early October, the Germans continued their withdrawal to positions on the new Hermann Line, roughly twenty-five kilometres northeast of the Canadian Corps.

Lieutenant-General Sir Arthur Currie was the first Canadian to command a corps. He was one of the finest military leaders this country has ever produced.

When patrols confirmed the enemy had left only rear-guards behind, the Canadians resumed their advance on October 17. Caution became the watchword, but there was now a definite feeling by all ranks that the end was near.

During the next week, the corps pressed deeper into the industrial coal regions of France, which included towns and cities that were less damaged and a lot more populated than the ones left behind. The Canadians faced light opposition but their progress was hindered by demolished bridges, ripped-up railroads, and cratered streets. These obstacles particularly delayed the movement forward of artillery guns and ammunition, as well as a vast array of other supplies, including water and fuel. The rain and cooler temperatures that greeted the hungry troops on their long marches were offset by spontaneous and joyful receptions at liberated villages (see Map XVI).

Wherever they went, the Canadians were hugged, kissed, and treated like heroes by people who had spent four years under harsh German occupation, and who had been robbed of what little food they had by the retreating enemy. In one village east of Douai the Germans had taken every cow, pig, sheep, and chicken they could find on fields and in farmyards. The plight of the liberated but starving masses placed added pressure on the Canadian Army's logistical capabilities. Its own food supply system lagged well behind the forward troops.[2] Through it all, however, scenes of generosity played out from one town to the next as soldiers willingly shared their meagre rations with civilians.[3]

Thomas Hazlitt, who enrolled at Valcartier on September 22, 1914, at the age of seventeen, had been on the Western Front with the Canadian Motor Machine Gun Brigade since late June 1915.

The Toronto teen had left home without telling his mother, but when she learned of her youngest child's whereabouts she contacted Valcartier and demanded his immediate release. The authorities agreed, but before Hazlitt could be formally discharged he took advantage of an opportunity to board a ship bound for England.

Any further attempts by his mother to gain his release were ignored or buried in bureaucracy.

While crossing the North Atlantic in a ship loaded with horses and other soldiers, Hazlitt toughed it out and got used to the food, and the smells. His voluntary service was indeed part of a larger, nobler cause spiced with adventure, but it was a life far removed from the days of being "fussed over and petted" as child. Years later, in an interview with the CBC, he recalled that even with his delicate stomach he got used to eating porridge without cream or sugar on board the ship.

In England and in war-torn France, the teenager soldiered through the unpredictable nature of war, relying — just as other men had — on experience and luck. For him there had been no turning back as he marked one birthday after another; moving through the latter stages of adolescence on a rotting landscape that claimed thousands of boys his age.

A lot of what Hazlitt witnessed occurred while he was wedged between two machine guns in one of Raymond Brutinel's bizarre-looking armoured cars. The car's armour was between two and a half and five centimetres thick, but the crew was still at risk of being hit by shrapnel or small arms fire because it had no covered top. Hazlitt compared it to an open "sardine can on wheels."

During the enemy's massive 1918 spring offensive, Hazlitt witnessed the sad and defeated demeanour of refugees streaming westwards out of Villers Bretonneux, ahead of the advancing Germans. By October he had switched from armoured cars to motorcycles, running cross-country errands while attached to the Canadian Light Horse as a dispatch rider. He remembered that the brigade had "fifty motorcycles" and "five of us — the best drivers — used to get five machines a week as replacements."

Now, assigned to deliver a message to the town of Béthune, some sixty-five kilometres northwest of Cambrai on the other side of Lens, Hazlitt kicked off in a swirl of dust over the shattered landscape. He skirted slag heaps, roofless farmhouses, charred vehicles, and passed one smashed village after another. "Every crossroad was blown up, every bridge was blown up and the only place I had any trouble was going over the freight yard at Douai." That large town was deserted and partly burned; only the wind was left to sweep the dust along the debris-filled streets where Hazlitt found he could enter any house — left standing — if he wanted to.

Deftly steering his motor bike around piles of smashed brick and mangled timbers, Hazlitt was determined to get through the town on time, but became increasingly frustrated trying to access the one remaining bridge across the River Scarpe. "You couldn't find it because when you got down to the river, you'd see it and you'd go back and get lost getting down to it." Finally across, Hazlitt accelerated to make up for lost time. Northeast of Vimy Ridge he approached the huge coal-mining centre of Lens and got a good look at what the war left behind. It looked as if the entire city had been turned upside down. In the midst of it the young Canadian spotted an old French soldier looking at a pile of rubble with tears streaming down his face. "He had just come back, I guess."[4]

Meanwhile, north of Cambrai, Private A. N. Davis was on the move with the 47th (British Columbia) Battalion, which he had joined as part of a reinforcement draft. Davis was also only sixteen when he enrolled in late 1915 at New Westminster, British Columbia. His father had died the year before, and being the oldest boy he felt it was his duty to join the army.

The young lad fudged his age and within a year he was in England, where he managed to avoid being sent to the Young Soldiers Battalion. In France, the 47th fought through Vimy Ridge, Hill 70, Passchendaele, Amiens, and the Drocourt-Quéant Line. Near Cambrai, Davis was knocked out of action by a gas shell that "lit right alongside" him. "Of course you got a whiff of it before you could get your gas mask on." The fast-acting chemical seared Davis's eyes — blinding him — before he was found and evacuated to hospital. Davis regained his eyesight, but the wound kept him out for the remainder of the war.[5]

Will Ogilvie was also counting his blessings after a few near misses.

The young signaller from Lakefield, Ontario, was subbing for a linesman who, like Davis, had been blinded in both eyes. Ogilvie and another linesman were running telephone wire from brigade headquarters to the forward gun positions when they were nearly cut down. Hauling a heavy spool of wire, the two soldiers cautiously picked their way across the scarred landscape as the wire played out behind them. They were well into their dangerous journey when they heard the familiar whistle of an approaching shell. Instinctively, both soldiers hit the ground, causing the spool to roll away. The shell exploded just as its nose touched the ground, sending razor-sharp shrapnel in all directions. "Daisy-cutters, we called them," remembered Ogilvie. "They were a new menace that the enemy had planned for our quicker extermination." Somehow, the red-hot fragments sailed past, missing the men by millimetres.

Signaller Will Ogilvie strikes a pose in a training trench.

When the dust settled, the two soldiers picked themselves up and carried on beneath the roar of more shelling, knowing how close they were to being killed.[6]

On the evening of October 23, the advance elements of the Canadian Corps were within a few kilometres of Valenciennes and the banks of the Canal de l'Escaut north of the city. Renowned for its fine lace, Valenciennes had prospered with the founding of the first French coalfield, and an ironworks industry.[7] Occupied by the Germans since 1914, the city was an important part of the Hindenburg Line, the enemy's last substantial line of defence.

With the British flanking forces some distance behind the Canadians, Currie ordered a halt until the British caught up. Reconnaissance and other sources of information indicated the Germans intended to make a determined stand at Valenciennes, where they had caused extensive flooding to the north and west of the city, leaving the only available approach from the south. To block this approach, the Germans stationed five divisions across it, three of them anchored on Mount Houy, a wooded hill situated roughly two and a half kilometres south of the city.

With heights of 150 metres, Mount Houy dominated the battlefield.[8] It was the key to taking Valenciennes, and to unhinging the Hindenburg Line.

A single British battalion captured this feature on October 28, only to be pushed off by strong counterattacks. First Army Headquarters staff, flustered that the delay might upset the general advance Haig had ordered for November 3, called on the Canadians yet again. Currie refused to take the hill unless he was allowed to do it his way. He was resolved to preserve the lives of his men by using shells instead of soldiers to achieve victory. The next day First Army Headquarters reluctantly agreed, but told Brigadier-General Andy McNaughton, commanding the corps heavy artillery, to use guns sparingly. McNaughton flatly refused and produced a solid and well-thought out bombardment plan, employing 108 heavy guns and three divisions' worth of field artillery.[9]

On November 1, at 5:15 a.m., under cover of the heaviest artillery barrage ever to support a single infantry brigade during the entire war, 4th Division's 10th Brigade attacked.[10] The 44th (New Brunswick) Battalion led the way up Mount Houy, followed by the 46th (South Saskatchewan) and 47th Battalion — minus the wounded Davis. Within three hours they had captured the hill and advanced four thousand metres into the southern outskirts of Valenciennes.

That afternoon reconnaissance patrols were sent into the city. For four separate acts of bravery that day, twenty-one-year-old Sergeant Hugh Cairns of the 46th Battalion became the last of seventy-two Canadians to earn the Victoria Cross during the First World War.

The former plumber's apprentice and noted football player from Saskatoon was not underage, but he had been only eighteen when he enrolled in August 1915.[11] On the day he earned his VC, Cairns kept fighting after being shot in the shoulder and then knocked to the ground by another bullet. He quickly killed the German officer who fired that shot and then helped mow down several more desperate Germans who had picked up their discarded weapons and fired on the Canadians. Cairns died of

Sergeant Hugh Cairns (photographed here while still a corporal) of the 46th (South Saskatchewan) Battalion was the last of seventy-two Canadians to earn the Victoria Cross during the First World War.

his wounds the next day at a casualty clearing station.

By November 2, Valenciennes was captured. Any German soldier lucky enough to survive the superbly coordinated artillery bombardment and well-planned infantry attack was either a prisoner — wounded or otherwise — or retreating to the east. It was also clear from the positions of various dead Germans that in the heat of battle little mercy was granted to an enemy whose stubborn resistance had claimed Canadian lives. The streets and enemy strongpoints were filled with hundreds of dead, including some who had been shot trying to surrender.[12] These latter deaths were an understandable consequence of war, considering that Canadians had been killed by Germans who had raised their hands in surrender just before picking up a discarded weapon. But despite such anger and cold-blooded vengeance, nearly 1,380 prisoners were taken by the Canadians during two days of fighting at Valenciennes.

Private William Thom of 1st CMR was not an underage soldier, but remembered several German youth in uniform fortunate enough to be captured, noting "the kids asked all kinds of questions" and were not any older than sixteen or seventeen. "But you had to watch them… They told us all kinds of rotten stories about their country … how they were treated and so on — just kids."[13]

Slowly the city's frightened and hungry citizens emerged from dark cellars and shelters, squinting against the daylight as they reached out — many with gifts — to thank their liberators. The Canadians, however, remained cautious as they moved through the city, watching for booby traps and listening to rumours about how the war was about to end.

With the possibility of peace hanging in the autumn air, "nobody wanted to take a chance, naturally," recalled Private W. A. Crouse, the young runner with the 102nd (North British Columbians) Battalion. "We used to toss [a coin] then to see who was going to take messages. We were leaving it to fate and I guess probably that's a good way to do it."[14]

Will Ogilvie adopted the same philosophy, noting years later in his memoir that "life became more precious than ever before ... the few scattered shells which the retreating Germans were able to fire were treated with the utmost respect." The signaller also recalled how the drivers were constantly pushed to the limits of their endurance to move the guns forward to new locations every day. Meanwhile, he and the other signallers attached to the headquarters party were busy laying more communications wire or moving forward with officers who had the task of registering the guns and locating new targets.[15]

As the Canadians moved into Valenciennes they collected intelligence from local citizens, who shared heart-breaking stories about how they and their families had been treated by the enemy. Crouse was treated royally by a French family and their relatives who had been hiding in a cellar. The family was so grateful they welcomed him in and shared bottles of their best wine, which Crouse and his mates enjoyed to the fullest — enough to make them forget details of the pleasantly long social call.[16]

Thomas Hazlitt, meanwhile, had returned from his motorcycle trip to Béthune and was enjoying his temporary accommodations in a beautiful home with several furnished rooms, including a library. "It was a lovely place to play poker. The chap that owned it — a French officer — knocked at the door and said, 'This is my home' and then looked around and went out and got in a car and just drove away."

Before settling into his billet in the little house along the city's main street, David Low met grateful citizens who had witnessed some of the Germans fleeing east to the unmistakable sound of Canadian machine guns coming from the south. For many, including Low, one of the town's greatest assets was its brewery. Throughout the night he and the other men could hear the barrels bouncing and rolling down the cobblestone streets.[17]

After Valenciennes, the Allies continued their rapid pursuit of the Germans, forcing them back while not allowing them to concentrate their reserves, such as they were. The final major battle of the war took place south of the Canadians in and around the Forêt de Mormal as troops advanced through the forest against a determined, last-ditch stand by the Germans. The countryside was perfect for German delaying actions, fought from behind hills, hedges, and slag piles. There were also swollen streams and thick forests to slow the Allies down. Crouse's 102nd Battalion captured the village of Marchipont and advanced to Baisieux, roughly twenty kilometres west of Mons.[18]

The next day, 2nd Division took over the lead, while 3rd Division moved forward on the left flank, where it too ran up against a German rearguard. By now most of the leading elements of the corps were in Belgium, where the population had not suffered nearly as badly as the French: shops seemed undamaged and had goods in them, the land had not been as devastated, and there were civilians moving about, offering food, wine, and coffee to the Canadians, who were cheered as liberators.

Private C. P. Keeler, a former Edmonton sign painter who had enrolled at age seventeen in 1915, was with the 49th (Edmonton Regiment) Battalion as it moved closer to Mons, the city where the British first met the Germans in 1914. Keeler had obviously matured considerably during the war. During his time on the Western Front, his pride had swelled every time he and his fellow Canadians went into action. Months into the war, he no longer saw himself as a teenager, but as a soldier with a job to do and a clear understanding of the enemy. "There was a good feeling among us men..." For some time the men had realized "we were just as good as the Germans. We thought of the Germans as wonderful fighters, which they were. That was on account of the discipline they had. After ... meeting so many prisoners in barbed wire enclosures ... we found out that they didn't want this any more than we did... We began (after Vimy) to feel we were a little better than the Germans."

That pride and intense feeling of comradeship remained, although many of the soldiers were clearly not looking forward to another battle.

While facing Mons, Keeler could empathize with men who knew the war had to be won, but openly questioned the need to advance any further. In their minds were recent examples of good, experienced men killed during the last few days, including several casualties from a Canadian platoon decimated by a shell.[19] The resentment reached well beyond Keeler's company. None of the men, he recalled, wanted any part of the Mons show. "They were all grumbling to beat hell. They knew the war was coming to an end and there was going to be an armistice. 'What the hell do we have to go any further for?' they grumbled.'" Their bitterness grew when the battalion — like other battalions in the corps — suffered several casualties that morning. At the end of the day the men were furious about the losses.[20]

George Cruickshank of the 29th (Vancouver) Battalion was riding what he called "an old plug" toward the right side of Mons. He was in charge of a group of men, having been in the army since joining with his older brother at Chilliwack, British Columbia, in 1914. That was shortly after his seventeenth birthday.

Now sitting atop his tired old horse, Cruickshank passed "dead fellows" lying along the road. "It was pretty tough to see those guys. They must have known the same as we did that it was only a matter [of time]." When Cruickshank got word that a runner had arrived with an "important" message, he took off in a gallop; noting later he never saw the old horse move so fast.[21]

By November 9, battalions of 7th Brigade reached the outskirts of beautiful Mons, a city the Germans had occupied for four years.[22] On November 10, as Canadians fought their way through and around densely clustered villages and shapeless slag heaps, German resistance stiffened. Late that same day, patrols singled out and attacked enemy strongpoints while working across bridges and wading through stagnant, foul-smelling moats. It was morning but still dark by the time RCR and 42nd (Royal Highlanders of Canada) Battalion patrols got into the streets, where they attacked pockets of stiff resistance.[23]

Hours earlier, W. J. Home, who had enrolled underage in 1914, was watching out for enemy snipers who remained concealed and active on the outskirts of the city. A member of the RCR, Home recalled that his company was at the time attached to the 42nd Battalion. "It was obvious that there weren't many Germans there ... but you couldn't expose yourself too much."

Home, who noticed that the buildings were not nearly as damaged as the ones he had seen in France, was in a house that served as company headquarters when a stranger arrived at the door. The man was a newspaper correspondent — the first journalist correspondent the young soldier had ever seen. "He said something about an armistice and I probably didn't even know what the word meant. It was the very first time I heard it."

Soon, Home's unit was ordered forward into the city. They moved in and gathered on a frontage of two or three hundred metres. "Daylight was breaking when the windows opened up, the Belgian flags came out and people streamed out into the

Representatives of the Allies and the Germans signed the Armistice inside this train car in the Forêt de Compiègne, France, on November 11, 1918.

streets with cake and brandy ... and there was no firing ... It seemed such a shock you could hardly believe it."[24]

Two days earlier — on November 8 — representatives of the Allies and the Germans had met in a railway car in the Forêt de Compiègne to discuss terms.[25] The next day, after being told his army would no longer fight for him, the kaiser abdicated and fled to neutral Holland. Germany then became a republic. On November 10, the Germans agreed to the Allied demands; the shooting would stop on the morning of November 11 at 11 o'clock. In Mons, the Germans had left, and all along the Western Front the agony of more than four years of carnage was over.

On the same day, after spending the night in the nearby village of Jemappes, where litres of wine appeared miraculously from the cellars of grateful citizens, young David Low moved with his unit into an abandoned cavalry barracks in Mons. Along the way the men stepped over dead Germans while accepting floral tributes from smiling girls.[26]

While the civilian population spilled over with gratitude, most of the soldiers were exhausted and just wanted a good meal, a hot shower, and a comfortable bed. They were glad the war was over, but for many it was not a cause for celebration because of the many friends they had lost.

Private William White, who had enrolled as a drummer in Vancouver at the age of fifteen and served with the 102nd Battalion, did not see a lot of excitement among the men he was with. Many were still deeply annoyed by what they perceived as a senseless loss of men in the last two days. "There was some jumping around and things like that ... but I was kind of fed up, glad it was over, so was everybody else ..."[27]

The same impression stuck with Private M. E. Parsons, who recognized that most soldiers were low-key and just wanted to get home to Canada. However, they also expected it would take a tremendous amount of organizing to repatriate some 120,000 men.[28] That evening he was standing with a few buddies on one of the main streets in Mons when he noticed a throng of humanity heading toward them like a giant wave. "Bands were playing and people were waving flags ... they just carried everybody with them." Parsons and his friends were swept up and carried through the streets most of the night. But even as that was going on, the young soldier noticed funerals being planned for the last soldiers to die in the war.

For Parsons, who had earned the Military Medal, and for many others it had been a very long war, one that had aged them before their time. Boys were no longer boys, but battle-hardened men; their teenaged years spent far from home on fields of fire and death. For many it was hard to contemplate what sort of adult life awaited them back home.

In his thirty-three months on the Western Front, Parsons

Canadian soldiers and Belgian civilians celebrate the signing of the Armistice in the town square of Mons a short while after the city's liberation.

missed only a dozen or so days with his company.[29] It would be hard to get used to anything else.

Will Ogilvie, meanwhile, was squeaky clean after taking a hot shower in the change room of the mine headquarters at Cuesmes, a little town southwest of Mons. That night — following a rugby game — he drifted off to sleep on a bed of straw put down by the owners of the house in which he was billeted.[30]

That same evening, Walter King, the schoolteacher from Wainwright, Alberta, who had enrolled as a teenager with his father Henry and older brother Arthur, settled down in his billet to write a letter to his mother, Florence. It was raining, and for the time being the street outside was quiet. "The great European war is over!" he wrote. "All last night we expected the news to come through, but we did not know officially until ten o'clock this morning… No doubt London, Paris, Washington and Rome are seething with excitement at the conclusion of the world's greatest struggle, but there are no celebrations of any kind here tonight. Probably it is because most of the boys cannot yet realize that what they set out to do has been accomplished … Today we had a general inspection and stood out six hours in the cold rain. Parades are going on as usual, and it appears as though the period of demobilization is only going to leave everyone with a more bitter memory of army life than is necessary."

Walter's father survived the war, but Arthur, who served as a stretcher-bearer during the Battle of Vimy Ridge, did not. He was slightly wounded on February 13, 1918, and then killed in action on April 13, during the Germans' final spring offensive.

Walter was hunkered down in a trench when he got word of his brother's death. The young soldier later retrieved Arthur's effects, which included a notebook he carried in his breast pocket. While flipping through its pages, Walter found notes and photographs of his brother's fiancée, Margaret Brade, of Calgary. That was when he noticed shrapnel had pierced her photograph and part of the notebook.[31]

In less than one hundred days, the Canadian Corps had achieved tremendous gains and sharpened its reputation as an elite fighting force. The cost, however, was high. Between August 8 and November 11, the corps suffered nearly forty-six thousand casualties, a cost that would be higher than the number of losses suffered by First Canadian Army in the Second World War.[32]

The entire cost of the war for Canada, the other Allied nations, and for Central Powers was staggering to say the least. Britain's estimates were 723,000 dead and more than 1.6 million wounded. France, meanwhile, suffered nearly 1.4 million deaths and Germany suffered well over two million.[33] The death toll for Canadian forces between 1914 and 1919 was 60,932. This figure does not include the more than 1,300 Newfoundlanders killed while serving with British forces, nor does it include those who died of their wounds soon after the war. The official figure used today by Veterans Affairs Canada is 66,655 dead and 172,950 wounded, statistics that include many boy soldiers.[34]

As the Canadians quietly reflected on their experiences and the loss of good friends, the excitement of war's end took hold in cities and towns far removed from the battle zones. Private Morris Searle was sitting in a London theatre on the night of November 11, waiting for the curtain to rise on a vaudeville show. The happiness and the relief among the patrons and the crowd outside were so intense the show was cancelled. "It was simply one wild mass of humanity giving into feelings that had been pent up for a number years."[35]

Private John Cadenhead of the 102nd Battalion also happened to be on leave in London that day. He recalled that the driver of a beer wagon did not stand a chance when he and his cargo were spotted by joyful soldiers. The barrels were pulled free and uncorked on the spot. After helping themselves to the brew, Cadenhead and about twelve other lads climbed into and onto a taxi, which they rode to Buckingham Palace. "It was really something."[36]

While the war was officially over, the suffering continued long past the victory speeches. The two Canadian divisions that had served the longest on the Western Front could not suddenly drop everything and head home. They had to remain behind as part of an occupation force that marched some four hundred kilometres through Belgium to the Rhine River, where they crossed into Germany at Bonn. That journey lasted about a month, ending under dark clouds in a cold, persistent rain.

From start to finish, the march was a logistical nightmare. Tempers flared as food supplies failed to keep up and men were repeatedly soaked to the skin by icy downpours. Worst of all, the tired troops were vulnerable to a virulent strain of flu that left men hacking up mucus and blood. Worldwide the flu epidemic killed some forty to fifty million people. [37] It also seemed to zero in on the young and healthy. Approximately 45,000 members of the CEF suffered from the Spanish flu, among whom roughly 780 died.[38] Ogilvie contracted it most likely before settling into his straw bed at Cuesmes. With a body temperature of 105°F he was transported in a drafty ambulance to a hospital in France. Luckily, he recovered.

For those that stayed behind the march to the Rhine was gruelling, but there were brighter moments. Private W. A. Crouse, who had been the benefactor of one family's prized wine in Valenciennes, was treated like a son while staying with a tailor, his wife, and their three children in Belgium.

Every day Crouse and a few buddies headed off to collect their rations, but when they returned the family made sure they did not eat the army food. Instead, the family fed the rations to the rabbits and sat the young soldiers down at the dining room table where they shared a more bountiful meal. "We lived with them as if we were part of the family."

The generous tailor took the lads into the city every weekend, where they bet on horse races with money given to them by their host. "We lived like kings all the time we were there. He was making a suit for each one of us when all of a sudden we got orders to move…" The boys never did get their suits, but all of them were eternally grateful for the hospitality.[39]

On December 13, General Sir Arthur Currie was brimming with pride as he stood soaking wet on the bridge over the Rhine to take the salute as the 1st and 2nd Canadian Divisions marched past. The cold rain did nothing to steal the moment away from the Canadian Corps, whose reputation as one of the most finely tuned fighting forces was now forever embedded in the war's history.

By the end of April, Ogilvie was in England and soon on his way back to Canada, where he was greeted at Toronto's Union Station by two of his sisters. In May, along with hundreds of others from 4th Brigade Artillery, he was handed his discharge papers and some money for civilian clothes.

Suddenly removed from the military culture, Ogilvie was frightened by the prospect of re-entering a world he hardly recognized.

The 19th (Central Ontario) Battalion marches across the Bonn Bridge past Lieutenant-General Currie and into Germany, December 1918.

Hopping on a train, he left the city behind and soon met his father on the laneway outside the family home in Lakefield. In his memoir, published years after the war, he describes walking up to the house for the first time in three years, and noticing how high the poplar trees had grown but how the house, the yard, and even his father seemed smaller. Within hours he pulled his canoe out of storage and was back on the river, where years earlier he and his friends had spent part of their summers diving for the white doorknobs they had tossed into the cool depths.

Slowly, all of the men were returned to England for embarkation to Canada. Most were home by late June 1919, including five thousand soldiers who served in northern Russia and eastern Siberia during the final days of the Russian revolution.[40]

Like many amputees, Private Fred Claydon, who earned the Military Medal, learned to walk with his artificial leg. But by the time he got to Manitoba he knew he could no longer work the ranch the way he used to. Instead, he performed what work he

A massive crowd of Torontonians celebrates the end of the war as tickertape and confetti stream down upon them.

could and survived on a small pension before moving further west.[41]

By the time Walter King returned to Alberta, he — like many Canadian soldiers — could speak French, one of many skills he transferred to his students during a long career that led to his becoming a school principal at Redcliff, Alberta. He married in 1927 and participated in the massive 1936 pilgrimage to Vimy Ridge for the unveiling of Walter Allward's towering memorial. Remarkably, King tried to enrol again at the outbreak of the Second World War but was turned down on account of being too old. Instead, he became a war services supervisor, offering assistance to Commonwealth military personnel posted in Canada as part of the British Commonwealth Air Training Plan. He died in 1947.

In Edmonton, Private C. P. Keeler paraded through the streets to the armouries, where he and the other veterans of his battalion turned in their rifles and revolvers, "took pay parade and walked out finished," and a whole lot older in many ways.[42]

CHAPTER 19

"WHAT IS THIS, A NURSERY? THIS KID CAN'T BE MORE THAN FIFTEEN. I WON'T PUT UP WITH THIS."
Canada's First Sailors and Airmen

Undeterred by the overwhelming odds, and with HMS *Good Hope*'s forward 9.2-inch turret burning furiously after a direct hit from the German cruiser *Scharnhorst*, Rear-Admiral Sir Christopher Cradock bravely steered his vessel toward the enemy squadron blasting away at his ships in the South Pacific Ocean off Coronel, Chile.

In a desperate attempt to get his 6-inch batteries into action, and perhaps ram *Scharnhorst* or launch torpedoes, Cradock managed to close the range to less than five kilometres. Several more German salvoes crashed into the British cruiser, setting fires, twisting metal into bizarre shapes, maiming and killing sailors. In the fast-fading light, an 8.2-inch shell struck between the mainmast and the after funnel, followed almost immediately by a tremendous explosion that spewed debris and a great geranium-coloured flame more than sixty metres skyward. A 6-inch casement managed to fire two more times before her guns went quiet.

Lit only by a dull red glow from fires raging throughout the ship, the outgunned cruiser slipped silently and unseen beneath the waves, taking all surviving crewmen with her, including four young midshipmen who were recent graduates of the first intake at Halifax's new Royal Naval College of Canada.

It was November 1, 1914, and the four "middies" were Canada's first combat deaths of the First World War.[1]

Canadian naval traditions, including boy sailors, are based upon those of the Royal Navy (RN). Early records about boys who were trained to become ordinary sailors aboard RN ships are generally scarce. One source is the records of the Marine Society, founded in London at the beginning of the Seven Years' War in 1756 to provide boys for the navy. With a combination of military, political, and philanthropic interests, its London-merchant founders were concerned about the navy's acute manning problem and believed a sailor's trade was best learned from an early age. They regarded the city's poor, abandoned, and unemployed youth as future sailors.

Providing the navy with boys was a high priority, as within a few years those youths would be able seamen and ease the manning problem. Since they would become accustomed to life at sea from an early age, the youths would also be well prepared for naval careers.

Although boys initially went aboard as captains' or other officers' servants, their actual role was as trainee sailors. A boy had to be at least fourteen years old — although several were accepted younger — or eleven if he were an officer's son. Although assigned to certain ship's tradesmen, the young boys were used for various other tasks. One of the most important was to act as powder monkeys, responsible for bringing powder and shot from a ship's magazine to the gun crews in battle.

The same aggressiveness that frequently brought youths into conflict with authority on land was a sought-after characteristic at sea, especially during wartime. The navy gave each officer a financial incentive to take one or more boys to sea with him, of which he was obliged to spend only one-fifth for clothing and other necessities for the boy. The Admiralty referred to the scheme as the navy's "nursery for seamen." Perhaps between 10 and 15 per cent of the crew of an eighteenth-century warship would have been boy servants. The number of boys might even be much higher, since there would also be boys aboard who had joined as men. Discipline was strict in the RN and, like older seamen, boy sailors were subject to corporal punishment — a common means of enforcing authority in the navy.[2]

Several boys from the British North America colonies who joined the navy became admirals, as some boys who joined the army became generals. One of the most remarkable former boy sailors was Halifax native Provo Wallis, second lieutenant in HMS *Shannon*, the RN frigate that broke an unprecedented string of single-ship American victories at sea during the War of 1812.

Wallis had been carried on the books of several ships from the age of four, a common practice at the time when promotion in the navy was based almost entirely on seniority. In later life he commented that his real career commenced when he joined the *Cleopatra* in October 1804, at thirteen. At fifteen he was appointed acting lieutenant and promoted lieutenant two years later.

In January 1812, Wallis joined the frigate *Shannon* under Captain Philip Broke, perhaps the pre-eminent gunnery officer in the navy. On June 1, 1813, *Shannon* and the USS *Chesapeake* met off Boston in the bloodiest single-frigate action in history. It was over in fifteen minutes, and although Broke was victor-

*Provo Wallis (pictured here)
was entered by his father
on the books of a naval ship
when he was four years old, a
common practice to establish
seniority.*

ious, he was severely wounded. With the other officers dead or incapacitated, the responsibility for bringing *Shannon* and the captured *Chesapeake*, along with the dead and wounded of both sides, into Halifax harbour fell to Wallis. He rose to the occasion and arrived on June 6 to a tumultuous welcome.

Wallis continued to rise through the ranks to become admiral of the fleet, receiving additional honours along the way. Benefiting from an 1870 ruling that allowed any officer who had commanded a ship during the Napoleonic Wars to remain on the active list, he received full pay until his death at one hundred, having served an incredible ninety-six years; a record that is likely to remain unbroken.[3]

Before the creation of the Royal Canadian Navy (RCN) in 1910, the RN was regarded as the empire's navy by the people of Britain's far-flung possessions. As such, many Canadian youths joined the navy as boy sailors throughout the colonial period and served full careers at sea without ever rising to senior rank.

As the empire grew and expanded during the nineteenth century, so did Britain's dependence on ocean shipping routes for trade and defence. At the same time, German naval power was increasingly offering a direct challenge to the RN; so much so that the adequacy of the navy to protect Britain's empire was in question. This concern gave rise in Britain to the Navy League in January 1895, an organization of ordinary citizens whose primary aim was to ensure an adequate naval defence. The movement proved to be popular and expanded quickly, with branches springing up throughout the empire. The first Canadian branch was established in Toronto in December that year; others followed over the next few years in Victoria, Halifax, and elsewhere. In Toronto, even before their branch was officially formed, the founding members were petitioning the Canadian government about the need for a naval reserve training program.[4]

In Newfoundland, a six-hundred-man Royal Naval Reserve was formed in 1902. When war broke out in 1914, it was the only trained military force in the colony and was called out for duty. Unfortunately, it could produce only seventy reservists as the rest were on the fishing grounds. Despite this temporary manning setback, Newfoundland Governor Davidson offered to increase the size of the reserve to one thousand men and to meet all local expenses. The British quickly accepted.[5]

In Canada, Minister of Marine and Fisheries Raymond Préfontaine drafted a bill in 1904 to create a naval militia and a naval academy. When the minister died suddenly in 1905, his bill died with him. The new minister, Louis-Philipe Brodeur, intended to continue the planning for the new service. Prime Minister Sir Wilfrid Laurier and his government, however, were more concerned with the final departure of the British navy and army from Halifax and Esquimalt and the subsequent takeover of the extensive facilities they would leave behind.

In 1905–06, the last of the RN ships and British army units left

Canada. Canada was now responsible for funding a larger share of her defence, an expense the new country had been largely avoiding. Although a naval reserve was not created just then, the Navy League did establish the Boy's Naval Brigade, a navy equivalent of the army's cadet program. Besides encouragement to pursue a seafaring life in the RN, basic training was provided in seamanship and citizenship. When the RCN was finally created in 1910, the Boy's Naval Brigades were renamed the Navy League Sea Cadets.

On January 10, 1910, Laurier introduced his *Naval Service Act* in the House. It proposed a fleet of eleven Canadian-built warships — five cruisers and six destroyers — for use in local waters, maintained by an annual expenditure of $3 million. On May 4, the Naval Service of Canada was created. Canada now had a navy, but only on paper. Before Laurier could do anything about making the navy a real force, his government was defeated in the general election of 1911, partly due to the naval issue. His successor, Conservative Robert Borden, who favoured direct financial support to the RN instead, was blocked in his efforts by the Liberal-controlled Senate. The net result was that when the First World War broke out three years later there was neither a proper Canadian navy nor any British warship financing by Canada.

On the morning of October 22, 1910, the aging ex-RN (some said "discarded"), 11,000-ton, Diadem class, lightly-armoured cruiser HMCS *Niobe* steamed into Halifax harbour, escorted by the Canadian Government Ships *Canada* and *Minto*. Flag- and bunting-bedecked — "dressed" in nautical terms — she fired her guns in salute of her new home port, as Citadel cannons echoed a welcome. Commissioned in 1898, the obsolescent *Niobe* was designed to have a wartime complement of seven hundred sailors. The entire strength of the RCN at the time was 350 officers and men. Rear Admiral Charles Kingsmill, a Canadian who had served in the RN and became the first director of the Canadian

Naval Service, went aboard and hoisted his pennant, the first time a Canadian flag officer did so in a major warship.[6]

Kingsmill had been born far from the ocean in Guelph, Canada West (now Ontario) in 1855, twelve years before the country whose navy he was eventually to head was even a nation. On September 24, 1869, at age fourteen, he joined the training ship HMS *Britannia*, the RN's training establishment for future officers at Dartmouth. He passed out near the bottom of his class.

Kingsmill's career could "be characterized as interesting, but certainly not extraordinary. Neither, however, could he conceivably be styled a laggard." Many of his early and middle years were spent on foreign stations. In 1908, he retired from the RN and accepted an invitation from Laurier to command the Canadian Fisheries Protection Service, having been promoted rear admiral before he retired. He played a prominent part in the founding of the RCN in 1910 and became the first director of the Naval Service. He was promoted vice-admiral in 1913, admiral in 1917, and was knighted in 1918. Kingsmill retired in 1920 and died in 1935 at his picturesque summer home on Grindstone Island in Big Rideau Lake near Portland, Ontario.[7]

But back in 1910, when Niobe went into Canadian service, to make up crew shortfalls, Britain loaned Canada six hundred RN sailors for a two-year term. These men would operate both *Niobe* on the east coast and her sister ship *Rainbow* on the west, while Canadians were recruited and trained. Recruiting did not begin in earnest until February 1911. Boys were accepted from the ages of fourteen to sixteen, and seamen could join between fifteen and twenty-three, while stokers had to be between eighteen and twenty-three. All had to engage for seven years after the age of eighteen.[8]

While the RN loaned sailors to Canada, several members of the Royal Naval Canadian Volunteer Reserve (RNCVR) — renamed to the more logical Royal Canadian Naval Volunteer

A very busy recruiting poster for the new Naval Service of Canada, almost immediately renamed the Royal Canadian Navy.

Reserve (RCNVR) in 1923 — served in British ships.

Walter Dodds was one. He had been born in Northumberland in northern England in 1864 and immigrated to the United States in 1888, but was in Ontario when he met Martha Laughton. The two were married in 1894 and went to the United States to live. The couple had six children by 1905, including twins Agnes and Gordon, who were born on March 2, 1899. In 1908, the family headed to Alberta before Walter began farming near Armstrong in British Columbia's Okanagan Valley.

Initially it was a hardscrabble existence. Several years later, Agnes recalled that the family lived in a number of rented homes until her father bought a farm. "There was an orchard on it, so for once we had apples to eat. The fields were covered with rocks and partially burned trees. Consequently, the land had to be cleared. We kids picked up stones daily, and stumps."[9] Agnes' twin, Gordon, joined the RNCVR on December 5, 1916, when he

The first group of recruits from Nova Scotia for HMCS Niobe *pose stiffly in their new uniforms. How many of them were underage?*

was seventeen. He first served in HMCS *Shearwater*, a west coast sloop, followed by service in *Niobe*. Dodds next went to Britain, where he underwent further training before he was assigned to the RN trawler *Lucknow*. Trawlers were small ships, about thirty metres long, and carried out a busy schedule of mine-laying, mine-sweeping, and anti-submarine patrols in British coastal waters. On May 18, 1917, *Lucknow* struck a mine in the English Channel off Portsmouth and sank quickly with her entire nine-man crew, which included two other Canadians besides Dodds.

Only three bodies were recovered; one of them that of Ordinary Seaman Dodds.[10]

If recruitment of sailors for the RCN drastically failed to achieve its manning goals, the same was only marginally true for officers. Once the RCN was created, the government established the Royal Naval College of Canada (RNCC) at Halifax in the old naval hospital at the extreme north end of the dockyard. It was a long, narrow, four-storey, red-brick building built in the 1860s. The applicants for the first two-year course responded to an advertisement that appeared across the country and were examined in November 1910. Candidates for the twenty-five cadet vacancies had to be between fourteen and fifteen years old, be British subjects, and they or their parents had to have resided in Canada for the last two years. Cost to the parents of those selected was estimated at $400 for the first year and $250 for the second, to cover board, accommodation, uniforms, and other expenses.

On January 11, 1911, the successful candidates for the first intake of officers for the RCN assembled in Halifax to begin their training. The new college was to train the prospective officers in naval science, tactics, and strategy. The commandant and uniformed instructional staff were supplied by the Admiralty, supplemented by three civilian schoolmasters who taught mathematics, science, and languages. For whatever reason — perhaps a lack of sufficient suitable younger candidates — the admission rules had been stretched and boys as old as sixteen and seventeen were part of the class. Even so, there were only twenty-one boys from across the country to fill the twenty-five vacancies.

Among the eager young boys were five who would be killed during the First World War, four of them in the same battle.[11]

Midshipmen Arthur Silver and William Palmer — both seventeen upon joining — were from Halifax. Malcolm Cann from Yarmouth and Victor Hathaway from Fredericton were both sixteen. Classmate John Grant remembered Hathaway as "very fine looking, modest, very nice, played the piano for our singsongs, a promising young officer," while Palmer was "very brainy, used to be top of the class apparently without having to work." Grant described Silver as "rather like Hathaway, very well-known Halifax family, keen fisherman and famous for his art in casting" and thought Cann was "a good mess mate." Based

The four midshipmen who died in the HMS Good Hope: *front row-Malcolm Cann (centre) and Arthur Silver, second row-Victor Hathaway, rear row-William Palmer.*

on their performance at the college, Silver became the chief cadet captain, while Hathaway became the senior midshipman.[12]

On completion of their training in January 1913, the nineteen graduates — now midshipmen — were assigned to Britain to get their "big ship time" in the RN training cruiser HMS *Berwick*; the next step on their path to commissions as sub-lieutenants. For the first time they received pay: two dollars per day. Training in *Berwick* was rigorous and thorough, intended to provide the practical side of the theory learned at the college, as well as to inculcate the traditions and esprit de corps of the RN. In early 1914, after completion of their on-board training year, the midshipmen returned to Canada. In the normal course of events they should have spent two more years at sea — but the RCN's only two ships were incapable of steaming. As a temporary expedient, the four were sent back to college to take a course in the new field of wireless communications. When that course ended in late spring, the middies were sent on leave. Then everything changed with the assassination of an Austrian archduke in an obscure Balkan town.

Two days before war was declared on August 4, the midshipmen had been ordered to report for duty at the nearest unit. Silver, Hathaway, Palmer, Cann, and three others reported to *Niobe*, which had been placed at the disposal of the Admiralty. When HMS *Suffolk* arrived in Halifax on August 13 for coaling, all seven action-hungry Canadian middies volunteered to join her and were accepted. *Suffolk* was not destined to be part of the squadron of two old heavy cruisers, a light cruiser, and a converted merchant ship auxiliary cruiser that would soon be dispatched to the Pacific in search of the German Asiatic Squadron under Admiral Graf von Spee, whose two heavy and three light cruisers were a threat to shipping in the Pacific.

On August 14, the armoured cruiser HMS *Good Hope* arrived in Halifax to take on coal and left the same day, meeting *Suffolk* at sea two days later, when Rear-Admiral Sir Christopher Cradock, commanding the force, changed his flag from *Suffolk* to the faster *Good Hope*. Cradock had discovered he was short four midshipmen and specifically requested that Silver and Palmer join his ship. The two others, Cann and Hathaway, were selected by lot. Cradock, his dog, a small staff, and the four midshipmen transferred to the larger ship by boat.[13]

On November 1, the South American Squadron was patrolling off Coronel, Chile, when it encountered the German flotilla. Outmatched, outgunned, and outranged, Cradock and his sailors bravely faced the enemy. In the hour-long gunnery duel that followed, a British cruiser was sunk and *Good Hope* was reduced to a flaming hulk. She went down with her crew, including the four Canadian middies.

It was a major blow to the future senior leadership of the RCN.[14]

Young Alan "Babe" McLeod pushed his Armstrong-Whitworth FK8 bomber for all it was worth.

He and his gunner/observer, Lieutenant Comber, were badly outgunned and outnumbered as they tried to outrun the three Fokker Dr.I triplanes on their tail. The two-seater "Big Ack," as the massive and ungainly aircraft was known, was slow in both speed and climb rate and was no match for the faster and more manoeuvrable fighters. Somehow, Comber was able to keep the Germans off with his rearward-firing Lewis machine gun, while McLeod used his considerable skills as a pilot to make it over Allied lines into safer territory. The Fokkers peeled off, unwilling to risk being shot down by British gunners. It was the chance for which McLeod had been waiting. He wheeled around in a wide circle, headed for the nearest German fighter, and managed to come up behind the unsuspecting pilot. When the enemy pilot filled his gun sight, McLeod let go with a deadly burst from his forward-firing Vickers machine gun. As the pilot slumped over, the Fokker reared up, stalled, fell over onto a wing, and crashed to the ground.

When they got back to their aerodrome, no one believed either McLeod or Comber; bombers did not shoot down fighters. They were credited with a "destroyed" only after a British balloon observer independently corroborated their story. McLeod was pleased; he had not joined the Royal Flying Corps to be a bomber pilot — he wanted to fly fighters. If the air force would not give him a fighter, well then, he would use his bomber like one. It was a winning combination.[15]

A JN4 does a loop over the Niagara Peninsula's Camp Beamsville training site, one of four established by the RFC in Canada.

When the First World War broke out in August 1914, Canada did not have an air force. Suddenly, Colonel Sam Hughes, the opinionated and autocratic minister of militia and defence authorized the formation of the Canadian Aviation Corps at Camp Valcartier on September 16 for attachment to the CEF. By May 1915 it had ceased to exist; neither its single plane nor its three personnel ever saw combat.[16] Although the Canadian government had not initially decided to create an air force, it did assist the air war by letting its young men join the British air services and in other ways. In December 1916 it loaned the British a million dollars to purchase an aircraft factory in Toronto and form Canadian Aeroplanes Ltd. The plant eventually manufactured twenty-nine hundred Curtiss JN4 (Canadian) Canuck training aircraft, as well as the Avro 504 trainer and the Felixstowe F5L flying boat for both Britain and the United States.[17]

By 1916 the British were suffering terrible losses in pilots and observers, and were unable to train replacements fast enough. The British government turned to Canada for help, and in less than six months a new training program was established in Canada at four sites in Ontario. The handful of no-nonsense men who established this scheme overcame enormous obstacles to build airfields, hangars, and training facilities; acquire training aircraft; set up courses; enrol recruits from across the country; and train them. In less than two years the plan graduated 3,135 pilots, 137 observers, and 7,453 ground crew for the British, plus another 456 pilots for the United States. Sadly, 137 young men were killed during training. The British government spent an enormous amount of money on the plan, some $40 million.[18]

In the minds of most Canadians who are aware that during the First World War their fellow countrymen fought in the Royal Air Force (RAF) and its precursors — the Royal Flying Corps (RFC) and the Royal Naval Air Service (RNAS) — "an impression was created that Canadian involvement in the air war could be summed up in the exploits of a small number of 'aces,'" a notion that "distorted the reality of Canada's air effort in that struggle."[19] In fact, more than twenty-two thousand Canadians were involved in the beginnings of military air power during the First World War. But because they served in the British air services and were not necessarily identified as Canadians, many of their details remain unknown to their fellow citizens.

Fortunately, the exploits of Alan McLeod are known.

The future pilot was born in the small Manitoba town of Stonewall on April 20, 1899, and was attracted to the military from an early age. After his family moved to Winnipeg he enrolled in the Fort Garry Horse, a cavalry unit, in 1913, when he was only fourteen. Although he was underage, it was peacetime, and officers simply looked the other way. McLeod's duties were hardly inspiring — grooming horses, shovelling manure, cleaning tack — but he did get to wear a uniform and attend summer camp. The young teenager was ecstatic. But when war broke out the next year, McLeod was sent home; he was too young for wartime soldiering.

If anything, McLeod was now more determined than ever to join the army and tried to enrol several times in Winnipeg. Each time the big-boned, six-foot-two-inch youth was rebuffed by recruiting sergeants, who sent him home and told him to stay in school. In 1916, he tried to enrol in the RFC, which was recruiting for its Canadian training program. The authorities insisted on a birth certificate. When they saw he was only seventeen they sent him home, but with a promise to process his application when he turned eighteen. True to form, McLeod showed up the next year, enrolled in the RFC, and was sent to Long Branch, Ontario, for initial pilot training. He was a natural and soloed after only three hours of experience. McLeod then proceeded to Camp Borden for intermediate training and graduated after fewer than fifty hours of flying. In August 1917, he sailed overseas as a new second lieutenant.

In England, after additional training, McLeod was sent to a squadron flying scouts, the type of aircraft in which most aces achieved their kills. Then, when his CO discovered his age, he told McLeod he was too young for combat and posted him to a home defence squadron flying antiquated BE12 fighters against Zeppelins at night. McLeod was bitterly disappointed, especially since some of his Canadian classmates went off to France and became high-scoring aces. Night flying was dangerous — airfields were not well lit, anti-aircraft balloons were tethered to the ground by long cables that could tear the wing off a BE12, and the Zeppelins were armed. McLeod even got shot down by a Zeppelin gunner; an experience he chalked up as simply part of war. All the while, as McLeod improved his flying abilities, he was trying to get to France. He finally convinced his group commander to change his age to nineteen on his records and he was sent across the Channel to a pilot pool. Instead of being assigned to a scout, though, he ended up as the pilot of a two-seat Armstrong-Whitworth FK8 bomber.

When his new CO first saw him, he exploded, "What is this, a nursery? This kid can't be more than fifteen. I won't put up with this."[20]

Accepting that he was stuck as a bomber pilot, McLeod resolved to use his aircraft as a fighter whenever he could and took to cruising behind enemy lines when his regular work was finished, looking for Germans to shoot down. Usually it was the Germans who found him. On March 27, 1918, McLeod and his observer at the time, Lieutenant Arthur Hammond, were on a bombing mission behind enemy lines when a Fokker appeared out of the clouds about two hundred metres away and slightly below them. McLeod manoeuvred his bomber so that Hammond could get a shot at the faster and much more agile fighter. After three bursts from the gunner's Lewis gun, the triplane flipped over on its back and plummeted to earth. As they congratulated each other, seven more Fokkers dove on them.

It did not look good.

The German fighters swarmed like angry hornets — diving, firing, and then pulling up. McLeod positioned the bomber so that Hammond got off a sustained burst at a particularly close Fokker, which shattered the German airplane and actually broke it apart. Another Fokker came up under the bomber and fired into its belly, wounding both pilot and observer and puncturing the fuel tank, which set the aircraft on fire. As another German closed in for the kill, Hammond, who had the use of only one arm, struggled to get a volley off that caused the Fokker to fall away.

Alan McLeod climbs out onto the wing of his burning "Big Ack" bomber to side-slip the aircraft and fan the flames away from the cockpit.

The situation seemed hopeless. The Big Ack was on fire, they were behind German lines, surrounded and being fired on by enemy fighters, and both were wounded. McLeod calmly climbed out onto the lower left wing to avoid the fire and yawed the aircraft by controlling the joy stick with his right hand to fan the flames to the right. By now, Hammond had to lie along the gun ring above his cockpit because flames had destroyed the bottom of the aircraft and his seat had fallen out. Another Fokker dove in for the kill and hit McLeod again, but he managed to sideslip the Big Ack so Hammond could get some shots away. Hammond fired, and the Fokker spun out of control. Another fighter attacked repeatedly, putting Hammond's Lewis gun out of commission and hitting the aircraft again and again. Convinced the bomber was doomed — and as it was heading for British airspace — the German pulled away to look for other targets.

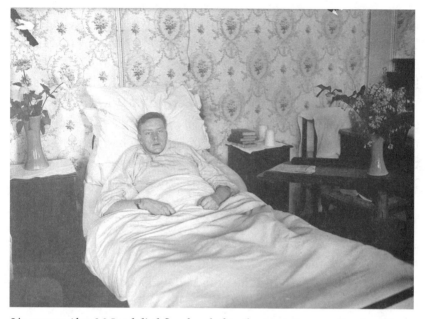

Lieutenant Alan McLeod died five days before the Armistice was signed, while recuperating from Spanish influenza at his parents' Winnipeg home.

But McLeod was far from finished.

The young pilot continued to sideslip the bomber over German territory and managed to flatten his glide so he crashed in no man's land. Miraculously, pilot and observer were still alive, although Hammond was unable to move, wounded six times and badly burned. With the fire approaching the aircraft's load of eight bombs and remaining ammunition, McLeod struggled to grab his comrade and haul him clear before the Big Ack exploded. When it did, McLeod was injured again and flaming debris scattered all around them. As they sheltered in a shell hole, front-line German soldiers fired at them, wounding McLeod for a sixth time. The two badly injured flyers stayed in the shell hole until nightfall, when some South African soldiers rescued them and carried them to a dressing station.

McLeod and Hammond were evacuated through the medical

chain, where bullets were removed and wounds patched up. Eventually they were separated and McLeod ended up in a London hospital. For several months he lay between life and death, but by late summer he appeared to be on his way to recovery. While he was convalescing, he was awarded the Victoria Cross in a ceremony at Buckingham Palace on September 4. He returned to Canada a few days later with his father, who had made the trip to London for the investiture. While recuperating in Winnipeg, McLeod caught the Spanish influenza then sweeping the world and died in November, five days before the Armistice.[21] Because Newfoundland was not a part of Canada when Tommy Ricketts earned his VC at seventeen, McLeod is Canada's youngest Victoria Cross recipient.

In March 1918, around the time McLeod and Hammond were on their bombing run behind enemy lines, Robert Morrison, an adventuresome teenager from the small eastern Ontario town of Chesterville, arrived in France to train on Caudron and Curtiss biplanes. Although Morrison had enrolled in Ottawa with the Signal Corps at age seventeen, he transferred to the Royal Naval Air Service in November 1917.

Pushing himself to the limit, the young pilot trained hard overseas, but always left room for fun. While learning to fly seaplanes off the south coast of England, Morrison took great delight in buzzing the ferry boats and flying as close as he could over the waves. He racked up more flying time in the fall of 1918 while stationed in the Mediterranean. Following the Armistice, Morrison participated in patrols over Gallipoli and a bomber escort patrol over Mount Athos, Greece.

When Allied forces, including the Royal Air Force (RAF), sought volunteers to fight the Bolsheviks, who had seized power in Russia, Morrison was quick to answer the call along with other members of 266 Squadron. Their destination in March 1919 was the Caspian Sea, the largest enclosed inland body of water on

Earth. Morrison's wartime diary offers a rare glimpse of a young man's service in a forgotten theatre of war. It notes the seaplanes, which were carried on small ships or tenders, had to be lowered onto the water by cranes. When the mission was over, the planes would land on the water, be recovered by crane, and deposited back on the tender.

On May 17, 1919, while trying to take off in heavy seas by repeatedly going down the side of one wave and up next, Morrison and his observer decided their aircraft was too heavy for takeoff so they got rid of their bombs. The ploy worked, but just as they were gaining airspeed the aircraft slammed into a large wave and spun "tail to wind." With the plane's elevator now broken, Morrison steered toward the ship, where he and his observer fought hard against the swell to get their crippled aircraft alongside. At one point the port wing struck the ship, smashing the aileron. On at least two occasions both men nearly fell into the wild, frigid water.

Less than a week later Morrison and his observer were busy again, this time attacking enemy ships moored along a pier. After dropping their bombs, they "machine gunned the whole harbour." Another plane, arriving later, successfully targeted a destroyer. "When we went over next we saw the thing was sinking fast," noted Morrison.

By the end of June the young airman's service in Russia was over, and he was on his way back to London. It was truly the experience of a lifetime for the Canadian fly boy who never lost his taste for adventure. Morrison's last diary entry was on August 20, 1919 — the day after he turned twenty.

"Ye gods," he wrote. "I'm out of my teens. I'm really getting old."[22]

After government inaction and procrastination since its formation in 1910, the RCN was totally unprepared to fight when the
First World War broke out. Very little changed during that conflict, and parsimonious Canadian politicians did not provide the
navy with the men, ships, or money for expansion much beyond a
coastal patrol and a local shipping protection force. The result was
a motley collection of small drifters, trawlers, and even donated
private yachts, but few purpose-built warships. Boy sailors played
their part in this small force, some of whom died for the empire.
That the navy survived and grew was testimony to the drive and
vision of the men who led it, despite the view of the prestigious
Cambridge History of the British Empire, which in 1930 sniffed
with disdain that "Canada's … naval contribution to the World
War was so small … that no Canadian naval history need be
recorded here."[23]

In the air, it was a different story. There was no distinct Canadian air force until after the hostilities ended, but thousands of
young Canadians, many under the age of eighteen, participated
in the air war, a few as aircrew and a much larger number as
ground crew. An estimated 22,812 Canadians eventually served
in the British flying services, initially in the Royal Flying Corps
and Royal Naval Air Service, then in the merged Royal Air Force
after April 1, 1918. By the end of the war, one-third of uniformed
RAF members were Canadians. Of the top fifty British Empire
aces with more than twenty-five victories, seventeen came from
Canada.

Although neither the RCN nor the CAF met the enemy in
combat during the First World War, that would change all too
soon, and many brave deeds at sea and in the air would belong
to lads who slipped in underage.

"THE MEDAL NO MOTHER WANTS"

The   Memorial   Cross

This book is dedicated to Canada's boy soldiers, but in many respects belongs to the mothers who saw their sons off to war. One can only imagine the loneliness and the fear they felt while awaiting word from their boys who were "somewhere in France or Belgium."

By the time "the war to end all wars" was over, 620,000 Canadians had served in the armed forces, of whom 66,000 had lost their lives and another 170,000 were wounded.[1] Among these totals were many young lads — the exact numbers will never be known — who were under the age of eighteen when they enrolled. Apart from the dead and wounded, no group was more affected by these losses than Canada's women.

During the First World War, Canadian women received the franchise. The controversial *Wartime Elections Act* of 1917 extended the vote to women in the armed forces and to female relatives of military men. On May 24, 1918, female citizens

The Memorial Cross was proposed by a Toronto author in 1916 as a tribute to mothers who lost sons in the First World War.

aged twenty-one and over became eligible to vote in federal elections, regardless of whether or not they could vote provincially. Surprisingly, throughout the debates that immediately preceded the granting of women's suffrage, the key argument put forth was women's service, sacrifice, and competence during the war. Women's service even trumped any argument based on democratic rights.[2] In 1916, William Alexander Fraser, a Toronto novelist and essayist, wrote a letter to the editor that appeared in the *Toronto Star.* In it, he proposed a tribute, in the form of a silver cross, to mothers who had lost sons. "The mothers are the heroines of the bitter home trenches. They suffer in silence with no reward but the sense that they have answered the call with their heart's blood — their sons." Fraser envisioned the respect the medal would accord its wearer: "Men could take off their hats when they met a woman with this medal on her breast, they could get up, even if tired, and give her a seat on a crowded car."

In October, Fraser followed up with a one-sentence letter to Prime Minister Sir Robert Borden, enclosing the newspaper clipping of his letter. "I ask for your kind consideration of this," he wrote, "and, if it meets with your appreciation, help." Fraser's suggestion took root. On December 1, 1919, King George V approved such an award. The Canadian government took Fraser's suggestion a step farther by including the mothers *and* widows of

Canadian soldiers who died on active duty or whose deaths were later determined to be attributable to their active duty.

Officially, the award is called the Canadian Memorial Cross; unofficially it is referred to as the Silver Cross. Many people have termed it "the medal no mother wants." The first Silver Cross Mother was Charlotte Wood of Winnipeg, who had several sons that served during the war. After the war she was active in veterans' affairs, in particular with the Canadian Legion, the Imperial Veterans of Canada (absorbed into the Legion in 1926), Comrades of

Mrs. Charlotte Wood of Winnipeg was Canada's first Silver Cross Mother. She participated in the pilgrimage to France for the dedication of the Vimy Memorial.

the World, and the Association of War Widows. In 1928, she travelled to the Western Front for the first time as part of a British Legion visit to France and Flanders.

In 1936, she was among several thousand Canadian and British veterans and their families who made the pilgrimage to France to attend the dedication of the Vimy Memorial. On the eve of departure she told reporters, "I would rather have all my twelve [sons and stepsons] about me tonight than all your pilgrimages, so I would." In one of the few official acts of his short reign, King Edward VIII unveiled the memorial when he removed the Union Flag covering the central figure of a woman in sorrow, symbolizing Canada mourning her lost sons.

Charlotte Wood wore the medals of several of her sons that

day. One of them, Percy, had been killed at Vimy Ridge when he was seventeen. Wood was one of three mothers presented to the king just before the ceremony. As he held her hand, he was informed that eleven of her sons had fought in the war and five had been killed. "Mrs. Wood," he asked, "Where are you from?" When she replied "Winnipeg, Sir" he responded solemnly, "I wish your sons were all here." "Oh! Sir," she cried. "I have just been looking at the trenches and I just can't figure out why our boys had to go through that." The king immediately replied, "Please God, Mrs. Wood, it shall never happen again."[3]

The next of kin of all British Empire service personnel killed as a result of the First World War received a memorial scroll with the individual's name, a letter signed by King George V, and a memorial plaque, popularly known as the "Dead Man's Penny."

ACKNOWLEDGEMENTS

Books such as this are neither researched nor written in isolation. While making extensive use of published histories of the various components of the Canadian military, discovering the stories detailed in the preceding pages required widespread research at organizations ranging from small local libraries and military museums to national institutions. Many people who work at these organizations assisted us in bringing this largely unknown Canadian story to fruition. They range from professional historians, archivists, curators, and authors to individual Canadians who freely shared their stories of boy soldiers with us.

At the Commonwealth War Graves Commission Canadian Agency, Johanne Neville prepared lists of all Canadian servicemen under the age of eighteen buried in the commission's cemeteries around the world. Her compilation provided us with an excellent starting point. At Library and Archives Canada we reviewed hundreds of service files, war diaries, and other important documents. Thankfully, many of the personnel files have been digitized and are available online. These files represent a national treasure and are in very good hands. The assistance provided by LAC staff was first-rate from the moment we began our research. In particular we are grateful for the assistance provided by Sarah Hurford, Mary Munk, and Debbie Jiang.

At the Canadian War Museum's Military History Research Centre we were greatly assisted by collections manager Carol Reid and other staff. We are also deeply indebted to Veterans Affairs Canada for its virtual war memorial website and other online resources; to the Canadian Letters and Images Project for its excellent website; to the Reginald Roy Collection at the University of Victoria, including the in-depth interviews conducted by Chris Bell with veterans Fred Claydon and Roy Henley; and especially to the Canadian Broadcasting Corporation for having the incredible foresight to interview dozens of First World War veterans in the early 1960s for the Flanders Fields radio documentary. The insightful questions and answers in these interviews continue to put a voice to history. Not to be forgotten are the boy soldiers from the First World War who took the time to write memoirs (listed in the bibliography), which have proven such a valuable source in our research. We must also thank the Provincial Archives of Newfoundland and Labrador, which has provided researchers and relatives with an invaluable tool by putting online the complete service files of all Newfoundlanders who served in the colony's forces during the First World War.

All good military history requires good maps to help explain the battles and campaigns. Graphic artist and designer Jason Duprau rose to the occasion for us and drew the outstanding maps used in the book. With minimal direction he produced excellent maps, which are works of art.

For his encouragement of our project and writing the foreword to this book, we thank Senator Roméo Dallaire, who has done invaluable work in bringing to the world's attention the story of modern child soldiers. For their kind support we thank historians/authors Ted Barris, Mike Bechthold, Carl A. Christie, Tim Cook, Colonel (Ret'd) John Gardham, Donald E. Graves, Hugh A. Halliday, Bill Rawling, and Kevin R. Shackleton. We are also greatly indebted to Geraldine Chase for sharing the story of Willie Dailey and locating details on various other young soldiers; Ron Leblanc, President of the British Columbia Regiment Museum Society, for details of Bill Barrett's career; Dale McClare for sharing images of his uncle, "Winnie" McClare; Al Lloyd, webmaster for the excellent 21st Battalion website for information about Harold Salisbury; and Mark Peapell for useful leads on Canadian airmen of the First World War. Timely assistance also came from Sharon Adams, Bill Beswetherick, Ted Dailey, Bill Fitsell, Dale Henley, Ethel King-Shaw, librarian Mary-Kate Laphen, Frances C. Lawrie, Doug and Madeline Prosser, and Jim Wellheiser. The ownership of any errors or omissions lies entirely with us and no one else. On the research side, we owe much to Tom Rankin, who pored over countless files and offered solid feedback throughout.

When our idea was first outlined to publisher Jim Lorimer, he immediately grasped its historical significance and readily agreed to publish it and a following volume that will begin where this volume ends. At Lorimer's editorial offices, initially Diane Young, followed by Cy Strom, were the very model of the type of editor with whom authors want to work. Also, thank you to Kendra Martin, Nicole Habib, indexer Wendy Scavuzzo, and all of the staff at Lorimer who made substantial contributions to the finished product. Additionally, reader Laurie Miller's succinct and thoughtful comments and observations were most useful to the writing process.

Finally, it goes without saying (but we will) that our wives, Alice and Miriam, and our families and closest friends have been outstanding in their encouragement and support of this project. We could not have done it without them.

ENDNOTES

PREFACE

1 At least two ten-year-olds enrolled in the CEF but never made it overseas.

INTRODUCTION

1 www.victoriacrosssociety.com/events.htm. Flynn is spelled Flinn in some references.

2 Max Arthur, *Symbol of Courage: The Men Behind the Medal* (London: Pan, 2005), pp. 73, 100.

3 Jonathon Riley, *A Matter of Honour: The Life, Campaigns and Generalship of Isaac Brock* (Montreal: Robin Brass Studio, 2011), p. 11.

4 *Dictionary of Canadian Biography Online*, www.biographi.ca/index-e.html, James Wolfe.

5 Ibid., Louis-Joseph de Montcalm.

6 W. Austin Squires, *The 104th Regiment of Foot (The New Brunswick Regiment) 1803–1817* (Fredericton: NB, 1962), pp. 18-19, 234.

7 Ibid., p. 44.

8 Ibid., pp. 43–44.

9 A.W. Cockerill, *Sons of the Brave: The Story of Boy Soldiers* (London: Leo Cooper, 1984), pp. 136–137.

10 Squires, p. 213, 228, 232.

11 *Dictionary of Canadian Biography Online*, www.biographi.ca/index-e.html, Sir Isaac Brock.

12 Ibid., Charles-Michel d'Irumberry de Salaberry.

13 Ibid., Sir Samuel Benfield Steele.

14 Ibid., Sir Frederick Dobson Middleton.

15 George F. G. Stanley, *Canada's Soldiers: The Military History of an Unmilitary People* (Toronto: Macmillan, 1974), pp. 254–55; Bob Beal and Rod Macleod, *Prairie Fire: The 1885 North-West Rebellion* (Toronto: McClelland & Stewart, 1994), pp. 229–33; John Marteinson, *We Stand on Guard: An Illustrated History of the Canadian Army* (Montreal: Ovale, 1992), pp. 43–48; Norman Black, *History of Saskatchewan and the Old North West* (Regina: North West Historical Company Publishers, 1913), p. 303.

16 *Dictionary of Canadian Biography Online*, www.biographi.ca/index-e.html, Sir Samuel Benfield Steele.

17 John Boileau, *Canada's Soldiers in South Africa: Tales from the Boer War, 1899–1902* (Toronto: Lorimer, 2011), pp. 11–24.

18 Ibid., pp. 33–37.

19 *Queen's Own Rifles of Canada Museum/Archives*, qormuseum.org/soldiers-of-the-queens-own/non-commissioned-officers/williams-douglas-f/.

20 "Remembering QOR Bugler Douglas Williams," *The Powder Horn*, Fall 2007, p. 8.

21 Boileau, pp. 38–39.

22 Ibid., pp. 43–51.

23 Ibid., p. 68.

24 Ibid., p. 74.

25 Ibid., pp. 77–78.

26 Ibid., pp. 105–16.

27 William Beahen, "Filling out the Skeleton: Paramilitary Support Groups 1904–1914," *Canadian Defence Quarterly* vol. 13, no. 4 (Spring 1984), pp. 34–35. Between 1903 and 1914, the Permanent Force grew from nine hundred to more than three thousand, while the NPAM trained numbers rose from twenty-five thousand to fifty-five thousand during the same period.

28 Beahen, pp. 37–38.

29 Ibid., pp. 38–39.

30 G.W.L. Nicholson, *The Fighting Newfoundlander: A History of the Royal Newfoundland Regiment*, (McGill-Queens: Montreal and Kingston, 2006), p. 92.

31 Ibid., pp. 92–97.

32 Beahen, p. 39.

33 Nicholson, pp. 93, 97.

CHAPTER 1

1 Martin Gilbert, *First World War* (London: Weidenfeld & Nicolson, 1994), pp. 11–12.

2 J. Castell Hopkins, *Canada at War: A Record of Heroism and Achievement 1914–1918* (Toronto: Canadian Annual Review, 1919), p. 24.

3 Debates, House of Commons, Session 1914, 1st June, vol. V, col. 4580.

4 Barbara W. Tuchman, *The Guns of August* (New York: Macmillan, 1962), pp. 91–92.

5 British Blue Book Cd. 7860, Document No. 160, "Report of late British Ambassador in Berlin, rendered on his return to London, 8th August 1914."

6 Debates, House of Commons, Session 1910, 12th January.

7 Col. A. Fortescue Duguid, *Official History of the Canadian Forces in the Great War 1914–19*, General Series, vol. 1 (Ottawa: Minister of National Defence, 1938), appx. 16, p. 15.

8 Hopkins, p. 42.

9 Although only 22,500 men were required for a division, some 36,000 were enrolled initially. Of the 1,500 officers, fully two-thirds were Canadian-born, while of the 34,500 men less than 30 per cent were born in Canada; 65 per cent were born in Britain or the British Empire.

10 Gwatkin became the country's chief of the general staff from 1913–19 and was promoted major-general in 1914.

11 Duguid, appx. 11, p. 11.

12 An additional twelve infantry battalions served with the 5th Division in England (commanded by Sam Hughes's son, Major-General Garnet Hughes, promoted for the occasion), while several others were converted to pioneer, forestry, or railway units and served on the Western Front.

13 Duguid, appx. 44, p. 37.

14   Desmond Morton, *When Your Number's Up: The Canadian Soldier in the First World War* (Toronto: Random House, 1993), p. 71. The doctors conducting the physicals often worked quickly, making note of visible scars, bruises, deformities, or underdeveloped features. They often conducted these cursory exams with several naked men awaiting their turns in the same room or just outside the door.

15   LAC, RG 150, Accession 1992-93/166, Box 6153-49, Attestation Paper Russell Mick.

16   Ibid.

17   Desmond Morton and J. L. Granatstein, *Marching to Armageddon: Canadians and the Great War 1914–1919* (Toronto: Lester & Orpen Dennys, 1989), p. 30.

18   Tim Cook, "'He was determined to go,' Underage Soldiers in the Canadian Expeditionary Force," *Histoire sociale/Social History* vol. 41, no. 81 (May 2008), p. 48, n. 25.

19   Morton and Granatstein, p. 31.

20   James M. Pitsula, *For All We Have and Are: Regina and the Experience of the Great War* (Winnipeg: University of Manitoba, 2008), p. 149.

21   Cook, p. 41.

22   Cockerill, p. 137.

23   Daphne Read, ed., *The Great War and Canadian Society: An Oral History* (Toronto: New Hogtown Press, 1978), pp. 107–08. "Frank Bell" is a pseudonym for a veteran of the First World War interviewed in Toronto in 1974 as a part of the War and Canadian Society Project. Pseudonyms were used to guarantee privacy.

24   LAC, MG 30 E100, Sir Arthur Currie papers, vol. 3, file A H.

25   Read, p. 101. "Burton Woods" is also a pseudonym.

CHAPTER 2

1   Daniel G. Dancocks, *Welcome to Flanders Fields: The First Canadian Battle of the Great War: Ypres, 1915* (Toronto: McClelland and Stewart, 1988), pp. 48–49; Morton, pp. 20–21.

2   Duguid, p. 106.

3   If the number of underage soldiers in the first contingent compares proportionally with the total number who served, then there were about twelve hundred adolescents in it. For an analysis of the estimated total numbers, see Cook, "'He was determined to go.'

4   The CEF was technically a part of the much larger British Expeditionary Force and subject to its rules and regulations.

5   Cook, p. 51.

6   Hansard, House of Commons Debates, April 25, 1916, p. 3049. It seems that the prime minister never did report back to MPs.

7   Cook, p. 59.

8   This quote and other aspects of Thompson's story appeared in a series of three newspaper articles written by John Thompson in the Mildmay, Ontario *Town Crier* in early 2009. In them, it is erroneously stated that Thompson initially

enlisted when he was thirteen.

9   LAC, RG 150, Accession 1992–93/166, Box 9655-14, Attestation Paper Robert Clarence Thompson.

10   Ibid.

11   Fred Claydon, Reginald Roy Collection, 1982. University of Victoria (hereinafter UVIC). Interviewed by Chris Bell.

12   Statistics Canada, "Average wage of farm help in Canada, by province, 1909, 1910 and 1914 to 1916."

13   Roy Edward Henley, Reginald Roy Collection, 1982, UVIC. Interviewed by Chris Bell. Henley's birth certificate shows he was born on August 22, 1901.

14   Cockerill, p. 139.

15   LAC, RG 150, Accession 1992–93/166, Box 4267-31, Attestation Paper Roy Edward Henley.

16   LAC, RG 9, III-A-I, vol. 90, 10-12-15, Adjutant General Reid to Minister OMFC Perley, November 8, 1916.

17   L. C. Giles, *Liphook, Bramshott and the Canadians* (Bordon, England: Bramshott and Liphook Preservation Society, 1986), p. 6.

18   LAC, RG 9, III-A-I, vol. 90, 10-12-8, Order 2483, September 18, 1917.

19   LAC, RG 150, Accession 1992–93/166, Box 6922-37, Attestation Paper Daniel Sayre Mackay.

20   Bruce Tascona, *From the Forks to Flanders Field: The Story of the 27th City of Winnipeg Battalion 1914–1919* (Winnipeg: self-published, 1995), pp. 10–22.

21   LAC, RG 9, III, vol. 4708, 90/21, YSB Historical Record, December 8, 1918.

22   Henley, Reginald Roy Collections, UVIC.

23   Giles, p.8.

24   LAC, RG 9, III, vol. 2859, 11–33, Adjutant General to CGS, June 3, 1918.

25   Report of the Ministry Overseas Military Forces of Canada (London: H. M. Stationery Office, 1918), p. 24.

26   This and other quotations are taken from interviews with John Babcock published in various magazines and newspapers, such as *MacLean's*, June 11, 2007.

27   LAC, RG 150, Accession 1992–93/166, Box 325-25, Attestation Paper John Foster Henry Babcock.

28   A few months later, Kinmel Park was the location of an infamous incident involving Canadian troops. The men were dissatisfied with long delays in returning home and, on March 4–5, 1919, a riot and mutiny broke out in which five Canadians were killed and twenty-three wounded.

CHAPTER 3

1   Cook, p. 47; LAC, RG 150, Accession 1992–93/166, Box 3644-44, Donald Gordon; Bruce Tascona, *Little Black Devils* (Winnipeg Frye Publications for Royal Winnipeg Rifles, 1983), p. 77.

2   Marteinson, p. 101.

3   Tim Cook, *At The Sharp End: Canadians Fighting The Great War, 1914–1916* (Toronto: Viking, 2007), p. 69.

4 Marteinson, pp. 101–102; Nathan M. Greenfield, *Baptism Of Fire: The Second Battle of Ypres and the Forging of Canada, April 1915* (Toronto: HarperCollins, 2007), p. 13.

5 Colonel Kenneth Cameron, *History of No. 1 Canadian General Hospital, 1914–1919* (Sackville, NB: Tribune, 1938), pp. 130–31.

6 Meningitis and pneumonia also killed many soldiers on the Western Front, among them Lieutenant-Colonel John McCrae, author of "In Flanders Fields."

7 Canadian Broadcasting Corporation, LAC, RG 41, vol. 8.

8 Marteinson, p. 103.

9 Cook, "He was determined to go," p. 47.

10 Dancocks, pp. 102–03.

11 Cook, "He was determined to go," p. 47.

12 Tascona, p. 77.

13 The Canadian Letters and Images Project, www.canadianletters.ca (hereinafter CLIP), William Lockhard Campbell letter, 21 April 1915.

14 Ibid.

15 LAC, RG 150, Accession 1992–93/166, Box 1461-40, Attestation Paper William Lockhard Campbell.

16 CLIP, Private James McGill letter, undated.

17 Ibid.

18 LAC, RG 150, Accession 1992–93/166, Box 6932-39, Attestation Paper John Wilfred McKay; Commonwealth War Graves Commission (hereinafter CWGC), Canadian Agency, Casualty List for Soldiers aged 14–17; Mentioned in Despatches, 31 May 1915 from Field Marshal Sir John French.

19 Ibid.

20 LAC, RG 150, Accession 1992–93/166, Box 6602–12 Private George McCahon.

21 Biography, Private William Barrett, 7th (British Columbia) Battalion, BCR Museum Society.

22 Lieutenant-Colonel H. M. Urquhart, *The History of the 16th Battalion (The Canadian Scottish) Canadian Expeditionary Force In The Great War, 1914–1919* (Toronto: MacMillan, 1932), p. 67.

23 Biography, Private Barrett.

24 Urquhart, p. 67.

25 Greenfield, p. 242. The same book notes that MacArthur attached himself to a British unit later in the day, but had "left his Ross rifle in the German, whose earlier wounds had been dressed by a Canadian."

26 Jonathan F. Vance, *Maple Leaf Empire: Canada, Britain, and Two World Wars* (Don Mills, ON: Oxford University Press, 2012), p. 63.

27 D. J. Goodspeed, *The Road Past Vimy: The Canadian Corps 1914–1918* (Toronto: Macmillian, 1969), p. 35.

CHAPTER 4

1 Sergeant Fred Bagnall, *Not Mentioned in Despatches: The Memoir of Sergeant Fred Bagnall, 14th Canadian Infantry Battalion, Royal Montreal Regiment Canadian Expeditionary Force 1914–1917* (CEF Books, Hartland Molson Library,

Canadian War Museum, 1933), p. 74; Goodspeed, p. 42.

2 Bagnall, p. 74.

3 Toronto World newspaper, October 4, 1915.

4 Ibid.

5 Urquhart, p. 78.

6 Goodspeed, p. 43.

7 CWGC, Canadian Agency, Casualty List for Soldiers aged 14–17.

8 Ibid.

9 LAC, RG 150, Accession 1992–93/166, Box 1298-3, Attestation Paper Frank Wilfrid Burnley.

10 Cameron, p. 194.

11 CWM, Letters from Lance Corporal Howard Salisbury; LAC, RG 150, Accession 1992–93/166, Box 8615-30, Howard Salisbury.

12 Ibid.

13 Ibid.

14 Ibid.

15 Ibid.

16 Ibid.

CHAPTER 5

1 LAC, RG 150, Accession 1992–93/166, Box 7407-8; LAC, RG 150, Accession 1992–93/166, Box 7407-8; Experience of David Stephen O'Brien In World War (1)-1914–1918, LAC, MG 30 E4261, p. 1.

2 Ibid. A profile on O'Brien contains information that is contrary to his memoir at LAC. The account at www.4cmr.com notes O'Brien sailed from Canada on the SS *Missanabie* on October 9, 1915, while his memoir states he arrived in England in August 1915 and was in France by December that year. The profile also notes on January 28, 1916, O'Brien was transferred for Overseas Service with the 8th Infantry Brigade, the same day landed in France as part of the contingent to build up the 4th CMR, and on February 21 was taken on strength with that unit.

3 Ibid., O'Brien, pp. 1–2.

4 O'Brien, p. 2.

5 Kevin R. Shackleton, *Second To None: The Fighting 58th Battalion of the Canadian Expeditionary Force* (Toronto, Dundurn Press, 2002), pp. 16–33.

6 LAC, RG 41., vol. 15., Albert Fallon.

7 CWGC, Canadian Agency, www.cwgc.org/search/casualty_details, Private Keith Bruce Crosby, 24th Battalion, CEF.

8 Casualty reports of service personnel aged 14 to 17, CWGC Canadian Agency; Veterans Affairs Canada, Virtual War Memorial, Private Keith Bruce Crosby.

9 CLIP, www.canadianletters.ca/letters, Keith Bruce Crosby.

10 Cook, *Sharp End,* p. 332.

11 Nicholson, p. 146.

12 LAC, RG 150, Accession 1992–93/166, Box 6215-30; Veterans Affairs Canada, Canadian Virtual War Memorial, Private Hubert Mills.

13 *Hamilton Spectator*, May 11, 1916.

14 Cook, *Sharp End*, p. 350.

15 Geraldine Chase and Bill Beswetherick, *Gananoque Remembers: A Tribute To The Men Who Gave Their Lives For Our Freedom* (Gananoque, ON, 2005), p. 33; 1901 Scottish Census; genealogical research on the family of David and Annie Drummond of Dunfermline, Fife, Scotland.

16 Ibid.

17 Chase and Beswetherick, p. 110.

18 Geraldine Chase and Bill Beswetherick, genealogical research on the Drummond family.

19 Morton, pp. 199–200.

20 Chase and Beswetherick, genealogical research.

21 O'Brien, p. 2.

22 O'Brien, p. 3. In *When Your Number's Up*, Desmond Morton notes on page 209 that a 4th CMR soldier, Corporal Peter Thornton, wounded in the chest, right leg, and jaw, was shot in the back and shoulder when he was unable to march further. He also notes that the soldier was loaded onto a stretcher and survived. The soldier O'Brien said he saw shot was "simply shot … through the head … the German guards paying no more attention to this cold-blooded murder than if it had been a dog."

23 O'Brien, p. 6.

24 Morton, p. 211.

CHAPTER 6

1 The Newfoundland Regiment and the Great War Database, www.therooms.ca/regiment/part3_database.asp (hereinafter The Rooms), John Fielding Chaplin.

2 Nicholson, p. 131.

3 Gary F. Browne, *Forget-Me-Not: Fallen Boy Soldiers, Royal Newfoundland Regiment, World War One* (St. John's: DRC Publishers, 2010), p. 25.

4 Nicholson, pp. 89–91, 97, 101–04.

5 Col. G. W. L. Nicholson, *Official History of the Canadian Army: The Canadian Expeditionary Force, 1914–1919* (Ottawa: Department of National Defence, 1964), p. 507.

6 www.heritage.nf.ca/greatwar.

7 Nicholson, *Fighting Newfoundlander*, pp. 121, 155, 159, 161–63.

8 Anthony Livesey, *The Viking Atlas of World War I* (London: Viking, 1994), p.60.

9 Nicholson, *Fighting Newfoundlander*, pp.169–70.

10 Sir Andrew MacPhail, *Official History of the Canadian Forces in the Great War 1914–19: The Medical Services* (Ottawa: King's Printer, 1925), pp. 290–93.

11 The Rooms, William Morgan.

12 The Rooms, William Frank Hardy, Edward Hardy.

13 Ibid, p. 172.

14 The Rooms, Edward Hardy.

15 Nicholson, *Fighting Newfoundlander*, pp. 173, 177.

16 The Rooms, Edward Hardy.

17   www.veterans.gc.ca/eng/collections/hrp/audio/details/414.

18   Nicholson, Fighting Newfoundlander, pp. 181-83.

19   The Rooms, Norman Coultas, Stephen Fallon.

20   Nicholson, *Fighting Newfoundlander*, pp. 185–92.

21   The Rooms, Edward Hardy.

22   Browne, p. 31.

23   Nicholson, *Fighting Newfoundlander*, pp. 227-33.

24   The Rooms, William Morgan; Nicholson, *Fighting Newfoundlander*, p. 228.

25   Gordon Corrigan, *Mud, Blood and Poppycock: Britain and the First World War* (London: Cassell, 2004), p. 220.

26   The Rooms, Stephen Fallon, Norman Coultas.

27   Martin Marix Evans, *The Battles of the Somme* (Toronto: Little, Brown, 1996), pp. 15, 18.

28   Nicholson, *Fighting Newfoundlander*, pp. 268, 274.

29   The Rooms, William Morgan, Stephen Fallon, Norman Coultas.

30   www.veterans.gc.ca/eng/collections/hrp/audio/details/414.

31   Nicholson, *Fighting Newfoundlander*, pp. 229, 273–76, 281, 284, 301–02, 306–07.

32   The Rooms, Edward Hardy.

33   Nicholson, *Fighting Newfoundlander*, pp. 310–15.

34   The Rooms, Edward Hardy.

35   The Rooms, George Graham Crosbie.

CHAPTER 7

1   Chase and Beswetherick, *Gananoque Remembers*, pp. 38–39; LAC, RG 150, Accession 1992–93/166, Box 2263-38, William Dailey; Archival files and William Dailey letters, Geraldine Chase, Seeley's Bay, ON.

2   Chase, archival files and William Dailey letters.

3   Ibid.

4   Shackleton, pp. 29, 79, 84.

5   Cook, *Sharp End*, pp. 437–38.

6   LAC, MG 31 G29, Lance Cattermole papers, vol. 1.

7   Shackleton, p. 84.

8   CWM, AQN 20030308, Owen Brothers papers: James Hector Owen, Cecil William Owen, Iorwerth Richard Owen.

9   Cook, *Sharp End*, p. 502.

10   LAC, RG 41, vol. 13.

11   LAC, RG 41, vol. 10.

12   James L. McWilliams and R. James Steel, *The Suicide Battalion* (Edmonton, Hurtig, 1978), pp. 16, 27, 46–48, 67.

13   Marteinson, pp. 151–52.

14   McWilliams and Steel, p. 67.

15   Cook, *Sharp End*, p. 521.

CHAPTER 8

1 Claydon, Reginald Roy Collections, UVIC.
2 Cook, *Sharp End*, p. 423 and www.somme-1916.com/albert.htm.
3 Claydon, Reginald Roy Collections, UVIC.
4 Shackleton, p. 93.
5 Brereton Greenhous and Stephen J. Harris, *Canada and the Battle of Vimy Ridge, 9–12 April, 1917* (Ottawa: Canada Communication Group Publishing, 1992) p. 49.
6 Herbert Fairlie Wood, *Vimy!* (Toronto: Macmillan, 1967), p. 71.
7 LAC, RG 150, Accession 1992–93/166, Box 6334-30, Private Percival Moore.
8 Tim Cook, *Shock Troops: Canadians Fighting The Great War, 1917–1918* (Toronto: Viking Canada, 2008) pp. 74, 76.
9 Claydon, Reginald Roy Collections, UVIC.
10 Major Michael Boire, "The Underground War: Military Mining Operations in support of the attack on Vimy Ridge, 9 April 1917," *Canadian Military History Journal* vol. 1, nos. 1 and 2 (Autumn 1992), pp. 15–23; www.nztunnellers.com/history/warunderground.html. The geophone was a device that consisted of two wooden discs about ten centimetres in diameter by thirty-seven millimetres thick. In the centre of each was a layer of mercury contained between mica plates, and each disc was connected to rubber tubes leading to earpieces. By placing the discs of the stethoscope against the tunnel, the operator could hear picks being used to carve out a passageway or underground gallery, or the muffled sound of sandbags or boxes of explosives being dragged into position.
11 J. C. Neill, ed., *The New Zealand Tunnelling Company 1915–1919* (Christchurch: Whitcombe and Tombs, 1922).
12 Claydon, Reginald Roy Collections, UVIC.
13 Pierre Berton, *Vimy* (Toronto: McClelland and Stewart, 1986), p. 56; Cook, *Shock Troops*, p. 6; Morton and Granatstein, pp. 55, 138.
14 Nicholson, *Official History*, p. 90.
15 Wood, p. 95.
16 Cook, *Shock Troops*, p. 77.
17 Claydon, Reginald Roy Collections, UVIC.
18 Wood, p. 46
19 Norah L. Lewis, ed., *"I Want to Join Your Club": Letters From Rural Children, 1900–1920* (Waterloo, ON: Wilfrid Laurier University Press, 1996), pp. 220–21.
20 R. E. Henley, interviews, 1982, Reginald Roy Collections, UVIC.
21 Claydon, Reginald Roy Collections, UVIC.
22 Cook, *Shock Troops*, p. 57.
23 Claydon, Reginald Roy Collections, UVIC.

CHAPTER 9

1 Andrew B. Godefroy, "A Lesson in Success: The Calonne Trench Raid, 17 January 1917," *Canadian Military History Journal* vol. 8, no. 2 (Spring 1999), pp. 25–34.
2 Arthur Esdon diary, 21stbattalion.ca.
3 Charles Ernest Hyderman, 21stbattalion.ca.

4   Esdon diary.

5   Godefroy, p. 29.

6   Cook, *Shock Troops*, p. 59.

7   Esdon diary. The word "fishtail" was soldier slang for a small, but deadly type of German mortar that was propelled by a launcher or "machine."

8   Hyderman, 21stbattalion.ca.

9   Cook, "He was determined to go," p. 59.

10   Nicholson, *Official History*, p. 241.

11   Morton and Granatstein, p. 140.

12   Cook, *Shock Troops*, p 85.

13   Norm Christie, *Winning The Ridge: The Canadians at Vimy Ridge, 1917* (Ottawa: CEF Books, 2004), pp. 10–11.

14   Cook, *Shock Troops*, p. 96.

15   Thomas P. Rowlett, "Memoirs of a Signaller, 1914–1918" (unpublished memoir, CWM Military History Research Centre), p. 19.

16   Fred Claydon, interviews, 1982. Reginald Roy Collections, UVIC.

17   Rowlett, p. 20.

18   Gordon Hamilton, interview with Cyril Smith (*Vancouver Sun*, April 9, 1999).

19   Cook, *Shock Troops*, p. 80.

20   Greenhous and Harris, p. 78.

21   Nicholson, *Official History*, p. 250.

22   Cook, *Shock Troops*, pp. 97–98.

23   David Moir, "At What Price," *Legion Magazine*, 1977), pp. 16–17.

24   *Peterborough Examiner* interview, April 1992.

25   Family history from Bill Fitsell of Kingston, ON, Jack Fitsell's son.

CHAPTER 10

1   Wood, pp. 130–31.

2   Jack Sheldon, *The German Army on Vimy Ridge 1914–1917* (Barnsley, South Yorkshire: Pen & Sword, 2008), p. 292–94.

3   LAC, RG 150 Accession 1992–93/166, Box 4811-24, John Jenken.

4   21sbattalion.ca, Frank Edmund Davern.

5   21stbattalion.ca, Archibald Barrow, with biographical research by Laura Huxley; William Powell, *Oxford's Heroes — Lost But Not Forgotten: A Tribute To The Men and Women of Oxford County Who Gave Their Lives In Service of Their Country* (self-published, 2009), p. 11.

6   War Diary 24th Battalion.

7   Dale McClare, ed., *The Letters of a Young Canadian Soldier During World War I, P. Winthrop McClare of Mount Uniacke, N.S.* (Dartmouth, N.S.: Brook House, 2000), pp. 106–08.

8   Claydon, Reginald Roy Collections, UVIC.

9   LAC, RG 150 Accession 1992–93/166, Box 6279-10, David Moir.

10   Moir, p. 17.

11   Claydon, Reginald Roy Collections, UVIC.

12   LAC, RG 150 Accession 1992–93/166, Box 1544-22, Harold Carter.

13 Wood, pp. 146–47.
14 Col. John Gardam, *Seventy Years After, 1914–1984* (Stittsville, ON: Canada's Wings, 1983), pp. 29–33.
15 Ibid.; LAC, RG 150 Accession 1992–93/166, Box 3204-6, Edward Charles Forrest.
16 LAC, RG 150 Accession 1992–93/166, Box 6334-30, Percival Moore.
17 Ibid.; Gardam, pp. 29–33.
18 Gardam, pp. 29–33.
19 Cook, *Shock Troops*, p. 133–34.
20 Gordon Hamilton, *Vancouver Sun*, April 9, 1999.
21 Cook, *Shock Troops*, pp. 134–36.
22 LAC, RG 150 Accession 1993–92/166, Box 4267-31, Roy Edward Henley.
23 Ibid. "SS *Welshman* Sailing Info." LAC, RG 9-II-B-9, vol. 3, file FD 225.
24 Roy Edward Henley, interviews 1982. Reginald Roy Collections, UVIC.
25 LAC, RG 150 Accession 1993–92/166, Box 4267-31, Roy Edward Henley.

CHAPTER 11

1   The Rooms, Samuel Stuart Reid.
2   Nicholson, *Fighting Newfoundlander*, pp. 321–29.
3   The Rooms, Gordon C. Lewis; Browne, op. cit., pp. 86–87.
4   Nicholson, *Fighting Newfoundlander*, pp. 331–40.
5   Ibid., pp. 346–51.
6   The Rooms, Joseph Patrick Vaughan; Browne, pp. 92–93.
7   The Rooms, William Adams.
8   The Rooms, Alfred Edward Cake.
9   The Rooms, Harold G. Jacobs.
10 Nicholson, *Fighting Newfoundlander*, pp. 351–56.
11 On April 11–12, 1918, Forbes-Robertson earned the Victoria Cross for his actions as CO of the 1st Battalion, the Border Regiment at Vieux Berquin, France, where he repeatedly saved the situation and helped to stem the German advance. When the award was announced, Newfoundland newspapers treated him as one of their own.
12 Nicholson, *Fighting Newfoundlander*, pp. 361–400.
13 The Rooms, Otto Herbert Adams. Originally Adams's online file at The Rooms was blank, but it is no longer so. In *Fallen Boy Soldiers*, Browne discusses Adams on pp. 125–29 without ever mentioning his name, but on the website Maple Leaf Up (www.mapleleafup.ca), Great War historian Daniel James Murphy reveals Adams's name and additional details of his case.

CHAPTER 12

1   Letters of Private Walter King, Ethel M. King-Shaw, Calgary, Alta.
2   LAC, RG 41, vol. 16, Archie Brown.
3   Claydon, Reginald Roy Collections, UVIC.
4   Mike Bechthold, Army Biography on "Frank R. MacMackin, MM — Brave

Young Warrior," *Canadian Army Journal* vol. 10, no. 4 (Winter 2008), pp. 96–100; LAC, RG 150, Box 7098-32; *War Diary, 10th Battalion,* April to August 1917; biographical note compiled by Lieutenant-Colonel W. J. Osborne; files from Doug and Madeline Prosser, Petitcodiac, NB.

5   Nicholson, *Official History*, pp. 274–78.

6   LAC, RG 150, Accession 1992–93/166, Box 7604-29; www.vac-acc.gc.ca/virtual; Connie Cripps; Belle Isle Regional High School, Springfield, NB.

7   Private Eric Parlee letters, www.vac-acc.gc.ca/virtual.

8   LAC, RG 41, vol. 10.

9   William B. Woods, "A Private's Own Story of the First World War" (1989), LAC, MG 31 G30.

10   Bryan Joyce biographies on Pte. Thomas Davy and Shurley Asselstine, www.4cmr.com/davy.htm; www.4cmr.com/asselstine.htm

11   LAC, RG 150, Accession 1992–93/166, Box 8962-14; *Toronto Star,* July 31, 1917; www.vac-acc-gc.ca/content/collections/virtualmem.

12   Bechthold, pp. 99–100.

13   William G. Ogilvie, *Umty-Iddy-Umty: The Story of a Canadian Signaller in the First World War* (Erin, ON: Boston Mills Press, 1982) p. 24.

14   Marteinson, p. 168.

CHAPTER 13

1   LAC, RG 41, vol. 16, Jack MacKenzie.

2   Marteinson, p. 169.

3   Cook, *Shock Troops*, p. 316.

4   LAC, RG 41, vol. 16, Archie Brown

5   McWilliams and Steel, p. 107.

6   Claydon, Reginald Roy Collections, UVIC.

7   Marteinson, p. 177.

8   LAC, RG 41, vol. 10.

9   Ogilvie, pp. 26–29.

10   Ibid, p. 9.

11   Claydon, Reginald Roy Collection, UVIC.

12   Ogilvie, pp. 31–32.

13   Stephen Snelling, *VCs of the First World War: Passchendaele 1917* (Gloucestershire, England: Sutton, 1998), p. 242.

14   Claydon, Reginald Roy Collections, UVIC.

15   McWilliams and Steel, p. 111.

16   Ibid. p. 114–15.

17   Cook, *Shock Troops*, p. 338.

18   LAC, RG 41, vol. 16, Jack MacKenzie.

19   LAC, RG 41, vol. 16, Archie Brown.

20   LAC, RG 41, vol. 16, Jack MacKenzie.

21   LAC, RG 41, vol. 16, Archie Brown.

22   LAC, RG 41, vol. 10

23   Cook, *Shock Troops*, p. 364.

24   Claydon, Reginald Roy Collection, UVIC.

CHAPTER 14

1   The Rooms, Chesley Bennett.
2   Nicholson, *Official History*, pp. 333–36; Morton & Granatstein, p. 174.
3   Nicholson, *Fighting Newfoundlander*, pp. 409–10.
4   LAC, RG 150, Box 3676-42, John Gould.
5   The Peerage, www.thepeerage.com/p40719.htm.
6   LAC, RG 150, Box 10462-41, John Wilson.
7   Nicholson, *Fighting Newfoundlander*, p. 423.
8   Marteinson, pp. 181–82.
9   Nicholson, *Official History*, p. 338.
10   http://21stbattalion.ca/tributeos/salisbury_h.html.
11   Nicholson, *Official History*, pp. 366–67, 369.
12   Nicholson, Ibid, pp. 367–69.
13   Brereton Greenhous, *Dragoon: The Centennial History of the Royal Canadian Dragoons 1883–1983* (Ottawa: Guild of the Royal Canadian Dragoons, 1983), p. 223.
14   LAC, RG 150, Box 2275-6, Frank Daly; *Toronto Evening Telegram*, April 22, 1918.
15   Nicholson, *Official History*, p. 368.
16   Nicholson, *Fighting Newfoundlander*, pp. 447–54.
17   The Rooms, Frederick Bugden.
18   LAC, RG 150, Accession 1992–93/166, Box 9655-14, Attestation Paper Robert Clarence Thompson.
19   John Boileau, *Halifax and the Royal Canadian Navy* (Halifax: Nimbus, 2010), p. 24.
20   John Thompson, "1918 Child Soldier from Hillier," Mildmay (Ontario) *Town Crier*, March, 2009.

CHAPTER 15

1   Claydon, Reginald Roy Collection, UVIC.
2   Ibid.
3   Cook, *Shock Troops*, p. 437.
4   Marteinson, p. 189.
5   LAC, RG 41, vol. 15.
6   Ogilvie, pp. 40–41.
7   LAC, RG 41, vol. 15.
8   Nicholson, *Official History*, p. 399.
9   Cook, *Shock Troops*, p. 449.
10   LAC, RG41, vol. 17.
11   Claydon, Reginald Roy Collection, UVIC.
12   McWilliams and Steel, p. 150.
13   Ogilvie, p. 43.
14   McWilliams and Steel, p. 152.

15 LAC, RG 41, vol. 10.
16 LAC, RG 41, vol. 17.
17 Marteinson,p. 195; Cook, p. 451.
18 Nicholson, pp. 427–28.
19 LAC, RG 41, vol. 17.
20 LAC, RG 150, Accession 1992–93/166, Box 6279-10, David Moir.
21 *Legion Magazine*, "Last Post" death notice, Corporal David A. Moir.
22 Henley, Reginald Roy Collections, UVIC.
23 LAC, RG 150, Accession 1992–93/166, Box 4267-31, Roy Edward Henley.
24 Marteinson, p. 198.
25 McWilliams and Steel, p. 164.
26 Marteinson, p. 199.
27 McWilliams and Steel, p. 168.
28 LAC, RG 41, vol. 10.

CHAPTER 16

1 Cook, *Shock Troops*, p. 510.
2 Nicholson, *Official History*, p. 442; Cook, pp. 504–06.
3 Cook, *Shock Troops*, p. 505.
4 Ibid., p. 369.
5 LAC, RG 41, vol. 17, M. E. Parsons.
6 Cook, *Shock Troops*, p. 496. This was after breaking through the Drocourt-Quéant Line in early September 1918.
7 Ibid., p. 505.
8 Ibid., p. 510; Nicholson, *Official History*, p. 444.
9 Ogilvie, p. 50.
10 Ibid., p. 51.
11 LAC, RG 150, Box 6963-32, Arthur MacKenzie.
12 LAC, RG 41, vol. 16, Arthur MacKenzie.
13 *Legion Magazine*, "Last Post" death notice, 1986.
14 LAC, RG 41, vol. 16, John Cadenhead; LAC, RG150, Box 1368-25.
15 LAC, RG 41, vol. 13, David Low.
16 Files from Jim Wellheizer, Ayr, ON; LAC RG 150, Box 70-19, Louis John Albrecht.
17 LAC, RG 41, vol. 17, M.E. Parsons.
18 Marteinson, p. 203.

CHAPTER 17

1 The Rooms, Alexander Barter.
2 The Rooms, Charles Bennett.
3 The Rooms, John Russell.
4 Ricketts is also often listed as having won the Distinguished Conduct Medal, but that is because of an error by the Newfoundland Pay and Record Office; he was never awarded the DCM. The French government did, however, award him the Croix de guerre avec étoile de vermeil.

5   Unless otherwise noted, the details of Tommy Ricketts's life are based on co-author John Boileau's *Valiant Hearts: Atlantic Canada and the Victoria Cross* (Halifax: Nimbus, 2005), pp. 197–207.
6   The Rooms, Thomas Ricketts.
7   Ibid.
8   Ibid.
9   Only eight men under eighteen have been awarded the VC.
10 The Rooms, Thomas Ricketts.
11 Illuminated addresses were official certificates, usually hand printed, with elaborate lettering in many colours. From the 1880s to the 1930s they were a popular way to mark special occasions or outstanding service.
12 The Rooms, Thomas Ricketts.
13 Ibid.

CHAPTER 18

1   LAC, RG 41, vol.13, David D. Low.
2   Nicholson, *Official History*, p. 468–69.
3   Shane B. Schreiber, *Shock Army of the British Empire: The Canadian Corps in the Last 100 Days of the Great War* (St. Catharines, ON: Vanwell Publishing Ltd., 2004), p. 117.
4   LAC, RG 41, vol. 20, Thomas Hazlitt.
5   LAC, RG 41, vol. 14, A. N. Davis.
6   Ogilvie, pp. 52–53.
7   *Encyclopedia Britannica Online*.
8   Cook, *Shock Troops*, p. 556; Marteinson, p. 207.
9   Morton and Granatstein, p. 232.
10 Ibid., pp. 559–60.
11 www.veterans.gc.ca/eng/collections/virtualmem/detail/533791.
12 Cook, *Shock Troops*, p. 567.
13 LAC, RG 41, vol. 17, W. Thom.
14 LAC, RG 41, vol. 16, W. A. Crouse.
15 Ogilvie, p. 53.
16 LAC, RG 41, vol. 16.
17 LAC, RG 41, vol. 13.
18 Nicholson, *Official History*, p. 477.
19 Cook, *Shock Troops*, pp. 575-76.
20 LAC, RG 41, Vol. 14, C. P. Keeler.
21 LAC, RG 41, Vol. 12, George Cruickshank.
22 Nicholson, *Official History*, p. 480.
23 Cook, *Shock Troops*, p. 577.
24 LAC, RG 41, Vol. 18, W. J. Home.
25 Nicholson, Official History, p. 483.
26 LAC, RG 41, Vol. 13.
27 LAC, RG 41, Vol. 16.
28 Marteinson, p. 208.

29 LAC, RG 41, Vol. 17, M. E. Parsons.
30 Ogilvie, p. 55.
31 Walter King Letters, courtesy Dr. Ethel M. King-Shaw & family, Calgary, AB.
32 Schreiber, p. 131.
33 Cook, *Shock Troops*, pp. 611–12, 617.
34 www.veterans.gc.ca/eng/history/firstfar/canada
35 LAC, RG 41, Vol. 10, Morris A. Searle.
36 LAC, RG 41, Vol. 16, John Cadenhead.
37 www.britannica.com/EBchecked/topic/287805/influenza-pandemic-of-1918-19
38 Cook, *Shock Troops*, p. 584.
39 LAC, RG 41, Vol. 16.
40 Marteinson, p. 209.
41 Fred Claydon, interviews 1982, Reginald Roy Collections, UVIC.
42 LAC, RG 41, Vol. 14.

CHAPTER 19

1 Bryan Elson, *First to Die: The First Canadian Navy Casualties in the First World War* (Halifax: Formac, 2010), pp. 71–74.
2 Roland Pietsch, "Ships' Boys and Youth Culture in Eighteenth-Century Britain: The Navy Recruits of the London Marine Society," *The Northern Mariner/Le marin du nord*, vol. 14, no. 4 (October 2004), pp. 11–24.
3 John Boileau, *Half-Hearted Enemies: Nova Scotia, New England and the War of 1812* (Halifax: Formac, 2005), pp. 39–49; Dictionary of Canadian Biography Online, www.biographi.ca/index-e.html, Provo William Parry Wallis.
4 William Johnston, William G. P. Rawling, Richard H. Gimblett and John MacFarlane, *The Seabound Coast: The Official History of the Royal Canadian Navy, 1867–1939* (Toronto: Dundurn, 2010), pp. 38–39, 45.
5 Nicholson, *Fighting Newfoundlander*, pp. 90, 97, 101–03.
6 John Boileau, *Halifax and the Royal Canadian Navy*, pp. 8–11.
7 Richard H. Gimblett, "Admiral Sir Charles E. Kingsmill: Forgotten Father" in Michael Whitby, Richard H. Gimblett and Peter Haydon, eds., *The Admirals: Canada's Senior Naval Leadership in the Twentieth Century* (Toronto: Dundurn, 2006), pp. 31–47.
8 Johnston et al., p. 166.
9 Quoted in Elaine Brown, Nancy Lowry, and Kathy Schultz, *Historic Spallumcheen and its Road Names* (Armstrong, BC: Armstrong-Spallumcheen Museum and Archives Society, 1986), p. 20.
10 Leonard J. Gamble, *So Far from Home: Stories of Armstrong's Fallen of the Great War, 1914–1919* (Armstrong, BC: L. J. Gamble, 2008), pp. 107–09.
11 Elson, pp. 7, 9, 11–12. 15.
12 Boileau, *Royal Canadian Navy*, pp. 14–15.
13 Elson, pp. 24, 33–34, 41–42.
14 Boileau, *Royal Canadian Navy*, p. 15.
15 www.constable.ca/caah/mcleod.htm, Alan Arnett McLeod, VC.
16 S. F. Wise, *Canadian Airmen and the First World War: The Official History of the*

Royal Canadian Air Force, vol. 1 (Toronto: University of Toronto, 1980), pp. 26–29.

17   Ibid., pp. 44–45, 115–16.

18   Ibid., pp. 289, 318.

19   Ibid., p. x.

20   Arthur Bishop, *Our Bravest and Our Best: The Stories of Canada's Victoria Cross Winners* (Toronto: McGraw-Hill Ryerson, 1995), p. 91.

21   Carl A. Christie, "Alan Arnett McLeod VC: Canada's Schoolboy Hero," *CAHS Journal*, vol. 34, no. 1 (Spring 1996), pp. 16–21, 34; www.constable.ca/caah/mcleod.htm, Alan Arnett McLeod, VC.

22   Robert Morrison, "Diary Of A Teen Flyer," *Legion Magazine*, March/April 2013, pp. 48–50, taken from the diary of Robert George Kerr Morrison, preserved by his son Robert Morrison.

23   Quoted in Boileau, *Royal Canadian Navy*, p. 36.

EPILOGUE

1   Veterans' Affairs Canada.

2   John Boileau, *The Peaceful Revolution: 250 Years of Democracy in Nova Scotia* (Halifax: Nimbus, 2008) pp. 181–182.

3   At www.hellfire-corner.demon.co.uk/ceris.htm, researcher Ceris Schrader provides details of Charlotte Wood's life, including the eleven sons who enlisted and the five killed. Other researchers disagree with her findings. While all agree that she had twelve sons or stepsons, they vary considerably on the number killed, ranging anywhere from one to eight.

BIBLIOGRAPHY

BOOKS

Aries, Philippe. *Centuries of Childhood: A Social History of Family Life*. New York: Alfred A. Knopf, 1962.

Arthur, Max. *Symbol of Courage: The Men behind the Medal*. London: Pan, 2005.

Bagnall, Sergeant Fred. *Not Mentioned in Despatches: The Memoir of Sergeant Fred Bagnall, 14th Canadian Infantry Battalion, Royal Montreal Regiment, Canadian Expeditionary Force 1914–1917*. CEF Books, Hartland Molson Library, Canadian War Museum, 1933.

Beal, Bob and Rod Macleod. *Prairie Fire: The 1885 North-West Rebellion*. Toronto: McClelland and Stewart, 1994.

Berton, Pierre. *Vimy*. Toronto: McClelland and Stewart, 1986.

Bishop, Arthur. *Our Bravest and Our Best: The Stories of Canada's Victoria Cross Winners*. Toronto: McGraw-Hill Ryerson, 1995.

Boas, George. *The Cult of Childhood*. London: Warburg, 1966.

Black, Norman. *History of Saskatchewan and the Old North West*. Regina: North West Historical Company Publishers, 1913.

Boileau, John. *Half-Hearted Enemies: Nova Scotia, New England and the War of 1812*. Halifax: Formac, 2005.

———. *Halifax and the Royal Canadian Navy*. Halifax: Nimbus, 2010.

———. *Valiant Hearts: Atlantic Canada and the Victoria Cross*. Halifax: Nimbus, 2005.

———. *The Peaceful Revolution: 250 Years of Democracy in Nova Scotia*. Halifax: Nimbus, 2008.

———. *Canada's Soldiers in South Africa: Tales from the Boer War, 1899–1902*. Toronto: Lorimer, 2011.

Brown, Elaine, Nancy Lowry, and Kathy Schultz. *Historic Spallumcheen and Its Road Names*. Armstrong, BC: Armstrong-Spallumcheen Museum and Archives Society, 1986.

Browne, Gary F. *Forget-Me-Not: Fallen Boy Soldiers, Royal Newfoundland Regiment, World War One*. St. John's: DRC Publishers, 2010.

Cameron, Colonel Kenneth. *History of No. 1 Canadian General Hospital, 1914–1919*. Sackville, NB: The Tribune Press, 1938.

Chase, Geraldine and Bill Beswetherick. *Gananoque Remembers: A Tribute to the Men Who: Gave Their Lives for Our Freedom*. Gananoque, ON, 2005.

Christie, Norm. *Winning The Ridge: The Canadians at Vimy Ridge, 1917*. Ottawa: CEF Books, 2004.

Cockerill, A. W. *Sons of the Brave: The Story of Boy Soldiers*. London: Leo Cooper, 1984.

Cook, Tim. *At The Sharp End: Canadians Fighting The Great War, 1914–1916*. Toronto: Viking Canada.

———. *Shock Troops: Canadians Fighting the Great War, 1917–1918*. Toronto: Viking Canada, 2008.

Corrigan, Gordon. *Mud, Blood and Poppycock: Britain and the First World War.*

London: Cassell, 2004.

Cunningham, Hugh. *Children and Childhood in Western Society since 1500*. London: Longman, 1995.

Dancocks, Daniel G. *Welcome to Flanders Fields: The First Canadian Battle of the Great War; Ypres, 1915*. Toronto: McClelland and Stewart, 1988.

Duguid, Col. A. Fortescue. *Official History of the Canadian Forces in the Great War 1914–19, General Series Vol. 1*. Ottawa: Minister of National Defence, 1938.

———. *Official History of the Canadian Forces in the Great War, 1914–19, General Series. Vol. 1: Chronicle, August 1914–September 1915*. Ottawa: King's Printer, 1938.

Elson, Bryan. *First to Die: The First Canadian Navy Casualties in the First World War*. Halifax: Formac, 2010.

Evans, Martin Marix. *The Battles of the Somme*. Toronto: Little, Brown, 1996.

Gamble, Leonard J. *So Far From Home: Armstrong's Fallen of the Great War, 1914–1919*. Armstrong, BC: L. J. Gamble Publisher, 2008.

Gardam, Col. John. *Seventy Years After, 1914–1984*. Stittsville, ON: Canada's Wings, 1983.

Gilbert, Martin. *First World War*. London: Weidenfeld & Nicolson, 1994.

———. *The Battle of the Somme: The Heroism and Horror of War*. Toronto: McClelland & Stewart, 2006.

Giles, L. C. *Liphook, Bramshott and the Canadians*. Bordon, England: Bramshott and Liphook Preservation Society, 1986.

Gimblett, Richard M. "Admiral Sir Charles E. Kingsmill: Forgotten Father." In *The Admirals: Canada's Senior Naval Leadership in the Twentieth Century*, edited by Michael Whitby, Richard M. Gimblett, and Peter Haydon, pp. 31–53. Toronto: Dundurn, 2006.

Goodspeed, D. J. *The Road Past Vimy: The Canadian Corps 1914–1918*. Toronto: Macmillian, 1969.

Granatstein, J. L. and Dean F. Oliver. *The Oxford Companion to Canadian Military History*. Don Mills, ON: Oxford University Press, 2011.

Greenfield, Nathan M. *Baptism Of Fire: The Second Battle of Ypres and the Forging of Canada, April 1915*. Toronto: HarperCollins, 2007.

Greenhous, Brereton. *Dragoon: The Centennial History of the Royal Canadian Dragoons 1883–1983*. Ottawa: Guild of the Royal Canadian Dragoons, 1983.

Greenhous, Brereton and Stephen J. Harris. *Canada and the Battle of Vimy Ridge, 9–12 April, 1917*. Ottawa: Canada Communication Group Publishing, 1992.

Hindman, Hugh D. *The World of Child Labour: An Historical and Regional Survey*. Armonk, NY: M. E. Sharpe, 2009.

Hopkins, J. Castell. *Canada at War: A Record of Heroism and Achievement 1914–1918*. Toronto: Canadian Annual Review, 1919.

Johnston, William, et al. *The Seabound Coast: The Official History of the Royal Canadian Navy, 1867–1939, Vol. 1*. Toronto: Dundurn Press, 2012.

Lewis, Norah L., ed. *"I Want to Join Your Club": Letters From Rural Children, 1900–1920*. Waterloo, ON: Wilfrid Laurier University Press, 1996.

Livesey, Anthony. *The Viking Atlas of World War I*. London: Viking, 1994.

MacPhail, Sir Andrew. *Official History of the Canadian Forces in the Great War 1914–*

19; *The Medical Services*. Ottawa: King's Printer, 1925.

Marble, Allan E. *Nova Scotians at Home and Abroad: Biographical Sketches of over Six Hundred Native Born Nova Scotians*. Hantsport, NS: Lancelot Press, 1989.

Marteinson, John. *We Stand On Guard: An Illustrated History of the Canadian Army*. Montreal: Ovale Publicatons, 1992.

McClare, Dale, ed. *The Letters of a Young Canadian Soldier During World War I, P. Winthrop McClare of Mount Uniacke, N. S*. Dartmouth, NS: Brook House Press, 2000.

McWilliams, James L. and R. James Steel. *The Suicide Battalion*. Edmonton: Hurtig, 1978.

Morton, Desmond. *A Military History of Canada: From Champlain to the Gulf War*. Toronto: McClelland & Stewart, 1992.

———. *When Your Number's Up: The Canadian Soldier in the First World War*. Toronto: Random House of Canada, 1993.

Morton, Desmond, and J. L. Granatstein. *Marching to Armageddon: Canadians and the Great War 1914–1919*. Toronto: Lester & Orpen Dennys, 1989.

Neill, J. C., ed. *The New Zealand Tunnelling Company 1915–1919*. Christchurch: Whitcombe and Tombs, 1922.

Newman, Stephen K. *With The Patricia's in Flanders, 1914–1918, Then & Now*. Saanichton, BC: Bellewaerde House Publishing, 2000.

Nichol, Stephen J. *Ordinary Heroes: Eastern Ontario's 21st Battalion C.E.F. in The Great War*. Privately published, 2008.

Nicholson, Col. G. W. L. *Official History of the Canadian Army: The Canadian Expeditionary Force, 1914–1919*. Ottawa: Department of National Defence, 1964.

———. *The Fighting Newfoundlander: A History of the Royal Newfoundland Regiment*. Montreal and Kingston: McGill-Queen's University Press, 2006.

Ogilvie, William G. *Umty-Iddy-Umty: The Story of a Canadian Signaller in the First World War*. Erin, ON: Boston Mills Press, 1982.

Pitsula, James M. *For All We Have and Are: Regina and the Experience of the Great War*. Winnipeg: University of Manitoba Press, 2008.

Powell, William. *Oxford's Heroes—Lost But Not Forgotten: A Tribute to the Men and Women of Oxford County Who Gave Their Lives in Service of Their Country*. Self-published, 2009.

Read, Daphne, ed. *The Great War and Canadian Society: An Oral History*. Toronto: New Hogtown Press, 1978.

Reid, Brian A. *Named By The Enemy: A History of the Royal Winnipeg Rifles*. Montreal: Robin Brass Studio, 2010.

Riley, Jonathon. *A Matter of Honour: The Life, Campaigns and Generalship of Isaac Brock*. Montreal: Robin Brass Studio, 2011.

Schreiber, Shane B. *Shock Army of The British Empire: The Canadian Corps in the Last 100 Days of the Great War*. St. Catharines, ON: Vanwell, 2004.

Shackleton, Kevin R. *Second to None: The Fighting 58th Battalion of the Canadian Expeditionary Force*. Toronto: Dundurn Press, 2002.

Sheldon, Jack. *The German Army on Vimy Ridge 1914–1917*. Barnsley, South Yorkshire: Pen & Sword Books, 2008.

Snell, A. E. *The C.A.M.C. with the Canadian Corps during the Last Hundred Days of the Great War*. Ottawa: F. A. Acland, 1924.

Snelling, Stephen. *VCs of the First World War: Passchendaele 1917.* Gloucestershire, England: Sutton Publishing Limited, 1998.

Squires, W. Austin. *The 104th Regiment of Foot: The New Brunswick Regiment 1803– 1817.* Fredericton: Brunswick Press, 1962.

Stanley, George F. G. *Canada's Soldiers: The Military History of an Unmilitary People.* Toronto: Macmillan, 1974.

Swettenham, John. *To Seize The Victory: The Canadian Corps in World War 1.* Toronto: Ryerson Press, 1965.

Tascona, Bruce. *Little Black Devils.* Winnipeg: Frye Publications for Royal Winnipeg Rifles, 1983.

———. *From the Forks to Flanders Field: The Story of the 27th City of Winnipeg Battalion 1914–1919.* Winnipeg: self-published, 1995.

Thornhill, Bonnie and W. James MacDonald, eds. *In The Morning: Veterans of Victoria County, Cape Breton.* Sydney, NS: University College of Cape Breton Press, 1999.

Topp, Lieutenant-Colonel C. Beresford, DSO., MC. *The 42nd Battalion, C.E.F., Royal Highlanders of Canada, in the Great War.* Manotick, ON: Archive CD Books Canada Inc., 2007.

Tuchman, Barbara W. *The Guns of August.* New York: Macmillan, 1962.

Urquhart, Lieutenant-Colonel H. M. *The History of The 16th Battalion (The Canadian Scottish) Canadian Expeditionary Force In The Great War, 1914–1919.* Toronto: MacMillan, 1932.

Vance, Jonathan F. *Maple Leaf Empire: Canada, Britain, and Two World Wars.* Don Mills, ON: Oxford University Press, 2012.

Veterans' Review: A Collection of War Stories by the Veterans of Sunnybrook Medical Centre. Toronto, 1983.

Wigney, Edward H. *The C.E.F. Roll of Honour.* Ottawa: Eugene Ursual, 1996.

Wise, S. F. *Canadian Airmen of the First World War: The Official History of the Royal Canadian Air Force,* Vol. 1. Toronto: University of Toronto Press, 1980.

Wood, Herbert Fairlie. *Vimy!* Toronto: Macmillan of Canada, 1967.

Wood, Herbert Fairlie, and John Swettenham. *Silent Witness.* Toronto: Hakkert, Canadian War Museum, 1974.

Young, Albert Charles. *24 Good Men and True: Members of Branch #142 of the Royal Canadian Legion.* New York: Vantage Press, 1992.

GOVERNMENT PUBLICATIONS

British Blue Book Cd. 7860, Document No. 160, Report of late British Ambassador in Berlin, rendered on his return to London, 8th August 1914.

Debates, House of Commons, Session 1914, 1st June.

Debates, House of Commons, Session 1910, 12th January.

Debates, House of Commons, Session 1916, 26th January.

Hansard, House of Commons Debates, April 25, 1916.

Report of the Ministry Overseas Military Forces of Canada. London: H. M. Stationery Office, 1918.

Statistics Canada. Average wage of farm help in Canada, by province, 1909, 1910, and 1914 to 1916.

MAGAZINE, NEWSPAPER, AND JOURNAL ARTICLES

Bechthold, Mike. "Frank R. MacMackin, MM—Brave Young Warrior." *Canadian Military History Journal*, vol. 10, no. 4, (Winter 2008).

Beahen, William. "Filling out the Skeleton: Paramilitary Support Groups 1904–1914." *Canadian Defence Quarterly*, vol. 13, no. 4 (Spring 1984).

Boire, Major Michael. "The Underground War: Military Mining Operations in Support of the Attack on Vimy Ridge, 9 April 1917." *Canadian Military History Journal*, vol. 1, nos. 1 and 2 (Autumn 1992).

Christie, Carl A. "Alan Arnett McLeod VC: Canada's Schoolboy Hero." *Canadian Aviation Historical Society Journal*, Spring 1996.

Clark, Doug. "70 Years On." *Legion Magazine*, June 1987.

Cook, Tim. "He was Determined to Go": Underage Soldiers in the Canadian Expeditionary Force. *Histoire sociale/Social History*, vol. 41, no. 81 (May 2008).

———. "'A Proper Slaughter': The March 1917 Gas Raid at Vimy Ridge." *Canadian Military History Journal*, vol. 8, no. 2 (Spring 1999).

Fairbairn, Bill. "A Lifetime Later." *Legion Magazine*, June 1992.

Godefroy, Andrew B. "A Lesson in Success: The Calonne Trench Raid, 17 January 1917." *Canadian Military History Journal*, vol. 8, no. 2 (Spring 1999).

Hamilton, Gordon. Interview with Cyril Smith. *Vancouver Sun*, April 9, 1999.

Hamilton Spectator, May 11, 1916.

Legion Magazine "Last Post" death notice, 1986.

MacLean's, June 11, 2007.

Moir, David. "At What Price." *Legion Magazine*, 1977.

Peterborough Examiner interview, April 1992.

Pietsch, Roland. "Ships' Boys and Youth Culture in Eighteenth-Century Britain: The Navy Recruits of the London Marine Society." *The Northern Mariner/Le marin du nord*, vol. 14, no. 4 (October 2004).

"Remembering QOR Bugler Douglas Williams." *The Powder Horn*, Fall 2007.

Thompson, John. "Child Soldier from Hillier." Mildmay (ON) *Town Crier*, March 2009.

Toronto Star, October 11, 1916; July 31, 1917.

Toronto World, October 4, 1915.

WEBSITES

Alan Arnett McLeod, VC. www.constable.ca/caah/mcleod.htm.

Ceris Schrader, "'Lady Lost Five Sons,' Canada's War Mother and the Great War." www.hellfire-corner.demon.co.uk/ceris.htm.

Commonwealth War Graves Commission. www.cwgc.org.

Commonwealth War Graves Commission, Canadian Agency. www.cwgc-canadianagency.ca.

Dictionary of Canadian Biography Online. www.biographi.ca/index-e.html.

Encyclopedia Britannica Online. www.britannica.com.

Jim Vandergriff, "Factors Influencing the Development of the Idea of Childhood in Europe and America." www.web.grinnell.edu/courses/mitc/vandergr.

Maple Leaf Up. www.mapleleafup.ca.
Newfoundland and the Great War, Memorial University of Newfoundland. www.heritage.nf.ca/greatwar.
Queen's Own Rifles of Canada Museum Archive. www.qormuseum.org/soldiers-of-the-queens-own/non-commissioned-officers/williams-douglas-f.
The Canadian Great War Project. www.canadiangreatwarproject.com.
The Canadian Letters and Images Project. www.canadianletters.ca.
The Peerage. www.thepeerage.com.
The Rooms. www.therooms.ca/regiment/part3_database.asp .
Veterans Affairs Canada, *Canadian Virtual War Memorial.* www.veterans.gc.ca/eng/collections/virtualmem.
Victoria Cross Society. www.victoriacrosssociety.com/events.htm.
4th Canadian Mounted Rifles. www.4cmr.com. Biographies of Thomas Davy and Shurley Asselstine by Brian Joyce.
21st Battalion. www.21stbattalion.ca.
54th Battalion. www.54thbattalioncef.ca.

UNPUBLISHED MATERIALS

BCR Museum Society. Biography, Private William Barrett, 7th (British Columbia) Battalion.
CWM textual records, Letters from Lance Corporal Howard Salisbury.
CWM Military History Research Centre, Thomas P. Rowlett, *Memoirs of a Signaller, 1914–1918.*
CWM, AQN 20030308, Owen Brothers papers.
Commonwealth War Graves Commission, Canadian Agency, *Casualty List for Soldiers Aged 14–17.*
Experience of David Stephen O'Brien in World War I, 1914–1918, Library and Archives Canada, MG 30 E4261.
LAC, RG 150.
LAC, MG 30 E100, Sir Arthur Currie papers.
LAC, MG 31 G29, Lance Cattermole papers, vol. 1.
LAC, MG 31 G30, William B. Woods, *A Private's Own Story of the First World War,* 1989.
LAC, RG 9, Adjutant General Reid to Minister OMFC Perley.
Milton Historical Society *Soldier Summary.*
Lieut.-Col. W. J. Osborne, biographical note on Frank R. MacMackin.
"SS *Welshman* Sailing Info." LAC RG 9-II-B-9, vol. 3, file FD 225.
Walter King letters, courtesy Dr. Ethel King-Shaw and family, Calgary, AB.
War Diary, 10th Battalion, Canadian Expeditionary Force.
War Diary, 24th Battalion, Canadian Expeditionary Force.
William Dailey letters, Geraldine Chase, Seeley's Bay, ON.

INTERVIEWS AND CORRESPONDENCE

Canadian Broadcasting Corporation's interviews (conducted in the early 1960s) with First World War veterans for the radio program, *Flanders Fields.* LAC, RG 41.
Doug and Madeline Prosser, interview re Frank R. MacMackin, November 2009.

Dr. Ethel King-Shaw, interview re Walter King, 2012.

Fitsell family history from Bill Fitsell, Jack's son.

Geraldine Chase and Bill Beswetherick, genealogical research.

Jim Wellheizer, interviews and files on Louis Albrecht, 2012.

Reginald Roy Collection, interviews by Chris Bell with Fred Claydon and R. E. Henley, 1982. University of Victoria.

IMAGE CREDITS

FRONT COVER
Barrett, British Columbia Regiment Museum, Vancouer.
Over the Top, LAC C-046606.
RCN recruits, Maritime Command Museum, Halifax.
27th Battalion, LAC PA-016778.

BACK COVER
McClare cousins, Dale McClare.
Amiens-Roye Road LAC PA-002946
Strathcona's Horse, LAC C-000171.
Ottawa recruits, LAC PA-122937.
German POWs, LAC PA-000823.
4th Division, LAC PA-000832.
Cambrai, LAC PA-003246.
Dan Black, Jessica Moore.
John Boileau, Mark Doucette.

INTRODUCTION
Victoria Cross (25): Army Museum Halifax Citadel.
Wolfe (26): Attributed to Joseph Highmore, ca. 1742, oil on canvas, LAC C-003916.
Montcalm (27): After A. H. Clark, n. d., photomechanical print on wove paper, LAC
    C-021457.
Queenston Heights (29): After John David Kelly, 1896, photomechanical print, LAC
    C-000273.
Salaberry (30): E. H. De Holmfield, 1896, oil, Chateau Ramezay Museum and
    Historic Site of Montreal.
Red river expedition (31): Francis Anne Hopkins, 1877, oil on canvas, LAC
    C-002775.
Batoche (33): Sergt. Grundy, 1885, lithograph on wove paper, LAC C-002424
"Dawn of Majuba" (37): R. Caton-Woodville, 1900, oil on canvas, City of Toronto
    (on permanent loan to the Royal Canadian Military Institute).
Strathcona's Horse (39): Joan Wanklyn, 1999, oil on canvas (detail), Lord
    Strathcona's Horse Royal Canadians, Edmonton.
Toronto cadets (42): LAC PA-028887
Church Lads' Brigade (45): PANL NA-6066

CHAPTER 1
Laurier (48): John Wentworth Russell, 1913, oil on canvas, LAC C-147256.
Camp Sewell (51): LAC PA-022692.
Hughes (52): Harrington Mann, 1918, oil on canvas, CWM 8414.
224th recruiting poster (55): Unknown artist, 1914-18, lithograph, Archives of
    Ontario C233-2-0-4-196.
Chums recruiting poster (57): C. J. Patterson, 1914-18, offset lithograph on wove

paper, LAC C-147822.

Borden (58): Harrington Mann, 1918, oil on canvas, CWM 8413.

Ottawa soldiers (60): LAC PA-122937.

CHAPTER 2

Thompson (66): A. W. Cockerill, Sons of the Brave: The Story of Boy Soldiers (London: Leo Cooper, 1984).

Witley cook house (69): Anna Airy, 1918, oil on canvas, CWM 8009.

Bramshott camp (72): L. C. Giles, Liphook, Bramshott and the Canadians (Bordon, England: Bramshott and Liphook Preservation Society, 1986).

Tintown (73): L. C. Giles, Liphook, Bramshott and the Canadians (Bordon, England: Bramshott and Liphook Preservation Society, 1986).

Babcock (75), Dan Black.

Victory bonds poster (76): unknown artist, 1914-18, lithograph on wove paper, LAC Acc 1983-28-963.

CHAPTER 3

Saint-Nazaire (82): Edgar Bundy, ca. 1915, photomechanical print, LAC C-014144.

Artillery recruiting poster (83): unknown artist, 1914-18, offset lithograph, LAC C-095377.

Campbell (87): J. H. DeWolfe, Our Heroes in the Great War (Ottawa: Patriotic Publishing, 1919).

Ypres (90): Arthur Nantel, 1915, water colour with some gouache over pencil on paper, CWM 8629.

Barrett (92): British Columbia Regiment Museum, Vancouver.

Ypres (93): Richard Jack, 1917, photomechanical print, LAC C-014145.

Ypres houses (95): A. Y. Jackson, 1917, oil on canvas, CWM 8207.

CHAPTER 4

Enlist! recruiting poster (97): C. J. Patterson, ca. 1915, offset lithograph, LAC C-029568.

YMCA canteen (99): Claire Atwood, 1918, oil on canvas, Senate of Canada Chamber.

Canadian stationary hospital (102): Gerald Moira, 1918, oil on canvas, CWM 8555, 8556, 8557.

Cheering (105): LAC PA-022711.

No man's land (108): Maurice Cullen, 1919, oil on linen, CWM 8149.

CHAPTER 5

Victory bonds poster (110): Louis Abel-Truchet, 1914-18, lithography on wove paper, LAC 1983-28-469.

Waldron (113): Ian Waldron.

Sanctuary wood (123): Kenneth Forbes, 1918, oil on canvas, CWM 8157.

Uhlans (124): Arthur Nantel, 1915, watercolour paper on cardboard, CWM 8620.

Lavallée (126): Richard George Matthews, 1916, chalk on paper, LAC C-017368.

CHAPTER 6

Armoury (129): PANL VA-33-15.
Cape Helles (135): PANL B3-15a.
St. John's Road (137): PANL NA-3105.
Somme (138): The Saddness of the Somme, Mary Riter Hamilton, ca. 1920, oil on
     plywood, LAC C-104799.
Shelter trench (140): Mary Riter Hamilton, 1919, oil on cardboard, LAC C-104800.
Beaumont Hamel (141): PANL NA-6067.
Poppies (142): Mary Riter Hamilton, 1919, oil on commercial board, LAC C-104747.

CHAPTER 7

Dailey (146): Ted Dailey.
Black watch recruiting poster (149): unknown artist, 1914-18, offset lithograph, LAC
     C-095391.
Albert (151): Mary Riter Hamilton, 1920, oil on plywood, LAC C-101312.
Waldron (152): Ian Waldron.
Courcelette (154): Louis Weirter, 1918, oil on canvas (detail), CWM 8931.
Sunken road (156): Fred Varley, ca. 1919, oil on linen, CWM 8912.
Waldron (157): Ian Waldron.
Thiepval (161): Kenneth Forbes, 1918, oil on canvas, CWM 8158.
4th Division (164): LAC PA-000832.

CHAPTER 8

McKinnon (167): LAC PA-000867.
US recruiting poster (168): unknown artist, ca. 1914-18, offset lithograph on paper,
     LAC C-131327.
Harvest poster (169): unknown artist, 1911, photomechanical print, LAC C-056088.
Troops in snow (175): James Morrice, 1918, oil on canvas, CWM 8949.
Mont-Saint-Eloi (178): Mary Riter Hamilton, ca. 1919-20, oil on plywood, LAC
     C-101318.
Trench foot (181): LAC PA-149311.

CHAPTER 9

Night raid (186): Harold Mowat, ca. 1918, conté and grey wash with highlights of
     white on board, CWM 8564.
Trench fight (188): Harold Mowat, n. d., conté and wash on cardboard, CWM 8562.
St. Nazarius's Church (191): William Beatty, 1918, oil on canvas, CWM 8102.
Railway construction (194): Leonard Richmond, 1917, oil on canvas, Senate of
     Canada Chamber.
Ammunition (195): LAC PA-001262.
Night shoot (196): Thurstan Topham, n. d., water colour and pencil on paper, CWM
     8884.
Dugout (199): Thurstan Topham, 1916, watercolour on paper, CWM 8896.

CHAPTER 10

McClare (208): Dale McClare.

McClare letter and telegram (210-12): Dale McClare.

Vimy Ridge (215): Richard Jack, 1919, photomechanical print, LAC C-000148.

Grenadier recruiting poster (218): unknown artist, ca. 1916-18, lithograph on wove paper, LAC R1300-111.

Vimy crest (220): Gyrth Russell, 1918, oil on canvas, CWM 8756.

Henley (221): Dale R. Henley.

Victory bonds poster (222): unknown artist, 1917, lithograph on wove paper, LAC PA-001332 (photo), LAC C-097748 (poster).

CHAPTER 11

Monchy (226): G. W. L. Nicolson, The Fighting Newfoundlander: A History of the Royal Newfoundland Regiment (Montreal and Kingston: McGill-Queen's University Press, 2006).

Death certificate (228): PANL.

Elverdinge (232): Cyril Barraud, 1917, etching with surface tone, CWM 8039.

Newfoundland Regiment (234): PANL F-46-27.

Victory bonds poster (237): unknown artist, ca. 1914-18, photomechanical print, LAC C-097750.

CHAPTER 12

Irish recruiting poster (241): unknown artist, ca. 1914-18, lithography on wove paper, LAC C-148324.

Parlee (249): Belleisle Regional High School, Springfield, NB.

Mustard gas (254): LAC C-080027.

Gas attack (256): A. Y. Jackson, 1918, oil on canvas, CWM 8197.

Stretcher bearers (257): Cyril Barraud, ca. 1918, oil on canvas, CWM 8021.

CHAPTER 13

Dead horse (259): Maurice Cullen, 1918, oil on canvas, CWM 8140.

Haig & Currie (261): LAC PA-004666.

Pack horses (263): LAC PA-001229.

German prisoners (265): Fred Varley, ca. 1919, oil on canvas, CWM 8961.

Gunners (268): Canadian Gunners in the Mud, Alfred Bastien, 1917, oil on canvas, CWM 8095.

Passchendaele (271): LAC PA-002107.

Signaller recruiting poster (276): LAC C-131498, unknown artist, ca. 1915-18, lithograph.

Copse (278): A. Y. Jackson, 1918, oil on canvas, CWM 8204.

CHAPTER 14

Hessian screening (282): A. Y. Jackson, 1918, oil over pencil on linen, CWM 8188.

Strachan (285): LAC PA-002515.

Motor machine gun (290): LAC PA-002614.

Flowerdew (292): Joan Wanklyn, 1989, oil on canvas, Lord Strathcona's Horse Royal
Canadians, Edmonton.

Flowerdew charge (293): Alfred Munnings, ca. 1918, oil on canvas, CWM 8571.

The Maple Leaf (294): John Boileau.

Halifax explosion (297): Maritime Command Museum, Halifax.

CHAPTER 15

Amiens (302): LAC PA-003015.

230th recruiting poster (304): unknown artist, ca. 1914-18, lithograph on wove
paper, LAC C-095378.

Amiens-Roye Road (305): LAC PA-002946.

Strathcona (307): Strathcona's Horse on the March, Alfred Munnings, ca. 1918, oil
on canvas, CWM 8569.

13th Battalion (311): LAC PA-002894.

Arras (314): Arras, The Dead City, James Kerr-Lawson, 1919, oil on canvas, Senate of
Canada Chamber.

Fresnes-Rouvroy line (319): Over the Top, Neuville Vitasse 1918, Alfred Bastien,
1918, oil on canvas, CWM 8058.

CHAPTER 16

Tobacco fund (322): unknown artist (after Samuel 'Bert' Thomas), ca. 1914-18,
lithograph, Library of Congress USZC4-12681.

Hundred days (325): Alfred Bastien, 1918, oil on canvas, CWM 8092.

Canal du Nord (328): LAC PA-003287.

DH9 bomber (330): LAC C-028029.

Victory bonds poster (335): unknown artist, 1918, lithograph, LAC C-096812.

Trooper and horse (339): On the Edge of the Wood, Alfred Munnings, ca. 1917-19,
oil on canvas, CWM 8587.

Cambrai (340): CWM 8936, Gerald de Witt, n. d., etching and aquatone on paper.

CHAPTER 17

Ypres Cloth Hall (344): James Kerr-Lawson, ca. 1919, oil on canvas, Senate of
Canada Chamber.

Aid detachment poster (346): PANL P5-11.

Dugout (349): Mary Riter Hamilton, 1920, oil on cardboard laid down onto
cardboard, LAC C-132004.

Ricketts (350): Dolda Clarke.

Rhine (352): PANL VA-28-146.

Wandsworth hospital (354): PANL VA-37-29.

Ricketts (359): Dolda Clarke.

CHAPTER 18

Currie (362): Sir William Orpen, 1919, oil on canvas, CWM 8673.

Ogilvie (366): William G. Ogilvie, Umty-Iddy-Umty: The Story of a Canadian
Signaller in the First World War (Erin, Ont.: Boston Mills, 1982).

Cairns (368): LAC PA-006735.

Armistice (373): John Boileau.

Mons (375): Inglis Sheldon-Williams, 1920, oil on canvas, CWM 8969.

Bonn Bridge (379): LAC PA-003776 .

Toronto (380): CWM 8795, Ernest Simpson, ca. 1918, oil on canvas.

CHAPTER 19

Wallis (384): Robert Field, 1813, oil on canvas, Art Gallery of Nova Scotia 79.18.

Naval service recruiting poster(388): unknown artist, ca. 1910, lithograph, Library of
    Congress USZC4-12677.

McLeod (389): LAC PA-006763.

RCN midshipmen (391): Maritime Command Museum, Halifax.

JN4 (394): Frank Hans Johnson, 1918, watercolour on paper, CWM 8269.

McLeod (398): Doug Comeau.

McLeod (399): LAC PA-006736.

EPILOGUE

Memorial Cross (404): Army Museum Halifax Citadel.

Charlotte wood (405): LAC PA-148875.

Next of kin (406): Army Museum,Halifax Citadel.

INDEX